Remittances and Development

Remittances and Development

Lessons from Latin America

Edited by

Pablo Fajnzylber and
J. Humberto López

THE WORLD BANK
Washington, D.C.

1818 H Street NW
Washington DC 20433
Telephone: 202-473-1000
Internet: www.worldbank.org
E-mail: feedback@worldbank.org

1 2 3 4 11 10 09 08

ISBN: 978-0-8213-6870-1
eISBN: 978-0-8213-6871-8
DOI: 10.1596/978-0-8213-6870-1

Library of Congress Cataloging-in-Publication Data

Remittances and development : lessons from Latin America / edited by Pablo Fajnzylber and J. Humberto Lopez.

p. cm.—(Latin American development forum series)
Includes bibliographical references and index.
ISBN-13: 978-0-8213-6870-1
ISBN-10: 0-8213-6870-2
ISBN-13: 978-0-8213-6871-8 (electronic)
1. Emigrant remittances—Latin America. 2. Economic development—Latin America. I. Fajnzylber, Pablo. II. Lopez, J. Humberto. III. World Bank.
HG3915.5.R47 2007
338.98—dc22

2007036235

Cover design: ULTRAdesigns

Latin American Development Forum Series

This series was created in 2003 to promote debate, disseminate information and analysis, and convey the excitement and complexity of the most topical issues in economic and social development in Latin America and the Caribbean. It is sponsored by the Inter-American Development Bank, the United Nations Economic Commission for Latin America and the Caribbean, and the World Bank. The manuscripts chosen for publication represent the highest quality in each institution's research and activity output and have been selected for their relevance to the academic community, policy makers, researchers, and interested readers.

Advisory Committee Members

Other Titles in the Latin American Development Forum Series

New Titles

China's and India's Challenge to Latin America: Opportunity or Threat? (2008) by Daniel Lederman, Marcelo Olarreaga, and Guillermo Perry, editors

Fiscal Policy, Stabilization, and Growth: Prudence or Abstinence? (2007) by Guillermo Perry, Luis Servén, and Rodrigo Suescún, editors

Raising Student Learning: Challenges for the 21st Century (2007) by Emiliana Vegas and Jenny Petrow

Published Titles

Investor Protection and Corporate Governance: Firm-level Evidence Across Latin America (2007) by Alberto Chong and Florencio López-de-Silanes, editors

The State of State Reform in Latin America (2006) by Eduardo Lora, editor

Emerging Capital Markets and Globalization: The Latin American Experience (2006) by Augusto de la Torre and Sergio L. Schmukler

Beyond Survival: Protecting Households from Health Shocks in Latin America (2006) by Cristian C. Baeza and Truman G. Packard

Natural Resources: Neither Curse nor Destiny (2006) by Daniel Lederman and William F. Maloney, editors

Beyond Reforms: Structural Dynamics and Macroeconomic Vulnerability (2005) by José Antonio Ocampo, editor

Privatization in Latin America: Myths and Reality (2005) by Alberto Chong and Florencio López-de-Silanes, editors

Keeping the Promise of Social Security in Latin America (2004) by Indermit S. Gill, Truman G. Packard, and Juan Yermo

Lessons from NAFTA: For Latin America and the Caribbean (2004) by Daniel Lederman, William F. Maloney, and Luis Servén

The Limits of Stabilization: Infrastructure, Public Deficits, and Growth in Latin America (2003) by William Easterly and Luis Servén, editors

Globalization and Development: A Latin American and Caribbean Perspective (2003) by José Antonio Ocampo and Juan Martin, editors

Is Geography Destiny? Lessons from Latin America (2003) by John Luke Gallup, Alejandro Gaviria, and Eduardo Lora

About the Contributors

Pablo Acosta is an Economist in the Research Department of the Corporación Andina de Fomento, Caracas, Venezuela.

Maurizio Bussolo is a Senior Economist in the Development Prospects Group, World Bank, Washington, DC.

Cesar Calderón is an Economist in the Office of the Chief Economist for the Latin America and the Caribbean Region, World Bank, Washington, DC.

Massimo Cirasino is Head of the Payment Systems and Remittances Services Unit of the Financial and Private Sector Development Vice Presidency, World Bank, Washington, DC.

Pablo Fajnzylber is a Senior Economist in the Office of the Chief Economist for the Latin America and the Caribbean Region, World Bank, Washington, DC.

Mario Guadamillas is a Senior Financial Economist in the Finance and Private Sector Development Department of the Latin America and the Caribbean Region, World Bank, Washington, DC.

J. Humberto López is a Senior Economist in the Office of the Chief Economist for the Latin America and the Caribbean Region, World Bank, Washington, DC.

María Soledad Martínez Pería is a Senior Economist in the Development Research Group, World Bank, Washington, DC.

Yira Mascaró is a Senior Financial Economist in the Finance and Private Sector Development Department of the Latin America and the Caribbean Region, World Bank, Washington, DC.

Florencia Moizeszowicz is a consultant in the Financial Sector Assessment Program Unit of the Financial and Private Sector Development Vice Presidency, World Bank, Washington, DC.

Luis Molina is an Economist in the International Economics Division, Bank of Spain, Madrid, Spain.

Mette E. Nielsen is a doctoral candidate in the Department of Economics, Princeton University, Princeton, NJ.

Yoko Niimi is a consultant in the Development Research Group, World Bank, Washington, DC.

Pedro Olinto is a Senior Economist in the Development Economics Vice Presidency, World Bank, Washington, DC.

Çağlar Özden is a Senior Economist in the Development Research Group, World Bank, Washington, DC.

Emanuel Salinas, formerly a Financial Economist in the Finance and Private Sector Development Department of the Latin America and the Caribbean Region, World Bank, Washington, DC, is currently Associate Director of Structured Finance at Standard & Poor's, London.

Contents

TABLES

Foreword

Workers' remittances have become extremely important for many Latin American economies. Indeed, Latin America was the region that received the largest volume of remittances in 2006: more than US$50 billion. This amount multiplied by 25 over the past 25 years, and today represents about 70 percent of foreign direct investment flows and is almost eight times larger than official development assistance flows to the region. The largest absolute amount goes to Mexico, where annual remittances flows are above US$20 billion, and the highest as a percentage of GDP goes to Haiti, where remittances represent about 50 percent of GDP. In El Salvador, remittances are equivalent to US$400 per capita, and in the Dominican Republic, more than 20 percent of the families report receiving remittances.

Not surprisingly then, the past few years have witnessed a booming interest by academics, donors, policy makers, and international financial institutions in the potential development impact of these flows. This book is a response to that interest. It analyzes the characteristics of households that are remittances recipients and how these characteristics affect the poverty-reducing impact of observed remittances flows. It also devotes significant attention to the macroeconomic impact of these flows, and explores policies and interventions aimed at enhancing the development impact of remittances in the region.

On the whole, the main messages that emerge from this study are quite positive. Even though the estimated impact is moderate in most cases and country heterogeneity is very significant, higher remittances inflows tend to be associated with lower poverty levels and improvements in human capital indicators (education and health) of the recipient countries. Remittances also appear to contribute to higher growth and investment rates, and lower output volatility. This is particularly important in the Latin American context because compared with other regions, Latin America's investment rates are still relatively low and output volatility relatively high.

Against this background, remittances are to be welcomed and actions that lower the cost of remitting, and therefore attract additional flows, should be encouraged.

These positive results, however, come with a number of important qualifiers that deserve the attention of the region's policy makers. For one, the migration of workers that precedes remittances flows is not without costs. Besides the social disruptions that take place when a parent migrates and leaves his or her children behind, there are potential losses of income associated with migrants' absence from their families and communities. Moreover, as a result of migration patterns, some countries have lost significant portions of their college-educated populations.

Similarly, in countries where the magnitude of remittances flows is high relative to the size of the receiving economies, remittances pose important macroeconomic policy challenges. The book explores these challenges and studies potential policy responses—for example, countries experiencing Dutch disease effects may need to rely more on indirect than direct taxation, and on a stronger effort to increase productivity in tradable sectors. And in the vein of other World Bank reports, in which the impact of international financial flows such as aid have been found to depend on the policy environment of the recipient country, this volume shows that countries are not equally capable of exploiting the potential benefits of remittances: Countries with better institutions and economic management appear to obtain a higher payoff from these flows. In other words, remittances are a complement to, rather than a substitute for, good economic policies.

This volume is a valuable contribution to the ongoing debate on the impact of migration and remittances in the Latin American region. I am confident that policy makers will find its guidance useful in their efforts to enhance the development impact of remittances.

Guillermo Perry
Former Chief Economist for the Latin America and the Caribbean Region
The World Bank

Acknowledgments

Remittances and Development is based on the second volume of the 2006 Latin American and Caribbean Regional Study *The Development Impact of Workers' Remittances in Latin America* (World Bank Report No. 37026), and is the result of a collaborative effort of two units of the Latin America and the Caribbean Region of the World Bank: the Office of the Chief Economist and the Finance and Private Sector Development Group. We are most grateful to the contributors to this book for their efforts in the preparation of the various versions of the manuscript; to Guillermo Beylis, Namsuk Kim, and Paola Granata for their excellent research assistance; to Omar Arias, Makhtar Diop, Susan Goldmark, Ernesto López Córdova, Samuel Muzele Maimbo, Ernesto May, Edmundo Murrugarra, Guillermo Perry, Santiago Pombo, José Guilherme Reis, Maurice Schiff, and Annie Sturesson, for their comments, suggestions, and encouragement from the start; and to Denise Bergeron, Aziz Gokdemir, Santiago Pombo, and Shana Wagger for their support in the production of this book. The authors alone take responsibility for the content of the book and the views expressed here, which do not necessarily reflect the views of our colleagues in the World Bank Group.

Abbreviations

ACH	Automated Clearing House
AFDC	Aid to Families with Dependent Children
AML-CFT	Anti-Money Laundering and Combating the Financing of Terrorism
ATM	automated teller machine
Bansefi	*Banco de Ahorro Nacional y Servicios Financieros*
BOP	balance of payments
bp	basis points
CCT	conditional cash transfer
CET	constant elasticity of transformation
CGE	computable general equilibrium
CIME	*Coalición Internacional de Mexicanos en el Extranjero*
CNBV	*Comisión Nacional Bancaria y de Valores*
Comtrade	U.N. Commodity Trade Statistics Database
CPSS	Committee on Payments and Settlement Systems
CTR	currency transaction report
FATF	Financial Action Task Force on Money Laundering
FDI	foreign direct investment
FedACH	Federal Reserve Bank's Automated Clearing House
FUSADES	*Fundación Salvadoreña para el Desarrollo Económico y Social*
GDP	gross domestic product
HAZ	height-for-age
IDB	Inter-American Development Bank
IFPRI	International Food Policy Research Institute
IMF	International Monetary Fund
IV	instrumental variables
LAC	Latin America and the Caribbean
LES	linear expenditure system
LSMS	Living Standards Measurement Study

MTO	money transfer operator
NGO	nongovernmental organization
ODA	official development assistance
OECD	Organisation for Economic Co-operation and Development
OFAC	Office of Foreign Assets Control
OLS	ordinary least squares
PAHNAL	*Patronato del Ahorro Nacional*
PPP	purchasing power parity
PRAF	*Programa de Asignación Familiar*
PROFECO	*Procuraduría Federal del Consumidor*
PROGRESA	*Programa de Educación, Salud y Alimentación*
PUMS	Public-Use Microdata Samples
RPS	*Red de Protección Social*
RSP	remittances services providers
SAM	Social Accounting Matrix
SDN	Specially Designated Nationals
TRAINS	U.N. Trade Analysis and Information System
UNDP	United Nations Development Programme
USAID	United States Agency for International Development
WAZ	weight-for-age
WOCCU	World Council of Credit Unions
VAT	value added tax

1

The Development Impact of Remittances in Latin America

Pablo Fajnzylber and J. Humberto López

Remittances are extremely important in the Latin American context. In 2006, remittances to Latin America amounted to about US$52 billion, making them comparable to foreign direct investment (FDI) and much larger than official development assistance (ODA) flows to the region. Today, Latin America is the top recipient region of remittances both by volume and in per-capita terms. Yet some important questions remain. What is the impact of these flows on the poverty levels of the different countries? Are there costs associated with remittances—and more significantly—to the migration that logically precedes remittances flows? What are the main challenges that policy makers face in countries experiencing a surge in remittances flows? In short, what is the development impact of remittances in Latin America, and how can it be enhanced?

Introduction

According to the World Bank's *Global Economic Prospects 2006*, remittances to middle- and low-income countries in 1990 amounted to about US$31 billion. Fifteen years later, they were estimated to have reached about US$200 billion, of which about one-fourth was directed toward the Latin America and the Caribbean region (Latin America henceforth). While this dramatic increase may to some extent reflect improvements in data collection, together with growing migration flows, the magnitude of remittances flows during recent years has attracted a great deal of attention among academics and development practitioners, who have grown increasingly interested in understanding their potential development impact and corresponding policy implications.

Existing evidence on these issues, however, is mostly restricted to a small number of countries, notably Mexico and El Salvador in the case of Latin America. To the extent that patterns of migration and remittances vary considerably across countries and regions—for instance in terms of the social and economic background of migrants and their families—the impact of growing remittances flows is also likely to differ in ways that at present are still largely unknown. This provides the main motivation for undertaking the research summarized in this book, which is aimed at uncovering possible cross-country differences in the development impact of remittances, while at the same time providing evidence that could help policy makers in taking advantage of those flows. To that end, we combine microeconometric country case studies based on household surveys with the analysis of aggregate data on remittances flows for a large sample of countries.

There are four main messages that emerge from this book. First, no matter how we look at the issue, remittances are extremely important in the Latin American context. With remittances estimated to have topped more than US$50 billion in 2006, Latin America is now the main destination of these flows. Today, remittances are comparable to foreign direct investment (FDI) flows and more than six times larger than official development assistance (ODA). The importance of remittances for some countries in the region can be best illustrated by expressing them as a ratio to GDP, while in others the percentage of recipients in the population or the absolute total of per-capita value of remittances flows are more revealing. In Guyana, for example, remittances represent about 25 percent of GDP. In the Dominican Republic, more than 20 percent of the households report receiving remittances on a regular basis. In Jamaica, remittances are close to US$700 per person per year, whereas in Mexico, they add up to more than US$20 billion per year. Policy makers and development practitioners should therefore pay due attention to the issue.

Second, remittances generate a number of important positive contributions to economic development. In particular, they tend to reduce poverty and inequality in recipient countries, as well as increase aggregate investment and growth. Moreover, thanks to their countercyclical behavior, remittances significantly reduce growth volatility and help countries adjust to external and macroeconomic policy shocks. At the microeconomic level, remittances allow poor recipient households to increase their savings, spend more on consumer durables and human capital, and improve children's health and educational outcomes. Remittances should thus be welcomed, encouraged, and facilitated.

Third, even though remittances have a positive impact on the development indicators of the recipient economies, the magnitude of the estimated changes tends to be modest. There are two main explanations for this finding. One is related to the fact that in the Latin American context, remittances are not necessarily targeted to the poorest segments of the population. Instead, in a number of cases, they seem to flow to better-off households. This distributional profile will clearly lower the potential poverty-reducing impact of remittances. The other explanation is related to the costs associated with remittances flows and the migration that logically precedes them. In particular, in addition to the emotional hardships endured by migrants and the family members that are left behind, the departure of migrants who were active in the labor market should lead to reductions in other sources of household income. In the case of some small Caribbean islands, this may be aggravated by the fact that many migrants come from among the most educated segments of the population. The impact of this phenomenon, which has often been termed "brain drain," is such that countries like Haiti, Jamaica, Grenada, and Guyana have lost more than 80 percent of their college graduates. Remittances, therefore, should not be considered a panacea or an alternative to sound economic policies.

Fourth, policy makers may take actions to enhance the development impact of remittances. For example, the empirical evidence in this book indicates that remittances increase the reservation wage of recipient households. Similarly, countries experiencing a surge in remittances tend to also experience a real exchange rate appreciation. In the absence of any policy action, these elements will have a negative impact on the international competitiveness of the tradable sector, and therefore somewhat offset the positive effect of remittances. Another area where policy interventions can make a difference is the financial sector. There is now ample evidence of the positive impact that a well-developed financial sector has on growth (Beck, Levine, and Loayza 2000) and poverty (Beck, Demirgüç-Kunt, and Levine 2007) so that to the extent that policy makers can enhance the impact of remittances on the financial sector of the recipient country, they will also be enhancing their development impact. This issue is particularly relevant to the region because as discussed in this book, remittances appear to have a modest impact on the development of the Latin American financial sector. One important message of this book is that the way countries benefit from remittances appears to be positively related to the countries' own institutional and macroeconomic environments.

We next summarize in more detail the main findings of the studies included in this book, starting with a description of aggregate remittances trends and the position of recipients in the income distribution of their home countries (chapter 2), and with an analysis of the profile of Latin American migrants and its relationship with the volume of remittances that they send home (chapter 3). We then summarize the main findings of the book on the impact of remittances on poverty, inequality, growth, and output volatility (chapter 4), and their effect on household expenditures, educational attainment, and labor supply (chapter 5). This is followed by a review of the links between remittances and the deepening of financial markets (chapter 6), the issues associated with possible real exchange rate overvaluations (chapter 7), and the possibility that remittances are crowded out by conditional cash transfer programs (chapter 8). Finally, we review the main regulatory issues involved in reducing transaction costs (chapter 9), and we report on our findings regarding complementarities between remittances flows and development policies (chapter 10).

Remittances Trends and Their Distribution

Over the past two decades, workers' remittances to Latin America and the Caribbean have increased 10-fold in real terms. As described by Acosta, Fajnzylber, and López in chapter 2, Latin America is at the top of the ranking of remittances-receiving regions both by volume (US$48 billion in 2005) and on a per-capita basis (an average of about US$90 per person in 2005). Within the region, remittances are particularly important for countries in Central America and the Caribbean. For example, remittances in 2005 represented about 25 percent of Guyana's and Haiti's GDP, whereas in Honduras, Jamaica, and El Salvador, they were 22 percent, 19 percent, and 17 percent of GDP, respectively. In terms of volume, the country with the highest absolute remittances flows is Mexico, which is estimated to have received US$21.8 billion in 2005. This would represent 45 percent of total flows to Latin America in that year and would make Mexico the third-largest world recipient (after China and India). In the region, Mexico is followed by Brazil and Colombia, which were ranked 19th and 20th, respectively, among the top remittances-receiving countries in the world, with flows of US$3.5 billion and US$3.3 billion, respectively, in 2005.

To gain insights about the characteristics of those at the receiving end of those flows, chapter 2 also uses national representative household surveys that contain specific questions on remittances. That information is available for 11 Latin American countries, which together represent more than two-thirds of remittances to the Latin America region: Haiti, El Salvador, Honduras, Nicaragua, Guatemala, the Dominican Republic, Ecuador, Paraguay, Mexico, Bolivia, and Peru. These surveys suggest that the fraction of households receiving remittances varies significantly across Latin American countries. For example, in Haiti, more than 25 percent of the households reported having received remittances in 2001. At the other extreme, only 3 percent of Peruvian households benefited from these flows. In between, remittances reached between 10 percent and 25 percent of the households in the Dominican Republic, El Salvador, Nicaragua, and Honduras; between 5 percent and 10 percent in Mexico and Guatemala; and between 3 percent and 5 percent in Bolivia, Ecuador, and Paraguay. Thus, remittances are a common element of household income in these countries.

There is also considerable heterogeneity in terms of the position along the income distribution of households that receive remittances. For instance, in Mexico, the recipients of remittances are predominantly poor: 61 percent of the households that report receiving remittances fall in the first quintile of nonremittances income, whereas only 4 percent of them are in the top quintile. Similarly, in Paraguay, 42 percent of recipients are in the lowest quintile of the distribution, and only 8 percent are in the top quintile. The other countries where at least 30 percent of the recipients of remittances are in the first quintile are Ecuador, El Salvador, and Guatemala.

By contrast, in Peru and Nicaragua, the distribution of remittances across households is completely different. For example, in Peru, fewer than 6 percent of the households that receive remittances belong to the lowest quintile, while 40 percent belong to the top quintile. In the case of Nicaragua, where only 12 percent of the recipients are in the first quintile, 33 percent belong to the fifth quintile. Thus in these two countries, remittances seem to be flowing toward the richest. In between the group of Mexico, Paraguay, Ecuador, El Salvador, and Guatemala, and the group of Peru and Nicaragua, there are four countries (Bolivia, Honduras, the Dominican Republic, and Haiti) where remittances recipients are found at similar rates among households in the bottom and top income quintiles, exhibiting a U-shaped distribution—that is, remittances flow at a higher proportion toward the poorest 20 percent and the richest 20 percent of the population, and to a lesser extent toward the three middle quintiles.

Overall, we find that the distribution of remittances income is quite unequal. In the cases of Mexico, El Salvador, Guatemala, and Paraguay, however, remittances are less unequally distributed than total income, with the poorest 60 percent receiving 41 percent of remittances, compared to 29 percent of income. By contrast, in the other seven countries, the first three quintiles receive only 16 percent of total remittances, compared to 26 percent of total income. These statistics suggest that remittances should have quite different impacts on inequality and poverty across the various countries of the region.

Migration Patterns and Remittances

To understand the volume of remittances that a given country may receive, it is critical to have some knowledge about its migrant population. Niimi and Özden explore this issue in chapter 3 by analyzing the profile of Latin American migrants living in developed countries. Due to data limitations, we are not able to cover the "South-to-South" migrants. We find, first, that while most Mexican and Latin American migrants go to the United States, for many South Americans, Europe continues to be a major destination. In some cases, migrants to the United States from South America represent less than 50 percent of those countries' migrants. That is the case for migrants to the United States from Brazil, Chile, Paraguay, and Uruguay. Among Latin Americans who migrate to European countries, language seems to play an important role; the Caribbean migrants prefer the United Kingdom as a destination, and the South American migrants choose Spain.

The total number of Latin American migrants in the United States increased from 8.6 million in 1990 to about 16 million in 2000 (an 86 percent increase). Among the countries in the region, Honduras experienced the most rapid growth in migrants in the United States—from 112,000 in 1990 to 281,000 (a 150 percent increase) 10 years later. The second-largest relative increase is found for Brazil, whose migrants in the United States increased from around 95,000 to about 210,000 in the same period, and Mexico, which also more than doubled its migrant population in the United States. Mexico is also the country with the largest number of migrants in the United States (close to 10 million in 2000), followed by Cuba (870,000), El Salvador (820,000), the Dominican Republic (680,000), Jamaica (550,000), and Colombia (510,000). When comparing numbers of migrants in the United States with the corresponding population of their home countries, the small islands of the Caribbean stand out, with an average of 30 percent of their labor force living abroad. In comparison, for non-Caribbean countries, the ratio of migrants in the United States to home country population averages about 10 percent (6 percent for South America).

The schooling levels of Latin American migrants in the United States are relatively low, especially in the case of those from Mexico and Central America. Yet there are significant differences in the education distribution when comparing different countries. Thus, while only 4 percent of Mexican migrants have tertiary education, the figures are 7 percent for Central America, 12 percent for the Caribbean, 24 percent for the Andean region, and around 30 percent for other South American countries. Even larger cross-country differences are found with regard to the share of migrants occupied in high- and medium-skilled jobs. That ratio is about 10 percent for Mexicans and Central Americans, and between 40 percent and 50 percent for Caribbean and South American migrants.

Most Mexican and Central American migrants are drawn from the lower end of the education spectrum of their home countries. By contrast, migrants from the Caribbean and South America tend to be proportionally more educated than those who remain behind. For example, even though education levels in Brazil and Mexico are similar, their migrants are starkly different in their education profiles. One possible explanation of this finding is that it is relatively easy for Mexicans and Central Americans to migrate to the United States, either through legal channels using family preferences, or without proper documentation.

So-called brain drain appears as a problem for many small Caribbean countries. More than 80 percent of people born in Haiti, Jamaica, Grenada, and Guyana who have college degrees live abroad, mostly in the United States. However, fewer than 10 percent of college graduates from South American countries have migrated, even though they form a large portion of the migrant population. This is mainly owing to the low levels of overall migration from South America. For Mexico and Central America, the migration level of college graduates is about 15 percent to 20 percent, which is relatively high in comparison to that of South America, but not as alarming as the situation found in the Caribbean.

The econometric analysis in this chapter relating remittances to the stock of migrants living abroad indicates that the ratio of remittances to GDP of a given country increases with its stock of migrants. However, larger migrant stocks are associated with lower remittances sent per migrant, which renders the impact on remittances received per capita ambiguous. In addition, increases in the overall education levels of migrants tend to reduce remittances sent, but remittances sent by migrants increase with the level of financial development and the rates of economic growth of their home countries.

The Impact of Remittances on Poverty, Inequality, and Growth

Since the position of migrants and remittances recipients in the income and educational distribution varies considerably across countries, the social and economic impact of remittances flows is also likely to vary across countries. To assess whether there is indeed heterogeneity in the effect of remittances on inequality and poverty, Acosta, Calderón, Fajnzylber, and López use both micro- and macroeconomic data and techniques in chapter 4. Those analyses are based on household survey data for 11 Latin American countries, and on the estimation of cross-country regressions for a large sample of countries, using balance of payments statistics on aggregate remittances flows.

In the first approach, we first compare Gini coefficients and poverty head count estimates obtained using observed total household income and nonremittances income. This simple analysis indicates that 9 out of 11 countries—the exceptions being Nicaragua and Peru—exhibit higher Gini coefficients for nonremittances income, suggesting that if remittances were exogenously eliminated, inequality would increase.[1] Quantitatively, however, the estimated potential changes in the Gini coefficient are small, which can be attributed to the generally very unequal distribution of remittances income, and to remittances reaching relatively well-off households in most countries. On the other hand, this simple methodology suggests large reductions in poverty head counts derived from remittances, especially in those countries where migrants tend to come from the lower quintiles of the income distribution.

In a second methodological approach, we take into account the potential losses of income associated with the migrants' absence from their families and communities. In particular, for remittances-recipient households, we impute the value of household income in a counterfactual scenario where migration hypothetically does not take place. Using this imputed income we find that the Gini coefficients that prevailed before remittances *and* migration were indeed larger than those currently observed, with the largest differences obtained for Haiti (7.7 percent), followed by Guatemala (2.9 percent), El Salvador (2.1 percent), Nicaragua (1.8 percent), and Honduras (1.1 percent). We also find that on average, migration and remittances reduce moderate and extreme poverty by 0.37 percent and 0.29 percent, respectively, for each 1 percentage point increase in the remittances to GDP ratio.

Similar results are obtained using cross-country regression analysis, building on the work of Adams and Page (2005) and the IMF's *World Economic Outlook* (2005). But this analysis considers the fact that remittances vary by region, and attempts to capture the impact that remittances have on poverty due to the increases in per-capita income, as well as the changes they trigger in income inequality. The results suggest that remittances tend to reduce poverty to a larger extent in Latin America than elsewhere in the developing world, partly because they lead to less income inequality, while the opposite is observed for other regions.

We also use a cross-country approach to look at the growth-remittances link. We do so while correcting for reverse causality and other sources of endogeneity in remittances flows, for which we employ external and time-varying instrumental variables. Our results suggest that remittances have a positive and significant impact on growth, even after controlling for per-capita income, education, financial depth, openness to trade, the quality of institutions, government expenditures, inflation, and real exchange rate overvaluation. As mentioned above, we find that for the average Latin American country in the sample, the increase in remittances from 0.7 percent of GDP in 1991–95 to 2.3 percent of GDP in 2001–05 led to an increase of only 0.27 percent per year in per-capita GDP growth, as well as to a 2 percent increase in the share of domestic investment to GDP—which would correspond to about one-half of the estimated total impact of remittances on growth during that period.

Chapter 4 also presents robust evidence suggesting that remittances exhibit countercyclical behavior, thus helping to maintain macroeconomic stability. This suggests that remittances behave quite differently from other procyclical private capital flows, and appear to be dominated by compensatory transfers sent by migrants to their families in order to offset or prevent income shortfalls due to negative external shocks. Remittances also appear to increase significantly after financial crises and natural disasters.

Remittances and Household Behavior

In chapter 5, Acosta, Fajnzylber, and López address the links between remittances and three aspects of household behavior—namely the pattern of household expenditures exhibited by recipients in comparison with nonrecipients, the extent to which the former keep their children in school for longer periods of time, and the different labor supply behavior of individuals living in recipient households. To that end, we use household survey data for seven Latin American countries. In particular, we test whether the share of different expenditure categories varies across recipient and nonrecipient households that share similar demographic characteristics and are in the same quintile of the household income distribution (prior to migration). We find that remittances' recipients direct a smaller share of their total expenditures toward food, thus suggesting that Adams' (2005) findings for Guatemala also apply to other Latin American countries with considerable remittances receipts. The reduction in food expenditures among remittances recipients is complemented by an increase in expenses for other nondurable goods, durable goods, housing, education, and health.

There is, however, considerable heterogeneity in the relative importance of these various increases across countries, as well as in the patterns observed for recipient households with different levels of income. In the case of Mexico, for instance, recipients in the lower income quintiles exhibit the same pattern observed for the overall recipient population, but their richer counterparts increase expenditures for nondurable goods and lower the share of expenditures for housing improvements and education. On the other hand, in the remaining countries under analysis, remittances only have the beneficial effect of changing consumption patterns toward higher educational and health expenditures among middle- and upper-class households. For those in the lower quintiles of the income distribution, the results tend to confirm the popular perception that remittances tend to tilt household expenditures mainly toward nondurable goods, with some effects on durable consumption, but with limited impacts on housing and human capital investments.

The above results indicate that, at least for some segments of the income distribution, remittances can help overcome borrowing constraints that limit human capital investments. However, a priori, this effect could be compensated for by the fact that migration can have disruptive effects on family life, with potentially negative consequences on the schooling of children. Moreover, to the extent that most migrants tend to work in occupations that require limited human capital in destination countries, the returns from investments in education may be lower for those who are envisaging international migration. We complement previous evidence on the impact of remittances on education by taking an approach similar to that employed by Hanson and Woodruff (2003) for Mexico. We find that remittances are positively and significantly associated with higher educational attainment among children ages 10 to 15, with larger effects obtained for children whose parents have low levels of schooling. While there are large differences in the magnitude of the effects across countries, and by gender and urban status (for example, in some countries the effects are stronger for girls or for rural areas, while in others they also affect boys and urban areas), it appears that remittances tend to relax budget constraints that otherwise would force children to leave school, especially in households with low levels of adult schooling.

Complementing the evidence on changes in household expenditure and children's school attendance, we explore whether remittances also affect labor force participation and the number of hours worked by individuals in recipient households. Simple comparisons with nonrecipient households suggest that remittances may also have a large effect on this dimension of household behavior. This is confirmed by more detailed analyses that control for individual and household characteristics associated both with access to remittances and with labor supply decisions. Thus, in all the 10 countries for which data are available, remittances have the effect of reducing both the number of hours worked per week and, with some exceptions, the probability of participating in the labor force. Moreover, we find that in most cases the reductions in labor supply caused by remittances are larger among individuals with lower levels of schooling.

Remittances and Financial Sector Development

It is a priori not clear whether remittances should be linked to higher or lower levels of financial development. Indeed, to the extent that a fraction of the money received from abroad is saved, remittances may increase the demand for savings and other financial products and services. Moreover, even if higher bank lending to remittances recipients does not materialize, overall credit in the economy might increase if banks' loanable funds surge as a result of deposits linked to remittances flows. On the other hand, remittances might not increase bank deposits if they are immediately consumed or if remittances recipients distrust financial institutions and prefer other ways to save these flows. In addition, because remittances can help relax individuals' financing constraints, they might lead to a lower demand for credit and have a dampening effect on credit market development. In this context, Maria Soledad Martínez Pería, Yira Mascaró, and Florencia Moizeszowicz investigate in chapter 6 the association between remittances and financial development in the specific case of Latin America, using both macro- and microlevel data and techniques.

In the first approach, the chapter shows that remittances have a positive and significant impact on both bank deposits and bank credit, but this effect is smaller in Latin America than in the rest of the world. Moreover, within Latin America, we find that in five countries—Belize, Dominica, St. Kitts and Nevis, St. Lucia, and St. Vincent and the Grenadines—remittances appear to have no statistically significant impact on financial development. For the remaining countries, a 1 percentage point increase in remittances results in an approximately 2 percentage point to 3 percentage point rise in bank deposits and credit. We do not have definitive explanations for the smaller impact on financial development for Latin American countries relative to other developing economies.

Possible explanations include the fact that financial crises have been more recurrent and severe in Latin America, which could make remittances recipients in that region more distrustful of financial institutions. Second, as suggested by surveys of remittances senders performed by the Inter-American Development Bank, in 2004 only 7 percent of remittances were sent through banks. Third, access to physical banking outlets is more limited in this region than in other countries, and the costs of banking are higher in the region, as suggested, for instance, by data collected by Beck, Demirgüç-Kunt, and Martínez Pería (2005). Finally, even if the supply of loanable funds increases with remittances, credit might not rise in Latin America because of weak creditor protection and poor contract enforcement.

The chapter also presents microeconomic evidence on the topic using household-level survey data to investigate the association between remittances and the use of financial services. All in all, simple comparisons of the use of financial services among remittances-recipient and nonrecipient households provide some evidence consistent with the hypothesis that the former have a higher degree of access to those services. This is particularly the case for deposit holdings, and less so for credit. However, this evidence needs to be taken with a grain of salt for at least two important reasons. First, the tests conducted do not control for other household characteristics that might account for differences in the use of financial services. Second, these simple statistics suggest a correlation between remittances and the use of financial services, but are in no way proof of causality.

To mitigate the first problem, we use household survey data from three countries that have been analyzed elsewhere in the study—Guatemala, the Dominican Republic, and Haiti—and find that households with access to remittances are significantly more likely to report deposit accounts. However, at least in Haiti and the Dominican Republic, recipients are also less likely to have bank and nonbank outstanding credit. An additional, more detailed analysis is performed using data from El Salvador and Mexico, which also allows for controlling for the possibility that remittances might be endogenous. For El Salvador, the results consistently indicate that households that receive remittances have a higher likelihood (between 0.12 percentage point and 0.16 percentage point higher) of owning a deposit account, but the likelihood of having outstanding bank debt does not seem to be affected by whether households receive remittances. We also find that the likelihood that remittances recipients have bank accounts is twice as large if remittances are channeled through the banking sector. On the other hand, no such effect is present on the credit side.

A second detailed case study is performed for Mexico, which is Latin America's largest recipient of remittances in dollar terms. To that end, chapter 6 combines information from the 2000 Mexican Census on the share of households across Mexican municipalities that receive remittances, with municipal-level information from the Comisión Nacional Bancaria y de Valores (National Banking and Securities Commission) on the size of the commercial banking sector and the use of its services across municipalities. We find that municipalities where a larger percentage of the population receives remittances also tend to have higher ratios of deposit accounts per capita, larger deposit amounts to GDP, and a higher number of branches per capita. However, contrary to the findings on deposits and branches, there does not appear to be a significant association between remittances and credit across municipalities.

Remittances and the Real Exchange Rate

In Chapter 7, López, Molina, and Bussolo discuss the possibility that when remittances flows are very large relative to the size of the receiving economies, they may also bring the undesired consequence of a loss of external competitiveness derived from an appreciation of the real exchange rate. The mechanism would operate through the increased consumption levels of recipients, which would raise the relative prices of nontradable goods and services (for which competition is likely to be somewhat limited) relative to those of their tradable counterparts. In turn, a number of additional macroeconomic effects can result from a real exchange rate appreciation associated with remittances flows. They include: (i) adverse effects on the tradable sector of the economy; (ii) widening of the current account deficit; and (iii) weaker monetary control, inflationary pressures, and sectoral misallocation of investment.

Both descriptive and econometric evidence presented in chapter 7 indicate that, at least in the Latin American context, remittances may indeed lead to real exchange rate appreciations. Depending on the specification of the model and the estimation method, a doubling of remittances would lead, on average, to a real exchange rate appreciation of between 3 percent and 24 percent. Of this impact, it is estimated that about one-half of the estimated appreciation would be consistent with the evolution of economic fundamentals, while the rest would be related to transitory factors or temporary overvaluations.

The chapter also discusses possible policy responses. The first is the use of *fiscal restraint*. However, our estimates also indicate that the adjustment needed to stabilize the real exchange rate may be quite large and therefore be constrained by political economy considerations. The chapter also argues against relying on the *sterilization* of remittances inflows, as the corresponding quasi-fiscal costs may be too large, and because sterilization could put pressure on domestic interest rates, a development that might put even more pressure on the exchange rate. Other alternatives include *microeconomic interventions*, including, for instance, actions aimed at making the economy more competitive and domestic markets more efficient and flexible. However, recognizing the extent to which fiscal adjustment and microeconomic interventions may not be sufficient to correct the upward pressures in the real exchange rate, it is possible that Latin American policy makers will have to accept some real appreciation, especially in those countries with substantial inflows.

We also note that since additional microeconomic interventions aimed at increasing the competitiveness of the economy may require increased public spending, they may not necessarily be consistent with the recommended tightening of fiscal policies. Several considerations have to be taken into account in this context. First, for a given taxation structure, the increase in national income associated with a surge in remittances would *ceteris paribus* result in higher tax revenues. Second, countries should try to avoid taxes on incoming remittances[2] for two main reasons: (i) this type of action likely would discourage the formalization of remittances flows; and (ii) directly taxing remittances would conflict with one of the general recommendations of this book, namely, making efforts to reduce the costs of sending remittances. Third, even in those cases where policy makers facing a surge in remittances do not consider it a priority to raise fiscal revenue, it is possible that they could experience some competitiveness gains by shifting from payroll taxes to value added taxes (VAT) or sales taxes. In fact, the evidence presented by López, Molina and Bussolo in chapter 7 for Jamaica indicates that such a policy, accompanied by a compensatory increase in VAT rates, can maintain the government balance unchanged and sterilize most of the negative labor supply effect of rising remittances.

Do Public Transfers Crowd Out Remittances?

Conditional cash transfer (CCT) programs have become an important antipoverty tool in many Latin American countries. CCTs currently reach 60 million people, representing approximately 60 percent of the extremely poor in Latin America (Lindert, Skoufias, and Shapiro 2006). As argued by Lindert, Skoufias, and Shapiro (2006), cash transfer programs tend to be well targeted and have strong performance in terms of their marginal contribution to social welfare, outranking not only social insurance schemes but also social assistance programs. Moreover, Olinto (2006) reports that impact evaluations of conditional cash transfers in Mexico,

Brazil, Honduras, and Colombia indicate that these programs have had large impacts on transition rates and secondary school enrollment (especially for girls), and in delaying student dropout.

One concern, however, is that CCTs could crowd out private transfers, particularly remittances. In fact, there is evidence that in the United States, private assistance in the form of both cash and time help were crowded out by Aid to Families with Dependent Children (AFDC) benefits, and unemployment insurance crowds out interfamilial transfers (Schoeni 1996, 2002). Moreover, Cox, Eser, and Jimenez (1998) have found that social security benefits crowd out the incidence of private transfers in Peru. With regard to CCT programs, however, studies utilizing experimental data provide more mixed results. Thus, while Attanasio and Rios-Rull (2001) find some weak evidence supporting the crowding out hypothesis for Programa de Educación, Salud y Alimentación (PROGRESA), Teruel and Davis (2000) reject that hypothesis on the basis of additional rounds of survey data.

In chapter 8, Pedro Olinto adds to this literature by exploiting experimental data from the evaluations of two CCTs in Central America—the *Red de Protección Social*[3] in Nicaragua and the second Programa de Asignación Familiar[4] (PRAF-II) in Honduras—to assess the link between the access to conditional cash transfers and the incidence and volume of private transfers. The author's findings are in line with those of Teruel and Davis (2000) for PROGRESA, as the chapter finds no evidence that CCTs crowd out remittances transfers in either Nicaragua or Honduras. These results should help dispel concerns that CCTs could be displacing private networks and informal insurance schemes and therefore add little to the utility of the recipient parties. In particular, it appears that as long as transferred amounts continue to be small, and programs are targeted to those who are more likely to be poor (and therefore less likely to receive remittances), CCTs are not likely to crowd out remittances and other forms of private insurance.

The Regulatory Framework: How to Facilitate Remittances Flows

For migrants who send money home, remittances services are still expensive, with fees of up to 20 percent of the principal sent, depending on the size and type of the transfer, as well as on its origin and destination. Fee structures themselves have been opaque (with hidden charges and poor exchange rates), and have penalized transfers of small amounts of the type commonly made by migrants. Not surprisingly, reducing the price of remittances services has been a major target for many multilateral initiatives and regulatory efforts. However, authorities have generally shied away from imposing direct price controls, favoring instead mechanisms aimed at enhancing competition in the system, increasing transparency, and reducing barriers for users to access a wider range of service providers.

While the incentives for incumbent remittances services providers (RSPs) to realize cost savings and reduce prices may be naturally limited in smaller corridors where the limited volume of operations represents a natural barrier to entry for new operators, many of the benefits of competition can be realized through increased market contestability. In this respect, the role of the authorities encompasses: (i) eliminating unnecessary regulatory entry requirements to new operators; and (ii) ensuring appropriate access to domestic payment infrastructures under fair conditions.

A complementary, crucial set of actions is related to the improvement of payment and settlement systems. The degree of development of those systems, and the extent to which new RSPs can access them, largely determines the potential for competition in the market. In this respect, technological barriers for the access of new RSPs to existing payment systems are less important than formal restrictions. Indeed, direct access to national payment systems is normally granted only to well-capitalized and established banking institutions. In this context, regulation of payment and settlement systems should ensure that indirect access to RSPs—for example, through banks—is provided under fair conditions.

An additional challenge is that of building cross-border payment systems, with appropriate coordination and adoption across borders of, for example, communications standards and payment message formats that facilitate greater interoperability, as well as rules, procedures, and operating hours that support straight-through processing. Cross-border initiatives may require a high level of bilateral (or possibly multilateral) cooperation on technical, regulatory, and oversight matters.

In parallel, it is also important to take measures directed at guaranteeing transparency and accessibility in the remittances market, so that users can make informed decisions and have the ability to choose their best service option. In particular, remittances senders are often unaware of the different direct and indirect costs and fees charged by RSPs, and therefore ignore the total price of their remittances transaction until the money is delivered to their relatives. In this respect, regulators can actively facilitate transparency through the collection and publication of comparative prices and conditions of service among different RSPs. These efforts can be complemented by the provision of basic financial literacy to users.

The recent entry of financial institutions into the remittances market has made available more cost-efficient transactions, such as account-to-cash and account-to-account remittances. These are slowly gaining market share but are constrained by the fact that a large percentage of migrants do not have access to banking facilities, partly because of their irregular status. Indeed, at least in the case of the United States, federal regulation does not expressly forbid the provision of financial services to undocumented applicants, but the issue is far from being clear, creating concerns among both financial institutions and a large segment of prospective clients.

Accessibility issues and the quality of the financial services infrastructure in recipient countries are also critical to ensure security and efficiency of remittances services. Accessibility can be improved by enabling more financial institutions to participate in the remittances market. In particular, savings and loans, credit unions, and microfinance companies may be well positioned to act as disbursing agents, as their networks may be closer to the usual recipients of remittances than those of large commercial banks. In this sense, authorities in recipient countries should ensure that there are no unduly burdensome regulatory constraints to the participation of these entities.

Finally, since remittances channels can potentially be used for illicit purposes, including money laundering, fraud, and financing of terrorist activities, it is important to encourage and enable the use of formal systems (such as banks). Indeed, the risk of misuse of remittances channels is highest among informal providers that are completely unknown to the regulatory or supervisory bodies. Moreover, countries should ensure that oversight of formal providers is commensurate with the risk of misuse to avoid unnecessary costs, thus balancing the benefits of increased safety of the system with the possible inefficiencies that increased oversight might also create.

Policy Complementarities: What Can Policy Makers Do to Enhance the Development Impact of Remittances?

Since remittances are transfers between private parties, it is difficult to imagine which type of policies governments should follow to enhance their development impact. For example, if recipients and senders jointly decide that, given the country's existing economic environment and their personal situations, remittances should be directed toward consumption rather than toward savings or investment (a typical concern of policy makers in recipient countries), then it is difficult to imagine which type of *direct* policy interventions may induce these individuals to do otherwise, other than forcing recipients to save, as a number of African countries (such as Lesotho and Mozambique) and Latin American countries (Mexico in the 1940s) have done in the past. In fact, the latter is probably the type of policy recommendation to avoid. As argued by Maimbo and Ratha (2005), forcing remittances recipients to save more and consume less tends to reduce, rather than increase, consumer welfare.

Yet this is not to say that governments cannot do anything to increase the development impact of remittances, especially if we consider *indirect* policy interventions, that is, policies that try to change the remittances recipients' incentives to use their resources in one way or another. For example, as noted by Burnside and Dollar (2000, 2004), the impact of aid flows on the growth rate of recipient economies depends on whether the policy environment is favorable to private investment. Good policy environments will increase the return on investment (or reduce the risk associated with a given return), and thus will raise the opportunity cost of consumption. Chapter 10 explores whether a similar case can be made for the possibility that the development effectiveness of remittances depends, as that of official aid does, on the policy environment prevailing in recipient countries.

Our evidence suggests that indeed, remittances are more effective in both raising investment and enhancing growth in countries with higher levels of human capital, strong institutions, and good policy environments. Somewhat surprisingly, we also find that increases in remittances apparently have more of an investment and growth impact in countries with less developed financial sectors. One possible reason is that, as noted by Giuliano and Ruiz-Arranz (2005), remittances can be seen as relaxing liquidity constraints faced by the poor, and that those constraints would be more relevant in countries with less developed financial sectors.

The finding that remittances have more positive effects on growth in better policy contexts—encompassing more stable macroeconomic regimes, better institutional quality, and higher levels of human capital—is particularly important for Latin America. Indeed, in the three areas that seem to complement the impact of remittances on growth, the region has significant progress to make. Thus, during the first half of the 2000s, Latin America, together with the Middle East and Sub-Saharan Africa, were the regions with the worst combined indicators of inflation, trade openness, and excessive government burden.

Similarly, on the institutional front, Perry et al. (2006) note that a majority of Latin American countries (the exceptions being Brazil, Chile, Costa Rica, Mexico, Nicaragua, Panama, Trinidad and Tobago, and Uruguay) score below what would be expected in a combined index of the six institutional measures of the Kaufmann, Kraay, and Mastruzzi (2005) database. Finally, as noted in De Ferranti et al. (2003) even if the Latin American picture regarding net primary enrollment rates is quite encouraging, most Latin American countries have massive deficits in net enrollments in secondary education, even after controlling for income levels.

Overall, these results strengthen the basic conclusion of this study, namely that remittances have positive implications for growth and poverty reduction, but they are not a substitute for sound development policies. In particular, countries that have experienced sizable migration flows and now receive large volumes of remittances from their migrants have even stronger reasons to improve their policy environments, so as to enhance the positive impact of those flows and create better incentives for foreign and domestic investment.

Notes

1. Note that household surveys include remittances received from abroad and do not differentiate between those coming from developed or developing nations. Thus, these results encompass cases where South-South and South-North migration are predominant.

2. Today, most remittances-receiving countries do not impose explicit taxes on incoming remittances, although there are some cases of implicit taxation in the form of financial services taxes.

3. Social Protection Network.

4. Family Allowance Program.

References

Adams, R. 2005. "Remittances, Household Expenditure and Investment in Guatemala." Policy Research Working Paper No. 3532, World Bank, Washington, DC.

Adams, R., and J. Page. 2005. "Do International Migration and Remittances Reduce Poverty in Developing Countries?" *World Development* 33: 1645–69.

Attanasio, O., and V. Rios-Rull. 2001. "Consumption Smoothing and Extended Families: The Role of Government Sponsored Insurance." In *Shielding the Poor: Social Protection in the Developing World*, ed. Nora Lustig, 239–67. Washington, DC: Brookings Institution Press.

Beck, T., R. Levine, and N. Loayza. 2000. "Finance and the Sources of Growth." *Journal of Financial Economics* 58: 261–300.

Beck T., A. Demirgüç-Kunt, and R. Levine. 2007. "Finance, Inequality, and the Poor." *Journal of Economic Growth* 12 (1): 27–49.

Beck, T., A. Demirgüç-Kunt, and M.S. Martínez Pería. 2005. "Reaching Out: Access to and Use of Banking Services Across Countries." Policy Research Working Paper No. 3754, World Bank, Washington, DC.

Burnside, C.A., and D. Dollar. 2000. "Aid, Policies, and Growth." *American Economic Review* 90 (4): 847–68.

———. 2004. "Aid, Policies, and Growth: Revisiting the Evidence." Policy Research Working Paper Series 3251, World Bank, Washington, DC.

Cox, D., Eser, Z., and E. Jimenez. 1998. "Motives for Private Transfers Over the Life Cycle: An Analytical Framework and Evidence for Peru." *Journal of Development Economics* 55 (1): 57–80.

De Ferranti, D., G.E. Perry, I. Gill, J.L. Guasch, W.F. Maloney, C. Sanchez-Paramo, and N. Schady. 2003. *Closing the Gap in Education and Technology*. Washington, DC: World Bank.

Giuliano, P., and M. Ruiz-Arranz. 2005. "Remittances, Financial Development and Growth." IMF Working Paper 05/234, International Monetary Fund, Washington, DC.

Hanson, G.H., and C. Woodruff. 2003. "Emigration and Educational Attainment in Mexico." Unpublished, University of California, San Diego.

IMF (International Monetary Fund). 2005. *World Economic Outlook*. Washington, DC: International Monetary Fund.

Kaufmann, D., A. Kraay, and M. Mastruzzi. 2005. "Governance Matters IV: Governance Indicators for 1996–2004." Policy Research Working Paper No. 3630, World Bank, Washington, DC.

Lindert, K., E. Skoufias, and J. Shapiro. 2006. "Redistributing Income to the Poor *and* the Rich: Public Transfers in Latin America and the Caribbean." Regional Study Working Paper, World Bank, Washington, DC.

Maimbo S., and D. Ratha. 2005. *Remittances: Development Impact and Future Prospects*. Washington, DC: World Bank.

Olinto, P. 2006. "Do Conditional Cash Transfer Programs Crowd Out Private Transfers? Evidence from Randomized Trials in Rural Honduras and Nicaragua." Unpublished, World Bank, Washington, DC.

Perry, G.E., O. Arias, J.H. López, W.F. Maloney, and L. Servén. 2006. *Poverty Reduction and Growth: Virtuous and Vicious Circles*. Washington, DC: World Bank.

Schoeni, R. 2002. "Does Unemployment Insurance Displace Familial Assistance?" *Public Choice* 110: 99–119.

Schoeni, R.F. 1996. "Does Aid to Families with Dependent Children Displace Familial Assistance?" Rand Working Paper, DRU-1453-RC.

Teruel, G., and B. Davis. 2000. *Final Report: An Evaluation of the Impact of PROGRESA Cash Payments on Private Inter-Household Transfers*. Washington, DC: International Food Policy Research Institute.

World Bank. 2006. *Global Economic Prospects 2006: Economic Implications of Remittances and Migration*. Washington, DC: World Bank.

2

How Important Are Remittances in Latin America?

Pablo Acosta, Pablo Fajnzylber, and J. Humberto López

Workers' remittances have become a major source of financing in developing countries, reaching levels that are comparable to those of foreign direct investment (FDI) and doubling those of official development assistance (ODA). However, there are a number of questions that are critical for determining the development impact of remittances in Latin America: How important are those flows in the regional context, and how have they evolved over the past years? What do we know about remittances recipients at the country and household levels? Are they mostly among the poor, or instead do they belong to better-off classes? Are the observed patterns similar across various Latin American countries? Finally, can we rely on official statistics?

Introduction

Workers' remittances have become a major source of financing in developing countries. According to the World Bank's *Global Economic Prospects 2006*, remittances to middle- and low-income countries in 1990 amounted to about US$31 billion. Fifteen years later, they are estimated to have reached about US$200 billion, of which about one-fourth went to Latin America and the Caribbean (Latin America henceforth). Workers' remittances now account for about 30 percent of total financial flows to developing countries, are more than twice as large as official development assistance (ODA) flows, and represent the equivalent of 2.5 percent of the gross national income of the developing world.

The rising importance of remittances flows has been reflected in the increasing attention being devoted to the issue by development practitioners in both academic and policy circles. At the academic level, a number of recent papers have explored the impact of remittances on poverty (Adams and Page 2005; Page and Plaza 2005; Acosta et al. 2006, 2007), intertemporal consumption smoothing (Yang 2006), growth (Giuliano and Ruiz-Arranz 2005; Calderón, Fajnzylber, and López 2006b), risk management (Amuedo-Dorantes and Pozo 2004), education (Cox-Edwards and Ureta 2003), labor supply (Rodriguez and Tiongson 2001), and external competitiveness (Amuedo-Dorantes and Pozo 2004; Rajan and Subramanian 2005).

At the policy level, the International Monetary Fund (IMF), the World Bank, and the United Nations Development Programme (UNDP) have all addressed the growing importance of migration and remittances and their impact on development efforts in some of their flagship publications. For example, the IMF's *World Economic Outlook 2005* (IMF 2005b) devoted significant attention to the determinants and implications of inflows of workers' remittances, while the World Bank's *Global Economic Prospects 2006* (World Bank 2006) had as its central topic the economic implications of remittances and migration. The World Bank has also edited a number of volumes on migration and remittances issues (see Maimbo and Ratha 2005; and Özden and Schiff 2006). Similarly, the UNDP's 2005 *Human Development Report* for El Salvador (United Nations 2005) focused heavily on the development impact of remittances, and the UNDP organized a high-level meeting on the topic in New York in the fall of 2006.

Yet to a large extent, the existing works have focused on the role of remittances or migration at the global level, with relatively little attention paid to region-specific issues. This is an important limitation because if, as discussed in chapter 3, the migration patterns of the Latin American region differ significantly from those of other regions, it is possible that findings based on studies relying on global databases are not fully applicable to the Latin American context. True, there are also works based on country case studies that focus on Latin American economies. However, these tend to be based on a limited number of countries (typically Mexico, El Salvador, and Guatemala) and have important methodological differences among them, something that in turn makes it difficult to easily extend and generalize the results to the region.

This book tries to somewhat fill the existing knowledge gap for Latin America. To start with, in this chapter we explore the basic facts of remittances to the region. Among others, we address the following questions: How much and how relevant from an economic perspective are these flows? How have they evolved over the past few years? Are they leveling off or continuing to increase? What do we know about those at the receiving end of the remittances chain? Are they the poor, or do they belong to better-off classes? What is their level of education? Finally, to what extent can we trust statistics on officially recorded remittances?

The Magnitude of Remittances Flows: The Global Picture

According to balance of payments statistics,[1] officially recorded remittances flows to developing countries reached US$193 billion in 2005, of which about US$48 billion went to the Latin American region. This would make Latin America the top remittances-recipient region of the world (figure 2.1, panel A). Latin America would be followed by East Asia and the Pacific (East Asia henceforth) with US$45 billion, South Asia (US$36 billion), Europe and Central Asia (US$31 billion), the Middle East and North Africa (US$24 billion), and finally Sub-Saharan Africa, the region with the lowest official remittances flows (US$9 billion). Not only is Latin America the top recipient region of the world, but it is also (together with East Asia) the region that has experienced the highest growth in officially recorded remittances since 1980, with annual growth rates of 14 percent (figure 2.2, panel A). This would be in contrast to the Middle East and North Africa, where over the past 25 years remittances have increased at a rate below 6 percent. At the global level, remittances are estimated to have increased at an annual rate of 8 percent since 1980.

To put this number into context, it is worth noting that: (i) at this growth rate, remittances flows double approximately every nine years; and (ii) the median GDP per-capita growth rate for the developing countries over the past 25 years was below 1 percent per year.

The regional ranking, based on total remittances flows hides, however, an important factor regarding the relative regional importance of remittances

Figure 2.1 Regional Distribution of Remittances in 2005

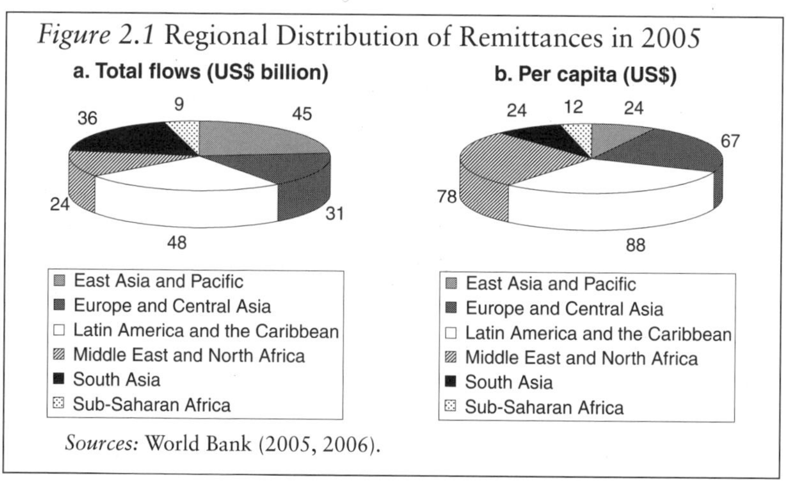

Sources: World Bank (2005, 2006).

Figure 2.2 Annual Growth Rate of Recorded Remittances, 1980–2005

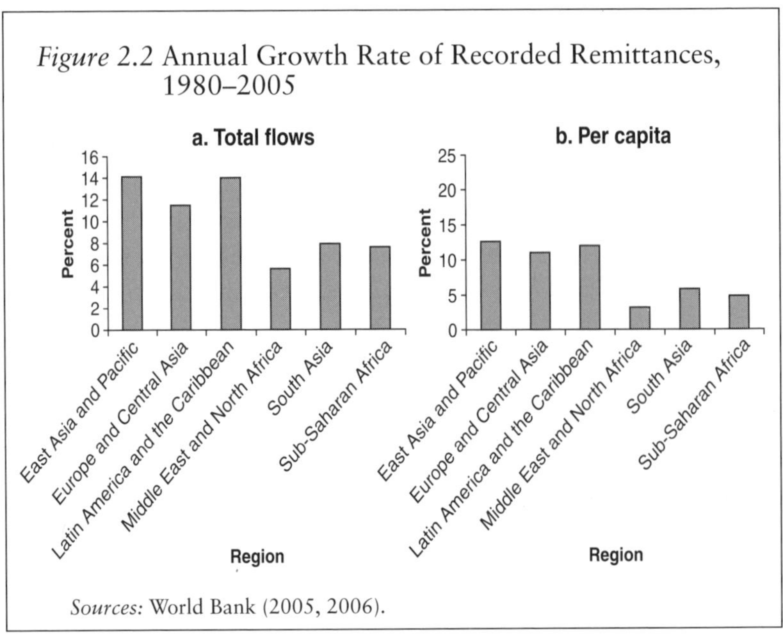

Sources: World Bank (2005, 2006).

Table 2.1 International Flows to Low- and Middle-Income Countries

Region	*Remittances (US$ billion)*	*Remittances per capita (US$)*	*FDI (US$ billion)*	*Private non-FDI (US$ billion)*	*ODA (US$ billion)*
EAP	45.1	24	96.9	33.3	9.5
ECA	31.4	67	73.7	110.2	5.7
LAC	48.2	88	70.0	28.9	6.3
MENA	24.0	78	13.8	7.2	26.9
SAR	35.6	24	9.9	13.4	9.3
SSA	8.7	12	16.6	9.8	32.6
Total	193.0	36	280.8	202.9	90.4

Sources: World Bank (2005, 2006).

Note: EAP = East Asia and Pacific; ECA = Europe and Central Asia; LAC = Latin America and the Caribbean; MENA = Middle East and North Africa; SAR = South Asia; SSA = Sub-Saharan Africa.

for development purposes—namely, the fact that the population of the different regions is also dramatically different. For example, East Asia has remittances flows that are similar to those of Latin America, but the population of East Asia is almost four times as large as that of Latin America.

In fact, when we take into account the existing differences in the population of the regions and compute remittances on a per-capita basis, Latin America would be the top receiving region (figure 2.1, panel B) with almost US$90 per person per year (table 2.1). This amount is more than twice as large as that of the developing world as a whole (US$36 per person per year). On a per-capita basis, Latin America would be followed by the Middle East and North Africa (US$78), Europe and Central Asia (US$67), East and South Asia (about US$24), and Sub-Saharan Africa, which with US$12 per person per year is also the lowest receiving region on a per-capita basis. Regarding growth rates of per-capita remittances, Latin America and East Asia continue to be the regions that have experienced the fastest growth, with annual rates of about 12 percent each (figure 2.2, panel B).

The relevance of workers' remittances is also apparent when we compare them with other international financial flows (both private and official) to low- and middle-income countries. As table 2.1 indicates, remittances represent 25 percent of the US$767 billion total international financial flows to the developing world, and are estimated to have reached levels equivalent to 70 percent of foreign direct investment (FDI) flows to developing countries (US$281 billion), and exceed ODA flows by about US$100 billion. Remittances are also larger than private non-FDI flows, such as portfolio investment and Bank and trade-related lending (US$203 billion). In relation to other financial flows, remittances are particularly important in South Asia, the Middle East and North Africa, and Latin America. In South Asia, they would account for more than half of the total international flows received, whereas in the Middle East and North Africa, and in Latin America, they would represent about 33 percent.

It is worth noting that this situation is radically different from that existing in 1990, when ODA accounted for about 40 percent of the financial flows to developing countries (figure 2.3). In fact, over the past 15 years private flows have increased dramatically at the cost of official flows. In this regard, workers' remittances are not an exception.

Figure 2.3 International Financial Flows, 1990 and 2005 (percent)

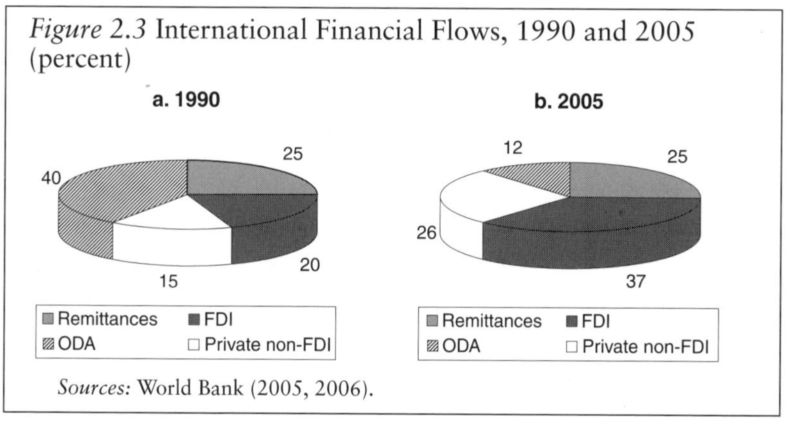

Sources: World Bank (2005, 2006).

The Magnitude of Remittances Flows: The Regional Picture

The growing importance of remittances to the Latin American region is reflected in figure 2.4, where we report the evolution of these flows (in current U.S. dollars) for 31 Latin American countries over the period 1980–2005.[2] This figure indicates that officially recorded remittances flows to Latin America have increased 25-fold since 1980, when remittances amounted to about US$1.9 billion. What is more relevant, this figure does not give any indication of remittances flows leveling off or stabilizing. If anything, the figure indicates that there is a clear upward tendency underlying the data to the point that a simulation of the evolution of remittances under the assumption of a continuous trend would result in remittances of about US$60 billion in 2007. While this estimate is likely to be on the high side of what one could expect,[3] it nevertheless highlights the fact that a collapse in remittances does not seem very likely over the short run. In other words, it is not unrealistic to assume that remittances are here to stay, at least in the short term.

It would be possible to argue that the previous figures have been artificially inflated by considering them in current rather than constant U.S. dollars. And in fact, once we take into account the contribution of U.S. inflation, the increase in remittances flows over time becomes less marked. Yet in 1980 prices, today's remittances flows would still be above US$20 billion (that is, in real terms, remittances have increased more than 10-fold over the past 20-plus years). Or consider the evolution in terms of the region's GDP. In that case, remittances have also increased dramatically since 1980, when they represented a mere 0.3 percent of GDP, to about 2.2 percent today. In other words, no matter how one looks at the evolution of remittances, the message that emerges is that they have increased significantly over a sustained period.

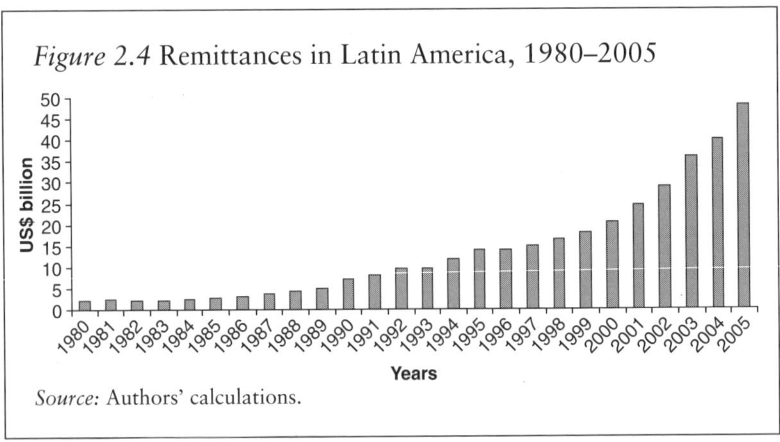

Figure 2.4 Remittances in Latin America, 1980–2005

Source: Authors' calculations.

At the country level, panel A of figure 2.5 reports the remittances to GDP ratio for a number of Latin American countries in 2005, and table 2.2 reports remittances' annual flows, and growth rates for each country in the region over 2002–05—using preliminary estimates for the latter year. The figures in table 2.2 indicate that remittances represent about one-fourth of GDP in Guyana (25.5 percent) and in Haiti (23 percent). A second tier of countries with high remittances to GDP ratios includes Honduras (21.6 percent), Jamaica (18.6), and El Salvador (16.7 percent). Similarly, in Nicaragua, Guatemala, and the Dominican Republic, remittances are between 9 percent and 12 percent of GDP. The importance of those flows can be illustrated by comparison with other private capital flows. Thus, in Guatemala remittances are 14 times higher than FDI flows. In Honduras, they are four times higher; El Salvador three times higher; and the Dominican Republic twice as high. Even in Ecuador and Colombia, where in relative terms remittances are lower than in several Central American and Caribbean countries, remittances represent about 100 percent and 200 percent of FDI, respectively.

The classification of recipients changes significantly on a U.S. dollar basis. Overall, the country with the highest absolute remittances flows (panel B of figure 2.5) is Mexico, which received US$21.8 billion in 2005. This would represent 45 percent of total flows to Latin America in that year, and would make Mexico the third-largest world recipient in 2005 after India ($23.7 billion) and China ($22.5 billion). Brazil and Colombia are ranked 19th and 20th among the top remittances-receiving countries in the world, with flows of US$3.5 billion and US$3.3 billion, respectively, in 2005. Other countries with more than US$2 billion of remittances inflows in 2005 (US$2.7 billion on average) include Guatemala, El Salvador, the Dominican Republic, and Ecuador. Also worthy of note are Honduras, Jamaica, and Peru, where remittances are well above US$1 billion in 2005.

On a per-capita basis (panel C of figure 2.5), the country with the highest level of remittances would be Jamaica with about US$700. It is followed by Barbados ($519) and El Salvador, with flows of approximately US$400. The average for the 29 countries being considered here would be close to US$150 per capita per year, but that amount increases to US$320 among the 10 countries with highest per-capita remittances—a group that also includes the Dominican Republic, Haiti, Trinidad and Tobago, Honduras, Antigua and Barbuda, Guatemala, and Mexico.

It is also worth noting that between 2002 and 2005, remittances to Latin America are estimated to have grown at a rate of close to 20 percent per year. While this rapid growth has been largely driven by Mexico's 25 percent annual growth in remittances flows, there are several countries with annual rates around 20 percent (table 2.2).

Figure 2.5 Remittances in Latin America in 2005

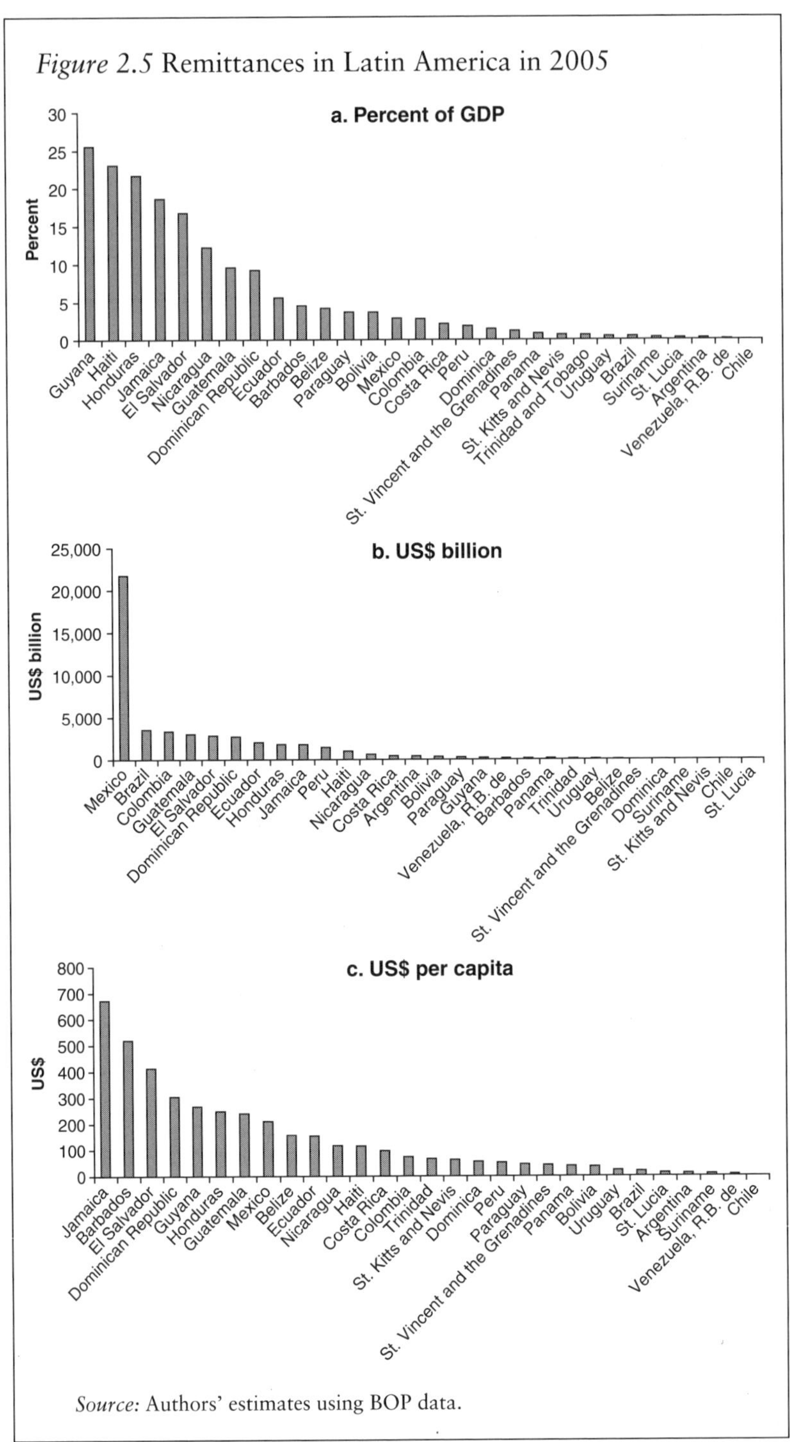

Source: Authors' estimates using BOP data.

Table 2.2 Remittances to Latin American and Caribbean Countries (US$ millions)

Country	*2002*	*2003*	*2004*	*2005e*	*Annual growth (percent)*	*Remittances/GDP*			
					2002–05	*2002*	*2003*	*2004*	*2005e*
Mexico	11,029	14,911	18,143	21,772	25.4	1.7	2.3	2.7	2.8
Central America									
Guatemala	1,600	2,147	2,592	3,033	23.8	6.9	8.6	9.5	9.6
El Salvador	1,953	2,122	2,564	2,842	13.3	13.7	14.1	16.2	16.7
Honduras	718	867	1,151	1,796	35.7	11.0	12.6	15.4	21.7
Nicaragua	377	439	519	600	16.8	9.4	10.7	11.5	12.2
Costa Rica	250	321	319	421	19.0	1.5	1.8	1.7	2.1
Panama	85	94	105	126	14.0	0.7	0.7	0.7	0.8
Belize	29	34	34	46	16.6	3.1	3.4	3.2	4.2
Caribbean									
Dominican Republic	2,195	2,326	2,501	2,717	7.4	10.2	14.2	13.6	9.2
Jamaica	1,261	1,399	1,623	1,783	12.2	14.7	17.0	18.3	18.6
Haiti	676	811	932	985	13.4	19.8	27.6	24.4	23.1
Guyana	51	99	153	201	58.0	7.1	13.3	19.5	25.5
Barbados	109	114	109	140	8.7	4.4	4.3	3.9	4.5
Trinidad and Tobago	79	87	87	87	3.3	0.9	0.8	0.7	0.6
St. Vincent and the Grenadines	4	4	5	5	7.7	1.1	1.0	1.2	1.2

(continued)

Table 2.2 Remittances to Latin American and Caribbean Countries (US$ millions) (*continued*)

					Annual growth (percent)	*Remittances/GDP*			
Country	*2002*	*2003*	*2004*	*2005e*	*2002–05*	*2002*	*2003*	*2004*	*2005e*
Dominica	4	4	4	4	0.0	1.6	1.5	1.5	1.4
St. Kitts and Nevis	3	3	3	3	0.0	0.9	0.8	0.7	0.7
St. Lucia	2	2	2	2	0.0	0.3	0.3	0.3	0.2
South America									
Brazil	2,499	2,822	3,576	3,540	13.1	0.5	0.6	0.6	0.4
Colombia	2,480	3,076	3,190	3,346	10.5	3.1	3.9	3.3	2.7
Ecuador	1,438	1,633	1,838	2,038	12.3	5.8	5.7	5.6	5.6
Peru	705	860	1,123	1,440	26.9	1.2	1.4	1.6	1.8
Argentina	189	256	292	413	29.8	0.2	0.2	0.2	0.2
Bolivia	113	159	210	338	44.1	1.4	2.0	2.4	3.6
Paraguay	202	223	238	268	9.9	4.2	4.8	4.7	3.7
Venezuela, R.B. de	19	21	20	148	98.2	0.0	0.0	0.0	0.1
Uruguay	36	62	70	78	29.4	0.3	0.6	0.5	0.5
Suriname	15	23	9	4	–35.6	1.6	2.3	0.8	0.8
Chile	12	13	13	3	–37.0	0.0	0.0	0.0	0.0
Latin America	28,083	34,932	41,425	48,179	19.7	1.7	2.0	2.1	2.0

Source: Authors' calculations using BOP and WEO data. e = Preliminary estimates.

Profile of Recipients

The BOP data reviewed in the previous section allows for a cross-country comparison of remittances. Yet it gives no information about those at the receiving end. For example, are those receiving remittances the poorest groups in society so that remittances can be expected to have a large impact on poverty reduction? Or instead are they from better-off classes so that remittances, while certainly increasing welfare in the recipient country, may not have that much of an impact on poverty? In order to address these issues, it is necessary to have household-specific information, and therefore a natural way forward is looking at household surveys.

Unfortunately, nationally representative household surveys with specific questions on remittances are only available for 11 Latin American countries: Haiti, El Salvador, Honduras, the Dominican Republic, Nicaragua, Guatemala, Ecuador, Paraguay, Mexico, Bolivia, and Peru.[4] On a more positive front, it is worth noting that in terms of BOP data, these countries would represent more than two-thirds of remittances to the region.

We next review the profile of recipients that emerges from these household surveys.

How Many Households Receive Remittances?

The number of households receiving remittances in the Latin American region varies significantly across countries (figure 2.6). For example, in Haiti more than 25 percent of the households reported having received remittances in 2001. At the other extreme, only 3 percent of the Peruvian households benefit from these flows. In between, remittances reach between 10 percent and 25 percent of the households in the Dominican Republic,

Figure 2.6 Share of Households Receiving Remittances, 2001

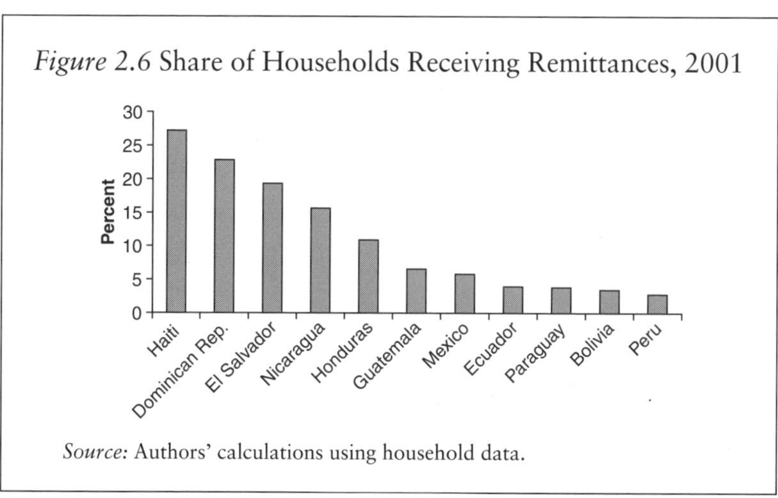

Source: Authors' calculations using household data.

El Salvador, Nicaragua, and Honduras; between 5 percent and 10 percent in Mexico and Guatemala; and between 3 percent and 5 percent in Bolivia, Ecuador, and Paraguay.

Who Receives Remittances in Latin America?

A natural question that arises from the previous discussion is with regard to the income distribution of those households receiving remittances. Figure 2.7 shows the relative position of Latin American recipient families according to income quintiles both for nonremittances income and for total income (including remittances) for the 11 Latin American and Caribbean countries for which remittances microdata are available. The figure was constructed by averaging the results for the individual countries (see below for country details).

Review of this figure reveals two important elements. First, the income data that excludes remittances indicate that, on average for the 11 countries under analysis, 30 percent of the households receiving remittances are in the lowest quintile of the income distribution; the remaining 70 percent are distributed more or less homogeneously over the four richest quintiles. In other words, remittances flows seem to be directed to all income groups, but the proportion that goes to the poorest families appears to outweigh

Figure 2.7 Households Receiving Remittances by Income Distribution Quintile

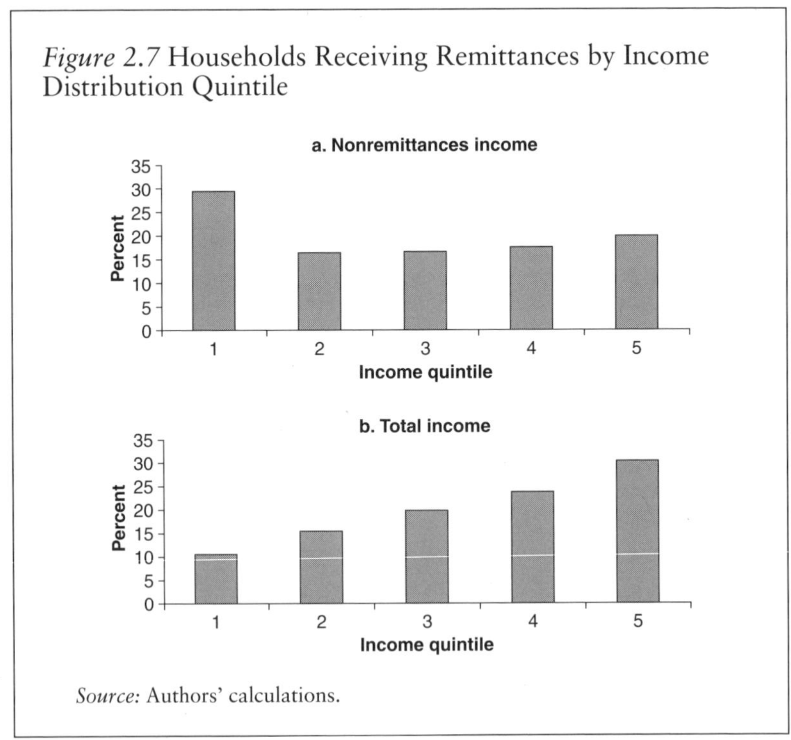

Source: Authors' calculations.

that which goes to any of the other four groups. Second, once we take into account remittances income, recipient households significantly climb the income ladder. In fact, after we take into account the role of remittances, only 10 percent of the households that receive them belong to the lowest quintile of the income distribution. In contrast, on the basis of total income, more than 30 percent of the households receiving remittances would now be in the highest income quintile. Thus, this aggregate analysis indicates that remittances seem to have a positive impact on the incomes of the poor.

The data underlying figure 2.7, however, show significant country heterogeneity (figure 2.8), as the socioeconomic segment from which migrants and recipient families come varies considerably across Latin American countries. For instance, in the case of Mexico, remittances recipients are predominantly poor: 61 percent of the households that report receiving remittances fall in the first quintile of nonremittances income, and only 4 percent are in the top quintile. Similarly, in Paraguay, 42 percent of recipients are in the lowest quintile, and only 8 percent are in the top quintile. Other countries where at least 30 percent of remittances recipients are in the lowest quintile (that is, where flows tend to be directed toward the lower quintile) are Ecuador, El Salvador, and Guatemala.

In contrast, in Peru and Nicaragua, the distribution of remittances across households is completely different. For example, in Peru, less than 6 percent of the households that receive remittances belong to the lowest quintile, while 40 percent belong to the top quintile. Or take the case of Nicaragua, where only 12 percent of the recipients are in the first quintile, while 33 percent belong to the fifth quintile. Thus, in these two countries, remittances seem to be flowing toward the richest.

In between the group of Mexico, Paraguay, Ecuador, El Salvador, and Guatemala, and the group of Peru and Nicaragua, there are four countries (Bolivia, Honduras, the Dominican Republic, and Haiti) where remittances recipients are found at similar rates among households in the bottom and top income quintiles, exhibiting a U-shaped distribution (that is, remittances flow toward the poorest and the richest in the same proportion, which is more than toward the three middle deciles).

This situation changes dramatically when we analyze the economic status of recipients on the basis of total income (including the value of remittances). In fact, figure 2.9 suggests that: (i) the share of recipients that belongs to the lowest quintile falls dramatically in all the countries; and (ii) with the exception of Mexico, and to a lesser extent Paraguay and El Salvador, where 50 percent, 40 percent, and 34 percent of recipients, respectively, continue to be in the first and second quintiles, in the rest of the countries more than half of the recipients are in the two highest quintiles. Not surprisingly, this concentration is particularly marked in those countries where migrants seem to come from richer classes. Figure 2.9 indicates that in Peru, more than 75 percent of recipients are now in the highest two quintiles of the income distribution. The situation is similar in Nicaragua, a country where more

Figure 2.8 Households Receiving Remittances by Quintile of Nonremittances Income Distribution

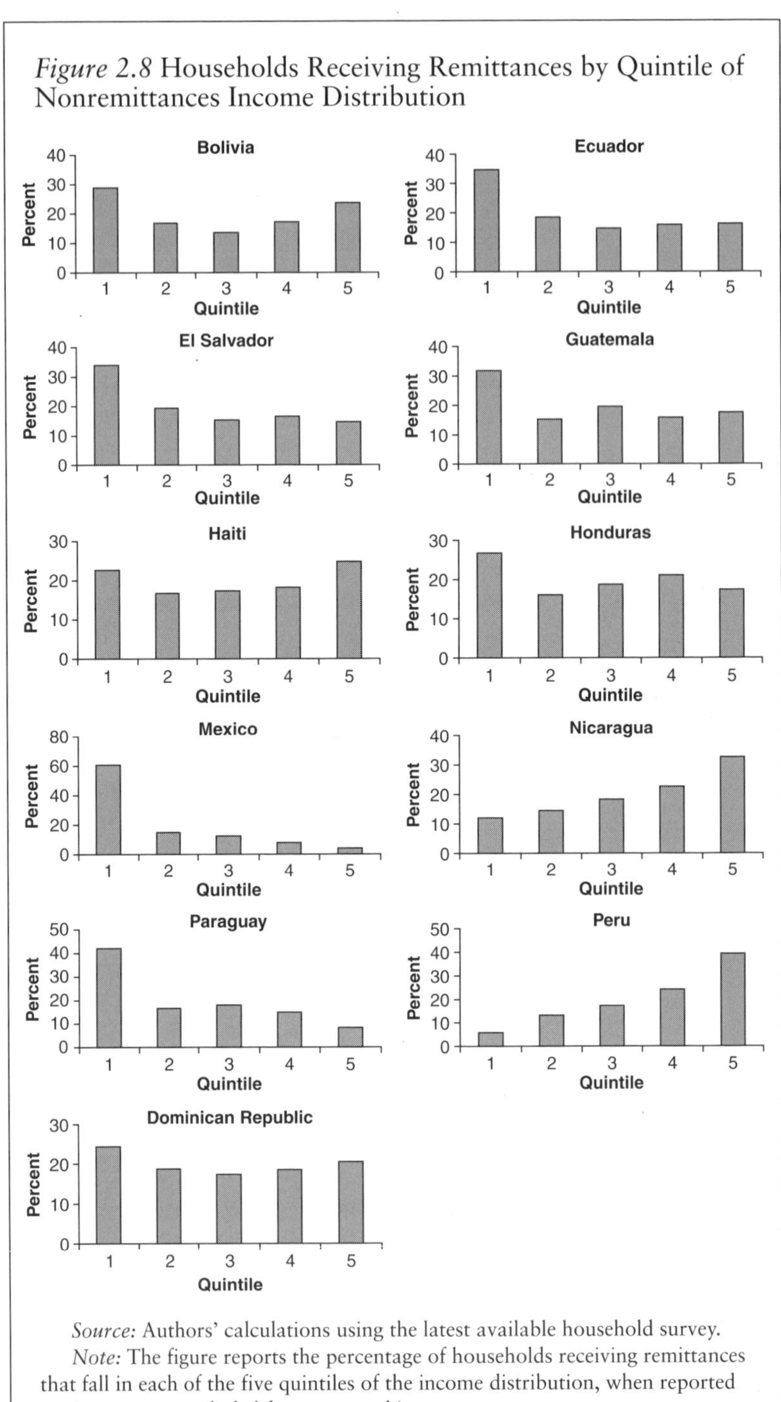

Source: Authors' calculations using the latest available household survey.

Note: The figure reports the percentage of households receiving remittances that fall in each of the five quintiles of the income distribution, when reported remittances are excluded from reported income.

Figure 2.9 Households Receiving Remittances by Quintile of Total Income Distribution

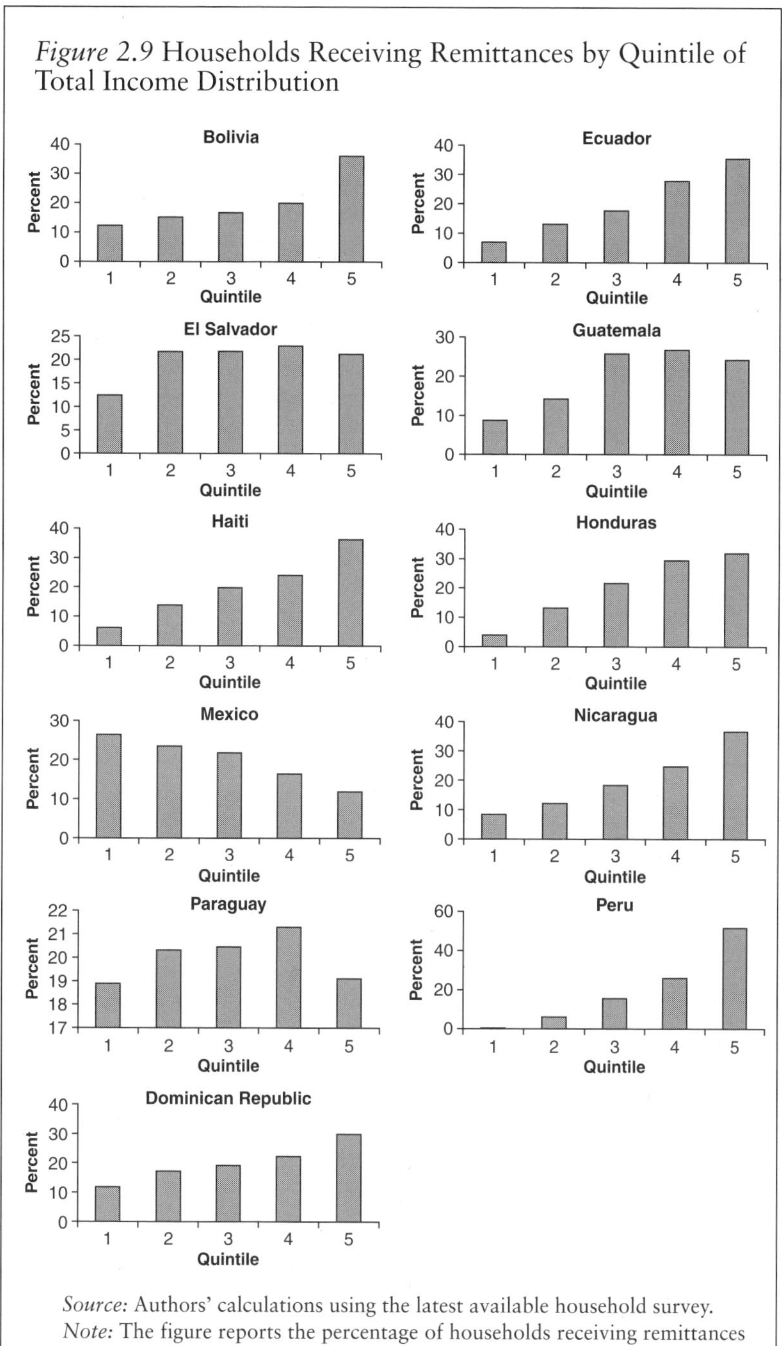

Source: Authors' calculations using the latest available household survey.

Note: The figure reports the percentage of households receiving remittances that fall in each of the five quintiles of the total income distribution, (when reported remittances are included in reported income).

than 60 percent of recipients belong to the top two quintiles. Thus, on the basis of this analysis, one would expect that remittances might have quite different inequality and poverty impacts in different countries.

Remittances and Education

Understanding the selectivity process of migration is important in order to evaluate the overall impact of migration on poverty and inequality (see Acosta, Calderón, Fajnzylber, and López 2007 for a technical discussion of the relevance of selectivity issues in this context; see also chapters 3 and 4 for a more basic discussion). One important dimension of the selection into the migration process is likely to be related to the patterns of educational attainment in the households with migrants, and ideally we would like to compare the educational attainment of migrants and nonmigrants. Unfortunately, the only country survey that contains information on migrants' education is Nicaragua (2001).

According to that survey, the average education of adult migrants is 6.83 years, while nonmigrant adults have on average 5.61 years of education, which reinforces the idea emerging from figures 2.8 and 2.9 that migrants are positively selected in Nicaragua. This result is similar to the one in Chiquiar and Hanson (2005), who, on the basis of the 1990 and 2000 Mexican and U.S. population censuses, find that Mexican immigrants in the United States are more educated than nonmigrants in Mexico. For the rest of the countries, the only relevant information available in our surveys relates to the schooling of migrants' family members. However, the evidence for Nicaragua suggests that the level of education of migrants closely resembles that of nonmigrant adult members in the same households.[5] In other words, it seems that one can get a good approximation of the patterns of educational selection in migration using data on adult family members left behind by migrants.

Figure 2.10 presents the incidence of remittances recipient households based on the average years of schooling of adults ages 16 to 65. For example, in the case of Nicaragua, only 10 percent of those without education receive remittances, whereas about 30 percent of those with 12 or more years do. Similarly, in Peru, only 2 percent of those without education are recipients, compared to 6 percent of those with 12 or more years. That is, remittances are relatively more important among those with higher education than among those with lower educational levels. In contrast, in Mexico, Paraguay, and Ecuador, recipients tend to be more represented among the less educated groups. Take the case of Mexico, where between 10 percent and 15 percent of those with less than four years of education receive remittances, compared to less than 2.5 percent among those with at least 12 years. Or take the case of Paraguay, where the corresponding shares for least and most educated groups would be 8 percent and 3 percent, respectively. In these two cases, remittances are relatively more relevant among less educated groups.

Figure 2.10 Educational Characteristics of Households Receiving Remittances

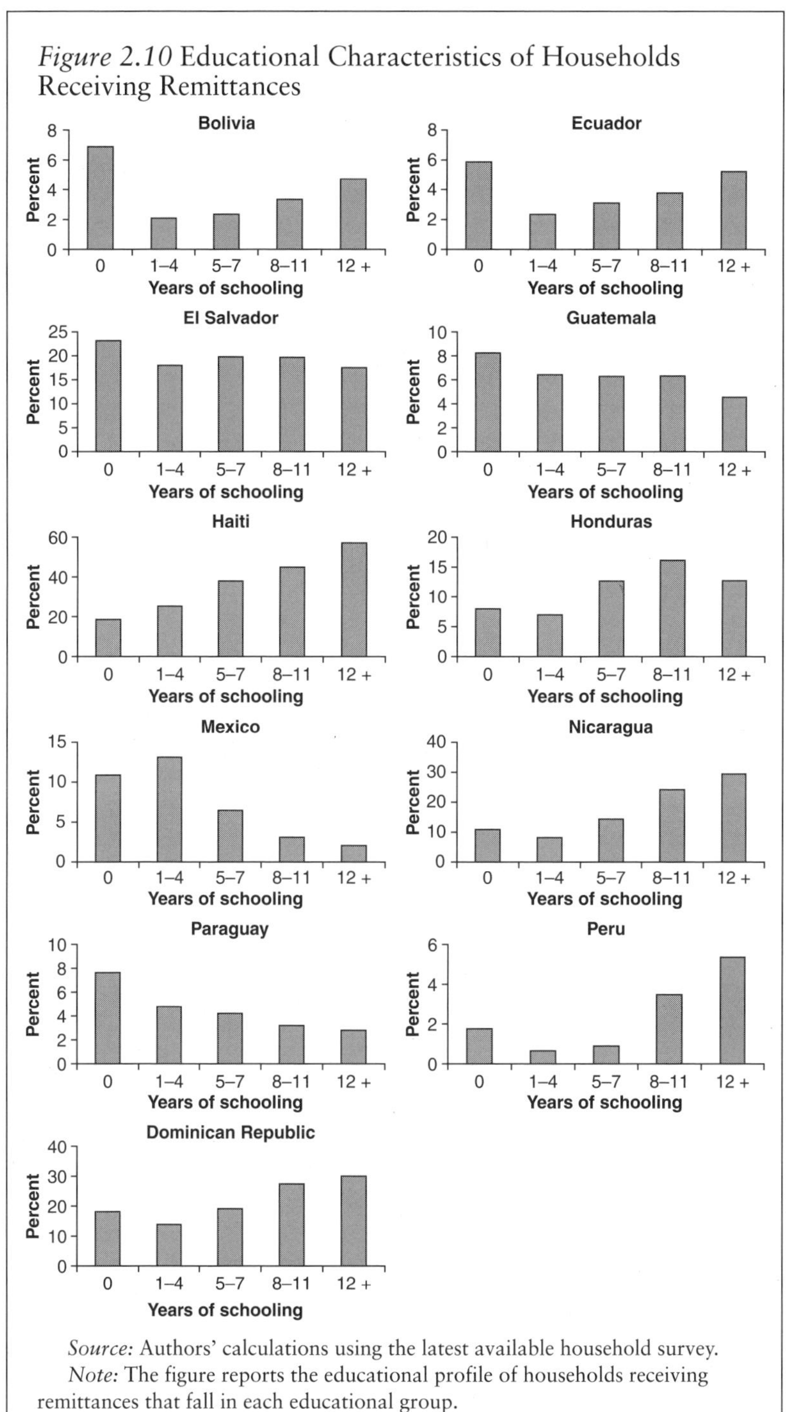

Source: Authors' calculations using the latest available household survey.

Note: The figure reports the educational profile of households receiving remittances that fall in each educational group.

Table 2.3 Percentage of Households with Migrants by Average Years of Adult Education (16–65 Years Old) in the Household

Years of adult education	*El Salvador*	*Honduras*	*Haiti*	*Nicaragua*
0	18.37	6.85	21.08	11.37
1–4	14.09	7.28	29.74	7.49
5–7	14.24	11.42	38.94	12.34
8–11	14.27	13.89	43.52	17.89
12 +	12.87	11.81	62.54	12.90
All households	14.46	10.04	29.92	12.04
Average education of adults in non-migrant households (years)	6.28**	5.17***	2.27***	5.39***
Average education of adults in all households (years)	5.93**	6.09***	3.91***	6.36***

Source: Authors' calculations using household survey data.
Note: ** significant at 5% level. *** significant at 1% level.

Table 2.3 shows the proportion of households with migrants across the educational distribution of the four countries (El Salvador, Haiti, Honduras, and Nicaragua) for which information is available not only on households with remittances receipts, but also on households with members who have migrated abroad. In El Salvador, 14.5 percent of the surveyed families reported having members who were international migrants, while 19.3 percent of the surveyed families receive remittances—including money received from distant family members and friends abroad. The equivalent figures for Haiti, Honduras, and Nicaragua show that, respectively, 29.9 percent, 10 percent, and 12 percent of the families have migrants, and 27.2 percent, 10.9 percent, and 15.6 percent, respectively, receive remittances.

Overall, the results indicate the presence of negative educational selection into migration in Guatemala, El Salvador, and Paraguay,[6] and of positive educational selection in Haiti, Peru, Honduras, the Dominican Republic, and Nicaragua. The evidence presented here is less conclusive for Bolivia, Ecuador, and Mexico, where migrants are likely to be drawn from several educational levels.

How Important Are Remittances for Recipients?

An issue of particular interest to infer the relevance of remittances in this context is the amount received by recipient households. Figure 2.11 addresses this issue and suggests that for the 11 countries under analysis, on average, the typical household receiving remittances reports about

Figure 2.11 Average Annual Amount Reported by Recipients

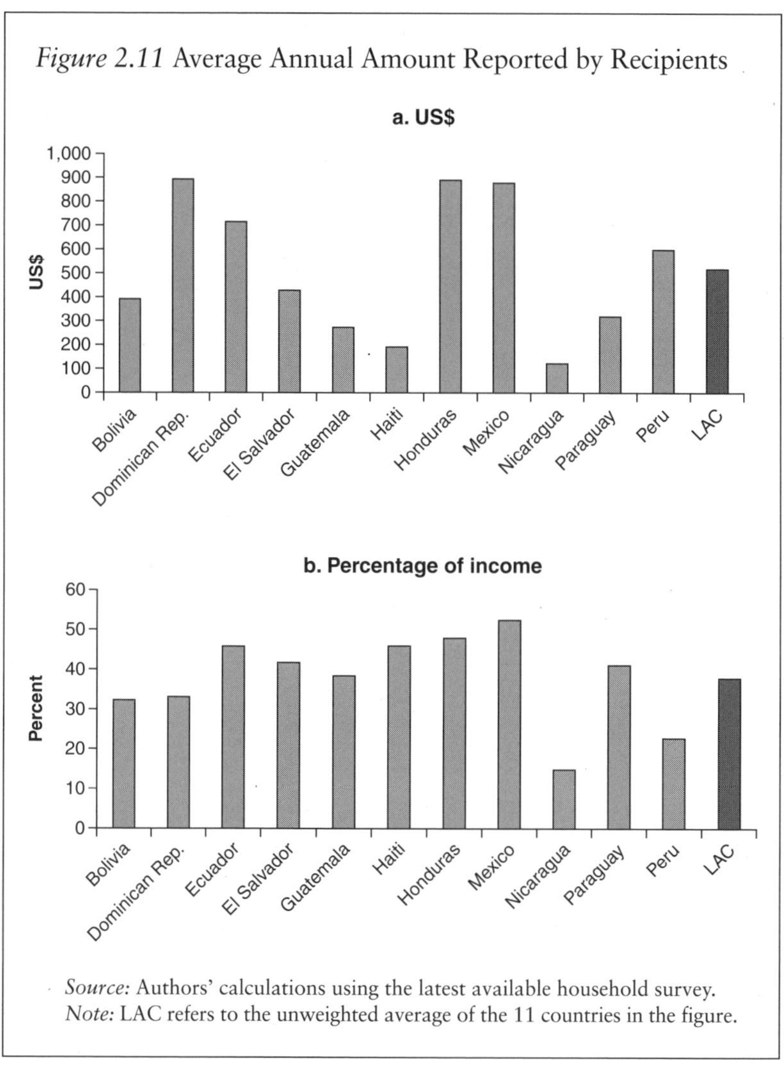

Source: Authors' calculations using the latest available household survey.
Note: LAC refers to the unweighted average of the 11 countries in the figure.

US$500 per year (panel A). Here, there is also significant variation. In the Dominican Republic, Mexico, and Honduras, remittances may be close to US$900 per receiving household per year; in Nicaragua and Haiti they are much smaller. In fact, in Nicaragua, household remittances are estimated at about US$120 per receiving household, while in Haiti, they are estimated at US$191. Among the remaining countries, Peruvian and Ecuadorian households report receiving between US$600 and US$700, Salvadoran US$430, and Guatemalan and Paraguayan between US$200 and US$400.

The country variability is much smaller when we look at remittances as a share of the income of the receiving families. In fact, apart from Nicaragua and Peru, remittances tend to represent between 30 percent and 50 percent of household income (panel B). However, much more variation across countries is observed in the manner in which the share of remittances in recipient households' income varies across income quintiles. Indeed, as seen in figure 2.12, while the income share of remittances is generally higher among recipient households located in lower income quintiles—the rich are less dependent on remittances than the poor—the decline in this share as one moves up the income distribution is quite slow in some countries and very fast in others. As an example, in Mexico, Haiti, Paraguay, and Bolivia, the decline in the share of remittances in income from the highest receiving quintile to the lowest receiving quintile is about 10 percent. In these countries, the share of remittances in income is very similar in poor and rich households. At the other extreme, in Guatemala and El Salvador, remittances represent, respectively, 63 percent and 55 percent of income in households located in the first income quintile, but fall to less than 20 percent of income among households in the fifth quintile. Similarly, in Peru and Nicaragua, remittances are 50 percent lower as a percentage of recipients' income in the bottom quintile, as compared to the top quintile. Honduras and Ecuador are intermediate cases, with declines in the income share of remittances among recipients of about 30 percent from the first to the fifth quintiles.

How Regressive is the Distribution of Remittances Income?

Given that a larger share of recipients tends to be located in the upper quintiles of the income distribution (figure 2.9)—the only exception being Mexico—the finding that remittances are higher as a percentage of income for poor recipients, compared to their richer counterparts, (figure 2.12) does not imply that remittances have a progressive effect on the distribution of income. In fact, as seen in figure 2.13, with the exceptions of Mexico, El Salvador, and to a lesser extent Paraguay and Guatemala, remittances are a bigger share of total income in the upper quintiles of the income distribution, considering all households in each quintile, regardless of their remittances recipient status. Thus, for instance, in Haiti, almost 25 percent of the income of households in the fifth quintile comes from remittances, compared to 5 percent and 10 percent for the first and second quintiles, respectively. Large differences of this sort are also found in the Dominican Republic and Honduras, where among the richest 20 percent, remittances represent, respectively, 11 percent and 8 percent of total income, compared to a respective average of 5 percent and 3 percent for households in the two lowest quintiles.

More direct evidence on the extent to which remittances have a regressive effect on the distribution of income is provided in figure 2.14, which

Figure 2.12 Income Share of Remittances by Income Quintile (Recipients Only)

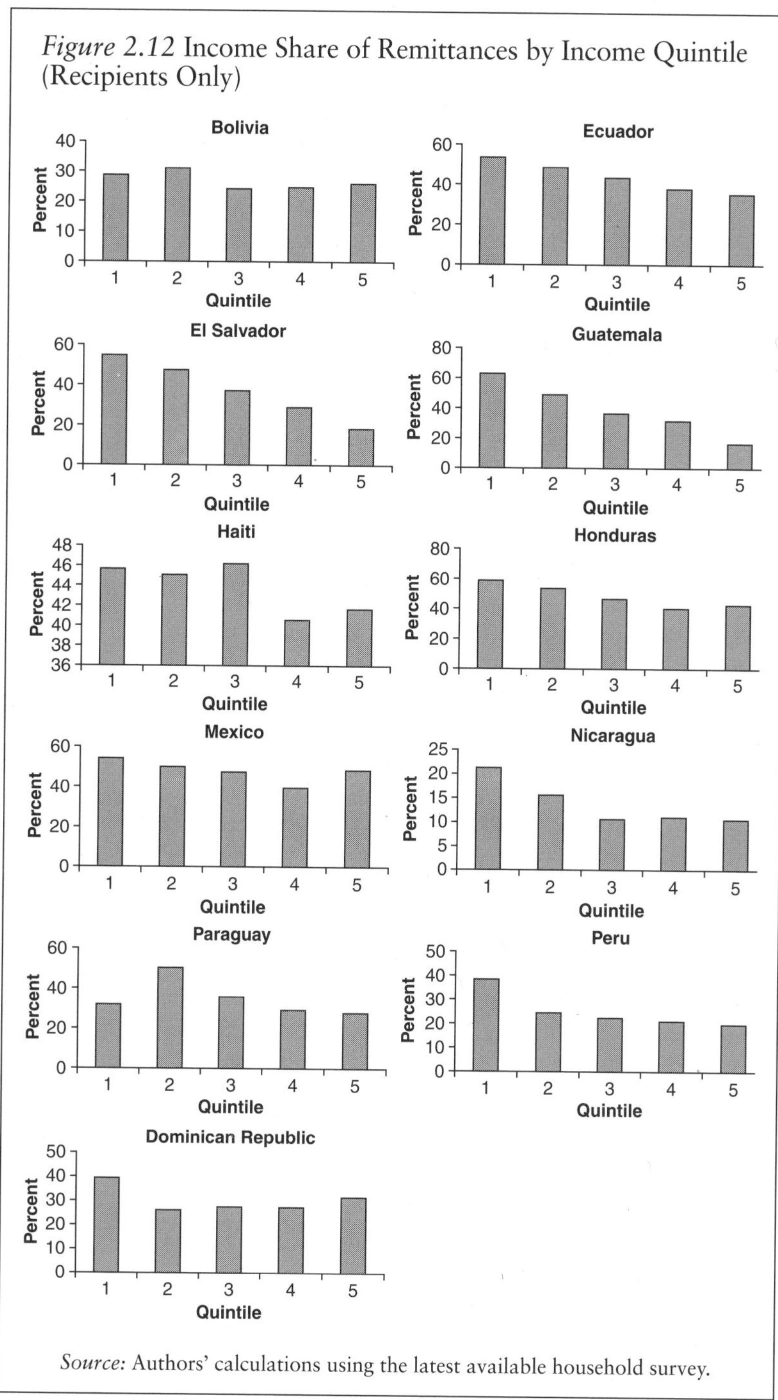

Source: Authors' calculations using the latest available household survey.

Figure 2.13 Income Share of Remittances by Income Quintile (All Households)

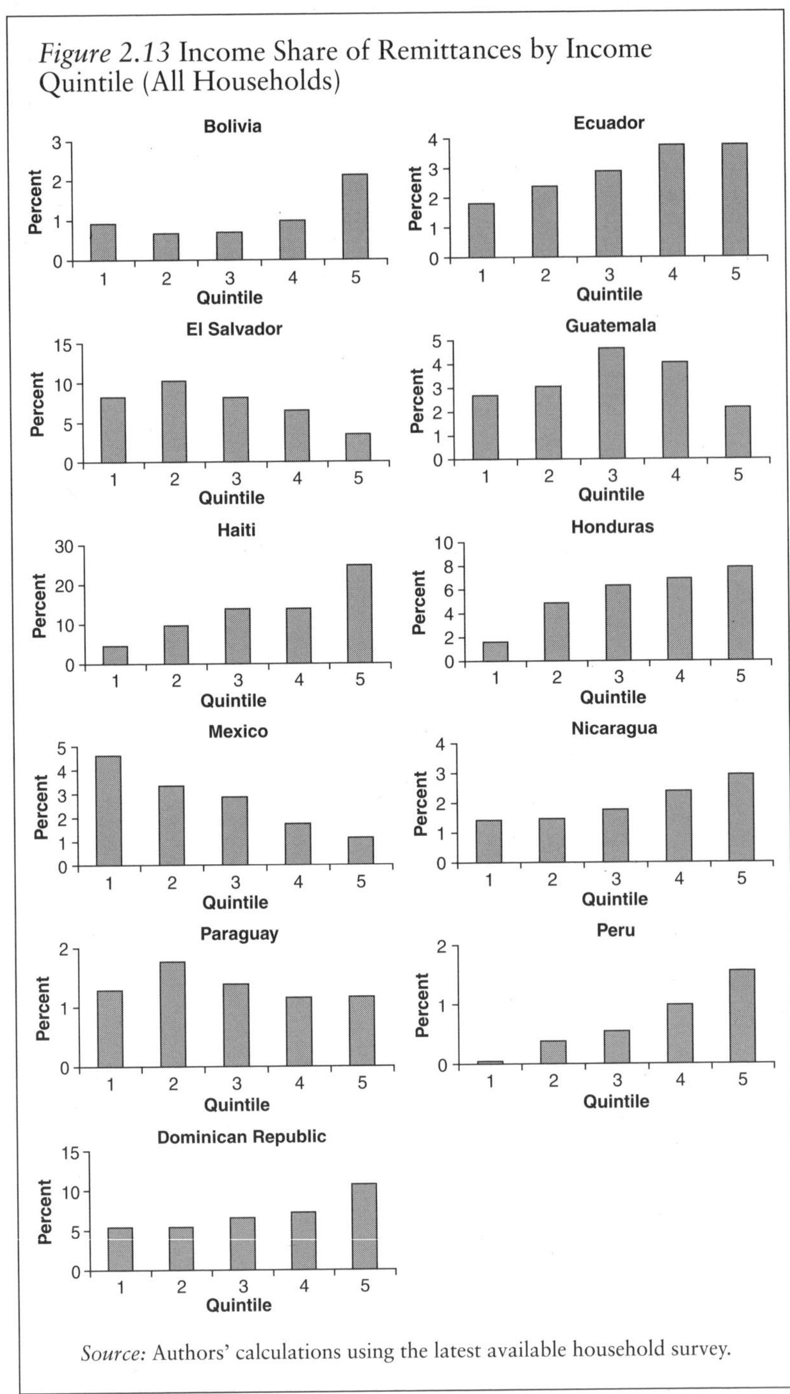

Source: Authors' calculations using the latest available household survey.

Figure 2.14 Income and Remittances Distribution by Income Quintile

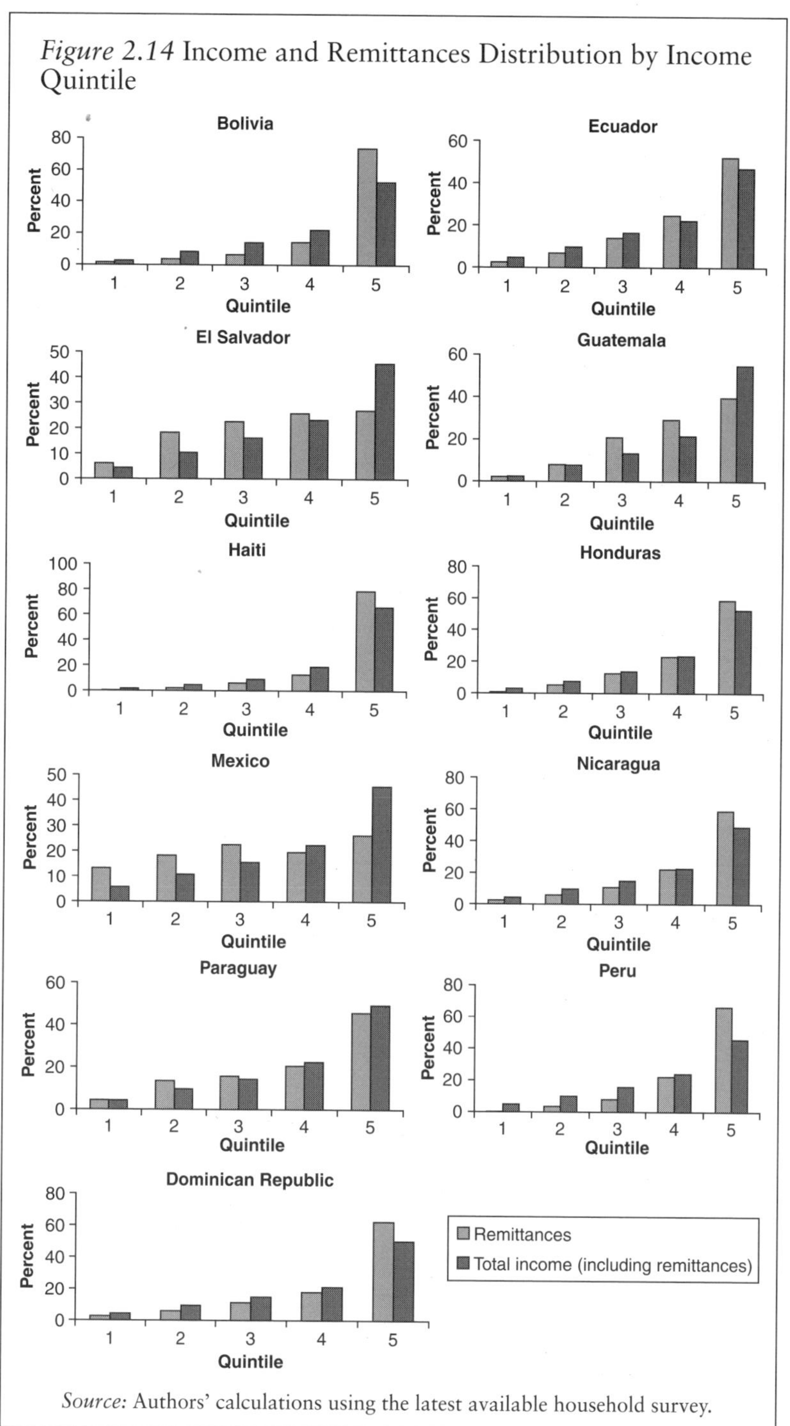

Source: Authors' calculations using the latest available household survey.

reports each quintile's share of both total income and total remittances. The results suggest not only that remittances are distributed in a quite unequal fashion, but also that they are generally distributed more unequally than total income. Thus, in the 11 countries for which we have data, the first three quintiles—the poorest 60 percent of the population—receive only a quarter of total remittances, while the top quintile receives on average 54 percent of those flows. For comparison purposes, on average, the richest 20 percent account for 51 percent of total household income, which suggests that the distribution of remittances is only slightly more unequal than that of income. Figure 2.14, however, reveals that in the cases of Mexico, El Salvador, Guatemala, and Paraguay, remittances are less unequally distributed than total income—for example, the poorest 60 percent receive 41 percent of remittances, compared to 29 percent of income. In contrast, in the other seven countries, the first three quintiles account for only 16 percent of total remittances, compared to 26 percent of total income, thus suggesting that remittances have a regressive effect on income distribution. While these calculations are subject to a number of caveats that we address in detail in chapter 3—for example, in the absence of remittances, households would probably have generated incomes that are likely to be higher than the observed nonremittances income—the evidence so far does not suggest that remittances could play an important role in reducing the very high levels of income inequality observed in Latin America.

How Reliable Are Remittances Figures?

So far we have reviewed the magnitude of remittances flows to the Latin American region, their evolution over time, and the profile of receiving households. Yet we have also mentioned that remittances data can be subject to significant mismeasurement issues to the point that it could be possible that part of the observed upward trend in observed remittances is simply driven by improvements in recording procedures. This raises many questions regarding the quality and coverage of the data with which we have been working, which could in turn affect the robustness of the analyses based on these data. In other words, casual evidence indicates that there may be important deficiencies with the officially recorded statistics on remittances. In this section we perform an exercise that we hope will give some indication of the extent to which the data described in this chapter can be trusted.

Remittances data are typically computed from balance of payments statistics for aggregate analysis, and from household surveys for country-specific studies. As argued in the World Bank's *Global Economic Prospects 2006*, there are a number of reasons why these two sources may not coincide.[7] To start with, there is not a single definition of remittances. Should they just include current transfers by migrants who are employed and resident in another country, or should they also include compensation of employees (that is, current transfers by nonresident workers)? Similarly, what should be the treatment of migrants' transfers (that is, financial items that arise from migration from one economy to another)?

Moreover, even when one agrees on a common definition, there are still a number of important issues that may affect the quality of the data. In addition to the implicit difficulties of capturing flows through informal channels, weaknesses in data collection may imply that many formal flows, especially if small, go unrecorded or are misclassified as tourism receipts or nonresident deposits.

On the other hand, household survey-based remittances have a number of associated problems. First, the corresponding household survey may not be as "nationally representative" as it should be. Moreover, even if the household is representative for the purposes of analyzing income levels, it may not be representative when the focus is the analysis of migration and remittances. A second aspect is related to possible recall bias estimates of remittances' receipts: Families usually decide to pool their income regardless of source, and therefore are presumably more likely to remember whether they received financial aid from abroad, rather than remembering the exact amount.

Finally, the timing of the survey data collection may also have an impact. Anecdotal references suggest that remittances' flows tend to be highly volatile within a year, with peaks at particular dates (Christmas, Mother's Day, and birthdays). If survey questions do not ask for the amount perceived as remittances during the entire year (as in the case of the Dominican Republic, Ecuador, Paraguay, and Peru, for instance), depending on the data collection period, remittances could be underestimated.

Similarly, in countries with volatile exchange rates, it is difficult to value (in dollars) the amounts remitted when they are reported in local currency values (as in the majority of household surveys). Yet, if official figures are reliable, one could also expect a strong positive correlation between the balance of payments–based and household-based estimates.

Figure 2.15 compares the estimates (as a ratio to GDP) obtained using the two available sources of data that we have for the 11 Latin American countries for which the household surveys report data on remittances. Review of this figure suggests a number of interesting issues. First, BOP-based estimates tend to be larger than household survey data estimates. The only case where the latter is higher is Mexico, and only by 0.1 percentage point. Second, the discrepancies can be very important. For example, in the cases of Haiti and El Salvador, BOP-based data produce estimates that are 10 percentage points of GDP higher than household survey data. In Nicaragua, the differences are smaller but still of a substantial magnitude (about 6 percentage points of GDP). The median remittances to GDP ratio for the 11 countries under analysis would be 4.7 percent on the basis of the balance of payments data, and 2.7 percent on the basis of household survey data.

It is worth noting, however, that these discrepancies may be more predictable than they appear. In other words, the observed discrepancies reflect systematic differences more than unexplained gaps. In fact, figure 2.15

Figure 2.15 BOP-Based versus Household Survey–Based Remittances

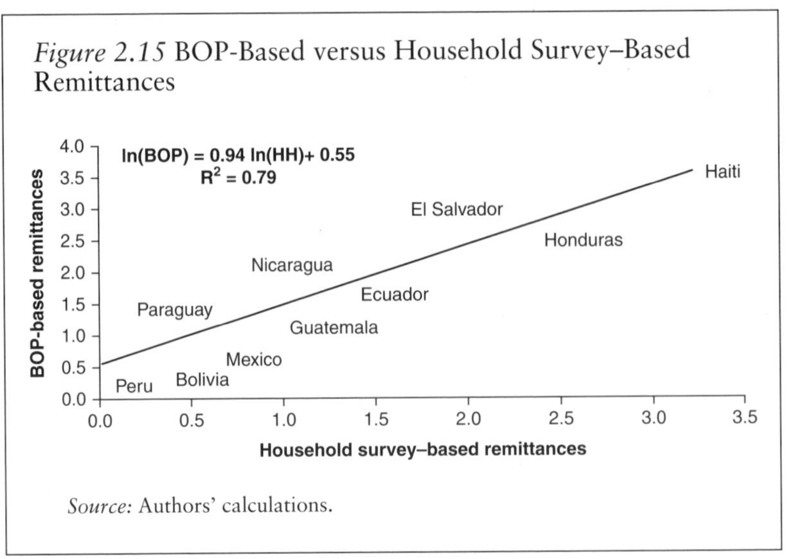

Source: Authors' calculations.

indicates that after a logarithmic transformation, the balance of payments– and household-based series of remittances are strongly correlated: the estimated R^2 of a simple ordinary least squares regression is almost 0.80, indicating that most of the variance in observed balance of payments–based figures can be explained with the findings of household survey data.

The slope of the regression line, estimated at 0.94, is also quite close to 1. By working with a sample size of just 11 observations, we cannot pretend to do a rigorous statistical inference, yet it is worth noting that the null hypothesis that this slope is equal to zero is rejected by the data, whereas the null hypothesis of a slope being equal to 1 cannot be rejected. In other words, the differences in the estimated remittances flows emerging from the two different sources of data seem to be more a question of scale.

These results, which are virtually unchanged when Haiti is eliminated from the sample to control for extreme values, would suggest that a good rule of thumb relating remittances from these two sources would be given by:

$$\text{BOP Remittances} = 1.73 \times (\text{HH Remittances})$$

In other words, balance of payments-based remittances statistics tend to be on average 70 percent to 75 percent larger than household-based data.[8]

Conclusions

This chapter has reviewed the evolution of remittances flows to Latin America using both balance of payments statistics and household survey data from 11 Latin American countries. It has also explored the varying economic and educational profiles of the households that receive remittances using household survey data from those countries. It has been argued that remittances flows to Latin American are very important regardless of whether one looks at them as total flows (about US$50 billion), per-capita flows (US$90 per person per year), their contribution to total financial flows (about 40 percent), or their share of regional GDP (2 percent). The chapter has also noted that remittances have dramatically increased over the past 25 years (20-fold in nominal terms and 10-fold in real terms), and that there is no indication of them leveling off. At the country level, they are relatively most important among Central American and Caribbean countries.

As for the characteristics of remittances-receiving households, the analysis of household survey data indicates that their distribution by income and adult educational attainment varies considerably across Latin American countries, with households with remittances income coming mainly from the bottom of the distribution in some countries—for example, Mexico and Paraguay—but an opposite pattern being found in others—for example, Haiti, Peru, and Nicaragua. This would indicate that the impact of remittances on poverty and inequality cannot be expected to be the same across the different countries of the region.

Finally, it has also been noted that balance of payments statistics and household survey data do indeed produce dramatically different estimates of the importance of remittances for receiving countries. However, the differences between those two data sources appear to be somewhat predictable, something that at least in our sample should ease concerns about data quality.

Notes

1. The BOP-based remittances figures used throughout this report do not exactly coincide with the line "workers remittance" of the BOP statistics. The data we use come from the *World Economic Outlook 2005* database (IMF 2005b) and are constructed as the sum of three BOP items of the *Balance of Payment Statistics Yearbook* (IMF 2005a): *workers' remittances* (current transfers made by migrants who are employed and resident in another economy); *compensation of employees* (wages, salaries, and other benefits earned by nonresident workers for work performed for residents of other countries); and *migrant transfers* (financial items that arise from the migration or change of residence of individuals from one economy to another).

2. Data on remittances' receipts are not available each year for all countries. In fact, it is possible to gather complete time series data for only 14 countries during this period: Mexico, Colombia, Brazil, Guatemala, El Salvador, Dominican Republic, Haiti, Jamaica, Honduras, Argentina, Costa Rica, Paraguay, Bolivia, and Barbados, in descending order, according to the total value of remittances received during 2003. On a more positive note, these countries were recipients of 90 percent of total officially recorded remittances flows to Latin America in 2002, a year for which information is available for all 31 countries (details on

available BOP data coverage for each country can be found in the appendix of Acosta, Calderón, Fajnzylber, and López 2006). Figure 2.4 then assumes that the 90 percent ratio has kept constant over time (that is, it extrapolates the data using a constant factor for every year).

3. It is highly likely that the evolution of officially recorded remittances is driven not only by an increase in actual remittances flows, but also by improvements in the quality of the statistics and in recording procedures by the different statistical offices. Once these statistics start reaching a good degree of accuracy, the increase in officially recorded remittances is likely to, ceteris paribus, decline significantly.

4. A 12th country with data on remittances receipts is Jamaica. Unfortunately as the household survey of reference does not include information on other income sources (i.e., labor income), it is not included in the analysis that follows. Nevertheless, the Jamaican case is explored in chapter 4 (remittances and household behavior).

5. In Nicaragua, the average years of schooling of adults in households with migrants is 6.66, compared to 6.83 for migrants, and 5.61 for adults in nonmigrant households.

6. It is also worth noting that Mexico, Guatemala, and El Salvador are the three Latin American countries whose migrants in the United States have the lowest educational levels (see chapter 3).

7. Indeed, remittances from these two sources of data rarely coincide for individual countries.

8. It must be admitted that this exercise does not tell us anything about errors in the temporal measurement of remittances and that this ratio could change if we had used earlier household surveys.

References

Acosta, P., C. Calderon, P. Fajnzylber, and H. López. 2006. "Remittances and Development in Latin America." *The World Economy* 29: 957–87.

———. 2007. "What Is the Impact of International Remittances on Poverty and Inequality in Latin America?" Policy Research Working Paper No. 4249. World Bank, Washington, DC.

Adams, R., and J. Page. 2005. "Do International Migration and Remittances Reduce Poverty in Developing Countries?" *World Development* 33: 1645–69.

Amuedo-Dorantes, C., and S. Pozo. 2004. "Workers' Remittances and the Real Exchange Rate: A Paradox of Gifts." *World Development* 32: 1407–17.

Calderón, C., P. Fajnzylber, and H. López. 2006a. "Remittances and Growth Volatility: An Investigation into the Business Cycle Properties of Workers' Remittances." Unpublished, World Bank, Washington, DC.

———. 2006b. "Remittances, Growth, and Policy Complementarities." Unpublished, World Bank, Washington, DC.

Chiquiar, D., and G.H. Hanson. 2005. "International Migration, Self-Selection, and the Distribution of Wages: Evidence from Mexico and the United States." *Journal of Political Economy* 113: 239–81.

Cox-Edwards, A., and M. Ureta. 1998. "International Migration, Remittances, and Schooling: Evidence from El Salvador." *Journal of Development Economics* 72: 429–61.

Giuliano, P., and M. Ruiz-Arranz. 2005. "Remittances, Financial Development and Growth." IMF Working Paper 05/234, International Monetary Fund, Washington, DC.

Ibarraran, P., and D. Lubotsky. 2005. "Mexican Immigration and Self-Selection: New Evidence from the 2000 Mexican Census." NBER Working Paper No. 11456, National Bureau of Economic Research, Cambridge, MA.

IMF (International Monetary Fund). 2005a. *Balance of Payment Statistics Yearbook*. Washington, DC: International Monetary Fund.

———. 2005b. *World Economic Outlook 2005*. Washington, DC: International Monetary Fund.

Maimbo, S., and D. Ratha. 2005. *Remittances: Development Impact and Future Prospects*. Washington, DC: World Bank.

Özden, C., and M. Schiff. 2006. *International Migration, Remittances, and the Brain Drain*. Washington, DC: World Bank.

Page, J., and S. Plaza. 2005. "Migration, Remittances, and Development: A Review of Global Evidence." Unpublished, World Bank, Washington, DC.

Rajan, R., and A. Subramanian. 2005. "What Undermines Aid's Impact on Growth?" Unpublished, International Monetary Fund, Washington, DC.

Rodriguez, E., and E. Tiongson. 2001. "Temporary Migration Overseas and Household Labor Supply: Evidence from Urban Philippines." *International Migration Review* 35, 1185–204.

United Nations. 2005. *Human Development Report*. New York, NY: United Nations Development Programme.

World Bank. 2005. *World Development Indicators*. Washington, DC: World Bank.

———. 2006. *Global Economic Prospects 2006: Economic Implications of Remittances and Migration*. Washington, DC: World Bank.

Yang, D. 2006. "Coping with Disaster: The Impact of Hurricanes on International Financial Flows, 1970–2001." NBER Working Paper No. 12794, National Bureau of Economic Research, Cambridge, MA.

3

Migration and Remittances in Latin America: Patterns and Determinants

*Yoko Niimi and Çağlar Özden**

Migration and remittances are inextricably intertwined. Whereas remittances would not occur if the senders had not migrated in the first place, migration is often motivated by the desire to improve the welfare of those left behind, mainly by sending them money. Migration profiles such as destination and migrant characteristics are likely to influence remittance patterns. This chapter aims to describe Latin American migration in an international perspective, and to relate it to the patterns of remittances sent by migrants. What do we know about the destinations that are chosen by Latin American migrants? What are the age and education profiles of the region's migrants and what is their labor market performance in destination countries? How do these characteristics affect remittances flows?

Introduction

Migration and remittances are two faces of the same coin. While workers' remittances would not occur if those sending them had not migrated in the first place, migration is often motivated by the desire to improve the welfare of those left behind, mainly by the remittances sent by the migrants. Thus, migrant profiles in terms of their destination choices, human capital levels, and other characteristics are key factors that influence remittances flows. The present chapter aims to describe Latin

* We would like to thank Maurice Schiff, L. Alan Winters, Pablo Fajnzylber, Caroline Freund, J. Humberto López, and Michel Beine for comments, and Ileana Cristina Neagu for her help with the data.

American migration patterns in an international perspective, and then link them to the remittances patterns.

Migration is a key economic and social development issue for a large number of countries in the world, many of them in Latin America and the Caribbean. For many small countries, like Tonga and Moldova, remittances account for the largest portion of their GDP. Larger countries, such as Sri Lanka, Bangladesh, and the Philippines, have millions of citizens who work abroad for several years at a time and accumulate enough savings to finance future investments. Countries like India, the Republic of Korea, and Taiwan (China), have seen some of their most educated workers migrate abroad over the last three decades, but they also have benefited tremendously through the closer economic links these migrants established between their native and adopted countries. For others with large diasporas in Europe, such as Turkey, the ex-Yugoslav republics, and the North African countries, migration poses complex cultural challenges.

Latin American and the Caribbean countries occupy a special place in the migration debate and research. As part of the "New World," they were among the main destinations for two centuries, and many countries in South America continued to receive migrants in large numbers until quite recently from Europe and, to a certain extent, from Asia. However, the pattern has shifted dramatically over the last two decades, and millions of people from the region have emigrated, with the vast majority choosing the United States as their destination. This is due to their geographic proximity, the existence of extended social networks, and the relative ease of social and economic assimilation. On the other hand, the vast majority of Latin American migrants have relatively low levels of human capital—even when compared to their fellow citizens who do not migrate—and they end up in unskilled jobs in the destination countries. Furthermore, a large portion emigrates without official documentation or residency status, which makes their presence, especially in the United States, a subject for contentious political debate, as recent events have shown.

A large potion of Latin American migration is permanent. A typical pattern is for a member to migrate, in many cases without proper documentation, and bring the rest of the family over time as legal and financial constraints are relaxed. All of these facts create a different emigration profile for Latin America when compared to other source regions such as Asia, Africa, or the Middle East. For example, a large portion of South Asian migrants obtain legal but temporary jobs in the Persian Gulf countries, typically with no intention of permanent settlement. African or Middle Eastern migrants predominantly choose Europe as their destination, are relatively more educated, and migrate on a relatively permanent basis. However, their economic and social integration is much slower, mainly due to cultural and legal differences between Europe and the United States.

The main motivation for Latin American migration is economic—most people migrate in order to provide better economic conditions for their families, whether they take their families with them or leave them behind. There is a very large gap in real wages between the United States and the countries in the region for the whole spectrum of skills in the labor market. In many cases, especially for some of the Central American and Caribbean countries, the wage gap for unskilled labor can be over 15 times. This gap encourages millions of people to take many economic and legal risks in order to migrate since the economic pull factors make it rather difficult to constrain migration pressures through legislation.

This chapter first reviews the patterns of emigration from Latin American countries. It relies on the censuses of the destination countries (mainly the United States), which offer a detailed picture of the existing stock of migrants. It then explores the profile of migrants in terms of age, education, and performance in the labor market of the destination country. Next, we relate the observed characteristics of the stock of migrants to the observed official flows of remittances. One group that is affected significantly by migration but tends to be overlooked is the families who are left behind. As such, along with the characteristics of migrants, we focus on remittances, the main channel through which migration impacts nonmigrants in the source countries.

Latin American Migrants Abroad

How many Latin Americans live abroad? In principle, countries with a larger population living abroad—both in absolute and relative terms—would experience more economically significant migration and remittances flows. Panels A and B of figure 3.1 present the overall number of migrants from the region using two different definitions and destinations. Panel A presents migration to the United States, while panel B focuses on migration from the region to all Organisation for Economic Co-operation and Development (OECD) countries. Finally, panel C presents the ratio of the labor force abroad to the total native labor force of the country of origin. In these panels, the countries have been grouped according to geographic region and economic similarity. First, we list Mexico, followed by the Central American countries, the Caribbean countries, the Andean countries, and finally the rest of South America.

Before proceeding, the reader should note that these figures use a logarithmic scale so that Mexican migration does not visually overwhelm the other, smaller countries. In fact, the differences between Mexico and the rest of the Latin American countries are very marked. Panel A indicates that, in 2000, there were close to 10 million Mexicans living in the United States. That same year, according to U.S. Census figures, the number of Cubans (870,000) or Salvadorans (820,000)—the countries with the second- and third-highest number of migrants, respectively, represented less than 10 percent of the Mexican figure. One common criticism of the

Figure 3.1 Latin American Migrants

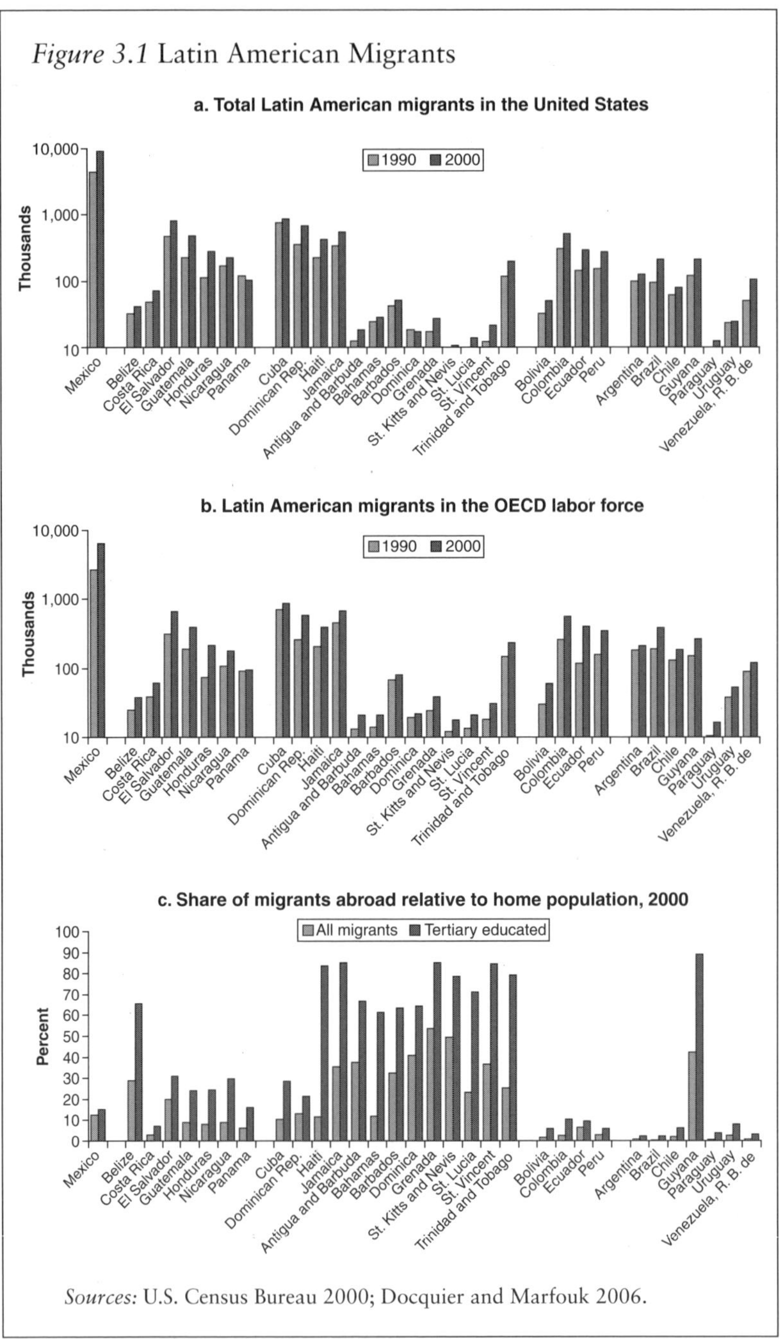

Sources: U.S. Census Bureau 2000; Docquier and Marfouk 2006.

Census is that it undercounts undocumented migrants for a variety of reasons. Among these, the desire of migrants to minimize their contact with the U.S. government out of fear of deportation is considered the most serious. However, the Census claims to have measures to correct for the problem, and many studies confirm that the problem is no greater than 10 percent of the population in most cases.

In addition to Cuba and El Salvador, there are several other countries with a stock of migrants between half a million and 1 million in the United States: the Dominican Republic (680,000), Jamaica (550,000), and Colombia (510,000). In absolute terms, and apart from the small Caribbean island of St. Kitts and Nevis, the country with the lowest number of migrants in the United States is Paraguay, with less than 13,000. The total number of Latin American migrants in the United States increased from 8.6 million in 1990 to about 16 million in 2000 (an 86 percent increase). Even excluding Mexico, which clearly dominates the absolute figures, migration to the United States from the other countries in the region increased by 63 percent, from 4.2 million migrants in 1990 to 6.8 million in 2000.

Among the countries in the region, Honduras experienced the most rapid growth in terms of migrants—from 112,000 in 1990 to 281,000 (i.e., a 150 percent increase) a decade later. It is followed by Brazil, with a 120 percent increase—from around 95,000 migrants to about 210,000—and Mexico, which more than doubled its migrant population in the United States. During this period, there were only two Latin American countries whose number of migrants in the United States declined: Panama (from 121,000 to 104,000) and Dominica (from 18,000 to 17,000). In absolute terms, the largest increases in migrants in the United States between 1990 and 2000 were from Mexico (4.7 million), followed by El Salvador (343,000).

Panel B of figure 3.1 presents the number of migrants from the region in the labor forces of all OECD countries. This data, which is based on the Docquier and Marfouk (2006) data set on brain drain, excludes children and other migrants who are not in the labor force. It is worth noting that there is significant correlation with panel A since the United States is the main destination for migrants from many of the countries. Yet, for many South American countries, Europe continues to be an important destination. In some cases, migrants to the United States from South America represent less than 50 percent of those countries' migrants.

Panels A and B of figure 3.1 fail to reflect an important issue. Even though there might be many migrants from a given country, such as Mexico, migration can be relatively more important for countries with much smaller populations. In fact, the number of Mexican migrants in the United States is larger than the total population of several countries in the region. To address this bias, panel C presents the ratio of migrants to the overall labor force in the home country.

The most striking feature of this panel is that there are significant levels of migration from a number of small countries, especially in the

Caribbean. For example, as of 2000, on average 30 percent of the labor forces of many Caribbean islands had migrated. An extreme case is that of Grenada, where close to 50 percent of the population had migrated. For the non-Caribbean countries, migrants as a share of the origin country population represent on average about 10 percent (6 percent for South America). Thus, even if Mexico and the Central American countries tend to top the ranking of migrants in absolute terms, the small Caribbean islands clearly dominate the migration charts when we look at migration flows in relation to each country's population.

The next issue is which countries migrants choose as their destinations. Figure 3.2 presents the destinations of migrants for 1990 and 2000. The United States is the main destination for migrants from Mexico and Central America. Mexico is the second most important destination for migrants from Central America since Mexico serves as the first stop on their way to the United States. For the Caribbean countries, Canada and the United Kingdom are the main destinations after the United States, accounting for 50 percent of the migrants for many countries. This is mainly due to colonial and linguistic links. Europe is a major destination for Andean and other South American countries, again due to colonial and ethnic links. An interesting example is the migration from Brazil to Japan, where grandchildren of the ethnic Japanese who migrated at the turn of the century are now going back to Japan for employment. In short, the United States is the destination for less than 50 percent of the migrants from South America, and slightly above 50 percent from the Caribbean countries. Nevertheless, over 90 percent of migrants from Latin America and the Caribbean end up in the United States since the vast majority of them are from Mexico and Central America.

Among the European destinations of Latin American migrants, figure 3.3 indicates that language seems to play an important role. This figure is restricted to the Caribbean and South American countries, and indicates that the Caribbean migrants' preferred destination is the United Kingdom, while South American migrants prefer Spain.

Age Profile of Migration

One of the main differences between Latin American migrants and those from other countries is that migration is permanent for a vast majority of those from Latin America. This implies that most migrants are young adults who want to start a new life—most often in the United States—and bring over their families once they have established themselves. As a result, the age profile of Latin American migrants is rather different from those from other countries.

Figure 3.4 presents the age profile of migrants *at the time of arrival,* according to the U.S. Census 2000. For every country in the region, the

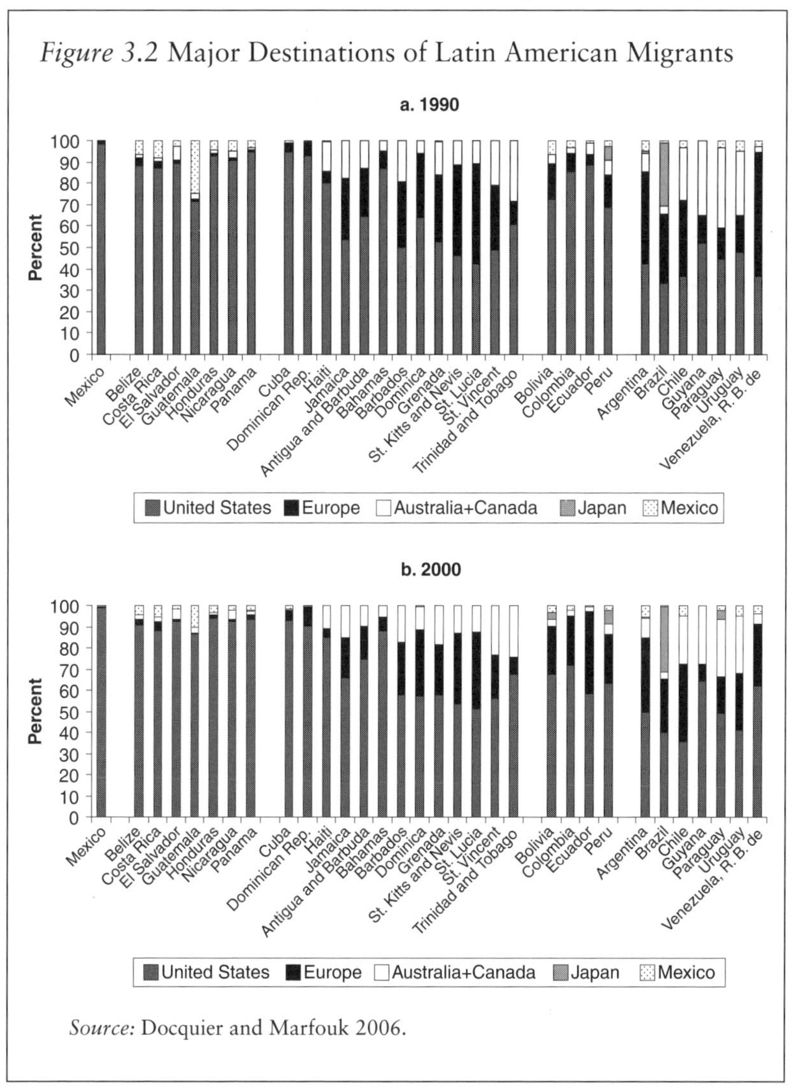

Figure 3.2 Major Destinations of Latin American Migrants

Source: Docquier and Marfouk 2006.

majority of migrants are below age 30 when they migrate. For Mexico and Central America, around 40 percent of migrants are between the ages of 18 and 30, and another 40 percent are below age 17. For other countries in the region, 70 percent of migrants are below the age of 30, and they are equally divided between those up through age 17, and those 18 to 30 years old.

Figure 3.5 presents the *current age distribution* of migrants in the United States. As a result of migration at a very young age, the age profile

Figure 3.3 Major European Destinations of Latin American Migrants, 2000

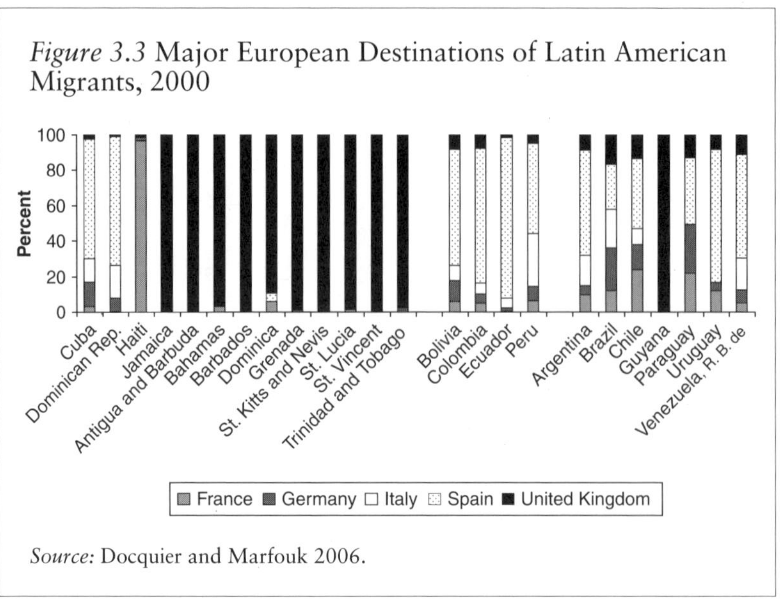

Source: Docquier and Marfouk 2006.

Figure 3.4 Age Profile at the Time of Arrival for Latin American Migrants

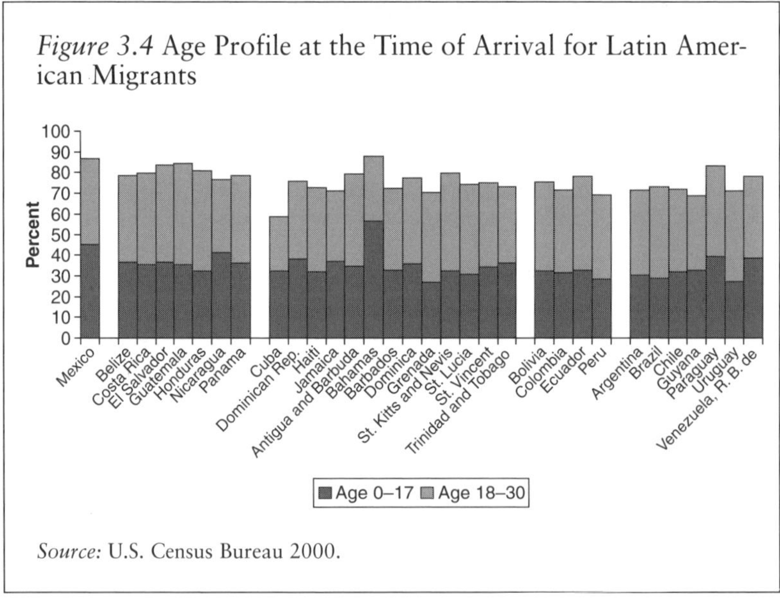

Source: U.S. Census Bureau 2000.

of migrants who are currently in the United States is also rather young, especially when compared to the native population or other migrant communities. For example, almost 50 percent of Mexican-born migrants are under age 30, with the majority between the ages of 18 and 30. These

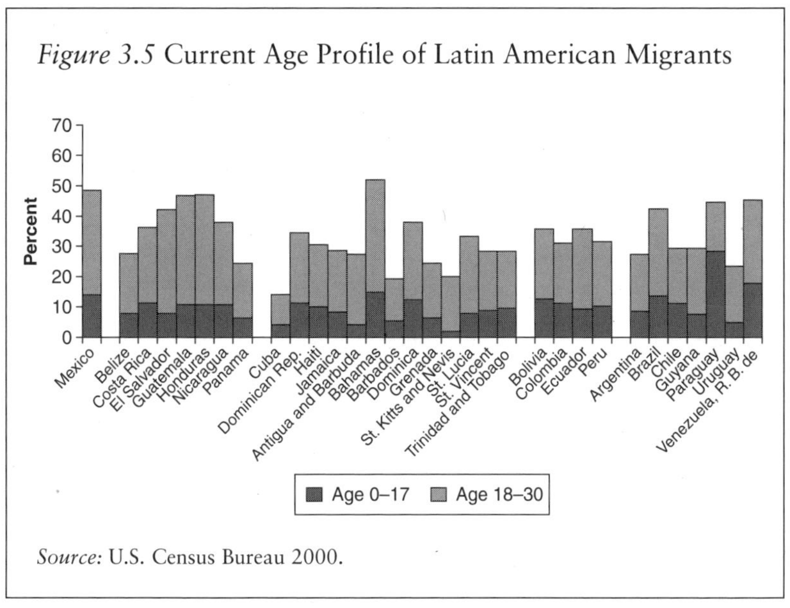

Figure 3.5 Current Age Profile of Latin American Migrants

Source: U.S. Census Bureau 2000.

numbers do not include the U.S.-born children of migrants since they receive automatic citizenship. Thus, the overall "Latin American community" in the United States is likely to be even younger in terms of age profile than that presented in figure 3.5.

The age profile has important implications for both the migrants and the United States. On one hand, it implies a steady source of new entry into the labor market, where the pressures due to the aging native population are beginning to be felt. This provides an added advantage to the U.S. economy. Many other OECD countries are experiencing steady declines in their labor supplies, which have negative implications for long-term sustainability of many government programs, especially those related to social security and welfare. On the other hand, it means a large number of young people need to be culturally and economically integrated, which can constrain many government resources. The recent political debates are a reflection of these challenges.

Finally, we should add that there are certain exceptions, such as Cuba, Belize, Panama, and Barbados, which are relatively small and had an extensive history of migration to the United States. As a result, their migrants tend to be older. We also do not have comparable data for the European countries. However, there is no indication that the overall migration from South America to Europe is different than the migration flows to the United States. Thus, at this point, it would be safe to assume that Latin American migrants in Europe present a similar profile.

Education Profile

One of the main differences between migrants from Latin America and the rest of the world is the educational distribution. For a variety of reasons, the Latin American migrant population is distributed toward the bottom end of the education spectrum. This is especially true for the people who migrate as adults after completing their education at home. Figure 3.6 presents the education distribution of migrants to the United States who arrived during the 1990s and were above the age of 22 at the time of their arrival. Most migrants, especially those from Mexico and Central America, have very little education. Since they account for the majority of the migrants from Latin America, they dominate the overall education profile as well.

An important observation is that there are significant differences in education distribution among different countries. Only 4 percent of Mexican migrants have tertiary education, compared to 7 percent for the Central American migrants, 13 percent for the Caribbean, 24 percent for the Andean, and around 30 percent for the other South American countries.

Educational differences are also evident from table 3.1, which reports the share of migrants with primary, secondary, and tertiary educations for three groups: Mexico and Central America, the Caribbean, and South America. In fact, a majority of migrants in the first group have only

Figure 3.6 Education Profile of 1990s Latin American and Caribbean Migrants (Age 22 and Older)

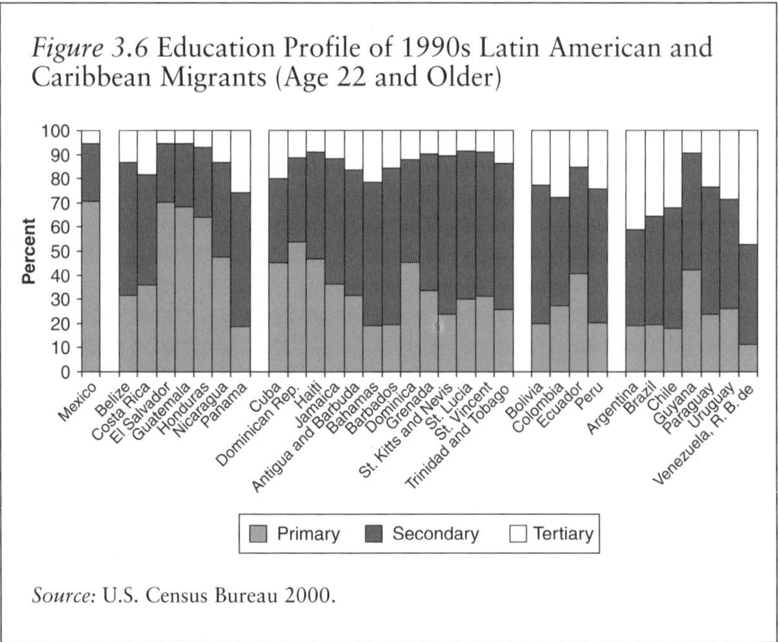

Source: U.S. Census Bureau 2000.

Table 3.1 Education Profile of Latin American and Caribbean Migrants (Percent with a Given Educational Level)

	Primary	*Secondary*	*Tertiary*
Mexico and Central America	51	37	12
Caribbean	34	53	13
South America	24	48	28

Source: U.S. Census Bureau 2000.

Figure 3.7 Education Profile of Native Population versus Migrants from Latin American and Caribbean Countries

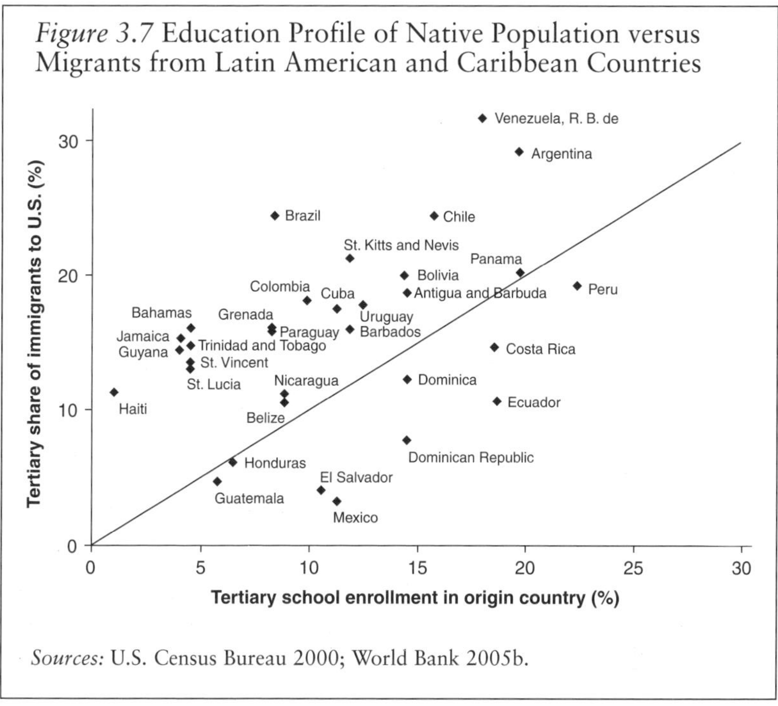

Sources: U.S. Census Bureau 2000; World Bank 2005b.

primary education. In contrast, a majority of Caribbean migrants have secondary education. Finally, the most educated migrants are those from South America, where more than three-quarters have secondary or tertiary education.

One of the key questions is what factors explain this divergence. One possibility is the overall educational level of the population in the home country. In figure 3.7, the horizontal axis presents the tertiary school enrollment in the home country. This ratio ranges from 1.5 percent in Haiti to 20 percent in many countries, such as Costa Rica, Panama, República Bolivariana de Venezuela, and Argentina. The vertical axis is the ratio of those with a tertiary education among the migrants who are currently in the United States. Mexico and most of the Central American countries are *below* the 45-degree line, whereas the Caribbean and the South American countries are above it. Although Brazil and Mexico have similar educational levels, their migrants are starkly different in their education profiles.

Figure 3.7 implies the migrants are drawn from the lower end of the education spectrum in Mexico and Central America and from the upper end for the Caribbean and South America. The main factor that explains the differences in these selection patterns is the ease of migration. It is relatively easy for Mexicans and Central Americans to migrate to the United States whether through legal channels using family preferences or without proper documentation. On the other hand, it is more costly due to the distance and the low number of informal networks of migrants for a Brazilian to migrate to the United States. As a result, we see that the educated form a higher portion of the migrants from South American countries. These are the people who can afford to migrate and they benefit more from migrating.

The Brain Drain

The next question related to the education profile of migrants is the degree of brain drain—the portion of educated workers who migrate, and its impact on their home country. Brain drain is one of the most debated and researched issues related to migration. There is a large amount of evidence pointing out the importance of human capital in development, and many developing countries spend significant public funds on education, especially tertiary education. When these workers migrate, their home countries lose on many fronts. First, there is the loss of potentially positive externalities generated by the educated workers, whether they are doctors, engineers, or entrepreneurs. Second, there is the loss of potential tax revenue from the incomes of these people. Third, there is the loss of public funds spent on their education. On the other hand, there are potential gains. They might earn significantly higher incomes in their destination countries and the remittances they send can be a significant source of income. They also establish important cultural and economic links between their home countries and the global economy. For example, Saxenian provides rather compelling evidence on the role played by the Silicon Valley–based Taiwanese and Indian engineers in the emergence of the computer industries in their home countries.

Figure 3.8 presents the portion of migrants who have at least a college degree. As discussed in the previous section, we see that the migrants become more educated as we go farther away from the United States. Only 6 percent of the Mexican-born migrant population has a college degree, while it is about 30 percent for Argentina and República Bolivariana de Venezuela.

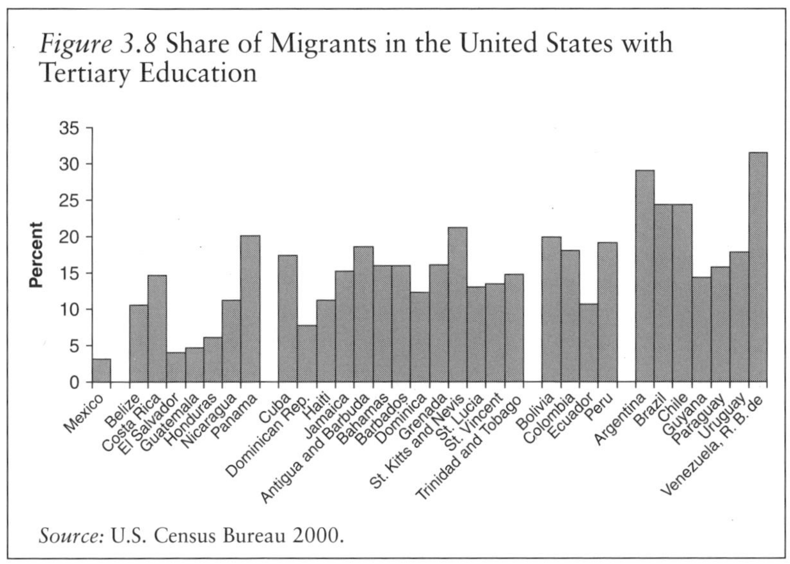

Figure 3.8 Share of Migrants in the United States with Tertiary Education

Source: U.S. Census Bureau 2000.

The brain drain debate centers more on the portion of the educated who migrate, rather than their portion within overall migration. An example might illustrate this point more clearly. Suppose 50 percent of a European country's population have a college degree and 5 percent of these people migrate abroad and nobody else does. On the other hand, 5 percent of an African country's population have a college degree and half of them migrate, along with 10 percent of the rest of the population. All of the migrants from the European country will have a college degree, whereas only 20 percent of the African country's migrants will. Even though European migrants are more educated, the brain drain will have a more significant impact on the African country.

Docquier and Marfouk's (2006) study was the first systematic effort to provide evidence on the extent of migration of highly educated people based on the censuses of the destination OECD countries. Fgure 3.9 is based on their data set and provides a very different picture. Many small and economically isolated countries in the region, especially island countries, have lost a very significant portion of their college-educated population to migration. Over 80 percent of people born in Haiti, Jamaica, Grenada, Guyana, etc., who have college degrees live abroad, mostly in the United States. On the other hand, less than 10 percent of the college graduates from South American countries have migrated, even though they form a large portion of the migrant population. This is mainly due to the low levels of overall migration. For Mexico and Central America, the migration level of college graduates is around 15 percent to 20 percent, which is relatively high but not as alarming as the Caribbean.

Figure 3.9 Share of Educated Workers Who Migrate

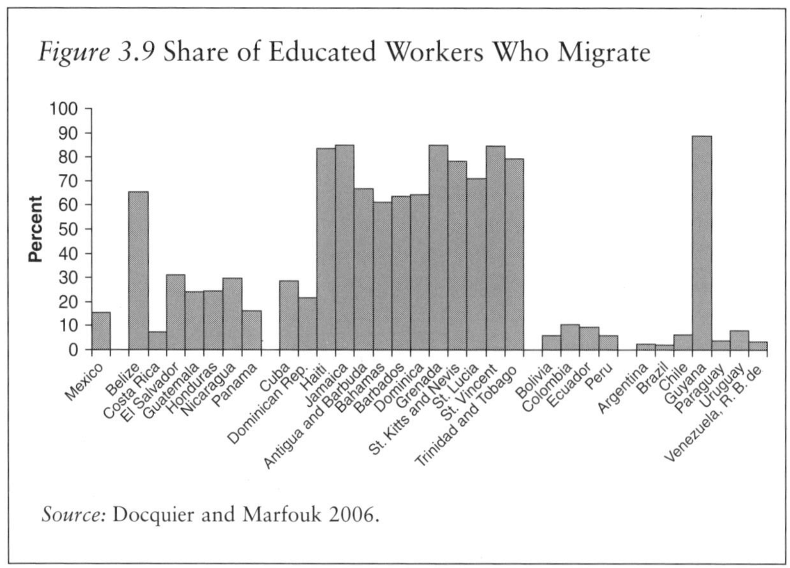

Source: Docquier and Marfouk 2006.

It is important to note that these numbers include people who went to the United States as children and completed their education there. This is an important distinction since, as shown in the previous section, a large portion of the migrants from the region enter as children. Even though they are foreign born and are considered migrants, it is debatable whether they would constitute brain drain since there is no guarantee they would receive the same level of education if they had not migrated. This is due to the limited capacity fo tertiary education institutions in many developing countries; the demand for tertiary education almost always exceeds the supply.

Figure 3.10 presents the ratio of college-educated migrants in the United States who received their degrees in their home countries. Around 40 percent of college-educated migrants from Mexico and Central America received their degrees at home; the other 60 percent finished their education in the United States. The level of those who completed their educations in the United States is much higher for Caribbean migrants, but much lower for South Americans. Even if we exclude U.S.-educated workers from the brain drain numbers, over 50 percent of college-educated workers have migrated from many Caribbean countries, which is still a very significant number.

Considering that a significant portion of the migrants from the region are very young, an important question regards the link between migration and the incentives to obtain tertiary education in destination countries. Figure 3.11 presents the portion of migrants from each subregion by the age of arrival and their likelihood of receiving a college degree. The first pattern is that the percentage of migrants who receive a college degree is inversely related to the age of arrival, regardless of the country of origin.

Figure 3.10 Share of College-Educated Workers in the United States Who Received Their Degrees at Home

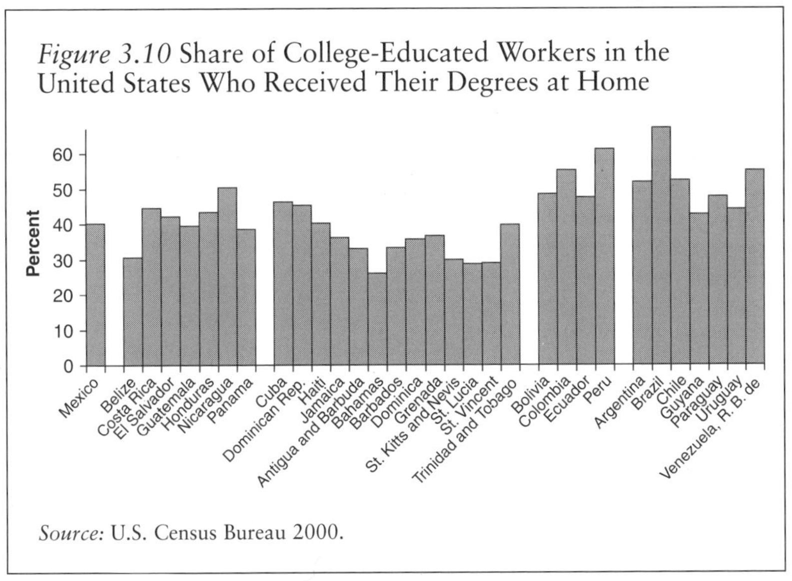

Source: U.S. Census Bureau 2000.

Figure 3.11 Share of Migrants in the United States with College Degrees According to Age of Entry

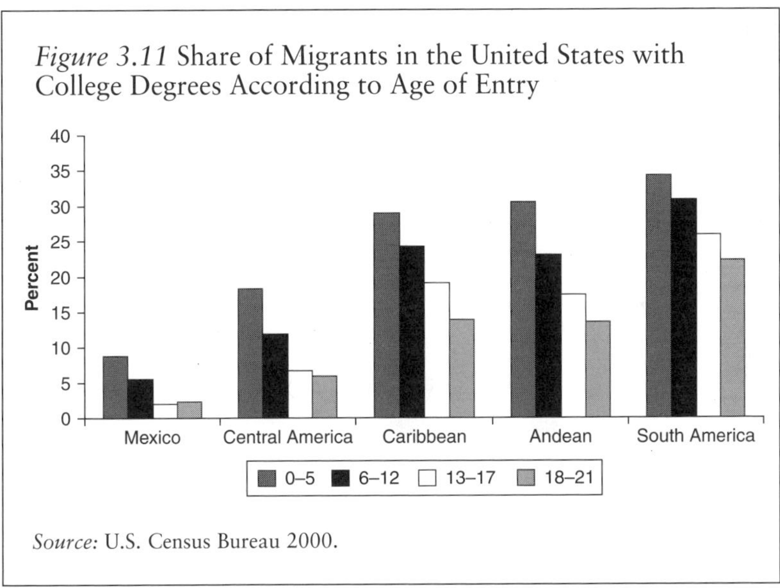

Source: U.S. Census Bureau 2000.

The younger the age of arrival, the higher is the likelihood of receiving a college degree. For example, 6 percent of Central American migrants who arrived between the ages of 18 and 21 received a college degree, whereas the same ratio is 18 percent for those arriving by the age of 5. The second observation is that the likelihood of receiving a college degree is increasing with distance from the United States. South American migrants are more likely to obtain a college degree in the United States, compared to Mexican or Central American migrants for all age groups. These observations are likely to be related to the social and economic status of the parents since South American adult migrants are also more educated than their counterparts in Central America. This issue obviously needs more research as it is crucial for the integration of migrants into the economy.

Labor Market Performance

The previous sections dealt with the age and education profiles of Latin American migrants. This section analyzes their performance in the labor market, which is the key determinant of their economic and social integration. Figure 3.12 presents the occupational distribution for all migrant working adults above age 22 in 2000, who were also above 22 when they arrived. In other words, these are the migrants who are less likely to continue their education in the United States. Once again, there are stark differences between different countries. Slightly above 10 percent of Mexican and Central American migrants work in high-skilled and medium-skilled jobs, whereas the same ratio is between 40 percent and 50 percent for the Caribbean and South American migrants. Naturally, this reflects the overall educational distribution of the migrants we analyzed above.

Figure 3.12 Occupational Distribution of Migrants in the United States Older than 22 at Time of Arrival (Current Age 22+)

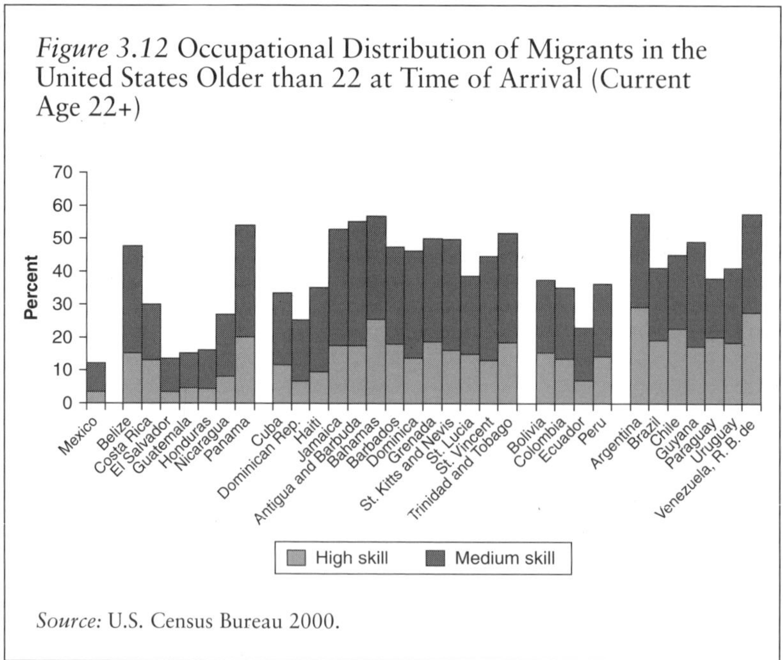

Source: U.S. Census Bureau 2000.

The situation improves significantly for migrants who arrived as children. Figure 3.13 provides the same data for people who arrived before age 17. We still see differences between Mexican and Central American migrants on the one hand, and Caribbean and South American migrants on the other. Under that scenario, over 20 percent of Mexican migrants and over 30 percent of Central American migrants are in high- or medium-skilled jobs. The same ratio is between 50 percent and 60 percent for those from the Caribbean and South America. The improvements are due to higher education levels, English proficiency, and other measures of social and economic integration.

These figures do not take into account the underlying educational distribution of the migrants. South American migrants might be obtaining better jobs compared to Central American migrants because they are more educated. The right comparison is between migrants with the same education levels. Figure 3.14 presents the labor market placement of college-educated migrants who were above age 25 at the time of arrival. In other words, these are the people who completed their education in their home countries and migrated to the United States as adults for employment. We refer to this as "brain waste" since there is significant "underplacement" of migrants from certain countries in the U.S. labor market. For example, only 33 percent of college-educated migrants from Mexico end up in highly skilled jobs, and 23 percent are in medium-skilled jobs. In other

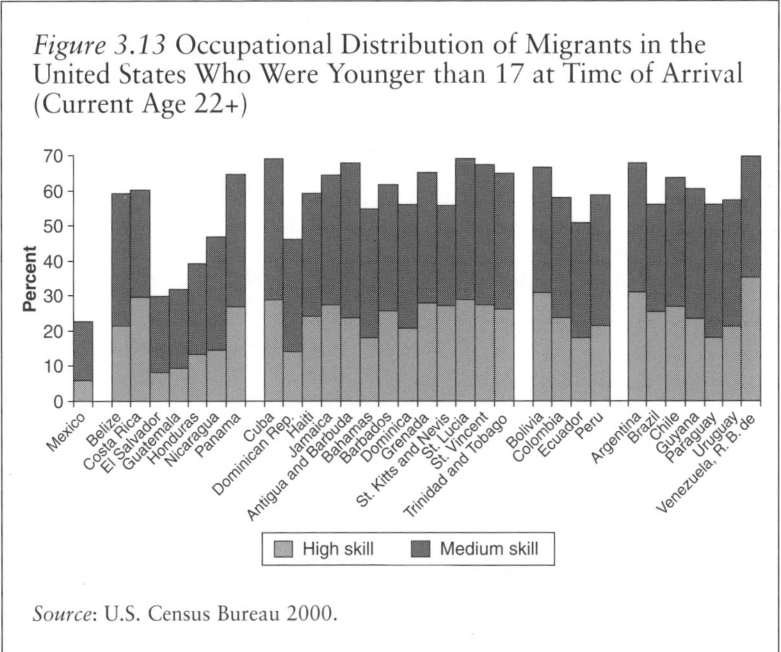

Figure 3.13 Occupational Distribution of Migrants in the United States Who Were Younger than 17 at Time of Arrival (Current Age 22+)

Source: U.S. Census Bureau 2000.

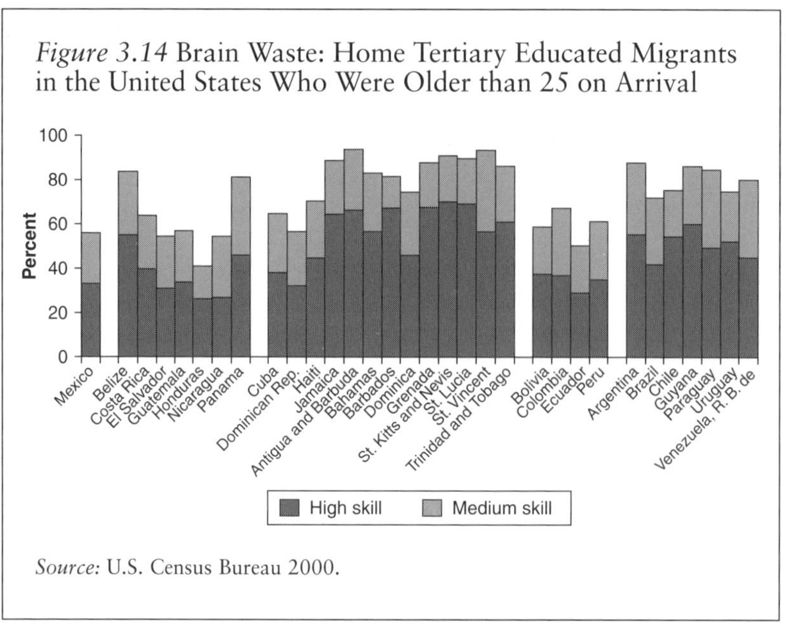

Figure 3.14 Brain Waste: Home Tertiary Educated Migrants in the United States Who Were Older than 25 on Arrival

Source: U.S. Census Bureau 2000.

words, 44 percent of them are in unskilled jobs, and this is a very high number. Whereas the fraction of college-educated Central American and Andean migrants in skilled jobs is similar to that of Mexican migrants, college-educated migrants from the Caribbean and South America are significantly more likely to hold skilled jobs.

Mattoo, Neagu, and Özden (2005) observe similar patterns for countries in other parts of the world and explore the differences between these outcomes. They point out two sets of answers—the first is related to the underlying quality of education in the home country. South American and Caribbean countries spend more on education and their migrants are likely to have high quality human capital. Still, this does not explain the large differences observed. The main reason seems to be a variant of the selection effects. South American and Caribbean migrants with college degrees seem to be among the best in their home countries. On the other hand, Mexican and Central American college graduates who migrate seem to be coming from the lower end of the quality distribution of all college graduates at home. Again, this is related to the ease of migration we mentioned earlier. For South American migrants, the main method of entry seems to be through employment preferences, which require the migrant to secure a job in the United States before emigration. This naturally favors more qualified migrants. On the other hand, Mexican and Central American migrants can more easily enter through family preferences or illegally. As a result, the overall quality of South American migrants seems to be higher even though all migrants, on paper, have college degrees. These observations have important implications for both migration and education policies of the source countries. For example, what skills should the potential migrants obtain to perform better in the U.S. labor market? Is it an economically efficient policy to provide free tertiary education if the migrant is likely to end up in an unskilled job in the United States?

Migration and Remittances

Now we turn to the remittances sent to families back at home. Remittances are a significant source of income in many countries and, in many cases, the largest source of foreign exchange earnings for the country. The emerging literature on remittances has established several facts. First, remittances have a large and significant effect on poverty reduction (Adams 2005; Yang and Martinez 2005). Second, they are invested in human and physical capital acquisition in larger proportions than other sources of income, and thus, have a large impact on long-term economic growth and development (Cox-Edwards and Ureta 2003; McCormick and Wahba 2003). Third, they tend to be rather stable and countercyclical, which means they are very important in smoothing out macroeconomic shocks, especially in small and vulnerable economies (Chami, Fullenkamp, and Jahjah 2005; Gupta 2005).

In the previous sections, we explored the characteristics of Latin American migrants. The question that we address now is whether these characteristics can be used to explain the remittances patterns. Previous efforts that have aimed at explaining the determinants of remittances include those contained in the World Bank's *Global Economic Prospects 2006,* where it is found that remittances tend to increase with the stock of migrants a country has abroad and with the level of financial development and per-capita income in the home country; and they decline with the service fee that migrants are charged for the transactions and with the existence of dual exchange rates (World Bank 2005a).

What do all of these facts imply for source countries in Latin America and the Caribbean, especially in terms of remittances flows? Figure 3.15 shows the average share of remittances in GDP, weighted by population, in three main subregions. Remittances were the largest portion of GDP for the Caribbean countries, at 12 percent as of 2000. In Central America and Mexico it was at 3 percent, and in South America it was at 1 percent. However, these numbers hide important variations across countries. For example, remittances are 15 percent of Haiti's GDP, but they are less than 1 percent for Argentina and Brazil. Another important pattern is the rapid increase in the remittances flows over the last two decades. This is partly due to increases in migration, increases in the incomes earned by the migrants, and better recording of remittances by official authorities.

Figure 3.15 Remittances as a Share of GDP

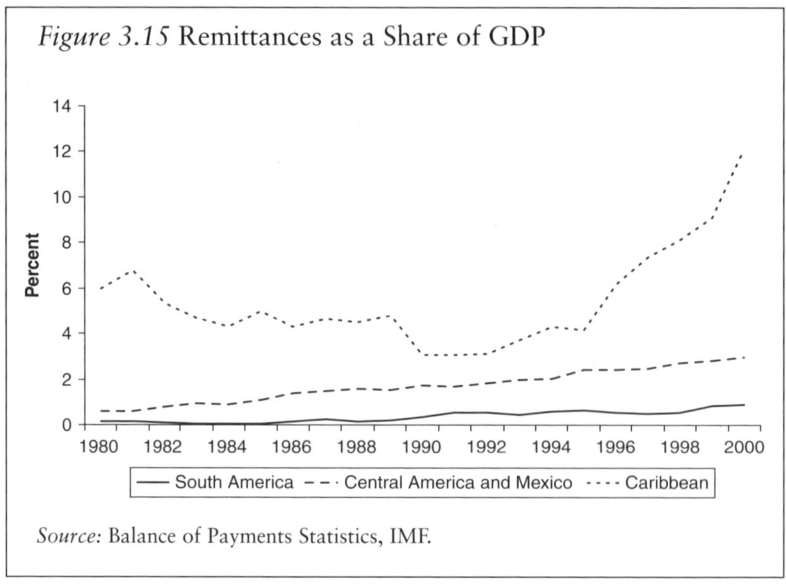

Source: Balance of Payments Statistics, IMF.

Another measure of remittances is the amount received per capita in the source country, which is presented in constant U.S. dollars (weighted by the population of each country) in figure 3.16. Again, the Caribbean is at the highest level, followed by Central America/Mexico and South America. However, the gap between the Caribbean countries and the rest of Latin America is much narrower. This is mainly due to lower levels of GDP per capita in the Caribbean countries relative to the rest of the region, which makes remittances to GDP numbers very high. Nevertheless, we see rapid increases over time for all of the regions in this figure as well. A final measure of remittances is the amount sent by each migrant. The previous two figures of *remittances as a share of GDP* and *remittances received per capita* might be biased if one region has a much larger share of its citizens migrating abroad. The previous sections have shown that this is actually the case. For example, over 30 percent of the population has migrated from many Caribbean island states. However, the proportion of migrants is around 10 percent for Mexico, 5 percent for Nicaragua, and less than 1 percent for Brazil and Argentina. Thus, figure 3.17 presents the *remittances sent per migrant* for each region, weighted by the migrant population of each country in each region.

The remittances behavior of Caribbean and Central American/Mexican migrants is much similar according to this figure, whereas remittances sent by South American migrants have increased considerably since 1990. There are several possible reasons for this rapid increase, which we will explore further in the next sections.

Figure 3.16 Remittances Received Per Capita

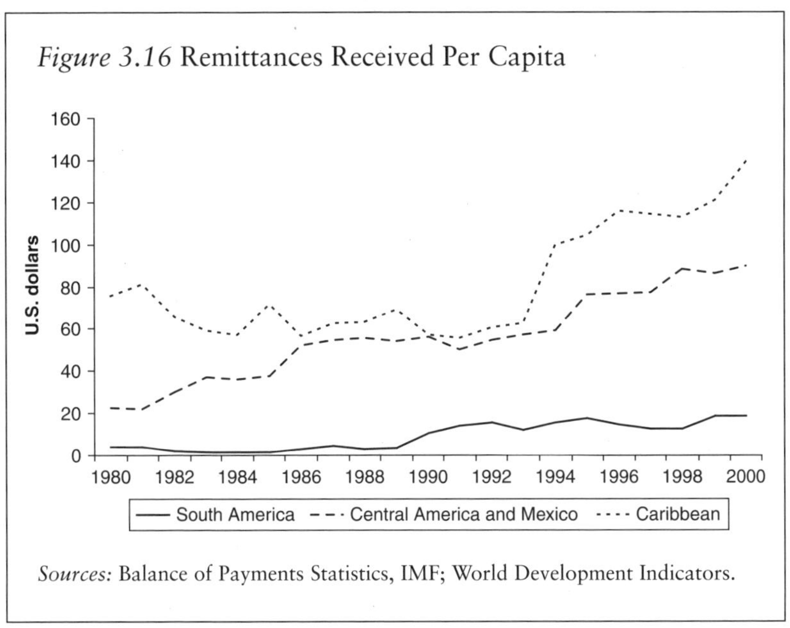

Sources: Balance of Payments Statistics, IMF; World Development Indicators.

Figure 3.17 Remittances Sent Per Migrant

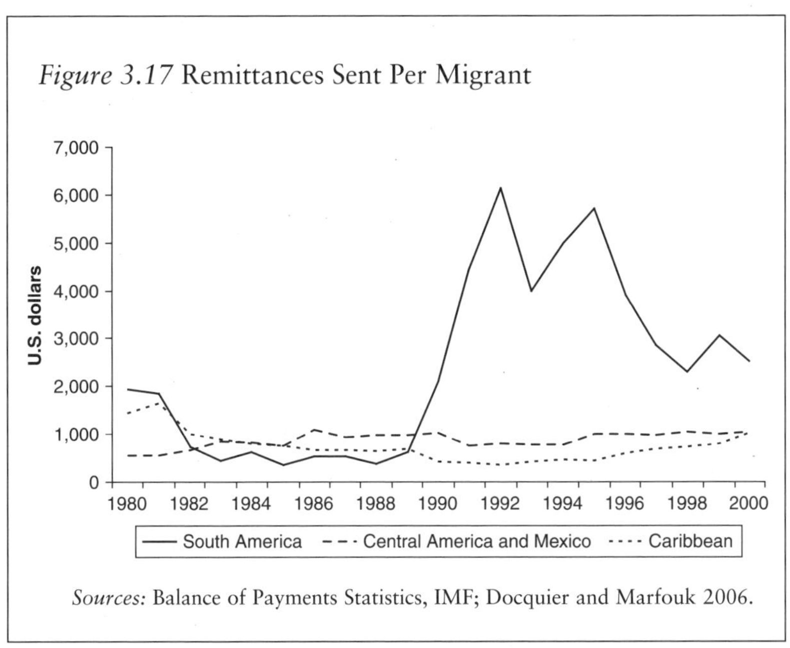

Sources: Balance of Payments Statistics, IMF; Docquier and Marfouk 2006.

Determinants of Remittances

Figures 3.15, 3.16, and 3.17 present interesting patterns in terms of remittances behavior across the three main regions in Latin America. There is actually a larger degree of variation if one were to draw the same graphs for different countries. The key question is what factors can explain these variations.

Migrant population. This is probably the most important determinant of remittances size, as figure 3.17 shows. Caribbean countries receive more in remittances as a share of their GDP and per capita, but this is mainly due to a very large level of migration. Figure 3.17 shows that they remit the same level as Central American/Mexican migrants and less than South American migrants. Figure 3.18 presents the average level of migration from each subregion. The Caribbean has the highest level of emigration—as of 2000, 15 percent of the population of the region had migrated abroad. This compares to slightly above 8 percent for Central America/Mexico and around 1 percent for South America in the same year.

Migrant characteristics. If the migrants from one country earn significantly higher levels of income compared to other countries, they are likely to send more remittances back to their families at home. Thus the income levels of the migrants, as well as other characteristics, will influence remittances behavior. Among such characteristics are the level of female migration

Figure 3.18 Migrants as a Share of Population

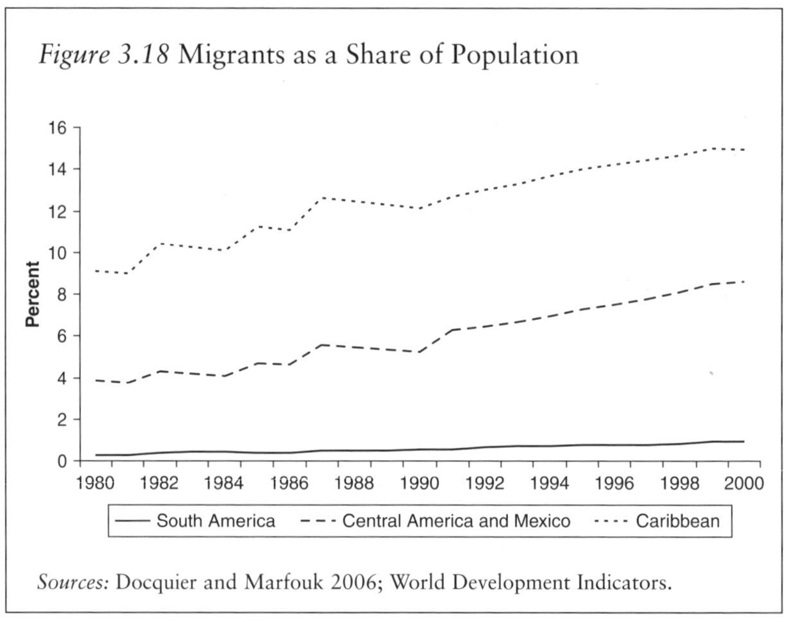

Sources: Docquier and Marfouk 2006; World Development Indicators.

and the ratio of college educated among the migrants. The female migration level is likely to have a negative correlation with remittances for two reasons. First, female labor force participation is generally lower and this is stronger in migrant communities. Second, higher female migration levels indicate that whole families have migrated and there are fewer family members at home who are relying on remittances. Figure 3.19 presents the portion of female migrants, and shows that the Caribbean has the highest level, followed by South America. Central America/Mexico has the lowest level of female migration—at 46 percent as of 2000—which indicates that the majority of migrants are young males, who have the highest likelihood of sending remittances.

Another important variable is the portion of the highly educated among the migrants, which is presented in Figure 3.20. Central American and Mexican migrants have much lower levels of education than the rest of the migrants from Latin America. There are various reasons for this divergence, which were explored in an earlier section. A high ratio of tertiary education implies a higher level of income and a higher level of remittances. However, there are countervailing forces. First, college-educated migrants are more likely to come from middle- and upper-class families, which would rely less on the remittances. Second, it is much easier for educated migrants to obtain legal residency in the destination country and bring their families with them. This would also decrease the incentives to

Figure 3.19 Share of Female Migrants

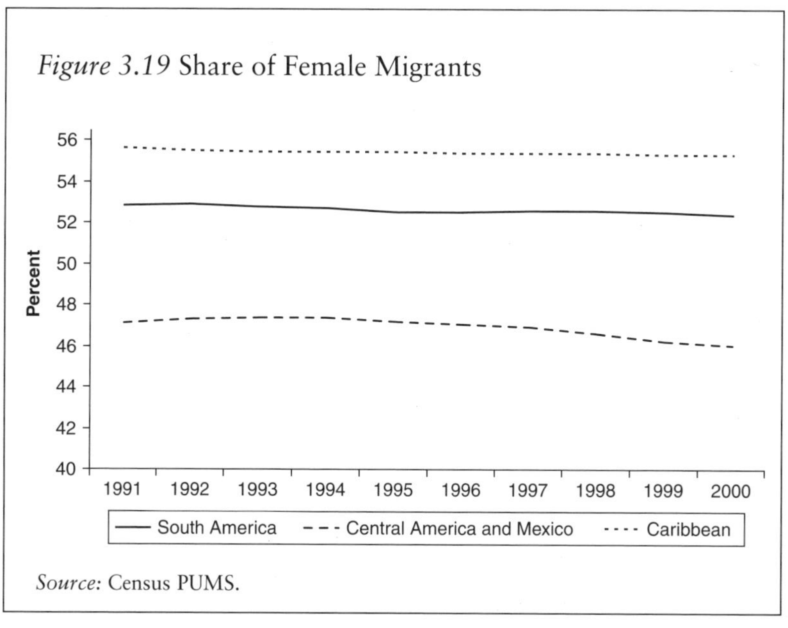

Source: Census PUMS.

Figure 3.20 Share of College Graduate Migrants

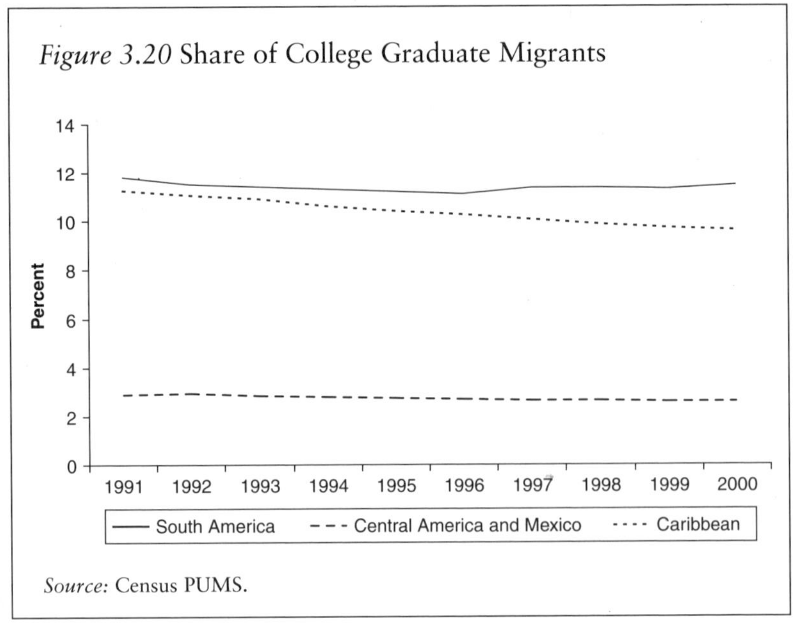

Source: Census PUMS.

remit money back home. Third, again due to ease of obtaining legal residency, they are more likely to stay permanently in the destination country and invest their assets there.

Financial market conditions in the receiving country. Recent literature has identified the positive effects that remittances have on the financial development of the recipient countries (Aggarwal, Demirgüç-Kunt, and Martínez Pería 2005; Freund and Spatafora 2005). The reverse is likely to be true as well—migrants would be more likely to send money back home if the financial sector were more developed and efficient. Furthermore, financial development is likely to increase the portion of remittances flowing through formal channels, which are, in return, more likely to be accurately captured in official remittances statistics. Figure 3.21 presents the bank deposit to GDP ratio for the three regions, which indicates the Caribbean is the more financially developed region, partially explaining the higher level of remittances.

Economic conditions in the receiving country. The final set of variables that influences remittances flows are related to macroeconomic conditions in the recipient countries. First is poverty. If income levels are low in a country, migrants might be more likely to remit money to their families. Second is economic growth. If the investment climate is positive and a country is growing rapidly, migrants might be more likely to remit for investment purposes. These take the form of real estate investments, which are highly

Figure 3.21 Ratio of Bank Deposits to GDP

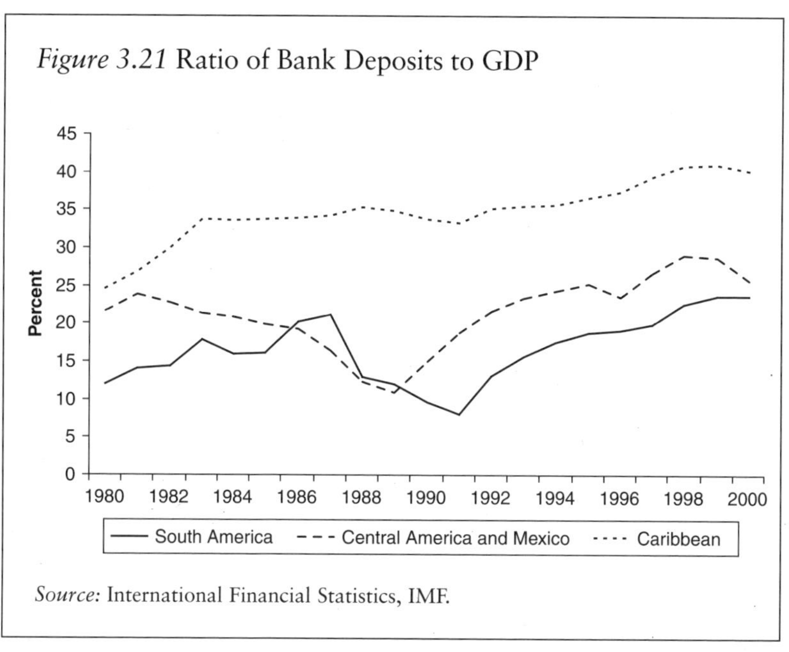

Source: International Financial Statistics, IMF.

favored by migrants in many countries; physical capital investment, such as businesses and capital goods; or human capital investment, such as the education of their children. Third is size of the country. There is much evidence that argues that smaller and isolated economies cannot sustain many economic activities, therefore prompting its citizens to migrate. Thus, smaller countries—controlling for the previous two factors—are likely to attract lower levels of investment.

Empirical Estimation

In this section, our goal is to identify which of the listed variables are significant determinants of remittances flows for the Latin American countries. The first step is to estimate the following equations for three different measures of remittances identified in the previous sections:

$$(1)\ \textit{Remittances/GDP}_{it} = \alpha + \beta_1\ \textit{Migrants/Population}_{it} + \beta_2\ \textit{BankDeposit/GDP}_{it} + \beta_3\ \textit{FemaleMigrantRatio}_{it} + \beta_4\ \textit{College EducatedRatio}_{it} + \beta_5\ \textit{GDPGrowth}_{it} + \beta_6\ \textit{Log GDP/capita}_{it} + \beta_7\ \textit{Log GDP}_{it} + \varepsilon_{it}$$

$$\begin{aligned}(2)\ Log\ Remittances/capita_{it} = \alpha &+ \beta_1\ Log\ MigrantsAbroad_{it}\\ &+ \beta_2\ BankDeposit/GDP_{it}\\ &+ \beta_3\ FemaleMigrantRatio_{it}\\ &+ \beta_4\ CollegeEducatedRatio_{it}\\ &+ \beta_5\ GDPGrowth_{it}\\ &+ \beta_6\ Log\ GDP_{it}\\ &+ \varepsilon_{it}\end{aligned}$$

$$\begin{aligned}(3)\ Log\ Remittances_{it} = \alpha &+ \beta_1\ Log\ MigrantsAbroad_{it}\\ &+ \beta_2\ BankDeposit/GDP_{it}\\ &+ \beta_3\ FemaleMigrantRatio_{it}\\ &+ \beta_4\ CollegeEducatedRatio_{it}\\ &+ \beta_5\ GDPGrowth_{it}\\ &+ \beta_6\ Log\ GDP/capita_{it}\\ &+ \beta_7\ Log\ GDP_{it} + \varepsilon_{it}\end{aligned}$$

The descriptions of the variables and how they were constructed are explained in annex A. For example, $Remittances/GDP_{it}$ is the remittance to GDP ratio for country *i* in year *t*. Each equation is first estimated using OLS with robust standard errors and the log of the native populations as weights to avoid attaching too much weight to smaller or larger countries in the sample. Next, we estimate the same equations using both country and year fixed effects to isolate country variables (such as the distance to the United States) and year variables (such as the business cycles in the United States).

Endogeneity

One of the crucial issues in the migration literature is that migrants are not a random sample of the underlying native population of the source country. In some cases, they are more educated than their fellow citizens, which is the case with Asian and Middle Eastern migrants in the United States. In other cases, they come from rural areas or are from a certain region. In the Latin American migration context, a large portion of the migrants, especially from Central America and Mexico, are relatively unskilled migrants who plan to send significant amounts of remittances back to their families to ease the impact of poverty. In other words, while the level of migration affects remittances levels, the desire to remit also influences migration levels. The endogeneity bias needs to be controlled in our estimation via instrumental variables. Thus, we add a first stage estimation to each equation listed above, where we use several instruments for the migration variables. These are the passport costs as a share of GDP per capita, the dependency ratio (i.e., the ratio of dependents to working-age population), and the population density in each country.

The qualifying requirement for being an appropriate instrument is that it should be correlated with a regressor for which it is to serve as an instrument, but uncorrelated with the dependent variable. In this context, the instruments should be correlated with the number of migrants abroad, but not with remittances flows. Our first instrument—passport costs—indicates the costs of migrating to destination countries. McKenzie (2005) examines the observed variation in the cost of obtaining a national passport across the world and finds high passport costs are associated with lower levels of outward migration. The other two instruments are thought to represent the demographic trends of home countries. As far as the dependency ratio is concerned, the lower figure informs us of a higher percentage of working-age population. Hence, this variable will be negatively correlated with the level of migration. On the other hand, population density in home countries is often thought to be a push factor for migration. It should be reasonable to assume that these variables are unlikely to be correlated with remittances flows and we therefore use them to instrument for the stock of migrants in our estimation.

Results

Each table in annex B corresponds to the estimation equation listed above. The first column in each table gives the results for the OLS estimation; the second column is the fixed effects estimation. The last column in each table reports the results from instrumental variables (IV) estimation. The first observation is that the OLS, the fixed effects, and the IV estimation results can be quite different for some coefficients. This indicates the importance of country and year variables, as well as the endogeneity problems. The results reveal the following patterns:

Migration levels increase remittances to GDP and remittances per capita levels, and decrease remittances per migrant. As expected, migration levels are positively correlated with remittances levels when remittances are measured as the remittances to GDP or the remittances to population ratio. For example, the coefficient of migrants per population in the first regression (table 3B.1) is 0.9, indicating if 1 percent of the population migrates, then the share of remittances in GDP increases by 0.9 percent. In other words, through their remittances, migrants more or less compensate for the loss in GDP due to their absence. On the other hand, in table 3B.3 in annex B, we see that a 1 percent increase in migrants boosts remittances by 0.1 percent, though the coefficient is not statistically significant. To put it differently, an increase in the number of migrants decreases remittances sent by each migrant, or each additional migrant sends less in remittances than the previous migrants. This might be influenced by the family reunification effect—as more people migrate the aggregate amount sent is divided among more senders, but can also become smaller as fewer relatives are left behind.

Increase in the overall education levels of migrants reduces remittances sent. This is actually a surprising result at the outset. One would expect higher education levels to be associated with higher incomes and higher remittances levels. However, more educated migrants are likely to come from wealthier families, which are less dependent on remittances. Furthermore, educated migrants can bring their families with them more easily, which also decreases the demand for remittances. Finally, educated migrants are more likely to settle permanently and invest in the destination country's assets. For example, in the third column of table 3B.1 in annex B, we see that a 1 percent increase in the share of college-educated migrants decreases the remittances to GDP ratio by 0.1 percent, and has a significantly negative effect on remittances per capita, as predicted. However, the effect loses some degree of significance in the other tables. It looks like a higher level of education among migrants increases total remittances, but this is not statistically significant.

Economic growth in the recipient country increases remittances levels. Higher economic growth is a sign of stability and more abundant investment opportunities. This is likely to encourage migrants to send remittances for investment purposes. Results in each table confirm this, as the coefficient of the GDP growth variable is significant and positive in almost every specification. The results indicate that 3 percent faster economic growth increases remittances flows by 0.2 percent of GDP (table 3B.1). Given the average remittances to GDP ratio is 3 percent in our sample, this translates into a 7 percent increase in remittances flows. This is almost perfectly confirmed by the results in tables 3B.2 and 3B.3.

Financial development variables do not have a significant effect on remittances. In all of the estimations, financial development variables have ambiguous signs. However, there are likely to be endogeneity issues as higher remittances encourage financial development. Furthermore, the financial development effect on remittances is likely to be captured by other variables in estimations, such as GDP per capita.

Share of female migrants has a significant negative effect on remittances flows. The coefficients of this variable in each case are negative, as predicted. There are two forces in play here. First, a higher level of female migration indicates that more people are migrating as families and are less likely to have relatives left behind. This implies that they are less likely to send money back home. The second effect is that female migrants' labor market participation levels and incomes are likely to be lower in the destination countries, which means there is less disposable income to be sent back as remittances.

Income per capita and size of the economy influence remittances flows. As stated earlier, overall economic prosperity is likely to be among the most important determinants of remittances flows. These variables, log GDP per capita and log GDP, have highly significant coefficients, especially in the IV estimation results. The correct approach is to analyze these coefficients together. Table 3B.1 indicates that a 1 percent increase in GDP per capita, with constant population, would decrease the remittances to

GDP ratio by around 0.077 percent. Similarly, the impact on total remittances (table 3B.3) is a decline of around 0.069 percent. In other words, poorer countries receive more remittances as a share of their GDP and in total. Finally, the coefficient on the log of GDP is statistically significant and positive in all the tables, which implies larger countries receive more remittances, as would be expected.

Conclusions

This chapter has reviewed the overall migration patterns from Latin American and Caribbean countries, especially in terms of the destinations chosen, age and education profiles of migrants, and their labor market performance in the United States. Even though most analysts categorize migrants from the region as a homogeneous group, we find that there are important differences across countries and subregions. Mexican and Central American migrants dominate overall migration flows in sheer numbers. They are also much younger, less educated, and tend to migrate primarily to the United States. South American migrants are older, more educated, and a large portion favors Europe due to ethnic and cultural linkages. While South American migrants are much more educated than the rest, brain drain is a more serious problem for other countries, especially smaller ones that do not provide many labor market opportunities for skilled workers. On the other hand, a large portion of the highly educated migrants from the region complete their education in the United States. Given that they might not have received the same education if they had stayed at home, migration provides them and their home countries with higher economic potential. We also observe significant "brain waste"—many college-educated migrants from the region end up in unskilled jobs that are not commensurate with their education levels.

As for the results relating the characteristics of migrants to observed remittances flows, the main findings of this chapter are the following: (i) migration levels increase remittances to GDP, remittances per capita levels, and total remittances; (ii) increases in the overall education levels of migrants reduce the level of remittances sent; (iii) economic growth in the recipient country increases remittances levels; (iv) financial development variables do not seem to have a significant effect on remittances; (v) the share of female migrants has a significant and negative effect on remittances flows; (vi) income per capita and size of the economy influence remittances flows, with larger and poorer economies receiving more remittances.

The patterns outlined in the chapter were aimed at providing an overview of general migration trends, not definite answers, in order to contextualize other sections, which primarily focus on remittances and their impact on home countries. The questions that were posed need to be explored in further detail if the goal is to design policies and institutions that lead to win-win-win outcomes for the migrants themselves, and for the destination and home countries.

Annex A Variable Description and Sources

Variable name	*Description*	*Source*
Remittances to GDP	Ratio of remittances to GDP (%), where remittances are defined as the sum of "compensation of employees," "workers' remittances," and "migrants' transfers" (see appendix A in Freund and Spatafora (2005)).	Balance of Payments Statistics (IMF)
Log of remittances per capita	Log of remittances per capita (constant 2000 US$).	Remittances: Balance of Payments Statistics (IMF) Population: World Bank (2005b)
Log of remittances	Log of remittances (constant 2000 US$).	Remittances: Balance of Payments Statistics (IMF) Migrants: www.ipums.org 2000: 5% Census PUMS 1990: 5% State
Migrants abroad to population	Ratio of migrants abroad (see above) to population of home countries (%).	Migrants in the United States: www.ipums.org 2000: 5% Census PUMS 1990: 5% State Population: (World Bank 2005b)
Log of migrants abroad	Log of cumulative number of migrants abroad by year. The estimates of the total number of migrants abroad was calculated based on the cumulative number of migrants in the United States and the ratio of migrants in	Migrants in the United States: www.ipums.org 2000: 5% Census PUMS 1990: 5% State

(continued)

Annex A Variable Description and Sources (*continued*)

Variable name	*Description*	*Source*
	the United States to the total number of migrants abroad. The ratio was obtained from Docquier and Marfouk (2006). The 1990 figure was applied for the years prior to 1991, and the 2000 figure was applied for the years between 1991 and 2000. As for the number of migrants in the United States, 1990–2000 values of indicator are based on Census 2000, whereas values before 1990 are based on Census 1990 (which reports intervals of arrival as opposed to years of arrival, therefore for some years the indicator takes the same value).	Ratio of migrants in the United States to total number of migrants abroad: Docquier and Marfouk (2006)
Bank deposit to GDP	Bank deposit to GDP calculated as: {(0.5)*[F(t)/P_e(t) + F(t–1)/P_e(t–1)]}/ [GDP(t)/P_a(t)] where F is demand and time and saving deposits, and GDP is line 99b, P_e is end-of-period CPI (line 64) and P_a is the average CPI for the year.	International Financial Statistics (IMF)
Share of female migrants	Share of females in migrant population by year (%); 1990–2000 values of indicator are based on 2000 U.S. Census, whereas values before 1990 are based on 1990 U.S. Census (which reports intervals of arrival as opposed to years of arrival, therefore for some years the indicator takes the same value).	www.ipums.org 2000: 5% Census PUMS 1990: 5% State

(*continued*)

Annex A Variable Description and Sources (*continued*)

Variable name	*Description*	*Source*
Share of college graduate migrants	Share of college graduate migrants (people with at least a bachelor's degree) in migrant population by year (%); 1990–2000 values of indicator are based on Census 2000, whereas values before 1990 are based on Census 1990 (which reports intervals of arrival as opposed to years of arrival, therefore for some years the indicator takes the same value).	www.ipums.org 2000: 5% Census PUMS 1990: 5% State
Log of GDP	Log of GDP (constant 2000 US$).	World Bank (2005b)
Log of GDP per capita	Log of GDP per capita (constant 2000 US$).	World Bank (2005b)
GDP growth	GDP growth (annual %).	World Bank (2005b)
Passport cost to GDP per capita	Passport cost normalized by the country's GDP per capita expressed in U.S. dollars, inflation adjusted (%): (passport cost/GDP current dollars per capita)*100/((1 + inflation90/100)(1 + inflation91/100) … (1 + inflation2004/100)).	McKenzie (2005); World Bank (2005b)
Dependency ratio	Age dependency ratio— ratio of dependents to working-age (15–64) population.	World Bank (2005b)
Population density	Population density (people per sq. km.).	World Bank (2005b)

Annex B Estimation Results

Table 3B.1 Regression Results for Determinants of Remittances to Latin America and the Caribbean

Dependent variable: Ratio of remittances to GDP (%)
Cross-country panel data spanning 1986–2000

Variable	*OLS*	*Fixed Effects*	*IV*
Migrants abroad/population	0.188**	0.218*	0.921***
	[0.043]	[0.125]	[0.223]
Bank deposit/GDP	0.402	-2.196	2.618
	[1.183]	[1.259]	[1.948]
Log of GDP	-0.044	3.283	5.243**
	[0.146]	[5.868]	[2.477]
Log of GDP per capita	-0.0955**	-6.366	-7.694**
	[0.379]	[5.827]	[3.487]
GDP growth (%)	0.043	0.048*	0.059*
	[0.035]	[0.026]	[0.031]
Share of female migrants (%)	-0.012	-0.192**	-0.318***
	[0.043]	[0.080]	[0.127]
Share of college graduate migrants (%)	-0.257***	-0.287*	-0.103***
	[0.053]	[0.152]	[0.272]
Constant	12.554***	-16.714	
	[3.902]	[106.671]	
Observations	290	290	290
R-squared	0.383	0.830	0.107
F test (p-value)	27.92	35.31	12.61
Overidentification χ^2 (p-value)			0.70 (0.40)

Robust standard errors in brackets.
*significant at 10%; ** significant at 5%; *** significant at 1%.

Table 3B.2 Regression Results for Determinants of Remittances to Latin America and the Caribbean

Dependent variable: Log of remittances per capita
Cross-country panel data spanning 1986–2000

Variable	*OLS*	*Fixed Effects*	*IV*
Log of migrants abroad	0.566***	–1.107	–0.987**
	[0.102]	[0.726]	[0.478]
Bank deposit/GDP	0.959	–0.071	–0.258
	[0.624]	[0.974]	[0.921]
Log of GDP	–0.344***	–0.270	2.331***
	[0.077]	[0.713]	[0.568]
GDP growth (%)	0.036	0.032**	0.026*
	[0.024]	[0.013]	[0.015]
Share of female migrants	0.038	–0.0297***	–0.181***
	[0.029]	[0.062]	[0.050]
Share of college graduate migrants (%)	–0.101***	0.024	–0.059
	–[0.032]	[0.070]	[0.109]
Constant	2.694	35.522	
	[2.197]	[23.766]	
Observation	290	290	290
R-squared	0.257	0.846	0.377
F test (p-value)	26.14(0.00)	83.18(0.00)	18.40(0.00)
Overidentification χ^2 (p-value)	4.73 (0.09)		

Robust standard errors in brackets.
* significant at 10%; ** significant at 5%; *** significant at 1%.

Table 3B.3 Regression Results for Determinants of Remittances to Latin America and Caribbean

Dependent variable: Log of remittances
Cross-country panel data spanning 1986–2000

Variable	*OLS*	*Fixed Effects*	*IV*
Log of migrants abroad	0.639***	–1.074	0.107
	[0.101]	[0.714]	[0.617]
Bank deposit/GDP	–0.833	0.161	–0.911
	[0.663]	[1.044]	[0.987]
Log of GDP	0.385***	–1.324	7.682***
	[0.089]	[2.511]	[2.114]
Log of GDP per capita	–0.111	1.215	–6.930***
	[0.155]	[2.405]	[2.472]
GDP growth (%)	0.020	0.031**	0.034**
	[0.024]	[0.013]	[0.015]
Share of female migrants (%)	0.020	–0.311***	–0.185***
	[0.025]	[0.067]	[0.046]
Share of college graduate migrants (%)	–0.100***	–0.008	0.095
	[0.030]	[0.071]	[0.134]
Constant	2.825	70.176	
	[1.900]	[50.655]	
Observations	290	290	290
R-squared	0.533	0.893	0.463
F test (p-value)	123.28 (0.00)	94.97 (0.00)	19.06 (0.00)
Overidentification χ^2 (p-value)			0.001 (0.97)

Robust standard errors in brackets.
* significant at 10%; ** significant at 5%; *** significant at 1%.

References

Adams, R.H. 2005. "Remittances, Poverty, and Investment in Guatemala." In *International Migration, Remittances and the Brain Drain*, ed. Ç. Özden and M. Schiff. Washington, DC: World Bank and Palgrave Macmillan.

Aggarwal, R., A. Demirgüç-Kunt, and M.S. Martínez Pería. 2005. "Do Workers' Remittances Promote Financial Development?" Unpublished, World Bank, Washington, DC.

Chami, R., C. Fullenkamp, and S. Jahjah. 2005. "Are Immigrant Remittance Flows a Source of Capital for Development?" *IMF Staff Papers* 52 (1): 55–81.

Cox-Edwards, A., and M. Ureta. 2003. "International Migration, Remittances and Schooling: Evidence from El Salvador." *Journal of Development Economics* 72 (2): 429–61.

Docquier, F., and A. Marfouk. 2006. "International Migration by Education Attainment, 1990–2000." In *International Migration, Remittances and the Brain Drain*, ed. Ç. Özden and M. Schiff. Washington, DC: World Bank and Palgrave Macmillan.

Freund, C., and N. Spatafora. 2005. "Remittances: Transaction Costs, Determinants, and Informal Flows." Policy Research Working Paper No.3704, World Bank, Washington, DC.

Gupta, P. 2005. "Macroeconomic Determinants of Remittances: Evidence from India." Working Paper WP/05/224, International Monetary Fund, Washington, DC.

Mattoo, A., I.C. Neagu, and Ç. Özden. 2005. "Brain Waste? Educated Migrants in the U.S. Labor Market." Policy Research Working Paper No. 3581, World Bank, Washington, DC.

McCormick, B., and J. Wahba. 2003. "Return International Migration and Geographical Inequality: The Case of Egypt." *Journal of African Economies* 12 (4): 500–32.

McKenzie, D. 2005. "Paper Walls are Easier to Tear Down: Passport Costs and Legal Barriers to Emigration." Policy Research Working Paper No. 3783, World Bank, Washington, DC.

MPC (Minnesota Population Center). 2007. *Integrated Public Use Microdata Series—International: Version 3.0*. Minneapolis: University of Minnesota. http://international.ipums.org/international/.

Ruggles, Steven, Matthew Sobek, Trent Alexander, Catherine A. Fitch, Ronald Goeken, Patricia Kelly Hall, Miriam King, and Chad Ronnander. 2004. *Integrated Public Use Microdata Series: Version 3.0* [Machine-readable database]. Minneapolis, MN: Minnesota Population Center [producer and distributor]. http://usa.ipums.org/usa/.

United States Census Bureau. 2000. 2000 Census. http://www.census.gov/main/www/cen2000.html.

World Bank. 2005a. *Global Economic Prospects: Economic Implications of Remittances and Migration*. Washington, DC: World Bank.

———. 2005b. *World Development Indicators*. Washington, DC: World Bank.

Yang, D., and C.A. Martinez. 2005. "Remittances and Poverty in Migrants' Home Areas: Evidence from the Philippines." In *International Migration, Remittances and the Brain Drain*, ed. Ç. Özden and M. Schiff. Washington, DC: World Bank and Palgrave Macmillan.

4

Do Remittances Lower Poverty Levels in Latin America?

Pablo Acosta, Cesar Calderón, Pablo Fajnzylber, and J. Humberto López

To the extent that remittances increase per-capita income, ease credit constraints, and compensate for negative shocks to recipient countries, they are likely to help reduce poverty and inequality, as well as boost domestic investment and economic growth. However, remittances also tend to be associated with a reduction in the income-generating capacity of households with migrants. Moreover, they may reduce labor supply and lead to real exchange rate appreciations, all of which could potentially increase income volatility. The question thus remains as to whether remittances do in fact improve social outcomes and bolster economic growth and investment. Are all the above potential impacts of remittances economically relevant? Are the positive effects of remittances offset by their negative effects? What is the net effect of remittances on poverty and growth?

Introduction

Have the large remittances flows received by Latin America contributed to reducing poverty in the region? In principle, given that in many cases remittances go to poor households and directly increase their level of income, an unequivocal positive answer could be expected. Moreover, to the extent that remittances ease credit constraints and reduce risk and volatility, they could also promote higher levels of investment in physical and human capital, and have dynamic effects on growth and poverty reduction.

There are, however, several reasons that warrant circumspection in the assessment of the development impact of remittances. First, as shown in the previous chapter, the position of migrants in the distribution of income and education varies considerably across sender countries. As a result, the impact of remittances on poverty reduction should also be expected to vary by country and region. Second, according to the New Open Economy Macroeconomics literature, if remittances lead to increases in a country's domestic wealth, they could reduce labor supply, increase the demand for nontradable goods, and generate real exchange rate appreciations which, in turn, could hurt competitiveness and growth. Third, to the extent that remittances are just one among other consequences of migration, they cannot be treated as exogenous transfers. Rather, it is reasonable to believe that in many cases, remittances and migration also entail potential losses of income associated with migrants' absences from their families and communities. Moreover, depending on the demographic characteristics of migrants, "brain drain" effects could have negative impacts on productivity and welfare.

In this chapter, we explore both the static and dynamic effects of remittances on development using micro- and macroeconomic data and techniques. In particular, we investigate the links between remittances, poverty, and inequality, using household surveys and cross-country regression analyses. We then analyze the macroeconomic effects of remittances in more detail, considering not only their impact on economic growth, but also that on volatility and investment.

Remittances, Inequality, and Poverty: A Microeconomic Approach

As argued in the seminal paper by Stark, Taylor, and Yitzhaki (1986), the impact of migration and international remittances on income inequality depends on the magnitude of remittances in relation to income from other sources, and upon the position of remittances-receiving households in the distribution of income. In their perspective, when migration is incipient, its costs and related uncertainty are likely to be high, so that migrants can be expected to come from among the better off. As a result, at this point remittances would tend to have an unequalizing effect. Over time, however, the uncertainty and costs involving migration are likely to diminish with the spread of information and contacts across a wider range of households, which may lead to increases in migration among the worse off, with potentially favorable effects on poverty and income inequality.

As a first pass at the issue, table 4.1 presents the estimates of the Gini coefficient obtained, with observed nonremittances household income and total income, respectively. As shown in this table, with the exception

Table 4.1 Income Gini Coefficient Before and After Remittances

Country	*Gini coefficient*	*Difference in Gini before/after remittances*	*Percent difference*	*Country*	*Gini coefficient*	*Difference in Gini before/after remittances*	*Percent difference*
Bolivia (2002)				Honduras (2002)			
Nonremittances income	0.557			Nonremittances income	0.572		
Total income	0.555	–0.002	–0.4	Total income	0.559	–0.013	–2.3
Dominican Republic (2004)				Mexico (2002)			
Nonremittances income	0.531			Nonremittances income	0.491		
Total income	0.520	–0.011	–2.0	Total income	0.481	–0.010	–2.1
Ecuador (2004)				Nicaragua (2001)			
Nonremittances income	0.505			Nonremittances income	0.517		
Total income	0.499	–0.006	–1.2	Total income	0.518	0.001	0.3
El Salvador (2000)				Paraguay (2003)			
Nonremittances income	0.514			Nonremittances income	0.520		
Total income	0.486	–0.028	–5.4	Total income	0.516	–0.004	–0.7
Guatemala (2000)				Peru (2002)			
Nonremittances income	0.596			Nonremittances income	0.476		
Total income	0.586	–0.010	–1.8	Total income	0.476	0.000	0.1
Haiti (2001)							
Nonremittances income	0.670						
Total income	0.669	–0.001	–0.1				

Source: Acosta et al. 2007.

of Nicaragua and Peru, the Latin American countries for which data on remittances is available exhibit higher Gini coefficients for nonremittances income, suggesting that if remittances were exogenously eliminated, inequality would increase. Thus, even though as noted in chapter 2, remittances have a very unequal distribution (in several countries remittances tend to go to relatively well-off households), in general we can say that with the exception of Nicaragua and Peru, the distribution of remittances is less unequal than the distribution of nonremittances income. Quantitatively, however, the estimated potential changes in the Gini coefficient are small. The exception is El Salvador, where the Gini coefficient of total income is almost 3 percentage points lower than the Gini coefficient of nonremittances income.

One implication of the results in table 4.1 is that in principle, remittances will contribute to lower poverty levels. After all, remittances raise income levels and in most cases lower inequality—even if marginally. However, what is the magnitude of the impact on poverty? To address this question, table 4.2 reports poverty head counts calculated before and after excluding remittances from the total income of recipients. We employ two commonly used head count poverty indicators, based on poverty lines of US$1 and US$2 per person per day, measured at purchasing power parity (PPP) values, corresponding respectively to "extreme" and "moderate" poverty.[1] As already noted, with this very simple approach, remittances lead to large reductions in poverty levels, especially in those countries where migrants tend to come from the lower quintiles of the income distribution—notably Mexico, El Salvador, and the Dominican Republic, where extreme poverty is estimated to fall by more than 35 percent (that is, the poverty rate would be reduced by more than one-third), and moderate poverty by an average of 19 percent.

One concern with the above simulations is that they are rather mechanical and make the unrealistic assumption that remittances can be treated as exogenous transfers by migrants. This is equivalent to assuming that the behavior—and hence the income—of the households is not affected by the remittances they receive and by the migration flows that logically precede those remittances flows. However, it is reasonable to believe that in many cases, migration also entails potential losses of income associated with the migrants' absences from their families and communities. In other words, remittances are not exogenous transfers, but rather they substitute for the home earnings that migrants would have had if they had not decided to work abroad.

In order to consider these effects, one needs to estimate the value that household income would have taken had migrants stayed in their households. To impute per-capita household income for migrant families in that counterfactual scenario, we predict per-capita income levels for households with remittances on the basis of a reduced-form specification for

Table 4.2 Poverty Head Counts Before and After Remittances

Country	*Less than US$ 1 a day (%)*	*Percent difference*	*Less than US$ 2 a day (%)*	*Percent difference*	*Country*	*Less than US$ 1 a day (%)*	*Percent difference*	*Less than US$ 2 a day (%)*	*Percent difference*
Bolivia (2002)					El Salvador (2000)				
Nonremittances income	18.400		35.261		Nonremittances income	12.116		23.743	
Total income	17.764		34.674		Total income	7.700		18.607	
Diff. before/after remittances	–0.6	–3.5	–0.6	–1.7	Diff. before/after remittances	–4.4	–36.4	–5.1	–21.6
Dominican Republic (2004)					Guatemala (2000)				
Nonremittances income	7.219		16.072		Nonremittances income	24.413		41.715	
Total income	4.688		12.836		Total income	21.578		39.087	
Diff. before/after remittances	–2.5	–35.1	–3.2	–20.1	Diff. before/after remittances	–2.8	–11.6	–2.6	–6.3
Ecuador (2004)					Haiti (2001)				
Nonremittances income	12.531		28.849		Nonremittances income	60.229		76.343	
Total income	11.198		27.147		Total income	53.425		71.414	
Diff. before/after remittances	–1.3	–10.6	–1.7	–5.9	Diff. before/after remittances	–6.8	–11.3	–4.9	–6.5

(continued)

Table 4.2 Poverty Head Counts Before and After Remittances (*continued*)

Country	*Less than US$ 1 a day (%)*	*Percent difference*	*Less than US$ 2 a day (%)*	*Percent difference*	*Country*	*Less than US$ 1 a day (%)*	*Percent difference*	*Less than US$ 2 a day (%)*	*Percent difference*
Honduras (2002)					Paraguay (2003)				
Nonremittances income	18.681		34.772		Nonremittances income	6.839		16.188	
Total income	16.155		31.731		Total income	6.057		15.333	
Diff. before/after remittances	–2.5	–13.5	–3.0	–8.7	Diff. before/after remittances	–0.8	–11.4	–0.9	–5.3
Mexico (2002)					Peru (2002)				
Nonremittances income	5.268		15.029		Nonremittances income	4.193		15.644	
Total income	3.165		12.695		Total income	4.185		15.539	
Diff. before/after remittances	–2.1	–39.9	–2.3	–15.5	Diff. before/after remittances	0.0	–0.2	–0.1	–0.7
Nicaragua (2001)									
Nonremittances income	8.763		23.323						
Total income	8.260		22.552						
Diff. before/after remittances	–0.5	–5.7	–0.8	–3.3					

Source: Acosta et al. 2007.

the determinants of income among households without remittances. The estimated model is the following:

$$\log Y_i = \alpha + \beta X_i + \gamma H_i + \mu_i \tag{1}$$

where Y_i represents per-capita nonremittances income, X_i is a vector of household characteristics (demographic and location covariates), H_i is a set of characteristics of the household head, and μ_i is unobserved heterogeneity in income generation. The procedure consists of estimating the equation (1) for the subsample of households that do not receive remittances, making a correction for possible selection biases. The estimated coefficients allow for predicting the counterfactual nonmigration income for remittances-recipient households. As explained below, in order to avoid the reduction in income variability for migrant families due to the use of predicted values, we follow Barham and Boucher (1998) in adding a simulated error component to the predicted values of income.

Several issues need to be discussed. First, in the absence of information on migrant characteristics—which is the case in 9 of our 11 countries—it is necessary to make some basic assumptions about the number and demographics of migrants. In this respect, we follow Rodriguez (1998)—and most of the evidence on international migration—in assuming that on average, remittances are sent by a single adult male family member. In addition, we assume that the migrant has the average years of education of other adults in the household. To test the robustness of our results with the above assumptions, we compare the corresponding results with those obtained when detailed data on migrants' demographics are employed in lieu of the above assumptions, which are possible only for Nicaragua and Haiti.

Second, ordinary least squares (OLS) estimates of equation (1) would be inconsistent if μ_i is not independent and identically distributed (i.i.d.). In other words, if migrants are not randomly selected from the pool of households, estimates of equation (1) based on the sample of households without migrants could suffer from selection bias. To control for that possibility, we add variables that approximate the "propensity to migrate" in the context of the two-step estimation framework proposed by Heckman (1979).[2] With the assumption stated before concerning migrant characteristics, the estimated coefficients for equation (1) are used to impute the counterfactual nonremittances per-capita household income for recipient families. With this variable, one can proceed to calculate the levels of poverty and inequality that would have prevailed had migration and remittances not taken place.

It must be noted, however, that as mentioned by Rodriguez (1998), the variance of the counterfactual income predicted on the basis of observable household characteristics is artificially small because it ignores unobserved determinants of income. To deal with this problem, we follow Barham and Boucher (1998) and add to the predicted household income a random error component drawn from a distribution with the same properties (mean, variance) of the actual estimated errors. We pursue this approach and obtain 1,000 different estimates of the imputed counterfactual non-remittances income for families with migrants, and the same number of estimates for the poverty and inequality levels that would have prevailed in the above counterfactual scenario. This allows us to report not only point estimates for those variables, but also 95 percent confidence intervals, based on the 25th and 975th estimates of the variables—after sorting them in ascending order. The resulting estimates for the impact of remittances on inequality and poverty are reported in tables 4.3 and 4.4, respectively.

Our results suggest that the Gini coefficients that would have prevailed in the absence of migration would have been generally higher, with the largest difference obtained for Haiti (7.7 percent), followed by Guatemala (2.9 percent), El Salvador (2.1 percent), Nicaragua (1.8 percent), and Honduras (1.1 percent). The negative effects of remittances on inequality are much smaller in the other countries, and a positive effect is even obtained for Mexico and the Dominican Republic. The results for the countries for which remittances' impact is minor or even favors inequality are consistent with the findings of previous studies that have made attempts to calculate counterfactual pre-remittances income for families with migrants.[3] Overall, the estimated inequality-reducing effects of remittances are found to be relatively small, at 2.7 percent on average. Yet they tend to be comparatively larger in countries where remittances represent a higher share of income.

As for the impact of migration and remittances on poverty, the results in table 4.4 suggest that the failure to correct for the reduction in income associated with the absence of migrants from their households may lead to grossly overestimating the poverty-reducing effect of remittances. In particular, we find that when the counterfactual of no migration is considered, remittances reduce poverty head counts in only 6 of the 11 countries for which data is available—the exceptions being the Dominican Republic, Mexico, Nicaragua, Paraguay, and Peru—and they reduce poverty gaps in only three cases—Ecuador, Guatemala, and Haiti.[4] In two cases, the Dominican Republic and Nicaragua, we even find that remittances are linked to increases in extreme poverty—of 7.4 percent and 0.4 percent, respectively. Thus, for very poor households in those countries, the income lost due to the absence of migrants from their households is less than compensated for by the money they send home, possibly because they also underperform in the job market in destination countries.

Considering all 11 countries and assuming that the remittances share in GDP is as given by balance of payments statistics, the average estimated impact of remittances on poverty head counts is such that a 1 percentage point increase in the remittances to GDP ratio reduces moderate and extreme poverty by, respectively, 0.37 percent and 0.29 percent.

Interestingly, the countries for which we find the largest inequality- and poverty-reducing effects are not necessarily those where remittances

Table 4.3 Income Gini Coefficient in Counterfactual Scenario of No Migration

Country	*Gini coefficient*	*Difference in Gini before/after remittances*	*Percent difference*	*Country*	*Gini coefficient*	*Difference in Gini before/after remittances*	*Percent difference*
Bolivia (2002)				El Salvador (2000)			
Nonremittances income	0.556			Nonremittances income	0.497		
95% confidence interval	(0.553; 0.561)			95% confidence interval	(0.494; 0.501)		
Total income	0.555	–0.001	–0.3	Total income	0.486	–0.011	–2.1
Dominican Republic (2004)				Guatemala (2000)			
Nonremittances income	0.519			Nonremittances income	0.603		
95% confidence interval	(0.514; 0.525)			95% confidence interval	(0.596; 0.615)		
Total income	0.520	0.001	0.3	Total income	0.586	–0.017	–2.9
Ecuador (2004)				Haiti (2001)			
Nonremittances income	0.501			Nonremittances income	0.725		
95% confidence interval	(0.500; 0.503)			95% confidence interval	(0.703; 0.756)		
Total income	0.499	–0.002	–0.5	Total income	0.669	–0.056	–7.7

(continued)

Table 4.3 Income Gini Coefficient in Counterfactual Scenario of No Migration (*continued*)

Country	*Gini coefficient*	*Difference in Gini before/after remittances*	*Percent difference*	*Country*	*Gini coefficient*	*Difference in Gini before/after remittances*	*Percent difference*
Honduras (2002)				Paraguay (2003)			
Nonremittances income	0.565			Nonremittances income	0.515		
95% confidence interval	(0.564; 0.567)			95% confidence interval	(0.514; 0.517)		
Total income	0.559	–0.006	–1.1	Total income	0.516	0.001	0.2
Mexico (2002)				Peru (2002)			
Nonremittances income	0.477			Nonremittances income	0.478		
95% confidence interval	(0.477; 0.478)			95% confidence interval	(0.476; 0.481)		
Total income	0.481	0.004	0.7	Total income	0.476	–0.002	–0.3
Nicaragua (2001)							
Nonremittances income	0.528						
95% confidence interval	(0.519; 0.539)						
Total income	0.518	–0.010	–1.8				

Source: Acosta et al. 2007.

Table 4.4 Poverty Head Counts in Counterfactual Scenario of No Migration

Country	*US$1 a day (%)*	*Percent difference*	*US$2 a day (%)*	*Percent difference*	*Country*	*US$1 a day (%)*	*Percent difference*	*US$2 a day (%)*	*Percent difference*
Bolivia (2002)					Ecuador (2004)				
Nonremittances income	17.999		35.052		Nonremittances income	11.665		28.082	
95% confidence interval	(17.842; 8.184)		(34.824; 5.279)		95% confidence interval	(11.594; 11.741)		(27.960; 28.221)	
Total income	17.764		34.674		Total income	11.198		27.147	
Diff. before/after remittances	−0.2	−1.3	−0.4	−1.1	Diff. before/after remittances	−0.5	4.3	−0.9	−3.3
Dominican Republic (2004)					El Salvador (2000)				
Nonremittances income	4.364		13.008		Nonremittances income	8.215		20.055	
95% confidence interval	(4.247; 4.488)		(12.777; 13.270)		95% confidence interval	(8.077; 8.375)		(19.824; 20.311)	
Total income	4.688		12.836		Total income	7.700		18.607	
Diff. before/after remittances	0.3	7.4	−0.2	−1.3	Diff. before/after remittances	−0.5	−6.3	−1.4	−7.2

(continued)

Table 4.4 Poverty Headcounts in Counterfactual Scenario of No Migration (*continued*)

Country	*US$1 a day (%)*	*Percent difference*	*US$2 a day (%)*	*Percent difference*	*Country*	*US$1 a day (%)*	*Percent difference*	*US$2 a day (%)*	*Percent difference*
Guatemala (2000)					Honduras (2002)				
Nonremittances income	23.630		41.379		Nonremittances income	16.715		33.155	
95% confidence interval	(23.335; 23.931)		(41.055; 41.710)		95% confidence interval	(16.608; 6.820)		(32.993; 3.307)	
Total income	21.578		39.087		Total income	16.155		31.731	
Diff. before/after remittances	−2.1	−8.7	−2.3	−5.5	Diff. before/ after remittances	−0.6	−3.4	−1.4	−4.3
Haiti (2001)					Mexico (2002)				
Nonremittances income	57.541		74.376		Nonremittances income	3.079		12.603	
95% confidence interval	(56.929; 58.138)		(73.793; 74.992)		95% confidence interval	(3.019; 0.145)		(12.480; 2.731)	
Total income	53.425		71.414		Total income	3.165		12.695	
Diff. before/after remittances	−4.1	−7.2	−3.0	−4.0	Diff. before/after remittances	0.1	2.8	0.1	0.7

(*continued*)

Table 4.4 Poverty Headcounts in Counterfactual Scenario of No Migration (*continued*)

Country	*US$1 a day (%)*	*Percent difference*	*US$2 a day (%)*	*Percent difference*	*Country*	*US$1 a day (%)*	*Percent difference*	*US$2 a day (%)*	*Percent difference*
Nicaragua (2001)					Peru (2002)				
Nonremittances income	8.226		22.848		Nonremittances income	4.186		15.555	
95% confidence interval	(8.012; 8.528)		(22.427; 23.345)		95% confidence interval	(4.186; 4.192)		(15.533; 15.888)	
Total income	8.260		22.552		Total income	4.185		15.539	
Diff. before/after remittances	0.0	0.4	–0.3	–1.3	Diff. before/after remittances	0.0	0.0	0.0	–0.1
Paraguay (2003)									
Nonremittances income	6.066		15.373						
95% confidence interval	(5.999; 6.145)		(15.256; 15.521)						
Total income	6.057		15.333						
Diff. before/after remittances	0.0	–0.1	0.0	–0.3					

Source: Acosta et al. 2007.

recipients tend to come from lower income groups. Consider, for instance, the cases of El Salvador, Guatemala, Mexico, and Paraguay, where remittances recipients tend to be relatively less educated than the general population (and there is "negative" selection into migration) and remittances are more progressively distributed than total income. Only in two of them (El Salvador and Guatemala) do we find that remittances are associated with significant reductions in both inequality and poverty. Moreover, in the other two countries where remittances appear to reduce poverty and inequality—Haiti and Honduras—remittances recipients are more likely to be found among highly educated individuals, and remittances income is distributed more unequally than total income. If anything, what the four countries where remittances have the largest effects on poverty and inequality have in common is that they are among those in which remittances are highest with respect to GDP.

One complementary approach proposed by Schiff (2006) is to estimate the impact of remittances on poverty, focusing exclusively on the population of households that receive remittances. The point is that while the impact of remittances on national poverty levels may be limited, the effect on the poverty status of the families with migrants could be much larger. Table 4.5 reports the results of such analysis, using as a reference group only remittances-recipient households rather than the entire survey sample, even though the latter continues to be used, as described above, for estimating the counterfactual income of recipients. The first interesting finding from this analysis is that the initial poverty rates (before migration) among households with migrants are lower than those found in the general population. In Peru and Nicaragua, for instance, moderate poverty levels in the no-migration counterfactual had been estimated to be close to 15 percent and 22 percent, respectively, at the national level, but they are close to 1 percent and 12 percent, respectively, when we only consider the households that receive remittances. Other countries where migrants are considerably less likely to be poor than the average household in the country include Haiti, the Dominican Republic, and Honduras. Second, as expected, we find that the effects of remittances on poverty are much larger than in the case when nonrecipient households are included in the calculations. The largest absolute reductions in extreme poverty are found in Haiti and Guatemala, with rates that are, respectively, 15 percentage points and 10.7 percentage points below those in the scenario of no migration. Similarly, in Haiti and Guatemala as well as Bolivia, Honduras, and Ecuador, the absolute reductions in moderate poverty are between 10 percentage points and 17 percentage points. In contrast, remittances are found to have the effect of slightly increasing poverty levels, even among households that receive remittances, in both Mexico and the Dominican Republic.

Table 4.5 Poverty Head Counts among Recipient Households in Counterfactual Scenario of No Migration

Country	*US$1 a day (%)*	*Percent difference*	*US$2 a day (%)*	*Percent difference*	*Country*	*US$1 a day (%)*	*Percent difference*	*US$2 a day (%)*	*Percent difference*
Bolivia (2002)					Ecuador (2004)				
Nonremittances income	15.103		32.610		Nonremittances income	7.357		22.977	
95% confidence interval	(10.297; 20.118)		(26.619; 39.209)		95% confidence interval	(6.060; 8.826)		(20.666; 25.539)	
Total income	8.570		22.181		Total income	2.953		10.934	
Diff. before/after remittances	–6.5	–43.3	–10.4	–32.0	Diff. before/after remittances	–4.4	–59.9	–12.0	–52.4
Dominican Republic (2004)					El Salvador (2000)				
Nonremittances income	1.715		7.746		Nonremittances income	5.255		17.870	
95% confidence interval	(1.195; 2.265)		(6.738; 8.864)		95% confidence interval	(4.555; 6.074)		(16.658; 19.327)	
Total income	3.266		7.349		Total income	2.774		10.757	
Diff. before/after remittances	1.6	90.4	–0.4	–5.1	Diff. before/after remittances	–2.5	–47.2	–7.1	–39.8

(continued)

Table 4.5 Poverty Headcounts among Recipients Households in Counterfactual Scenario of No Migration *(continued)*

Country	*US$1 a day (%)*	*Percent difference*	*US$2 a day (%)*	*Percent difference*	*Country*	*US$1 a day (%)*	*Percent difference*	*US$2 a day (%)*	*Percent difference*
Guatemala (2000)					Honduras (2002)				
Nonremittances income	20.995		38.085		Nonremittances income	7.694		22.785	
95% confidence interval	(17.362; 24.527)		(34.098; 42.246)		95% confidence interval	(6.703; 8.699)		(21.260; 24.318)	
Total income	10.307		21.341		Total income	2.769		10.124	
Diff. before/after remittances	–10.7	–50.9	–16.7	–44.0	Diff. before/after remittances	–4.9	–64.0	–12.7	–55.6
Haiti (2001)					Mexico (2002)				
Nonremittances income	47.225		63.877		Nonremittances income	1.719		12.967	
95% confidence interval	(45.053; 49.452)		(61.686; 66.060)		95% confidence interval	(0.835; 2.810)		(10.979; 15.185)	
Total income	32.238		53.030		Total income	3.632		15.942	
Diff. before/after remittances	–15.0	–31.7	–10.8	–17.0	Diff. before/after remittances	1.9	111.3	3.0	22.9

(continued)

Table 4.5 Poverty Headcounts among Recipients Households in Counterfactual Scenario of No Migration (*continued*)

Country	*US$1 a day (%)*	*Percent difference*	*US$2 a day (%)*	*Percent difference*	*Country*	*US$1 a day (%)*	*Percent difference*	*US$2 a day (%)*	*Percent difference*
Nicaragua (2001)					Peru (2002)				
Nonremittances income	3.348		12.309		Nonremittances income	0.051		1.269	
95% confidence interval	(2.049; 5.103)		(9.751; 5.363)		95% confidence interval	(0.018; 0.692)		(0.244; 2.530)	
Total income	3.730		10.815		Total income	0.000		0.804	
Diff. before/after remittances	0.4	11.4	–1.5	–12.1	Diff. before/after remittances	–0.1	–100.0	–0.5	–36.6
Paraguay (2003)									
Nonremittances income	4.052		14.799						
95% confidence interval	(2.098; 6.018)		(11.594; 18.158)						
Total income	3.979		14.127						
Diff. before/after remittances	–0.1	–1.8	–0.7	–4.5					

Source: Acosta et al. 2007.

Inequality and Poverty Effects: Macroeconomic Evidence

The poverty analysis in the previous section relied on isolating the effect of remittances on income using a purely static analysis. However, remittances can also have a poverty impact over time, for example, by accelerating the growth rate of GDP, or by affecting the sectoral composition of growth—impacts that in turn may affect the levels of income inequality. In this section we explore these issues following Acosta et al. (2007).

Briefly, we assume that per-capita income levels follow a lognormal distribution,[5] so that the effect on poverty of a change in remittances will depend on: (i) the impact that remittances have on growth; (ii) how growth is translated into poverty reduction; (iii) the simultaneous impact that remittances have on inequality (as measured by the Gini coefficient); and finally (iv) how inequality changes are translated into poverty reduction. Under fairly general conditions (see López and Servén 2006) it is possible to derive theoretical values for the impact of growth and inequality on poverty (that is, for the growth elasticity of poverty and the inequality elasticity of poverty). Hence, the empirical problem becomes one of estimating the impact of remittances on income growth and inequality.

In order to estimate the links between remittances and growth in the data, our empirical strategy is based on the addition of a measure of remittances to an otherwise standard empirical growth regression:

$$(y_{it} - y_{it-1}) = \delta y_{it-1} + \omega' x_{it} + \beta_1 r_{it-1} + \beta_2 r_{it-1} \times lac_i + \nu_i + \upsilon_{it} \quad (2)$$

where y is the log of per-capita income, r is a measure of remittances, x represents a set of control variables other than lagged income, which we shall discuss shortly, ν_i is a country-specific effect, and υ_{it} is an i.i.d. error term. According to (2), growth depends on initial income, remittances, and current and/or lagged values of the control variables, and the impact of remittances on growth for Latin America would be given by $\beta_1 + \beta_2$.

As for the impact of remittances on inequality, we follow a similar strategy and estimate the following specification:

$$g_{it} - g_{it-1} = \lambda g_{it-1} + \chi' x_{it} + \alpha_1 r_{it-1} + \alpha_2 r_{it-1} \times lac_i + \mu_i + \varepsilon_{it} \quad (3)$$

where g is the (logged) Gini coefficient, and μ_i and ε_i are a country-specific effect, and an i.i.d. error term, respectively. Analogous to equation (2), the impact of remittances on the changes in inequality for Latin America would be given by $\alpha_1 + \alpha_2$. Table 4.6 reports the results of this exercise.[6]

Overall, it appears that remittances tend to be good for growth (that is, a higher remittances to GDP ratio tends to be associated with higher

Table 4.6 The Impact of Remittances on Growth and Changes in Inequality

	(1)	(2) Distance level	(3) Distance growth	(4) Migration level	(5) Migration growth	(6) Distance level, growth	(7) Migration level, growth
Impact of remittances on growth							
Remittances (t–1)	0.005**	0.012	0.012	0.008*	0.013*	0.011*	0.009*
	(1.75)	(3.48)	(4.57)	(3.45)	(3.16)	(4.46)	(4.64)
Remittances (t–1) × LAC	0.000	0.002	–0.003	0.002	–0.008	0.000	0.003
	(–0.05)	(0.43)	(–0.66)	(0.49)	(–1.39)	(–0.22)	(1.10)
Remittances in LAC	0.005*	0.014*	0.009 *	0.010*	0.006**	0.011	0.012
p-value	0	0	0.005	0.001	0.07	0	0
Impact of remittances on inequality							
Remittances (t–1)	0.007*	0.010 *	0.011*	0.008*	0.009*	0.005*	0.008*
	(5.43)	(5.61)	(9.92)	(6.59)	(6.51)	(5.99)	(6.10)
Remittances (t–1) × LAC	–0.014*	–0.012 *	–0.011*	–0.011*	–0.012*	–0.011*	–0.013*
	(–10.80)	(–3.03)	(–9.41)	(–5.61)	(–11.01)	(–13.49)	(–7.73)

(continued)

Table 4.6 The Impact of Remittances on Growth and Changes in Inequality *(continued)*

	(1)	*(2)* *Distance level*	*(3)* *Distance growth*	*(4)* *Migration level*	*(5)* *Migration growth*	*(6)* *Distance level, growth*	*(7)* *Migration level, growth*
Remittances in LAC	–0.007	–0.001	0.000	–0.003	–0.003	–0.006	–0.006
p-value	0.000	0.600	0.950	0.030	0.140	0.000	0.000

Source: Acosta et al. 2007.

Note: The regressions are performed using the system General Method of Moments estimator. The first column uses only internal instruments. The second to seventh columns use lagged internal instruments for the Gini, average years of secondary education of the female and male population, and the measure of market distortion plus an external instrument that equals the per capita income level in the main migrant host countries weighted by distance ("Distance") or by number of migrants ("Migration"). "Level" indicates that the external instrument is the value of the host countries, per-capita GDP series. "Growth" indicates that the external instrument is the growth rate of the host countries, per-capita GDP series. "Level, growth" combines the levels and growth instruments.

The dependent variables are either logged changes in per capita income (upper panel) or the Gini (lower panel). Other explanatory variables: either lagged per-capita income or the lagged Gini (in logs), average years of secondary education of the female and male population, a measure of market distortion (given by the price of investment goods), remittances (as a percentage of GDP in logs), and remittances interacted with a regional dummy for Latin America. All regressions include a constant. The row "Remittances in LAC" presents the value corresponding to the impact of remittances on Latin American growth or inequality changes.

growth), both at the global level and in Latin America. In fact, we cannot reject the hypothesis that the impact of remittances on growth is the same in Latin America as it is in the rest of the world. On the other hand, remittances seem to lead to higher income inequality at the global level, but either reduce inequality or leave it unchanged in Latin America (something to be welcomed given the high inequality levels of the region). These basic messages are robust to the use of different instrumental variables to correct for the possible endogeneity of remittances—for example, the possibility of remittances also being affected by growth or inequality. These results suggest that remittances tend to reduce poverty in Latin America. In terms of the magnitude of the estimated effects, table 4.7 reports the elasticity of poverty with respect to the remittances to GDP ratio obtained for the average Latin American country, for each of the specifications used.

As seen in table 4.7, there is substantial heterogeneity in the effects of remittances on poverty, depending upon the country's initial conditions, as given by the ratio of per-capita income to the poverty line, and the Gini coefficient. In the Latin American context, however, this range can be substantially narrowed, as most countries in the region have Gini coefficients of around 0.5.[7] Thus, considering that in the average Latin American country remittances are 6 percent of GDP, a 1 percentage point increase in the remittances to GDP ratio is estimated to lead to reductions in poverty that vary from between 0.08 percent for poorer countries to 1.12 percent for richer countries, with an average estimated reduction of 0.37 percent, which is fully in line with our microeconometric results for moderate poverty.[8]

Remittances, Growth, and Investment

While the above reported results suggest that remittances are positively and significantly related to growth, they are based on a very parsimonious specification. Thus, the question remains as to the extent to which the link between remittances and growth is robust to the inclusion of additional control variables. This question is particularly relevant given that previous cross-national empirical evidence on the impact of remittances on growth has not been conclusive.

Faini (2002), for instance, has found that remittances have a positive impact on economic growth, thus confirming the predictions of the new economic migration literature (Stark and Lucas 1988; Taylor 1992), according to which remittances promote investment and entrepreneurial activities. However, a broader study conducted for the *World Economic Outlook* (IMF 2005b) finds that there is no significant relationship between remittances and growth in GDP per capita.[9] In addition, Chami, Fullenkamp, and Jahjah (2005) find a negative association between the growth rate of immigrant remittances and growth in GDP per capita for a sample

Table 4.7 Poverty Elasticity of Remittances in Latin America

GMM Gini coefficient					*GMM, distance, level Gini coefficient*				
v/z	0.30	0.40	0.50	0.60	v/z	0.30	0.40	0.50	0.60
6.0	–1.17	–0.68	–0.46	–0.33	6.0	–0.94	–0.51	–0.32	–0.20
3.0	–0.56	–0.34	–0.24	–0.18	3.0	–0.59	–0.33	–0.20	–0.14
2.0	–0.32	–0.20	–0.15	–0.12	2.0	–0.40	–0.23	–0.15	–0.10
1.5	–0.19	–0.13	–0.10	–0.08	1.5	–0.29	–0.18	–0.12	–0.08
1.0	–0.07	–0.06	–0.05	–0.04	1.0	–0.16	–0.11	–0.08	–0.06
GMM, distance, growth Gini coefficient					*GMM, migration, level Gini coefficient*				
v/z	0.30	0.40	0.50	0.60	v/z	0.30	0.40	0.50	0.60
6.0	–0.53	–0.29	–0.17	–0.11	6.0	–0.92	–0.52	–0.33	–0.23
3.0	–0.35	–0.19	–0.12	–0.08	3.0	–0.52	–0.30	–0.19	–0.14
2.0	–0.25	–0.14	–0.09	–0.06	2.0	–0.34	–0.20	–0.13	–0.10
1.5	–0.18	–0.11	–0.07	–0.05	1.5	–0.23	–0.14	–0.10	–0.07
1.0	–0.10	–0.07	–0.05	–0.03	1.0	–0.12	–0.08	–0.06	–0.05

(continued)

Table 4.7 Poverty Elasticity of Remittances in Latin America *(continued)*

	GMM, migration, growth Gini coefficient					*GMM, distance, level & growth Gini coefficient*			
v/z	0.30	0.40	0.50	0.60	v/z	0.30	0.40	0.50	0.60
6.0	–0.71	–0.40	–0.26	–0.18	6.0	–1.41	–0.80	–0.52	–0.37
3.0	–0.37	–0.22	–0.15	–0.11	3.0	–0.74	–0.44	–0.29	–0.21
2.0	–0.23	–0.14	–0.10	–0.07	2.0	–0.46	–0.28	–0.19	–0.14
1.5	–0.15	–0.10	–0.07	–0.05	1.5	–0.30	–0.19	–0.14	–0.11
1.0	–0.07	–0.05	–0.04	–0.03	1.0	–0.14	–0.10	–0.08	–0.06

	GMM, migration, level & growth Gini coefficient			
v/z	0.30	0.40	0.50	**0.60**
6.0	–1.49	–0.84	–0.55	**–0.38**
3.0	–0.80	–0.47	–0.31	–0.22
2.0	–0.49	–0.30	–0.21	–0.15
1.5	–0.33	–0.21	–0.15	–0.11
1.0	–0.15	-0.11	–0.09	–0.07

Source: Acosta et al. 2007.

Note: The table reports the estimated poverty elasticities of remittances/GDP for different values of the Gini coefficient and of per-capita income to the poverty line v/z. It assumes an initial level of remittances of 10 percent of GDP.

of 113 countries over the period 1970–98. Similarly, Giuliano and Ruiz-Arranz (2005) find that the impact of remittances on growth is not significant when remittances are simply added as an additional explanatory variable in a growth regression. They claim that it is likely that the impact of remittances on growth may depend on some structural features of the economy, and find evidence that remittances enhance growth in countries with shallower financial markets.

There have also been a few studies dealing with the specific case of the Latin American and Caribbean region. Solimano (2003) evaluated the impact of remittances on per-capita growth for two Andean countries, Colombia and Ecuador, during the period 1987–2002. He found that lagged remittances have a positive and significant impact on growth in Colombia, but the relationship is not significant for Ecuador. Mundaca (2005) evaluated the effects of workers' remittances on growth for countries in Central America, as well as Mexico and the Dominican Republic, during the period 1970–2003. She found that remittances promote growth in the region and that the impact is even stronger in the presence of an active banking sector in the credit market. In the same vein, using a sample of Caribbean countries, Mishra (2005) found that private investment rises by 0.6 percentage points of GDP in response to a 1 percentage point of GDP increase in remittances inflows.

The fact that the results on the growth-remittances link have been ambiguous is not surprising given the countercyclicality of those flows, which suggests that remittances tend to respond negatively to economic growth. Thus, failure to correct for reverse causality and other sources of endogeneity in remittances flows may lead to misleading conclusions regarding the causal relationship of remittances to economic growth. From a conceptual point of view, this relationship could be motivated by the possibility that workers' remittances may help ease credit constraints, thus allowing individuals to not only increase their consumption and reduce poverty, but also to lead to higher investments in physical capital, education, health care, and the creation or expansion of microenterprises, all of which could eventually be reflected in higher aggregate investment and economic growth. As seen in figure 4.1, even simple scatter plots showing remittances, growth, and investment using a large cross section of countries tend to suggest the presence of positive correlations among remittances, investment, and growth.

Panel data estimates on the impact of remittances and growth are presented in table 4.8, using a sample of 67 countries, of which 21 are from Latin America and the Caribbean. We find that remittances have a positive and significant impact on growth, and that this effect is robust to the use of external and time varying instrumental variables to control for the potential endogeneity of remittances.[10] All control variables are found to be significant and with the sign that would be a priori expected. That is, growth is found to be higher for countries with lower levels of

Figure 4.1 Scatter Plots of Remittances, Growth, and Investment

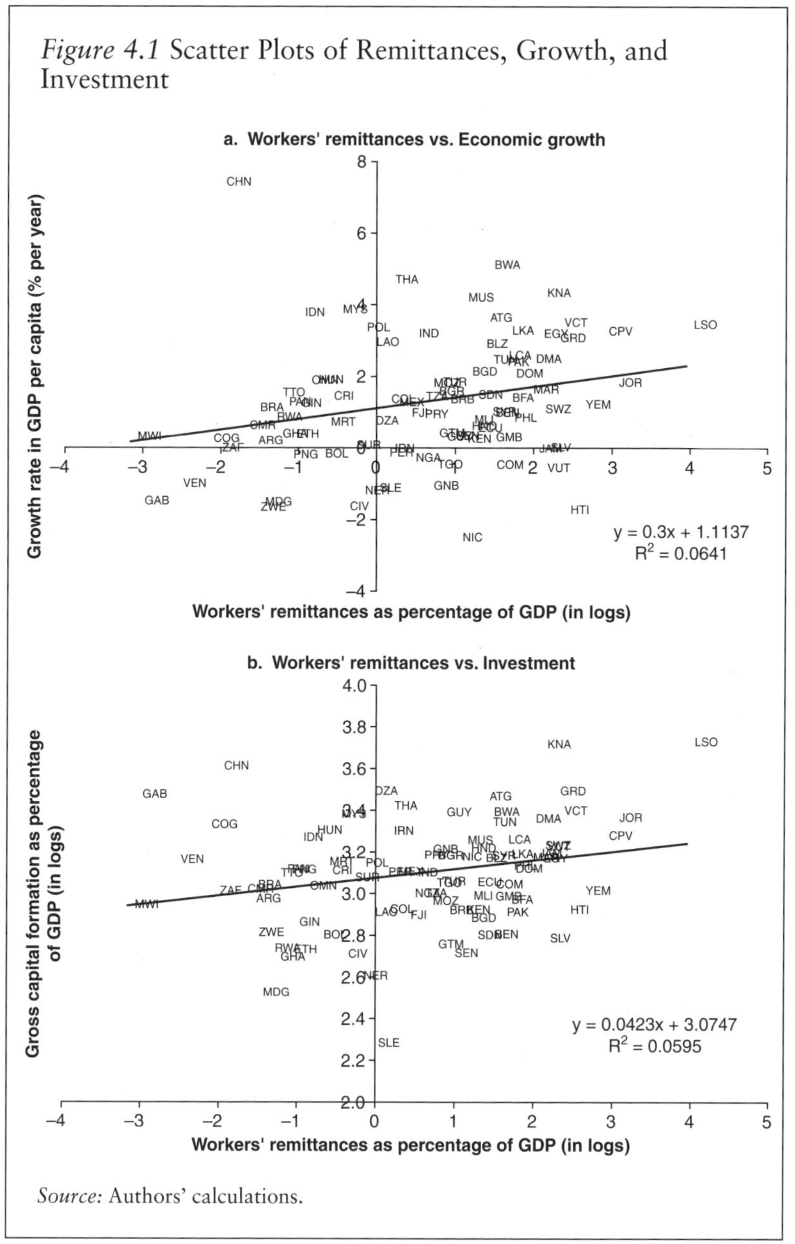

Source: Authors' calculations.

Table 4.8 Remittances and Economic Growth

Variable	Growth regressions without investment				Growth regressions including investment			
	[1] Exogenous remittances	*[2] Distance instrument*	*[3] Migration instrument*	*[4] Lagged remittances*[a]	*[5] Exogenous remittances*	*[6] Distance instrument*	*[7] Migration instrument*	*[8] Lagged remittances*[a]
Transitional convergence								
Initial GDP per capita (in logs)	–0.354**	–0.281**	–0.296**	–0.349**	–0.438**	–0.641**	–0.648**	–0.524**
	(0.08)	(0.08)	(0.09)	(0.08)	(0.09)	(0.07)	(0.08)	(0.09)
Investment								
Investment rate (as a percentage of GDP, in logs)	...	...	...	...	4.116**	6.645**	5.988**	4.325**
					(0.65)	(0.32)	(0.26)	(0.19)
Macroeconomic policies and institutions								
Education (secondary enrollment, in logs)	0.257**	0.258**	0.217**	0.346**	0.220**	0.303**	0.263**	0.219*
	(0.09)	(0.11)	(0.10)	(0.08)	(0.10)	(0.13)	(0.13)	(0.11)
Financial depth (private domestic credit to GDP, in logs)	0.620**	0.384**	0.499**	0.523**	–0.109	–0.448**	–0.226*	0.007
	(0.19)	(0.16)	(0.19)	(0.17)	(0.17)	(0.13)	(0.14)	(0.16)

(continued)

Table 4.8 Remittances and Economic Growth *(continued)*

	Growth regressions without investment				*Growth regressions including investment*			
Variable	*[1] Exogenous remittances*	*[2] Distance instrument*	*[3] Migration instrument*	*[4] Lagged remittances*[a]	*[5] Exogenous remittances*	*[6] Distance instrument*	*[7] Migration instrument*	*[8] Lagged remittances*[a]
Institutions (ICRG political risk index, in logs)	3.888** (0.31)	4.236** (0.27)	4.105** (0.31)	3.676** (0.29)	2.918** (0.41)	2.657** (0.35)	2.339** (0.39)	2.934** (0.41)
Trade openness (real exports and imports to GDP, in logs)	0.329** (0.11)	0.431** (0.11)	0.422** (0.10)	0.503** (0.12)	−0.095 (0.12)	−0.283* (0.15)	−0.305** (0.13)	−0.155 (0.11)
Lack of price stability (inflation rate, in log [100+inf.rate])	−0.007** (0.00)	−0.006** (0.00)	−0.007** (0.00)	−0.006** (0.00)	−0.008** (0.00)	−0.005** (0.00)	−0.007** (0.00)	−0.006** (0.00)
RER overvaluation (in logs, overvaluation if > 0)	−0.011** (0.00)	−0.012** (0.00)	−0.012** (0.00)	−0.010** (0.00)	−0.005** (0.00)	−0.001 (0.00)	0.000 (0.00)	−0.003* (0.00)
Government burden (general government consumption in logs)	−0.862** (0.18)	−0.882** (0.19)	−0.828** (0.16)	−0.942** (0.16)	−1.019** (0.16)	−1.061** (0.13)	−0.929** (0.11)	−1.026** (0.13)

(continued)

Table 4.8 Remittances and Economic Growth *(continued)*

	Growth regressions without investment				*Growth regressions including investment*			
Variable	*[1] Exogenous remittances*	*[2] Distance instrument*	*[3] Migration instrument*	*[4] Lagged remittances*[a]	*[5] Exogenous remittances*	*[6] Distance instrument*	*[7] Migration instrument*	*[8] Lagged remittances*[a]
Workers' remittances								
Remittances (workers remittances to GDP, in logs)	0.167**	0.226**	0.239**	0.025	0.063*	0.042	0.048	0.039
	(0.04)	(0.04)	(0.04)	(0.07)	(0.04)	(0.05)	(0.04)	(0.05)
No. of countries	67	67	67	67	67	67	67	67
No. of observations	273	273	273	273	273	273	273	273
Specification tests (p-values)								
Sargan Test	(0.34)	(0.28)	(0.31)	(0.37)	(0.64)	(0.56)	(0.55)	(0.53)
2nd order correlation	(0.19)	(0.19)	(0.19)	(0.19)	(0.20)	(0.29)	(0.29)	(0.21)

Source: Authors' calculations.

Note: All regressions include a constant and time dummies. * (**) denotes statistical significance at the 10 (5) percent level.

RER = real exchange rate.

a. Lagged levels and differences.

income, higher levels of education, deeper financial markets, more trade openness, and better institutions (as defined by the International Country Risk Guide index), and to be discouraged by excessive government burden, higher inflation, and real exchange rate overvaluation. These results improve upon previous estimates, which have either overlooked the issue of the possible endogeneity of remittances, or have addressed it using time-invariant instrumental variables (for example, IMF 2005a) or internal instruments only (for example, Giuliano and Ruiz-Arranz 2005).[11] Moreover, following Loayza, Fajnzylber, and Calderón (2005), we now use a wide set of control variables as potential growth determinants, thus reducing possible omitted variable biases.

The magnitude of the estimated effect of remittances on growth is, however, relatively small in economic terms. For the average Latin American country in the sample, for instance, the increase in remittances from 0.7 percent of GDP in 1991–95 to 2.3 percent of GDP in 2001–05 is estimated to have led to an increase in per-capita GDP growth of only 0.27 percent per year (27 basis points). Moreover, as seen in the final four columns of table 4.8, when domestic investment is included as an additional explanatory variable, the effect of remittances on growth ceases to be significant. This may imply that one of the main channels through which remittances affect growth is by increasing domestic investment.

Direct estimates of the effect of remittances on the ratio of investment to GDP confirm this hypothesis (table 4.9). In particular, the results suggest that from 1991–95 to 2001–05, the increase in remittances to LAC was responsible for a 2 percent increase in the share of domestic investment to GDP. Given the estimated effect of investment on growth from table 4.8, this implies that between 1991 and 2005, the impact of remittances on economic growth that took place through increased rates of investment was equivalent to 13 basis points per year, or about one-half of the total impact of remittances on growth estimated during that period. The remaining effects of remittances on growth could take place through other channels, including the reduction of aggregate volatility, the accumulation of human capital, and the possible increases in entrepreneurship. However, the finding of a relatively small overall impact of remittances on growth suggests that either the economic importance of those other channels is limited, or there are considerable negative compensating effects of remittances on labor supply and the real exchange rate. We next examine these issues in detail, starting in the next section with a direct analysis of the business cycle properties of remittances and their impact on growth volatility.

Remittances and Output Volatility

So far we have focused on how remittances affect household income levels, paying special attention to their impact on poorer households. Yet

Table 4.9 Remittances and Investment

Variable	*[1] Exogenous Remittances*	*[2] Distance Instrument*	*[3] Migration Instrument*	*[4] Lagged Remittances*[a]
Persistence				
Lagged investment ratio (in logs)	0.520** (0.02)	0.527** (0.02)	0.547** (0.02)	0.541** (0.01)
Growth				
Economic growth (in percentages)	0.037** (0.00)	0.035** (0.00)	0.034** (0.00)	0.037** (0.00)
Macroeconomic policies and institutions				
Education (secondary enrollment, in logs)	0.035** (0.02)	0.021 (0.01)	–0.032** (0.01)	0.020* (0.01)
Financial depth (private domestic credit to GDP, logs)	0.047** (0.01)	0.051** (0.01)	0.057** (0.01)	0.041** (0.01)
Institutions (ICRG political risk index, in logs)	0.319** (0.06)	0.347** (0.06)	0.415** (0.07)	0.235** (0.04)
Price of investment (in logs)	–0.055** (0.02)	–0.066** (0.02)	–0.058** (0.02)	–0.067** (0.02)

(continued)

Table 4.9 Remittances and Investment *(continued)*

Variable	*[1] Exogenous Remittances*	*[2] Distance Instrument*	*[3] Migration Instrument*	*[4] Lagged Remittances*[a]
Macroeconomic policies and institutions				
Lack of price stability (inflation rate, in log[100+inf.rate])	–5.81E–04** (0.00)	–3.55E–04** (0.00)	–2.99E–04 * (0.00)	–7.28E–04** (0.00)
Workers' remittances				
Remittances (workers remittances to GDP, in logs)	0.007** (0.00)	0.017** (0.01)	0.015* (0.01)	0.003 (0.00)
No. of countries	66	66	66	6s6
No. of observations	268	268	268	268
Specification tests (p-values)				
Sargan test	(0.36)	(0.30)	(0.20)	(0.27)
2nd. order correlation	(0.95)	(0.98)	(0.89)	(0.99)

Source: Authors' calculations.

Note: All regressions include a constant and time dummies. * (**) denotes statistical significance at the 10 (5) percent level.

a. Lagged levels and differences.

remittances can also contribute to household welfare by having an impact not only on the level of income but also on its volatility. This is particularly relevant in this context because output fluctuations in developing countries are substantially larger than those in industrial economies, with median welfare cost of business cycles ranging from 10 to 30 times the costs for industrial economies (Pallage and Robe 2003). To the extent that remittances exhibit countercyclical behavior, they could play a crucial role in smoothing out developing countries' output fluctuations, and helping maintain macroeconomic stability. This could be the case if remittances were dominated by compensatory transfers sent by migrants to their families in order to offset or prevent income shortfalls due to negative external shocks (natural disasters and financial crises, among others). Such transfers would raise household income at times when recipient economies are in downturn phases of their economic cycles. However, it is also possible that remittances respond to profitable investment opportunities in recipient economies, thus operating as standard private capital flows and behaving procyclically.

Previous evidence on the business cycle properties of remittances flows has so far been inconclusive. Chami, Fullenkamp, and Jahjah (2005) find that in general, remittances are negatively associated to the income gap of the recipient country with respect to the United States. Similarly, Mishra (2005) and Sayan (2006) show that remittances tend to be countercyclical among Caribbean countries and for low- and lower-middle-income countries. However, when analyzing the behavior of remittances sent by Turkish workers from Germany, Sayan (2004) finds that they are positively related to real output in Turkey, hence appearing to behave procyclically. Moreover, the evidence presented by Giuliano and Ruiz-Arranz (2005) suggests that in most cases, remittances comove directly with output fluctuations in recipient countries, with a higher degree of procyclicality in countries with shallower financial systems.

A common shortcoming of previous attempts at determining the cyclical properties of remittances flows is that they have not controlled for the potential endogeneity of output fluctuations. Table 4.10 presents the results of panel regression–based correlations between the cyclical components of remittances and real output in recipient countries for a sample of 26 Latin American countries, controlling for the possible presence of reverse causality from remittances to GDP, and for the fact that both variables could be affected by a common deterministic time trend, as well as by changes in the output of remittances-sending countries.[12]

We find that there is a negative and significant relationship between remittances and real output in the remittances-recipient country, regardless of the estimation technique used. Moreover, our estimates imply that reductions in real output below the trend are associated with more than proportional increases in the ratio of remittances to GDP above the trend. Thus, for instance, a one standard deviation reduction in real output of

Table 4.10 The Cyclical Behavior of Remittances in Latin America

	Pooled		*Fixed and time effects*	
Sample/filter	*Domestic GDP growth*	*Foreign GDP growth*	*Domestic GDP growth*	*Foreign GDP growth*
I. Ordinary least squares				
First-difference cyclical components	−1.1425**	1.7358	−1.2963**	−8.9426
	(0.491)	(1.281)	(0.533)	(28.801)
Band-pass filter cyclical components	−1.3736**	2.2620**	−1.5691**	−3.9082
	(0.581)	(1.029)	(0.529)	(25.843)
Hodrick-Prescott filter cyclical components	−1.1917**	1.9613**	−1.3809**	3.5604
	(0.597)	(0.990)	(0.529)	(24.636)
II. Instrumental variables (IV)				
First-difference cyclical components	−1.1575**	1.7269	−1.1601**	−9.0473
	(0.475)	(1.277)	(0.544)	(28.866)
Band-pass filter cyclical components	−1.2913**	2.1792**	−1.3976**	−3.7560
	(0.573)	(1.028)	(0.540)	(25.927)
Hodrick-Prescott filter cyclical components	−1.1293*	1.9001*	−1.2213**	3.7368
	(0.586)	(0.988)	(0.541)	(24.708)

Source: Authors' calculations.
Note: All regressions include a constant and time dummies.
* (**) denotes statistical significance at the 10 (5) percent level.

2.7 percent below the trend would be associated with an increase in the ratio of remittances to GDP above the trend of approximately 3.8 percent (using band-pass filter and instrumental variable estimates). On the other hand, we also find a positive association between remittances and the real output of remittances-sending countries—at least when time effects are not included.[13]

Similar calculations for other developing countries show that there is significant heterogeneity in the sensitivity of remittances to oscillations in the real output of both recipient and sending countries across regions (figures 4.2 and 4.3). Moreover, at least among developing countries, the countercyclicality of remittances appears to increase with income, being highest among upper-middle-income countries. However, the sensitivity of remittances with respect to fluctuations in the output of sending countries is largest among lower-middle-income countries.

One concern with the above estimates is that they reflect average responses of remittances to output in the whole sample of LAC countries. Figure 4.4 reports time series estimates obtained country by country. Although these results are statistically significant in only 8 of the 26 countries, they suggest considerable heterogeneity across Latin America. Indeed, we find that in 16 of 26 countries, remittances behaved countercyclically, with an average coefficient for the output of the recipient country of 2.88. The countries where these estimates are significant include Ecuador, Argentina, Costa Rica, and Mexico. On the other hand, in the remaining 10 countries,

Figure 4.2 Remittances' Sensitivity to Output Fluctuations in Recipient Countries

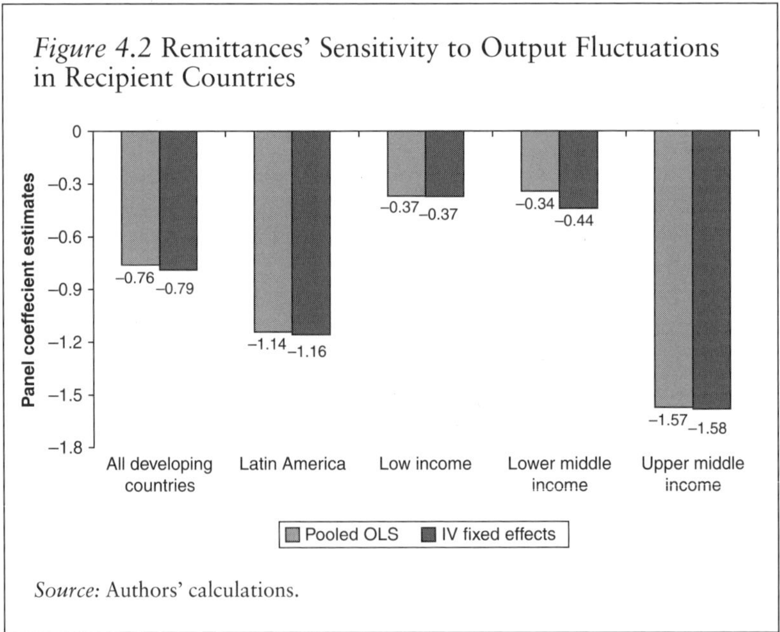

Source: Authors' calculations.

Figure 4.3 Remittances' Sensitivity to Output Fluctuations in Sending Countries

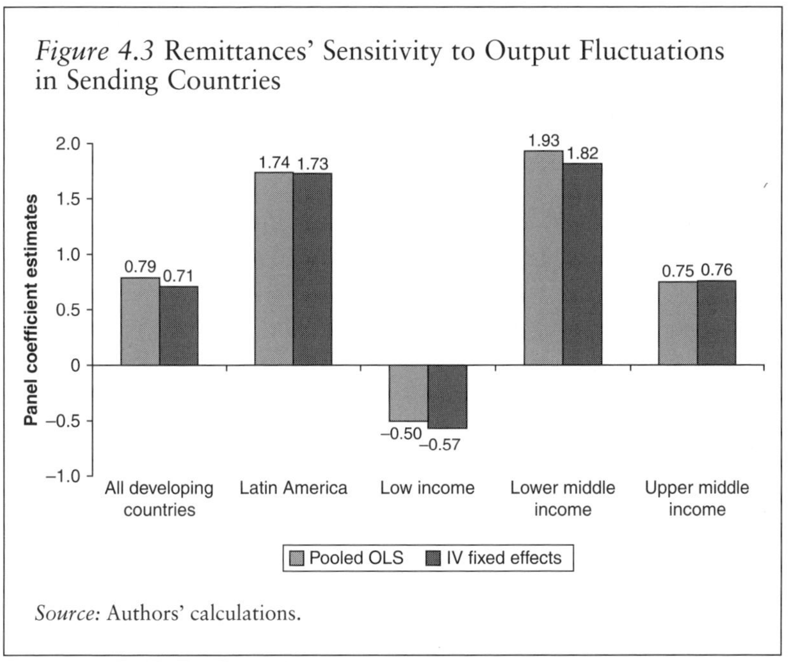

Source: Authors' calculations.

Figure 4.4 Country Estimates of Remittances' Sensitivity to Own Output

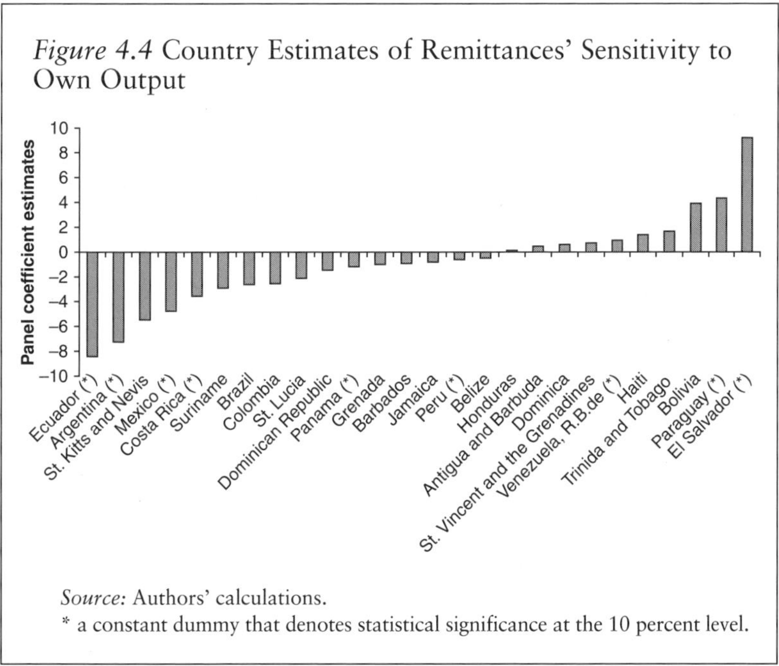

Source: Authors' calculations.

* a constant dummy that denotes statistical significance at the 10 percent level.

remittances appear to behave procyclically, with significant positive output coefficients for El Salvador, Paraguay, and República Bolivariana de Venezuela. It thus appears that the extent to which remittances operate as compensatory transfers or profit-driven capital flows differs considerably across countries.

Notwithstanding the somewhat conflicting results on the business cycle properties of remittances flows, several works have shown that workers' remittances play a critical role in reducing the vulnerability of home-recipient households to large negative shocks. Using aggregate data for 87 countries from 1970 to 2002, Yang (2006) finds that among poorer developing countries, remittances increase substantially in the aftermath of natural disasters. Kapur (2004) and Hysenbegasi and Pozo (2002) conclude that remittances increase sharply after large adverse macroeconomic shocks and currency crises. Using microeconomic data on Jamaican households, Clarke and Wallsten (2003) show that remittances have operated as a partial insurance mechanism, covering 25 percent of hurricane damages. Similar conclusions have been obtained by Yang and Choi (2005) for the Philippines, where workers' remittances replace approximately 60 percent of exogenous declines in income, and the World Bank (2005a), which shows that remittances have increased after floods in Bangladesh, and hurricanes in the Dominican Republic, Haiti, and Honduras.

Figure 4.5 shows the evolution of remittances in the wake of sudden stops in capital flows and currency crises.[14] We find that in Latin America, as well as in the rest of the developing world, remittances (as a percentage of GDP) have clearly declined in the periods preceding both types of severe negative shocks, but have increased considerably thereafter. In particular, in the year after a sudden stop in capital flows, remittances to Latin America have increased by 0.35 percent of GDP (0.43 percent for currency crises). By the fourth year, the average increase with respect to the level of remittances preceding the sudden stop is 0.75 percent of GDP (2.74 percent for currency crises).

The fact that remittances typically behave countercyclically and tend to increase after severe crises suggests that they should reduce the volatility of output per capita of recipient countries. This has been previously highlighted by the International Monetary Fund (2005a), which finds that a 2.5 percentage point increase in the ratio of remittances to GDP is correlated, on average, with a one-sixth decline in aggregate output volatility. Moreover, remittances are found to improve the creditworthiness of recipient countries, as illustrated by a positive and robust association between remittances and credit ratings for sovereign debt. For instance, model-based calculations show that including remittances in creditworthiness assessments would improve the credit rating of Haiti by two notches (from CCC to B-) and of Nicaragua by one notch (from CCC+ to B-). As shown by the World Bank (2005b), these improvements would imply a reduction in the sovereign spread of 334 and 209 basis points, respectively.

Figure 4.5 The Response of Remittances to Macroeconomic Crises

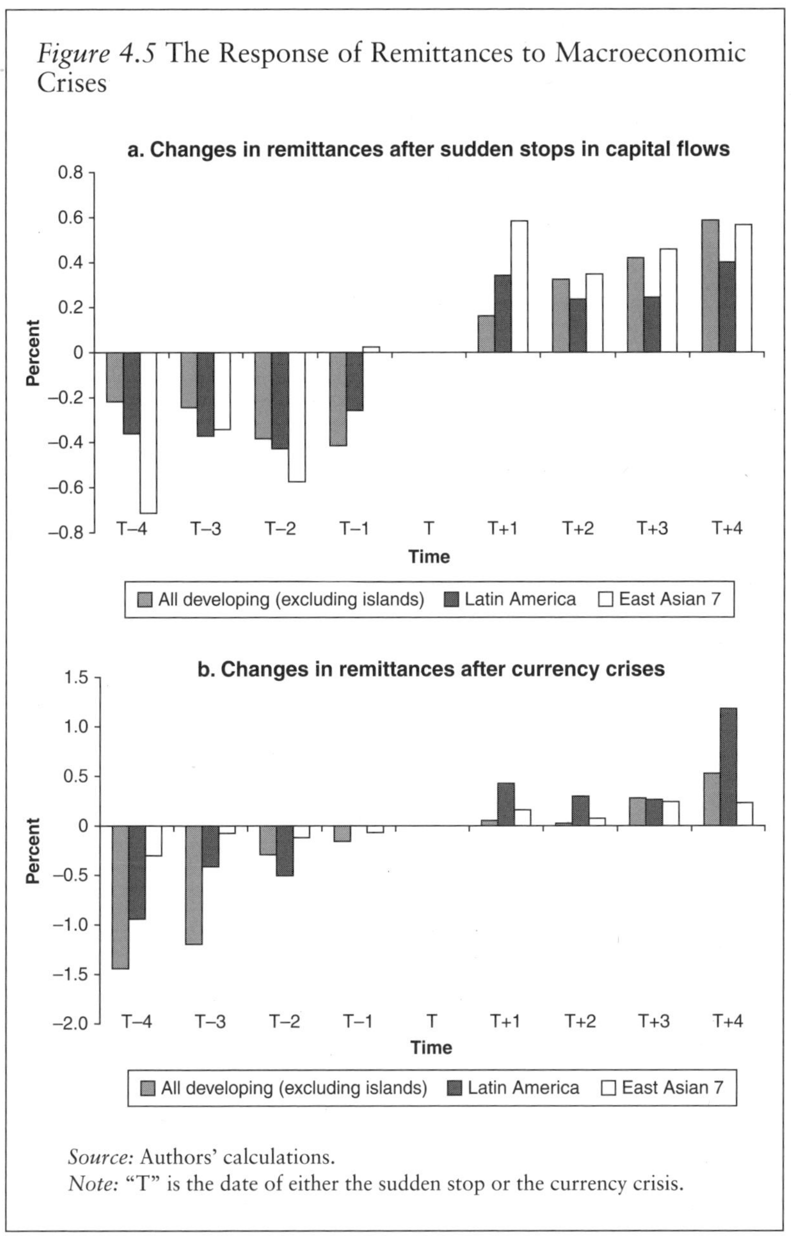

Source: Authors' calculations.
Note: "T" is the date of either the sudden stop or the currency crisis.

Table 4.11. Remittances and Growth Volatility

	S.D. growth in real GDP per capita		
Variable	*[1] Exogenous*	*[2] Distance*	*[3] Migration*
Macroeconomic policy variables			
Inflation volatility (S.D. annual log differences of CPI)	0.006** (0.00)	0.007** (0.00)	0.009** (0.00)
Monetary policy volatility (S.D. annual log differences of money)	0.133** (0.02)	0.133** (0.01)	0.135** (0.01)
Fiscal policy volatility (S.D. annual log differences of government consumption)	0.100** (0.01)	0.100** (0.01)	0.102** (0.01)
RER overvaluation (proportional index in logs, overvaluation if >0)	0.010** (0.00)	0.009** (0.00)	0.007** (0.00)
Systemic banking crises (frequency of years under crises: 0–1)	1.121** (0.07)	1.133** (0.06)	1.187** (0.06)
Trade openness (real exports and imports to GDP, in logs)	–0.541** (0.12)	–0.493** (0.12)	–0.266** (0.11)
Workers' remittances			
Remittances (workers remittances to GDP, logs)	–0.183** (0.02)	–0.202** (0.02)	–0.219** (0.02)
Volatility of foreign shocks			
Volatility of terms of trade changes (S.D. annual log differences of ToT)	0.009 ** (0.00)	0.010 ** (0.00)	0.011 ** (0.00)
Volatility of foreign growth (S.D. annual log differences of foreign growth)	0.105 ** (0.05)	0.113 ** (0.05)	0.044 (0.05)
Countries/observations	89/359	89/359	89/359

(continued)

Table 4.11. Remittances and Growth Volatility *(continued)*

	S.D. growth in real GDP per capita		
Variable	*[1] Exogenous*	*[2] Distance*	*[3] Migration*
Sargan test	(0.48)	(0.54)	(0.49)
2nd order correlation	(0.44)	(0.46)	(0.55)

Source: Authors' calculations.

Note: All regressions include a constant and time dummies.

* (**) denotes statistical significance at the 10 (5) percent level.

CPI = Consumer Price Index; RER = real exchange rate; S.D. = standard deviation; ToT = terms of trade.

Additional evidence on the impact of remittances on the volatility of output growth is provided in table 4.11, which shows the impact of workers' remittances on the standard deviation of GDP per-capita growth, controlling for standard determinants of growth volatility. The latter include macroeconomic policy variables, external shocks, and country- and time-specific effects. In this case, we find that there is a robust negative relationship between workers' remittances and growth volatility. This implies that countries with larger remittances flows (as a percentage of GDP) tend to have less volatile (or more stable) real output fluctuations. Economically speaking, a one standard deviation increase in remittances would reduce the standard deviation of growth in real output per capita by more than 10 percent. The volatility-reducing effects of remittances increase with per-capita income, as evidenced by the estimated negative sign of an interactive between remittances and GDP per capita. Quantitatively, the reduction in volatility that follows a one standard deviation increase in remittances is almost twice as large for countries close to the 80th percentile of the distribution of per-capita income (about US$3,000), compared to countries with the estimation sample's median income (about US$1,000). In contrast, for those countries with per-capita incomes below US$300 (the 15th percentile of the distribution), remittances are estimated to heighten macroeconomic volatility.

We also find evidence that external shocks, fiscal and monetary policy shocks, real exchange rate overvaluations, and banking crises have a smaller volatility-increasing effect in countries with higher levels of remittances. Indeed, interactives between measures of those various shocks and the share of remittances in GDP are found to have negative and significant coefficients in our volatility regressions. To illustrate this finding, table 4.12 reports the impact on volatility of various types of shocks for countries located in different deciles of the remittances distribution. In the case of external shocks, we find that for countries in the first decile of the

Table 4.12 Volatility Effects of External and Policy Shocks by Remittances Levels

	Shocks to growth volatility					
	Volatile external shocks		*Volatile policy shocks*		*Crises*	
Distribution of remittances (deciles)	*Terms of trade*	*Foreign growth*	*Monetary policy*	*Fiscal policy*	*RER overvaluation*	*Banking crises*
I	0.272**	1.062	1.286**	1.333**	0.819**	0.724**
	(0.04)	(0.19)	(0.16)	(0.13)	(0.16)	(0.07)
II	0.202**	0.708**	1.001**	1.097**	0.522**	0.599**
	(0.02)	(0.08)	(0.07)	(0.05)	(0.07)	(0.03)
III	0.162**	0.507**	0.838**	0.963**	0.354**	0.528**
	(0.01)	(0.05)	(0.04)	(0.03)	(0.04)	(0.02)
IV	0.130**	0.342 **	0.705**	0.852**	0.216**	0.469**
	(0.01)	(0.05)	(0.04)	(0.03)	(0.04)	(0.02)
V	0.102**	0.204**	0.593**	0.760**	0.100**	0.420**
	(0.01)	(0.03)	(0.03)	(0.02)	(0.03)	(0.01)
VI	0.077**	0.076*	0.490**	0.674**	–0.007	0.375**
	(0.01)	(0.04)	(0.03)	(0.03)	(0.03)	(0.01)
VII	0.052**	–0.048	0.390**	0.592**	–0.111**	0.331**
	(0.01)	(0.03)	(0.03)	(0.02)	(0.03)	(0.01)

(continued)

Table 4.12 Volatility Effects of External and Policy Shocks by Remittances Levels *(continued)*

Distribution of remittances (deciles)	*Shocks to growth volatility*					
	Volatile external shocks		*Volatile policy shocks*		*Crises*	
	Terms of trade	*Foreign growth*	*Monetary policy*	*Fiscal policy*	*RER overvaluation*	*Banking crises*
VIII	0.030**	–0.161**	0.299**	0.516**	–0.205**	0.291**
	(0.01)	(0.03)	(0.03)	(0.02)	(0.03)	(0.01)
IX	0.010	–0.264**	0.215**	0.448**	–0.292**	0.255**
	(0.04)	(0.03)	(0.03)	(0.03)	(0.01)	(0.01)
X	–0.033	–0.479**	0.042	0.304**	–0.472**	0.179**
	(0.02)	(0.12)	(0.10)	(0.08)	(0.10)	(0.04)

Source: Authors' calculations.
Note: Table shows changes in standard deviation of per-capita GDP growth after one standard deviation shock.
All regressions include a constant and time dummies.
* (**) denotes statistical significance at the 10 (5) percent level. RER = real exchange rate.

remittances distribution—with a share of remittances in GDP below 0.1 percent—a one standard deviation change in a country's terms of trade or in the volatility of its main trading partners increases the standard deviation of per-capita GDP growth by, respectively, 0.27 and 1.06. In contrast, the effect of those shocks for countries in the sixth decile of the remittances distribution—with an average remittances share of 2.3 percent of GDP—is only a 0.08 increase in volatility (for both types of shocks). Similarly, more volatile fiscal and monetary policies, higher real exchange rate overvaluations, and more frequent banking crises increase growth volatility to a much lower extent in countries with higher remittances shares.

Conclusions

This chapter has shown that migration and remittances have a significant poverty-reducing effect that appears to operate mainly through increases in the per-capita income of remittances-receiving countries. Our cross-country and micro-based estimates yield very similar conclusions, suggesting that for each percentage point increase in the share of remittances to GDP, the fraction of the population living in poverty is reduced by about 0.4 percent. However, the poverty and inequality impact of remittances varies considerably across countries, depending on their general level of development, initial inequality, and segments of the income distribution where remittances-receiving households are concentrated.

The chapter has also shown that remittances have a positive and significant impact on growth. This effect is robust to corrections for the potential endogeneity of remittances, and the use a wide set of control variables as potential growth determinants. However, the magnitude of the estimated effect of remittances on growth is found to be relatively small in economic terms. For the average Latin American country in the sample, for instance, the increase in remittances from 0.7 percent of GDP in 1991–95 to 2.3 percent of GDP in 2001–05 is estimated to have led to an increase of only 0.27 percent per year in per-capita GDP growth.

With regard to the channels through which remittances affect economic growth, direct estimates of the effect of remittances on the ratio of investment to GDP suggest that about one-half of the impact of remittances on growth takes place through increased rates of domestic investment. Another important channel is the reduction of aggregate volatility. Indeed, the evidence indicates that remittances behave countercyclically in most countries of the region, and they increase sharply after macroeconomic crises. Moreover, after controlling for various sources of external and policy shocks, we find that remittances significantly reduce growth volatility, both directly and by diminishing the impact on the economy of external and macroeconomic policy shocks.

Notes

1. The US$1 and US$2 a day are values measured in 1989 international prices and adjusted to local currency using purchasing power parities (PPP) to take into account local prices. Partly because of their simplicity, these are the standard indicators used for international poverty comparisons. For instance, they are periodically presented in the World Development Indicators (World Bank 2005b).

2. Ideally, we would like to count on fully convincing external instruments, such as distance to the border (López Córdova 2005) or something similar. However, given data limitations, we are forced to stick to variables available in household surveys. In this regard, for the exclusion restrictions for the nonremittances selection equation, we rely on an index of household assets, the percentage of households that receive remittances in the respective county or province of residence (a proxy for the presence of migrant networks), and their interaction. When information on household assets is missing (Bolivia, Ecuador, and Honduras), the network variable is interacted with the number of adult males, which ensures variability at the household level. Additional methodological details can be found in Acosta et al. (2006). Note that the percentage of households receiving remittances in the same county can be taken as a proxy for migration networks at the county level, and that previous literature has used migration networks as instruments for migration and remittances in order to assess their impact on development outcomes (Hanson and Woodruff 2003; López Córdova 2005; Woodruff and Zenteno 2007).

3. Rodriguez (1998), for instance, finds that remittances increase inequality in the Philippines, and the effect rises from 1.27 percent to 7.90 percent when using imputed income instead of reported nonremittances income. Similarly, Barham and Boucher (1998), in the case of Bluefields (Nicaragua), find that the Gini coefficient for household income falls from 0.47 to 0.43 when using reported figures, but inequality actually rises from 0.38 to 0.43 after correcting the pre-remittances distribution using imputed income for migrant families.

4. The results on poverty gaps are available in Acosta et al. (2006).

5. This is far from being a heroic assumption. In fact, Lopez and Serven (2006) compare the theoretical quintile shares according to a lognormal distribution with their empirical counterparts using data from 794 household surveys and argue that the lognormal approximation fits the empirical data extremely well.

6. With regard to the control variables, rather than adding to the huge variety of growth models, in this chapter we opt for considering a set of controls that has already been used in a number of empirical growth studies. This is the one used by Perotti (1996), Forbes (2000), Banerjee and Duflo (2003), and Knowles (2005), and it includes the average years of secondary education of the male population, the average years of secondary education of the female population, and a measure of market distortions: the price of investment goods relative to that in the United States. All these variables are measured in levels at the beginning of the period.

7. See, for example, figure 4.4.7 in Perry et al. (2006).

8. This is the estimated poverty effect of a 1 percentage point increase in the remittances to GDP ratio in a country where that ratio is 6 percent and the Gini coefficient is 0.5, using the average poverty elasticity from all alternative choices of instrumental variables reported in table 4.7.

9. This study uses a sample of 101 developing countries over the period 1970–2003.

10. The only exception is given in column [4], where we instrument remittances with their own lagged levels and differences. This may be inappropriate if remittances are influenced in an intertemporal optimizing framework by future shocks to economic growth.

11. We use two external instruments constructed by Aggarwal, Demirgüç-Kunt, and Martínez Pería (2005), based on the real output per capita of the countries where remittances originate.

12. For the sake of robustness, we use different filters to compute the cyclical components of remittances and GDP: first differences filter, Hodrick-Prescott filter, and band-pass filter. We also include country-specific and time-specific fixed effects. To instrument real output of remittances-recipient countries, we follow Fatas and Mihov (2003) in using lagged levels of this variable and current and lagged fluctuations in international crude oil prices. The real output of the remittances-sending country is approximated by the average foreign GDP growth of the top country destinations for migrants, weighted by the (inverse of the) distance between sender and recipient countries ("distance foreign GDP growth") and the average foreign GDP growth of the top five OECD country destinations for migrants, weighted by their share of migrants in each country ("migration foreign GDP growth").

13. The real output of remittances-sender countries is nonsignificant whenever we introduce time dummies, suggesting that time effects are largely capturing variations in the output of those countries.

14. We define and time those events following Cavallo and Frankel (2004) and, for currency crises, the episodes defined in Frankel and Rose (1996), Kaminsky and Reinhart (1999), and Goldstein, Kaminsky, and Reinhart (2000).

References

Acosta, P., C. Calderon, P. Fajnzylber, and H. López. "What Is the Impact of International Remittances on Poverty and Inequality in Latin America?" *World Development* (forthcoming).

———. 2006. "Remittances and Development in Latin America." *The World Economy* 29: 957–87.

Adams, R. 2006. "Remittances and Poverty in Ghana." Policy Research Working Paper 3838, World Bank, Washington, DC.

Aggarwal, R., A. Demirgüç-Kunt, and M. S. Martínez Pería. 2005. "Do Workers' Remittances Promote Financial Development?" Unbublished, World Bank, Washington, DC.

Banerjee, A., and E. Duflo. 2003. "Inequality and Growth: What Can the Data Say?" *Journal of Economic Growth* 8: 267–99.

Barham, B., and S. Boucher. 1998. "Migration, Remittances, and Inequality: Estimating the Net Effects of Migration on Income Distribution." *Journal of Development Economics* 55: 307–31.

Cavallo, E., and J. Frankel. 2004. "Does Openness to Trade Make Countries More Vulnerable to Sudden Stops, or Less? Using Gravity to Establish Causality." Working Paper No. 10957, National Bureau of Economics Research, Cambridge, MA.

Chami, R., C. Fullenkamp, and S. Jahjah. 2005. "Are Immigrant Remittance Flows a Source of Capital for Development?" Working Paper No. 03/89, International Monetary Fund, Washington, DC.

Clarke, G., and S.J. Wallsten. 2003. "Do Remittances Act Like Insurance? Evidence from a Natural Disaster in Jamaica." Working Paper, Development Research Group, World Bank, Washington, DC. http://ssrn.com/abstract=373480.

Faini, R. 2002. "Migration, Remittances and Growth." Manuscript, University of Brescia, Brescia, Italy.

Fatas, A., and I. Mihov. 2003. "The Case for Restricting Fiscal Policy Discretion." *Quarterly Journal of Economics* 118 (4): 1419–47.

Forbes, K. 2000. "A Reassessment of the Relationship between Inequality and Growth." *American Economic Review* 90 (4): 869–87.

Frankel, J., and E. Cavallo. 2004. "Does Openness to Trade Make Countries More Vulnerable to Sudden Stops, or Less? Using Gravity to Establish Causality." NBER Working Paper No. 10957, National Bureau of Economic Research, Cambridge, MA.

Frankel, J., and A. Rose. 1996. "The Endogeneity of the Optimum Currency Area Criteria." *Economic Journal* 108: 1009–25.

Giuliano, P., and M. Ruiz-Arranz. 2005. "Remittances, Financial Development and Growth." Working Paper 05/234, International Monetary Fund, Washington, DC.

Goldstein, M.G., L. Kaminsky, and C.M. Reinhart. 2000. *Assessing Financial Vulnerability: An Early Warning System for Emerging Markets*. Washington, DC: Institute for International Economics.

Hanson, G.H., and C. Woodruff. 2003. "Emigration and Educational Attainment in Mexico." Unpublished, University of California, San Diego.

Heckman, J. J. 1979. "Sample Selection Bias as a Specification Error." *Econometrica* 47: 153–61.

Hysenbegasi, A., and S. Pozo. 2002. "What Prompts Workers to Remit? Evidence Using a Panel of Latin American and Caribbean Nations." Unpublished, Department of Economics, Western Michigan University, Kalamazoo, MI.

IMF (International Monetary Fund). 2005a. *Approaches to a Regulatory Framework for Formal and Informal Remittance Systems: Experiences and Lessons*. Washington, DC: International Monetary Fund.

———. 2005b. *World Economic Outlook*. Washington, DC: International Monetary Fund.

———. (various issues). *International Financial Statistics*. Washington, DC: International Monetary Fund.

Kaminsky, G.L., and C.M. Reinhart. 1999. "The Twin Crises: The Causes of Banking and Balance-of-Payments Problems." *American Economic Review* 89 (3): 473–500.

Kapur, D. 2004. "Remittances: The New Development Mantra?" G-24 Discussion Paper No. 29, U.N. Conference on Trade and Development, Geneva, Switzerland.

Knowles, S. 2005. "Inequality and Economic Growth: The Empirical Relationship Reconsidered in the Light of Comparable Data." *The Journal of Development Studies* 41: 135–59.

Loayza, N., P. Fajnzylber, and C. Calderón. 2005. *Economic Growth in Latin America and the Caribbean: Stylized Facts, Explanations and Forecasts*. Washington, DC: World Bank.

López, H., and L. Servén. 2006. "A Normal Relationship? Poverty, Growth and Inequality." Policy Research Working Paper No. 3814, World Bank, Washington, DC.

López Córdova, E. 2005. "Globalization, Migration and Development: The Role of Mexican Migrant Remittances. *Economia, Journal of the Latin American and Caribbean Economic Association* 6(1): 217–56.

Mishra, P. 2005. "Macroeconomic Impact of Remittances in the Caribbean." Unbublished, International Monetary Fund, Washington, DC.

Mundaca, G. 2005. "Can Remittances Enhance Economic Growth? The Role of Financial Markets Development." Unpublished, Department of Economics, University of Oslo, Oslo, Norway.

Pallage, S., and M.A. Robe. 2003. "On the Welfare Cost of Economic Fluctuations in Developing Countries." *International Economic Review* 44 (2): 677–98.

Perotti, R. 1996. "Growth, Income Distribution and Democracy." *Journal of Economic Growth* 1: 149–87.

Perry, G., O. Arias, H. López, W. Maloney, and L. Servén. 2006. *Poverty Reduction and Growth: Virtuous and Vicious Circles*. Washington, DC: World Bank.

Rodriguez, E. R. 1998. "International Migration and Income Distribution in the Philippines." *Economic Development and Cultural Change* 46 (2): 329–50.

Sayan, S. 2004. "Guest Workers' Remittances and Output Fluctuations in Host and Home Countries." *Emerging Markets Finance and Trade* 40 (6): 68–81.

———. 2006. "Business Cycles and Workers' Remittances: How do Migrant Workers Respond to Cyclical Movements of GDP at Home?" Working Paper No. 06/52, International Monetary Fund, Washington, DC.

Schiff, M. 2006. "Trade and Factor Movement: Substitution in Markusen's Classic Complementarity Models." Policy Research Working Paper No. 3974, World Bank, Washington, DC.

Solimano, A. 2003. "Remittances by Emigrants: Issues and Evidence." Discussion Paper No. 2003/89, World Institute for Development Economics Research, United Nations University, Helsinki, Finland.

Stark, O., and R. Lucas. 1988. "Migration, Remittances and the Family." *Economic Development and Cultural Change* 36 (3): 465–81.

Stark, O., J. Taylor, and S. Yitzhaki. 1986. "Remittances and Inequality." *Economic Journal* 96: 722–40.

Taylor, J. 1992. "Remittances and Inequality Reconsidered: Direct, Indirect, and Intertemporal Effects." *Journal of Policy Modeling* 14: 187–208.

Woodruff, C., and R. Zenteno. 2007. "Remittances and Microenterprises in Mexico." *Journal of Development Economics* 82 (2): 509–28.

World Bank. 2005a. *The United States-Mexico Remittances Corridor Analysis*. Washington, DC: World Bank.

———. 2005b. *World Development Indicators Database*. Washington, DC: World Bank.

Yang, D. 2006. "Coping with Disaster: The Impact of Hurricanes on International Financial Flows, 1970-2001." Unpublished, University of Michigan, Ann Arbor, MI.

Yang, D. and H. Choi. 2005. "Are Remittances Insurance? Evidence from Rainfall Shocks in the Philippines." Ford School of Public Policy Working Paper Series No. 2005/005, University of Michigan, Ann Arbor, MI.

5

Remittances and Household Behavior: Evidence for Latin America

Pablo Acosta, Pablo Fajnzylber, and J. Humberto López

By increasing the income of recipient households, remittances can lead to changes in savings, expenditure patterns, and other household behaviors. For instance, remittances may allow previously poor families to meet their basic food needs and subsequently increase their expenditures on housing, education, or health. Expenditure patterns can also change if migrants tie remittances flows to specific expenditures, or if migration changes the preferences or incentives of those who are left behind. For instance, to the extent that migrants tend to work in occupations requiring limited schooling, the returns from investments in education may be lower for those who are envisaging international migration. Health outcomes can also change, possibly through a combination of increases in income and information transferred by remittances senders. Finally, by affecting local labor market conditions and household budget constraints, remittances may alter labor force participation decisions, and tilt individuals' occupational choices toward home production or entrepreneurship.

Introduction

Do recipient households save a fraction of remittances income? Are remittances spent mostly on "conspicuous" consumption goods? Do households that receive remittances devote a larger fraction of their income to investments in housing? How do expenditures in education and health vary with remittances? Are they reflected in better educational and health outcomes? Are remittances associated with changes in labor market participation? These questions have usually been at the center of the public debate on the impact of remittances on recipient communities. However, there is little empirical evidence on a wide set of countries to inform that debate, which is thus often based on country case studies and anecdotal evidence. This chapter aims to reduce this gap through an exercise that examines how a number of household characteristics differ between households with and without remittances. To this end, we use the household survey data employed in chapters 2 and 4 to describe recipients' profiles and estimate remittances' effects on poverty. Since some of the behaviors under analysis exhibit different patterns by income level, gender, and across urban and rural areas, when appropriate we also allow the impact of remittances to vary along those dimensions.[1]

Remittances and Household Savings

One of the main channels through which migration and remittances can affect household welfare is by providing mechanisms to smooth consumption in the context of negative external shocks. Indeed, in the absence of efficient credit and insurance mechanisms, migration and remittances can play an important role by allowing households to diversify their income sources and thus operate as ex ante risk-coping mechanisms. In addition, households also react to negative shocks—ex post—by sending some of its members to work abroad, or by asking existing migrants for additional monetary assistance during bad times. That this effectively happens in practice is confirmed by the evidence presented in the previous chapter regarding the countercyclicality of remittances flows.

A third channel through which remittances could help households smooth out the effects of negative shocks and increase their welfare is by allowing increases in savings and the accumulation of assets. Once again, the macro-level evidence presented in the previous chapter on the positive effect of remittances on investment rates would suggest that aggregate savings are likely to be affected as well. Moreover, as shown in the next chapter, both macro and micro data indicate that remittances tend to increase bank deposits, which suggests that recipient households are able to save some of the income from those sources. Despite these indications, there is no direct evidence regarding the savings behavior of remittances recipients. This section attempts to fill that gap on the basis of household surveys from six Latin American and Caribbean (LAC) countries, which contain information on income (including remittances) and expenditures.[2]

We calculate savings rates as the difference between total income and expenditures as a fraction of the former. The darker bars in figure 5.1 show the differences between savings rates of recipients and nonrecipients: In four of the six countries, recipients save more than nonrecipients, with Mexico and El Salvador being the exceptions. However, since savings rates are known to increase with income,[3] the savings behavior of remittances recipients in the latter countries could be driven by the fact that, as shown in chapter 3, migrants in Mexico and El Salvador tend to come from lower income quintiles. To avoid potential spurious savings differentials between recipients and nonrecipients, we estimate a simple model of savings as a function of income quintiles—using the counterfactual premigration income variable calculated in the previous chapter—as well as other demographic characteristics of the household. The estimated equation is of the following form:

$$S_i = \alpha + \beta X_i + \gamma H_i + \delta R_i + \varepsilon_i \qquad (1)$$

where S_i represents the savings rate, X_i is a vector of household characteristics (including the income quintile to which it pertains), H_i is a set of characteristics of the household head, R_i is a "dummy" variable for households that receive remittances, and ε_i is a random error term.[4] The differences in savings rates between recipients and other households after controlling for income and other household characteristics are given by

Figure 5.1 Differences in Savings Rates by Remittances-Recipient Status

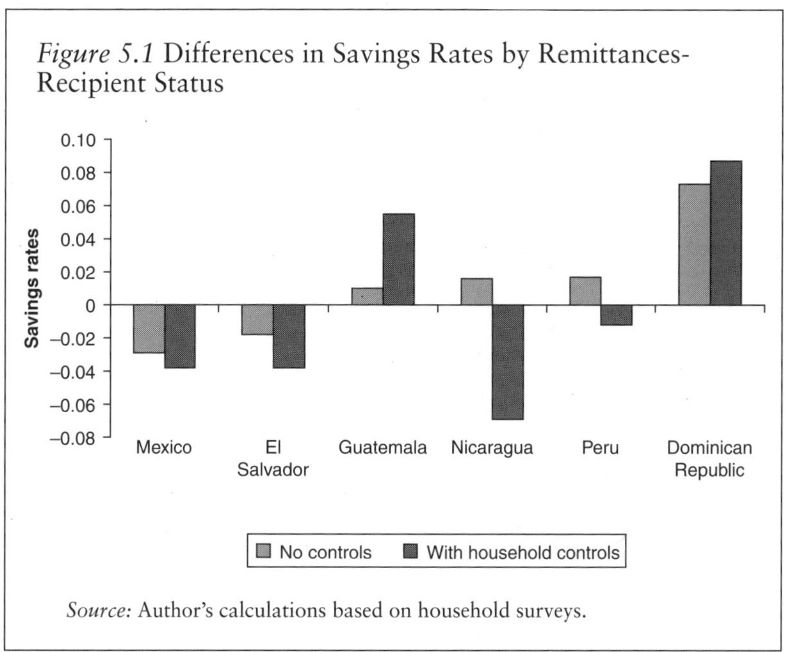

Source: Author's calculations based on household surveys.

the estimated δ coefficients, which are reported as the lighter bars in figure 5.1. Somewhat surprisingly, the savings rates of Mexican and Salvadoran recipients turn out to be even lower in comparison with those of nonrecipients in similar income ranges and sharing other common characteristics. Moreover, in the cases of Peru and Nicaragua, we now find lower savings rates for recipients. One possible interpretation of these results is that remittances may be largely operating as ex post risk-coping mechanisms for households that have suffered negative shocks to income. These shocks may have forced them to save a lower fraction of their income and even exhibit negative savings, which would explain the lower savings rates than nonrecipients, despite the higher income derived from remittances. The evidence for Guatemala and the Dominican Republic, however, suggests a different pattern, with recipient households saving between 5 percent and 9 percent more of their income than nonrecipients with similar demographic and income characteristics.[5]

In order to examine whether remittances affect household behavior throughout the income distribution, we have also calculated savings rates for the various income quintiles and compared them by remittances status. This is reported in table 5.1, which, for the six countries, shows the expected pattern of savings increasing with household income (column 1).[6] The same pattern is observed for nonrecipients (column 3). In the case of remittances recipients, however, savings rates increase with income only in the case of the Dominican Republic, with different patterns emerging in the other five countries (column 2). Thus, in Mexico, Peru, and Guatemala, savings rates do increase from the first to the second or even third income quintiles, but fall again for recipients located in the upper quintiles, thus creating an inverted-U pattern between savings and income. Possible explanations include the absence from the household—in the case of better-off recipients—of a larger number of income-generating migrants. See chapter 3 on the evidence that richer migrants tend to bring along most of their direct relatives. However, in El Salvador and Nicaragua, a U-shaped pattern is suggested by the data, with lower-income recipient households exhibiting savings rates that are above those of the middle class, which in turn saves less than households in the top income quintiles.

As for the differences between recipients and nonrecipients, in the six countries, recipients in lower income quintiles exhibit higher savings rates than nonrecipients (column 4). However, these differences tend to diminish and become negative for households located higher up in the income distribution. The same pattern is obtained when these differences are calculated in a regression framework, after controlling for other household characteristics, by adding to equation (1) a set of interactives between R_i and the income quintile "dummy" variables. Estimates for these interactives are reported in the last column of table 5.1. Once again, the results suggest that savings rates tend to increase for poorer remittances-receiving households, but tend to decrease for better-off households. One possible

Table 5.1 Savings Rates by Income Quintile and Remittances Recipient Status

Country	Counterfactual income quintiles	Savings rates				
		All	*Remittance recipient*	*Nonrecipient*	*Difference (recipient less nonrecipient)*	*OLS coefficients for remittances*
Mexico	Q1	–0.051	0.013	–0.054	0.067**	0.073**
	Q2	0.029	0.064	0.026	0.037*	0.001
	Q3	0.090	0.112	0.088	0.025	–0.016
	Q4	0.158	0.088	0.163	–0.075***	–0.112***
	Q5	0.244	0.017	0.249	–0.231***	–0.277***
El Salvador	Q1	0.285	0.514	0.252	0.262***	0.244***
	Q2	0.480	0.484	0.479	0.004	–0.007
	Q3	0.534	0.501	0.544	–0.043***	–0.037***
	Q4	0.592	0.503	0.621	–0.118***	–0.093***
	Q5	0.653	0.518	0.687	–0.170***	–0.167***
Guatemala	Q1	–0.418	–0.042	–0.479	0.437***	0.413***
	Q2	–0.184	0.057	–0.220	0.277***	0.308***
	Q3	–0.089	–0.070	–0.090	0.020	0.060
	Q4	0.020	–0.012	0.023	–0.035	0.021
	Q5	0.180	–0.025	0.201	–0.226***	–0.221***

(continued)

Table 5.1 Savings Rates by Income Quintile and Remittances Recipient Status *(continued)*

Country	*Counterfactual income quintiles*	*Savings rates*				
		All	*Remittance recipient*	*Nonrecipient*	*Difference (recipient less nonrecipient)*	*OLS coefficients for remittances*
Peru	Q1	0.035	0.105	0.034	0.071	0.061
	Q2	0.130	0.104	0.131	–0.027	–0.050
	Q3	0.199	0.278	0.196	0.081	0.088*
	Q4	0.268	0.181	0.273	–0.092	–0.081**
	Q5	0.388	0.192	0.398	–0.206***	–0.183***
Nicaragua	Q1	0.009	0.378	–0.005	0.383***	0.562***
	Q2	0.182	0.314	0.17	0.144**	0.141**
	Q3	0.286	0.258	0.291	–0.033	–0.012
	Q4	0.358	0.338	0.363	–0.025	0.020
	Q5	0.461	0.275	0.521	–0.246***	–0.149***
Dominican Republic	Q1	–0.363	–0.194	–0.388	0.194***	0.182***
	Q2	–0.32	–0.087	–0.373	0.286***	0.282***
	Q3	–0.191	–0.088	–0.226	0.138***	0.154***
	Q4	–0.08	–0.024	–0.103	0.078***	0.120***
	Q5	0.167	0.038	0.204	–0.166***	–0.118***

Source: Author's calculations based on household surveys.
Note: *** significant at 1% level; ** significant at 5% level; * significant at 10% level.
OLS = ordinary least squares.

interpretation of this finding is that for those in the lower quintiles, remittances operate more as an ex ante risk-coping mechanism, while for those located in the upper quintiles, remittances become significant *after* the corresponding households have been hit by negative income shocks that have reduced their savings capacity. Moreover, as mentioned above, it is also possible that the number of absent income-generating migrants is larger among richer households.

It must be noted, however, that the fact that some remittances recipients save less than other households with similar characteristics does not necessarily imply that they consume the income from remittances entirely (that is, that their savings rate is not positive). By itself, that result suggests only that the propensity to save out of the remittances income is lower than the corresponding savings rate from nonremittances income.

Remittances and Household Expenditures

Household savings has sometimes been defined in a broader sense, including not only the fraction of income that is not spent (as in the previous section), but also that which is designated for expenses that are likely to include important savings components, such as consumer durables, education, and health.[7] One problem with such an approach is the fact that it requires making the strong assumption that none of the above expenditures are associated with current consumption—that is, they can be entirely considered as an investment in future consumption. For this reason, rather than computing savings rates defined in such a broad fashion, and comparing them to remittances-recipient status, as in the previous section, we next examine the composition of household expenditures directly, trying to uncover evidence of whether remittances recipients set aside a different share of their total expenditures for items that are likely to embody a considerable savings component, such as education, health, and consumer durables.

Only a few previous studies have addressed the links between remittances and patterns of household expenditure. Using data on rural Mexico and controlling for observable household characteristics, Taylor (1992) found that remittances-recipient families tend to invest more in farm assets (for instance, livestock). Similarly, Adams (2005) has shown that with respect to their nonrecipient counterparts, Guatemalan families reporting remittances tend to spend a lower share of total income on food and other nondurable goods, and more on durable goods, housing, education, and health.

Most of the surveys used in this report—7 of 11—include detailed information on household expenditures, which can then be classified in several standard expense categories, for example, food, consumer durables, etc. While our surveys lack information on how the income of remittances is spent, the fact that money is fungible would render the utility of that sort of information quite limited. Thus, to assess the extent to which remittances alter expenditures, we proceed by focusing on the share of different expenditure categories and comparing them across recipients and nonrecipients who share similar demographic characteristics and are located in the same quintile of the household income distribution (prior to migration). We thus estimate models like the one shown in equation (1), but using as dependent variables the share in total expenditures of expenses for food, other consumer nondurables, durables (without housing), housing, education, and health.[8]

Figures 5.2 and 5.3 show the expenditure patterns of recipient and nonrecipient households in rural and urban areas, respectively. As is apparent in these figures, in all countries the share of food and other nondurable consumption goods tends to be higher in rural than in urban areas, and the opposite is true for expenses for durable goods (including housing), education, and health. Moreover, figures 5.2 and 5.3 show that both in urban and in rural areas, the households that report receiving remittances on average spend less than the rest for food, but spend more on durable goods, housing investments, education, and health.[9]

Figure 5.2 Expenditure Patterns by Remittances-Recipient Status—Rural Regions

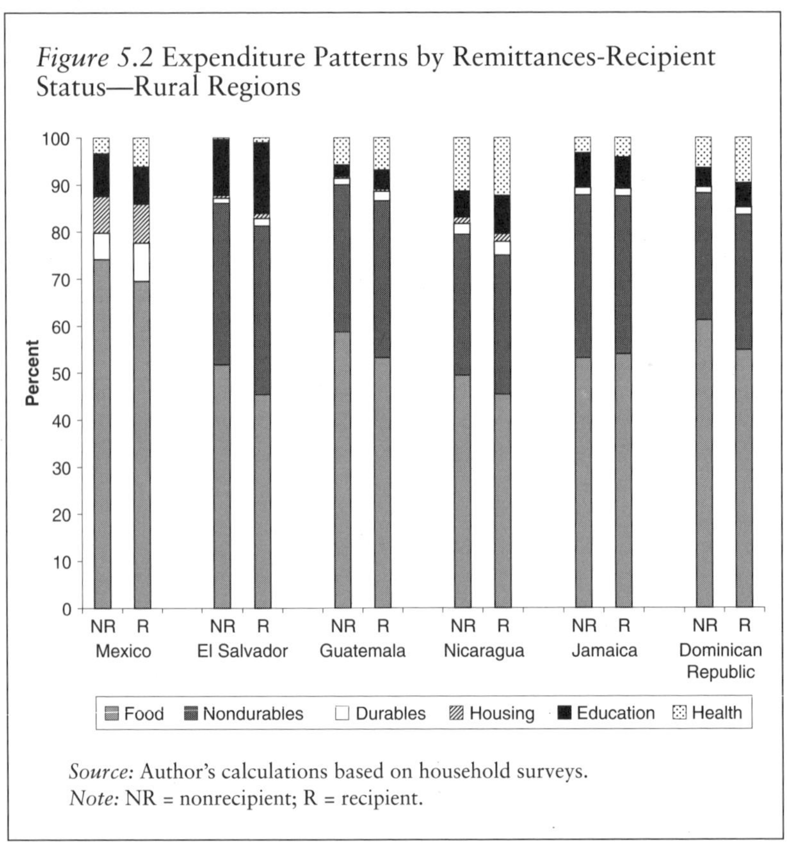

Source: Author's calculations based on household surveys.
Note: NR = nonrecipient; R = recipient.

Figure 5.3 Expenditure Patterns by Remittances-Recipient Status—Urban Regions

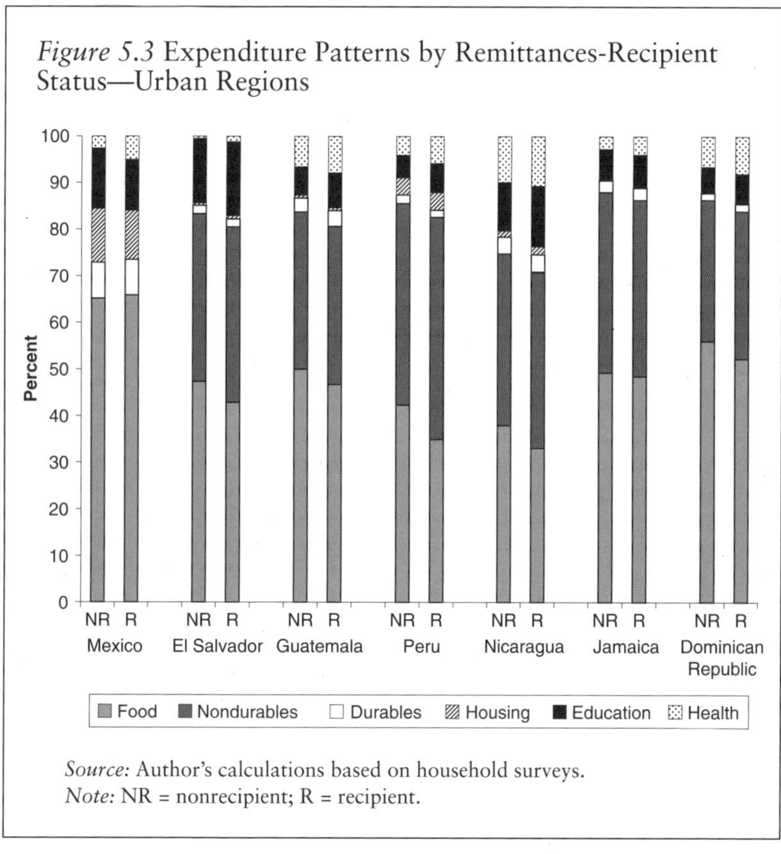

Source: Author's calculations based on household surveys.
Note: NR = nonrecipient; R = recipient.

While this preliminary evidence suggests that remittances tilt consumption patterns toward higher investments in physical and human capital, it does not necessarily imply a causal relationship between remittances and consumption patterns. Indeed, a third type of factor—income and demographics—could be driving both access to remittances and the distribution of household expenditures across different goods and services. To check whether this is indeed the case, we have estimated the impact of remittances on the above-mentioned expenditure shares in the context of regression models that control for household and location characteristics—household composition, educational levels, home ownership, quintile of the income distribution, relative importance of agricultural activities in the area, etc. Using this approach, table 5.2 reports the impact of remittances on expenditure shares for the seven countries for which the necessary data is available. With the exception of Jamaica, we find that remittances' recipients direct a smaller share of their total expenditures toward food, thus suggesting that Adams'

Table 5.2 Access to Remittances and Expenditure Shares

Dependent variable	*Food*	*Nondurables*	*Durables*	*Housing*	*Education*	*Health*
Mexico[a]	–0.031***	n.a.	0.014***	–0.006**	0.003	0.021***
	(0.006)		(0.004)	(0.003)	(0.004)	(0.003)
El Salvador	–0.038***	0.008**	0.002*	0.003**	0.019***	0.006***
	(0.004)	(0.003)	(0.001)	(0.001)	(0.003)	(0.001)
Guatemala	–0.034***	0.010*	0.006**	0.000	0.009***	0.009*
	(0.006)	(0.005)	(0.002)	(0.002)	(0.003)	(0.005)
Peru[b]	–0.043***	0.024***	–0.006	–0.001	0.009**	0.016***
	(0.008)	(0.007)	(0.004)	(0.003)	(0.004)	(0.005)
Nicaragua	–0.014*	–0.002	0.000	0.003	0.008	0.005
	(0.007)	(0.006)	(0.001)	(0.003)	(0.005)	(0.006)
Jamaica[c]	–0.002	–0.007	0.004***	0.003**	–0.005*	0.009***
	(0.005)	(0.005)	(0.001)	(0.001)	(0.003)	(0.002)
Dominican Republic[c]	–0.013***	–0.002	0.000	0.000	–0.003*	0.012***
	(0.004)	(0.003)	(0.001)	(0.001)	(0.002)	(0.003)

Source: Author's calculations based on household surveys.

Note: Table shows OLS differences with respect to nonrecipient households. Standard errors are in parentheses.

*** significant at 1% level; ** significant at 5% level; * significant at 10% level.

a. Food and other nondurable goods together.

b. Only urban areas.

c. Coefficients for housing in Jamaica and the Dominican Republic are multiplied by 10.

n.a. Not applicable.

(2005) findings for Guatemala also apply to other LAC countries with considerable remittances receipts.[10] While the estimates reported in table 5.2 are at the national level, separate estimates for rural and urban areas suggest that the changes in expenditure patterns are somewhat larger in rural areas.

The complement of the reduction in food expenditures among remittances recipients is an increase in expenses in nondurable goods, durable goods, housing, education, and health. The relative importance of these increases, however, varies considerably across countries. Thus, changes in nondurable goods consumption (excluding food) are significant only in Peru, El Salvador, and Guatemala. Moreover, only in the two latter countries, and in Mexico and Jamaica, do the share of durable goods increase significantly among remittances recipients, and more frequent housing improvements are apparent only in El Salvador and Jamaica, with the opposite effect found for Mexico. Increases in health expenditures, however, are present in six of seven countries (the exception being Nicaragua). Finally, higher educational expenditures are found for four of seven countries, with the opposite result found for Jamaica, and nonsignificant effects obtained for Mexico and Nicaragua.

Relatively similar results—reductions in food shares offset by increases in nondurables, durables, health, and education—are obtained when the per-capita amount of remittances received by each household is taken into account, and when the possible endogeneity of remittances is controlled for.[11] However, to the extent that savings and expenditure patterns vary with income (see previous section), the above estimates of average effects on all remittances recipients may be misleading in the sense that they could mask possible differences across households located in different parts of the income distribution. To investigate these possible differences, we allow the impact of remittances on household behavior to vary across quintiles of the distribution of per-capita household income. Moreover, in order to also capture the possible effect of remittances on expenditures that operate through increases in household income, we classify remittances recipients according to the income that they were estimated to have earned prior to migration (see chapter 4). The results, reported in table 5.3, indicate that remittances effects are quite different across segments of the income distribution, and vary considerably across countries.

In the case of Mexico, for instance, remittances recipients in the lower quintiles exhibit a pattern that is similar to the one observed for the population as a whole. Indeed, they increase expenditures on durable goods, housing, and human capital, mainly at the expense of nondurables. In contrast, their richer counterparts make higher expenditures for nondurable goods and lower expenditures for housing improvements and education. These results would suggest that, at least in Mexico, remittances are used in a more productive way by poorer households. Arguably, remittances have the effect of relaxing budget constraints that limit the housing and

Table 5.3 Remittances and Expenditure Shares by Counterfactual Household Income Quintiles

Country	*Coefficient*	*Food*	*Nondurables*	*Durables*	*Housing*	*Education*	*Health*
Mexico[a]	Remittances	–0.063***	n.a.	0.016*	0.013**	0.020*	0.015**
	Remittances × Q2	0.028	n.a.	0.000	–0.027***	–0.005	0.003
	Remittances × Q3	0.036*	n.a.	0.008	–0.023***	–0.025*	0.004
	Remittances × Q4	0.045**	n.a.	–0.012	–0.020**	–0.024*	0.011
	Remittances × Q5	0.074***	n.a.	–0.022	–0.020*	–0.051***	0.019
El Salvador	Remittances	–0.004	–0.011	0.012***	0.004	–0.003	0.002
	Remittances × Q2	–0.040***	0.018	–0.007*	0.001	0.026**	0.003
	Remittances × Q3	–0.046***	0.036**	–0.013***	0.000	0.020*	0.004
	Remittances × Q4	–0.043***	0.030**	–0.010**	–0.004	0.023**	0.004
	Remittances × Q5	–0.022*	0.001	–0.011**	–0.003	0.030***	0.006*
Guatemala	Remittances	–0.050***	0.040*	0.006*	0.016	–0.013**	0.001
	Remittances × Q2	0.003	–0.007	0.003	–0.018	0.014**	0.006
	Remittances × Q3	–0.003	–0.031	0.006	–0.015	0.025***	0.019
	Remittances × Q4	0.016	–0.046**	–0.005	–0.015	0.031***	0.019
	Remittances × Q5	0.049**	–0.047*	–0.002	–0.019	0.026***	–0.007
Peru[b]	Remittances	0.003	0.012	–0.004	–0.013***	–0.003	–0.008
	Remittances × Q2	–0.078	0.044	0.002	0.018*	0.008	0.024
	Remittances × Q3	–0.057	0.006	0.003	0.013**	0.020	0.027*
	Remittances × Q4	–0.055	0.015	0.005	0.016**	0.004	0.032**
	Remittances × Q5	–0.018	–0.001	–0.014**	0.004	0.015	0.018

(continued)

Table 5.3 Remittances and Expenditure Shares by Counterfactual Household Income Quintiles *(continued)*

Country	*Coefficient*	*Food*	*Nondurables*	*Durables*	*Housing*	*Education*	*Health*
Nicaragua	Remittances	0.056*	–0.013	0.007	–0.002	–0.041**	–0.008
	Remittances × Q2	–0.057	0.008	0.000	0.000	0.039*	0.009
	Remittances × Q3	–0.094***	0.015	0.003	0.003	0.050**	0.023
	Remittances × Q4	–0.074**	0.018	–0.009	0.005	0.042**	0.017
	Remittances × Q5	–0.067**	0.006	–0.015	0.007	0.064***	0.005
Jamaica[c]	Remittances	–0.026**	0.019*	0.007***	–0.001	–0.010	0.009*
	Remittances × Q2	0.021	–0.024*	–0.001	0.003	0.004	0.000
	Remittances × Q3	0.025*	–0.028**	–0.001	0.004*	0.005	–0.002
	Remittances × Q4	0.039**	–0.035**	–0.010**	0.006	0.006	–0.001
	Remittances × Q5	0.033	–0.052***	0.003	0.006	0.011	0.004
Dominican Republic[c]	Remittances	–0.016	0.024**	0.001	0.005	–0.010	0.000
	Remittances × Q2	–0.004	–0.013	0.004	–0.001	0.013*	0.001
	Remittances × Q3	–0.018	–0.023*	0.002	–0.008	0.010	0.030*
	Remittances × Q4	0.005	–0.027**	–0.002	–0.006	0.015*	0.010
	Remittances × Q5	0.028	–0.042***	–0.008***	–0.004	0.017**	0.005

Source: Author's calculations based on household surveys.
Note: *** significant at 1% level; ** significant at 5% level; * significant at 10% level.
a. Food and other nondurable goods together.
b. Only urban areas.
c. Coefficients for housing in Jamaica and the Dominican Republic are multiplied by 10.
n.a. Not applicable.

human capital investments of poorer families. For richer households, on the other hand, the results suggest that the above budget constraints are not binding, so that remittances have the effect of increasing consumption of food and nondurable goods. This is illustrated in figure 5.4, which shows that in Mexico, recipients in the first quintile experience a reduction in food and nondurable goods expenses, and an increase in educational expenditures in comparison with nonrecipients of similar characteristics, but both changes tend to become smaller—and even have their signs inverted—as one moves up in the income distribution.

In the remaining countries under analysis, however, a quite different pattern is observed across poorer and richer households. Thus, with the exception of Jamaica, whenever remittances are found to significantly increase educational and health expenditures of recipient households, the effects are restricted to those in the upper quintiles of the income distribution. For those richer families, higher human capital investments are achieved through lower expenditures in nondurable (three of seven countries) as well as durable goods (four of seven countries). Poorer recipient households, on the other hand, are found to reduce expenditures in education in Nicaragua and Guatemala, and they make higher expenditures for nondurables in the Dominican Republic, Jamaica, and Guatemala. The contrast with the Mexican case can be well illustrated by the pattern observed in Nicaragua, where as seen before, individuals tend to be positively selected into migration, as opposed to the negative pattern described in chapter 2 for Mexico. As seen in figure 5.5, a pattern of reduction in food and nondurable expenses, with an increase in educational expenditures, is also found among remittances recipients in Nicaragua, but that pattern is restricted to those in higher quintiles of the income distribution, as opposed to the lower quintiles in the case of Mexico. Moreover, an opposite pattern is obtained for poorer Nicaraguan recipients: relatively lower educational expenses and higher expenditures for food and nondurables.

Overall, our results indicate that except for Mexico, remittances only have the beneficial effect of changing consumption patterns toward higher educational and health expenditures among middle- and upper-class households. Among those in the lower quintiles of the income distribution, the results tend to confirm the popular perception that remittances tend to tilt household expenditures mainly toward nondurable goods, with some effects on durable consumption, but limited impact on housing and human capital investments. Putting this together with the results on the effect of remittances on savings in the previous section, the evidence indicates that poorer recipient households save a positive fraction of their remittances income, but they do not increase their share of expenditures in savings-intensive items—physical and human capital assets. Richer recipients, on the other hand, tend to lower their savings rates in comparison with nonrecipients, but they alter their expenditure patterns in the direction of goods and services with a high savings component.

Figure 5.4 Expenditure in Nondurables (Including Food) and Education by Remittances-Recipient Status and Counterfactual Income Quintile: Mexico

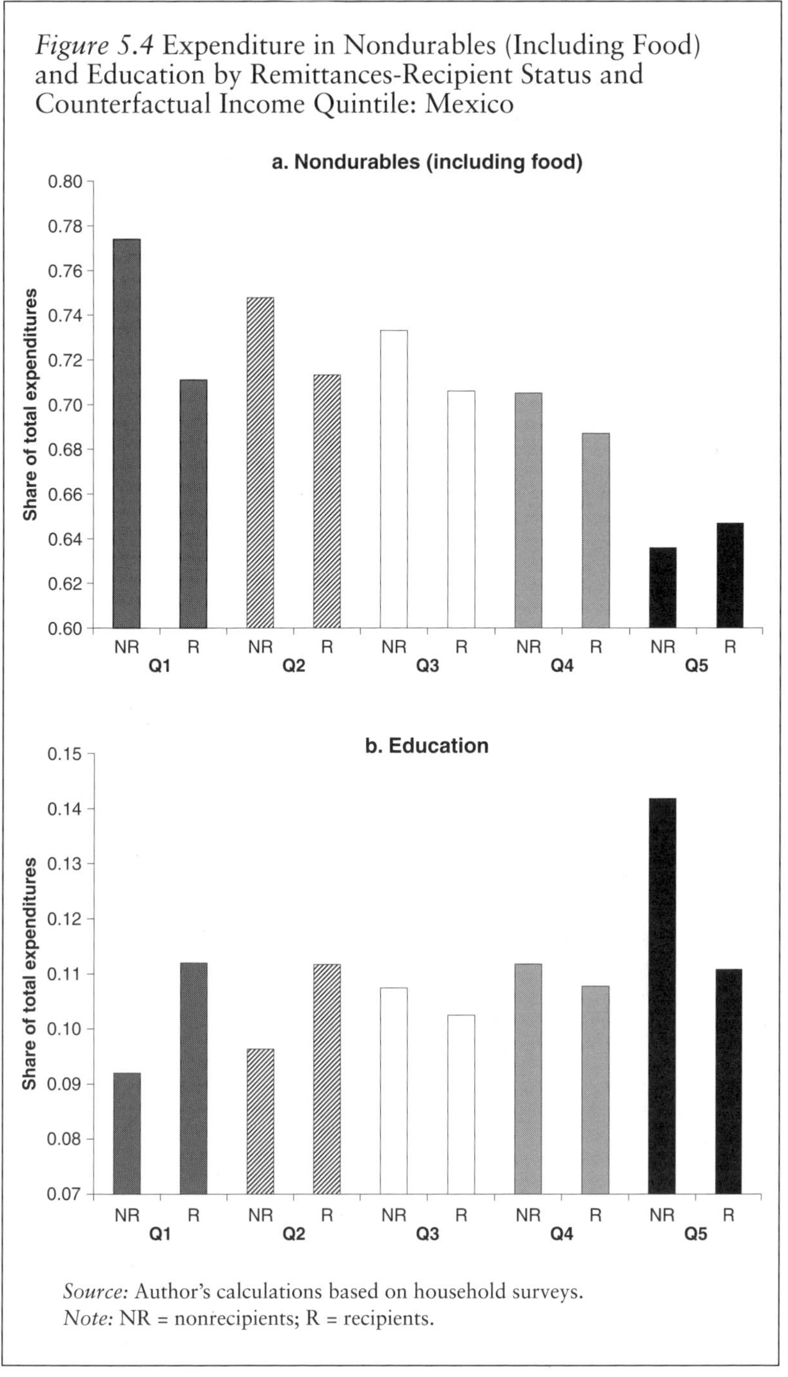

Source: Author's calculations based on household surveys.
Note: NR = nonrecipients; R = recipients.

Figure 5.5 Expenditure in Nondurables (Including Food) and Education by Remittances-Recipient Status and Counterfactual Income Quintile: Nicaragua

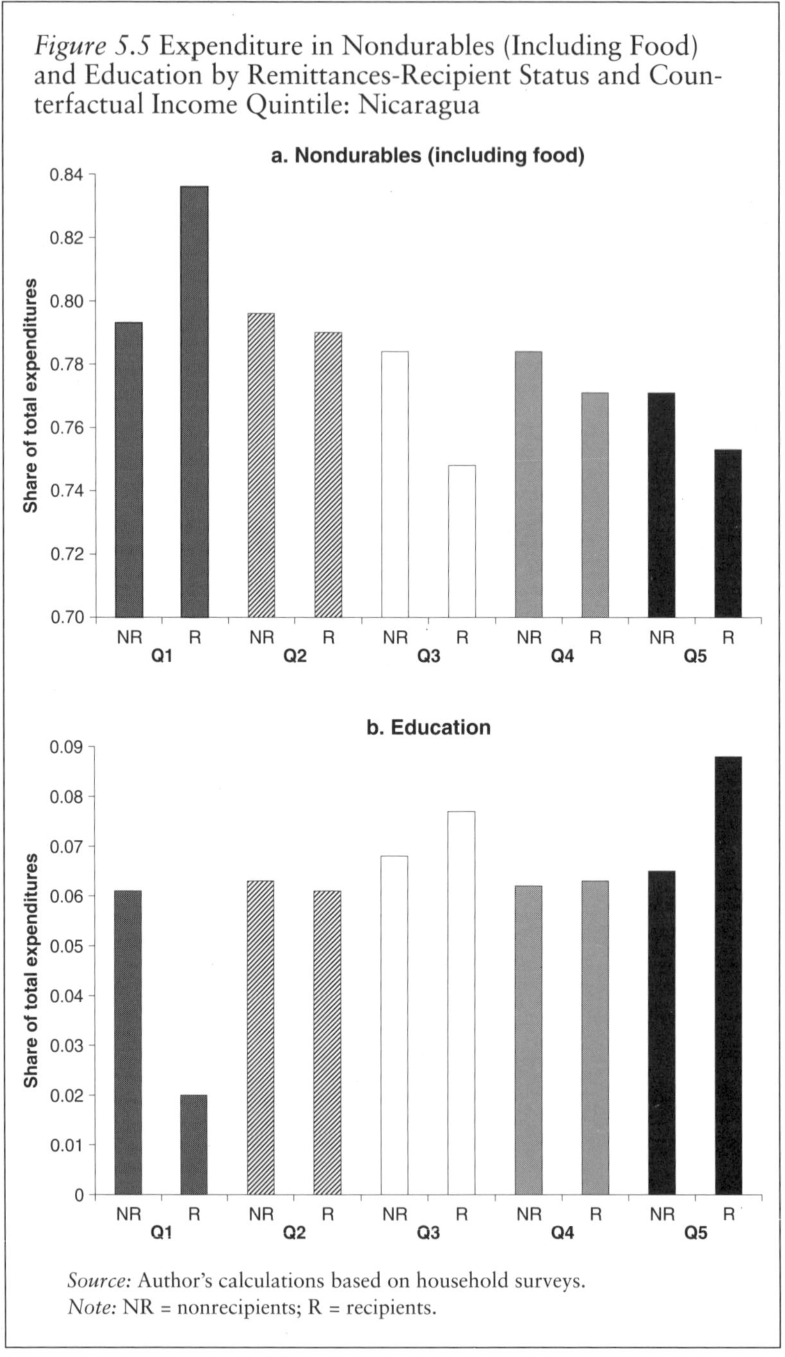

Source: Author's calculations based on household surveys.
Note: NR = nonrecipients; R = recipients.

Remittances and Human Capital

Educational Attainment

While remittances can help overcome borrowing constraints that limit the human capital investments of poor households, the migration of household members that precedes the receipt of remittances can also have disruptive effects on family life, with potentially negative consequences on the educational attainment of children. Moreover, to the extent that in destination countries most migrants tend to work in occupations requiring limited schooling, the returns from investments in education may be lower for those that are envisaging international migration, which also could tend to reduce the schooling of children in migrants' families.

Existing evidence on the impact of remittances on education in LAC is restricted to the cases of Mexico and El Salvador. For rural Mexico, Hanson and Woodruff (2003) find that remittances are associated with higher educational attainment, at least among 10- to 15-year-old girls whose mothers have low levels of schooling. Using a cross section of Mexican municipalities, López Córdova (2005) shows that remittances are associated with lower illiteracy among children, but the evidence on their impact on school attendance is mixed: the effect is positive only for 5-year-olds, becoming insignificant among 6- to 14-year-olds, and negative for those ages 15 to 17. Similarly, McKenzie and Rapoport (2005) show that Mexican children ages 16 to 18 who come from households with migrants have lower levels of educational attainment, and that this negative effect is even larger for those whose mothers have higher levels of schooling. For the case of El Salvador, Cox-Edwards and Ureta (2003) and Acosta (2006) show that children from remittances-recipient households are less likely to drop out of school, which they attribute to the relaxation of budget constraints affecting poor recipient households.

In the present section we investigate the extent to which previous findings on the impact of remittances on educational attainment also apply to other countries with significant remittances flows. Disparities in secondary enrollment rates are large in the LAC region, ranging from about 80 percent in countries such as Chile and Argentina, to less than 50 percent in high remittances-recipient countries such as Mexico, El Salvador, the Dominican Republic, Nicaragua, Honduras, and Guatemala. Moreover, as seen in figure 5.6, the above-mentioned countries, together with Haiti, exhibit among the lowest adult educational attainment rates in the region. That remittances could potentially have an important effect on education is illustrated by the comparison of enrollment rates among children ages 12 to 17 across recipient and nonrecipient households (see figure 5.7). With the exception of Mexico, children from families reporting remittances are more likely to stay in school. The largest differences

Figure 5.6 Average Years of Education for Adults (22–65 Years Old)

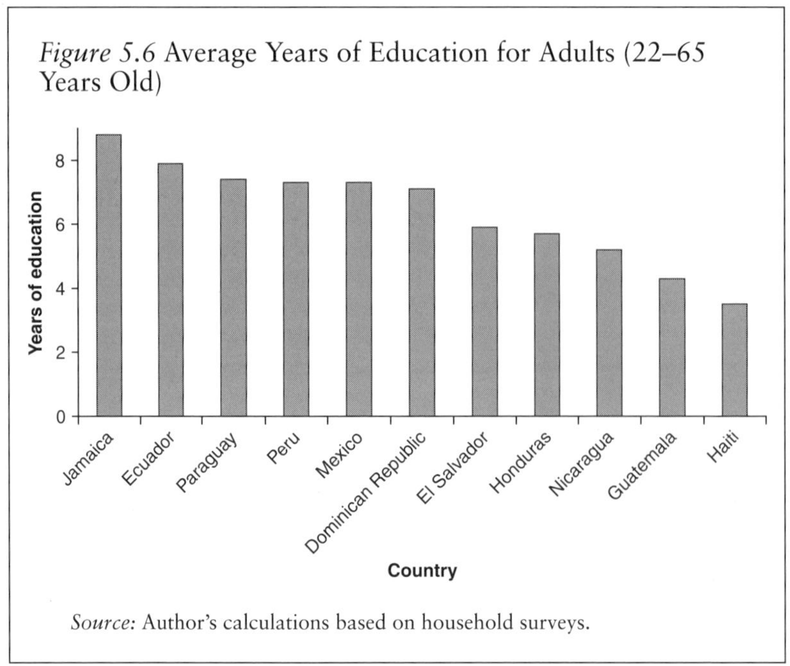

Source: Author's calculations based on household surveys.

Figure 5.7 Differences in School Enrollment Rates for Children 12–17 Years Old by Remittances-Recipient Status

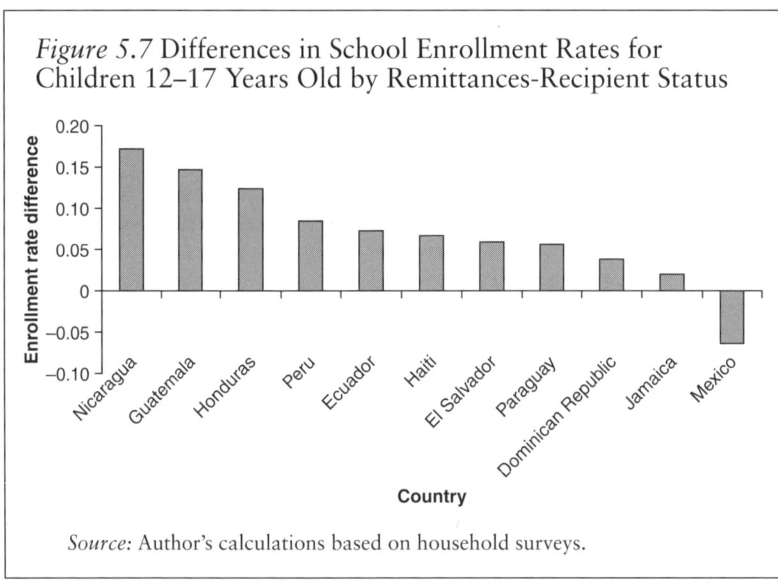

Source: Author's calculations based on household surveys.

are obtained for Nicaragua, Guatemala, and Honduras, where enrollment rates are between 12 percent and 17 percent higher for recipient families.

Some of these differences, however, could be attributed to the fact that, as shown in chapter 2, households that report remittances exhibit considerably different demographic and income characteristics than nonrecipients. We thus estimate regression models that attempt to deal with this problem, using a specification that closely follows Hanson and Woodruff's (2003), and focus on the accumulated schooling of children ages 10 to 15. The models, which follow equation (2) below, are estimated separately by gender, and urban and rural areas whenever possible (provided sufficient variability in remittances' receipts is available).

$$E_i = \alpha + \beta X_i + \gamma M_i + \lambda C_i + \delta R_i + \varepsilon_i \tag{2}$$

where E_i represents the number of school grades completed by child i, X_i is a vector of child and household characteristics (age of the child, a dummy for the child being the oldest in the household, indicators for the number of children of different ages in the household, presence of a newborn to 5-year-old child, family home ownership, counterfactual income quintile), M_i is a set of characteristics of the child's mother (indicators for mother's education, marital status, head of household status, and a quartic in mother's age), C_i represents community characteristics (the proportion of households with sanitary services in the county of residence, the proportion of household heads working in agricultural activities in the county of residence, and state or province indicators), R_i is a "dummy" variable for households that receive remittances, and ε_i is a random error term. Regression estimates for the δ coefficient are presented in table 5.4.

Our results suggest that access to remittances is positively and significantly associated with higher educational attainment in six of 11 countries—the exceptions being Mexico, Paraguay, Peru, Jamaica, and the Dominican Republic. The estimated positive impact of remittances varies by gender and across rural and urban areas—for example, in Ecuador an impact is found only for urban areas. Since the actual amount remitted is likely to have a differential impact depending on the magnitude of the transfer, we have also replicated this analysis looking at the impact of the per-capita value of remittances received by the household. The results suggest that higher remittances also increase schooling in the Dominican Republic, and among boys in urban Mexico.[12]

Previous evidence on Mexico has suggested that the positive effects of remittances on schooling vary with the educational attainment of the children's parents, being generally larger when the latter is low. Differential effects of this sort could be due to the fact that among poorer families with lower levels of adult schooling, remittances could have a more sizable effect in terms of relaxing budget constraints that keep children out of

Table 5.4 Access to Remittances and Children's Education—OLS

Age group	*10–15 years old*			
Dependent variable	*Accumulated schooling*			
	Rural		*Urban*	
Sample	*Boys*	*Girls*	*Boys*	*Girls*
Mexico	–0.149	0.113	–0.023	–0.235
	(0.129)	(0.095)	(0.177)	(0.192)
El Salvador	–0.482***	0.312***	0.245**	–0.010
	(0.110)	(0.097)	(0.098)	(0.097)
Guatemala	0.448**	0.313*	0.291	0.454**
	(0.177)	(0.164)	(0.230)	(0.177)
Honduras	0.427***	0.495***	0.298***	0.360***
	(0.100)	(0.098)	(0.078)	(0.080)
Ecuador	0.187	0.112	0.289**	0.314**
	(0.149)	(0.151)	(0.125)	(0.134)
Paraguay	–0.012	0.208		
	(0.195)	(0.182)		
Haiti			0.098	0.244**
			(0.107)	(0.098)
Peru			–0.070	0.157
			(0.146)	(0.120)
Nicaragua[a]	0.437***	0.375***		
	(0.153)	(0.133)		
Jamaica[a]	–0.114	–0.005		
	(0.150)	(0.113)		
Dominican Republic[a]	0.077	0.118		
	(0.107)	(0.094)		

Source: Author's calculations based on household surveys.

Note: *** significant at 1% level; ** significant at 5% level; * significant at 10% level.

Standard errors in parentheses.

a. Rural and urban areas together.

school. However, one could also expect an opposite effect—remittances having a smaller impact on education when the schooling of parents is low—if less-educated parents exhibit lower preferences for educational over other expenditures. To find out which effect dominates, we reestimate equation (2) adding an interaction term between remittances (R_i) and a variable that indicates whether the mother has four or more years or education. The corresponding results are reported in table 5.5.

Table 5.5 Remittances and Children's Education by Mother's Education

Age group		*10–15 years old*			
Dependent variable		*Accumulated schooling*			
		Rural		*Urban*	
Country	*Variable*	*Boys*	*Girls*	*Boys*	*Girls*
Mexico	Receive remittances	–0.082	0.329**	–0.041	–0.573
		(0.192)	(0.141)	(0.329)	(0.553)
	Receive remittances* Mother education 4 years or more	0.144	–0.417**	0.024	0.461
		(0.240)	(0.186)	(0.378)	(0.577)
El Salvador	Receive remittances	0.511***	0.251**	0.365**	–0.191
		(0.129)	(0.115)	(0.170)	(0.186)
	Receive remittances* Mother education 4 years or more	–0.116	0.229	–0.203	0.297
		(0.212)	(0.176)	(0.197)	(0.206)
Guatemala	Receive remittances	0.482**	0.223	0.412	1.109***
		(0.200)	(0.186)	(0.337)	(0.231)
	Receive remittances* Mother education 4 years or more	–0.179	0.450	–0.323	–1.336***
		(0.389)	(0.318)	(0.408)	(0.315)
Honduras	Receive remittances	0.581***	0.662***	0.731***	0.554***
		(0.142)	(0.155)	(0.178)	(0.209)
	Receive remittances* Mother education 4 years or more	–0.317*	–0.328*	–0.564***	–0.247
		(0.193)	(0.184)	(0.193)	(0.220)
Ecuador	Receive remittances	0.278	–0.106	0.502	0.805*
		(0.233)	(0.237)	(0.331)	(0.463)
	Receive remittances* Mother education 4 years or more	–0.138	0.386	–0.239	–0.547
		(0.277)	(0.287)	(0.344)	(0.475)
Paraguay	Receive remittances	0.056	0.433*		
		(0.271)	(0.235)		
	Receive remittances* Mother education 4 years or more	–0.133	–0.476		
		(0.374)	(0.345)		

(continued)

Table 5.5 Remittances and Children's Education by Mother's Education *(continued)*

Age group		*10–15 years old*			
Dependent variable		*Accumulated schooling*			
		Rural		*Urban*	
Country	*Variable*	*Boys*	*Girls*	*Boys*	*Girls*
Haiti	Receive remittances			0.043	0.273**
				(0.120)	(0.111)
	Receive remittances* Mother education 4 years or more			0.229	−0.111
				(0.237)	(0.220)
Peru	Receive remittances			0.187	0.393***
				(0.296)	(0.144)
	Receive remittances* Mother education 4 years or more			−0.362	−0.343*
				(0.338)	(0.207)
Nicaragua[a]	Receive remittances	0.577**	0.554**		
		(0.260)	(0.221)		
	Receive remittances* Mother education 4 years or more	−0.208	−0.296		
		(0.310)	(0.258)		
Jamaica[a]	Receive remittances	0.510	−0.236		
		(0.465)	(0.435)		
	Receive remittances* Mother education 4 years or more	−0.668	0.253		
		(0.484)	(0.443)		
Dominican Republic[a]	Receive remittances	−0.148	0.301		
		(0.242)	(0.208)		
	Receive remittances* Mother education 4 years or more	0.282	−0.242		
		(0.263)	(0.230)		

Source: Author's calculations based on household surveys.

Note: *** significant at 1% level; ** significant at 5% level; * significant at 10% level.

Standard errors in parentheses.

a. Rural and urban areas together.

Our findings confirm those of previous papers on Mexico, suggesting that the positive effect of remittances on education tends to be larger when the schooling of parents is low. For instance, among rural girls in Mexico, Paraguay, and Peru,[13] our previous results suggested no effect of remittances on educational attainment, but we now find a positive and significant effect for those whose mothers have at most three years of educational attainment, whereas for the remaining children the effect is estimated to be close to zero, although slightly negative in Mexico and Paraguay. Similarly, in Guatemala and Honduras, some of the previously estimated positive effects of remittances are now found to be larger in magnitude for children with uneducated mothers and considerably smaller for those whose mothers have at least four years of schooling.

Overall, with the addition of Paraguay and Peru to the list of countries where remittances affect educational attainment, we are left with only two countries (Jamaica and the Dominican Republic) in which those effects are always nonsignificant. As for the differences by gender and urban status, our estimation results do not allow easy generalizations and suggest that the various potential effects of migration and remittances—relaxation of budget constraints, social disruption, changes in the returns to schooling—carry different relative weights depending on the country and socioeconomic group involved. In any case, it appears that remittances tend to relax budget constraints that otherwise would force children to leave school and reduce their educational attainment, but this effect is sometimes restricted to those with less-educated mothers.

Health Outcomes

Few papers have addressed the impact of migration and remittances on children's health. The exceptions are mostly focused on infant mortality. Brockerhoff (1990), and Ssengonzi, De Jong, and Stokes (2002) investigate the effects of female migration on the survival chances of their children in Senegal and Uganda, respectively. They find that rural to urban migration significantly increases children's survival chances. Kanaiaupuni and Donato (1999) analyze the effects of village migration and remittances on infant survival outcomes in Mexico, and conclude that remittances reduce infant mortality. However, the authors reach an opposite conclusion for the effect of migration: higher rates of infant mortality in communities experiencing intense migration. Finally, with data on Mexican municipalities, López Córdova (2005) concludes that larger proportions of remittances and migrant households at the community level are associated with lower infant mortality rates.

Further evidence of the impact of migration on children's health has been provided by Hildebrandt and McKenzie (2005). The authors investigate the impact of international migration on several children's health outcomes in Mexico. Their results show that migrant households have lower rates of infant mortality and higher birth weights. Moreover, they find evidence that migration also raises maternal health knowledge and the likelihood that the child is delivered by a doctor. On the other hand, preventative health care (such as breastfeeding, visits to doctors, and vaccinations) seem to be less likely for children from migrant households.

No previous study has investigated the impact of remittances and migration on anthropometric indicators for young children (weight-for-age, height-for-age). Hoddinott and Kinsey (2001) present results on how external shocks drastically affect children's growth in developing countries. Both weight and height measures are good indicators of health status, with different consequences in the short run and long run. For instance, lower weight is associated with malnutrition and higher mortality risk. Similarly, lower stature in childhood is strongly correlated with smaller body size in adulthood, with negative consequences on earnings and productivity (Thomas and Strauss 1997), and increased risk of cardiovascular and lung diseases.

With this motivation, the present section aims to uncover evidence on the effect of international migrant remittances on anthropometric health indicators typically used in the health literature, and with well-known links with children's growth. We also estimate the impact of remittances on the probability that the delivery of children born in the year preceding the survey was assisted by a doctor, and on the probability that children ages 2 to 5 received the complete set of required vaccinations. The anthropometric measures on which we focus are the weight-for-age (WAZ) and height-for-age (HAZ) z-scores for children ages 1 to 5 years old. These are standardized measures of performance in weight and height, and consist of comparing each child of a given age to a reference group. The reference tables for WAZ and HAZ are taken from the CDC Growth Charts for the United States (Kuczmarski et al. 2000).[14]

Figures 5.8 and 5.9 show the distribution of weight-for-age and height-for-age anthropometric z-scores, using kernel density estimation, for Guatemala and Nicaragua, the only two LAC countries in which the household surveys used in this report provide the information needed for calculating the health indicators employed in this section. Plot densities of the above-described anthropometric indicators for children ages 1 to 5 years old from remittances-recipient and nonrecipient households are estimated using kernel densities. The figures show that children from recipient households have both higher weight-for-age and height-for-age z-scores. Kolmogorov-Smirnov tests for equality of distributions reject the equality of distributions for recipient and nonrecipient households, and suggest that remittances are in fact associated with better anthropometric scores for children.

In order to test whether these results are driven by the differential characteristics of households with and without migrants, we estimate a regression model similar to the one used for educational attainment (equation 2), changing only the dependent variable, from years of schooling to the four health indicators measured above. In addition to this basic specification, we estimate a modified version of equation (2), where the indicator for remittances recipients is interacted with a dummy variable for the second quintile of the income distribution—using the counterfactual income

Figure 5.8 Anthropometric Measures for Children Ages 1–5, by Remittances-Recipient Status: Guatemala

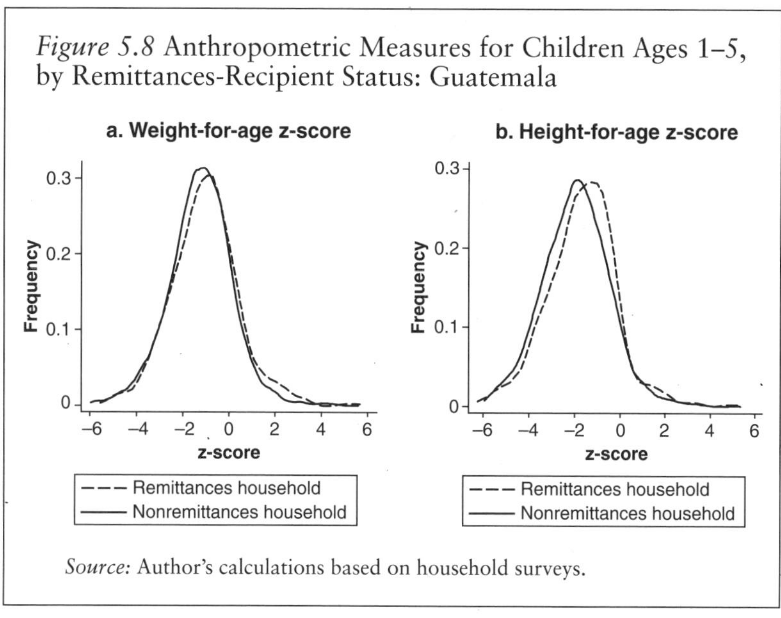

Source: Author's calculations based on household surveys.

Figure 5.9 Anthropometric Measures for Children Ages 1–5, by Remittances-Recipient Status: Nicaragua

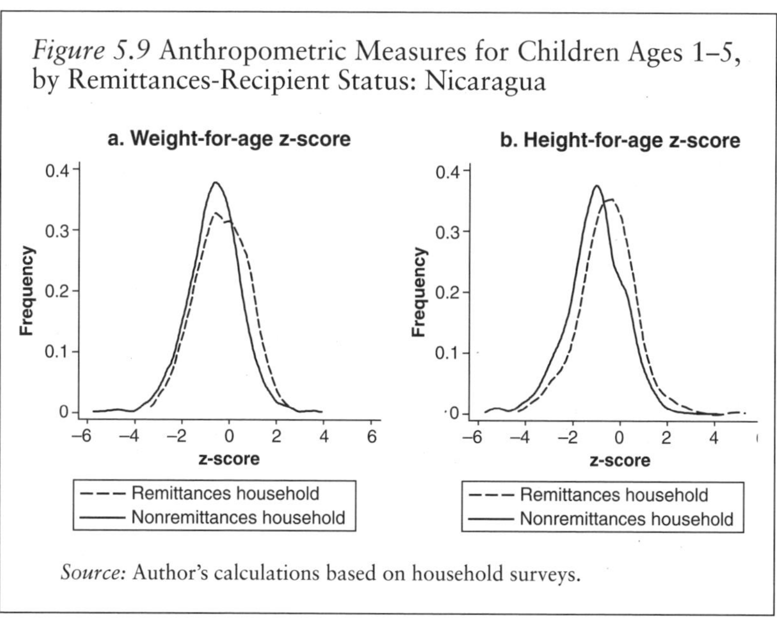

Source: Author's calculations based on household surveys.

prior to migration—and a dummy for households located in the third to fifth quintiles.[15]

Table 5.6 reports the corresponding results, including the coefficients on free-standing dummy variables for the second through fifth income quintiles. As confirmed by our estimates, both weight- and height-for-age indexes tend to increase monotonically and significantly with household income, and so does the likelihood of doctor-assisted deliveries in the case of Nicaragua. Moreover, controlling for premigration income, children from households that report receiving remittances tend to exhibit better health outcomes than those from nonrecipient households with similar demographic and socioeconomic characteristics. While the relatively small sample sizes make most of the estimated interactives between remittances and income quintiles nonsignificant from a statistical point of view, in most cases the results clearly indicate that the impact of remittances on children's health is concentrated on low-income households located in the first quintile of the income distribution.

Remittances and Labor Supply

The impact of remittances on labor supply is in principle ambiguous. For individuals from households with migrants, the net additional income derived from remittances could have the "income effect" of increasing the demand for leisure and reservation wages, with a consequent reduction in labor force participation. However, out-migration also has the direct effect of reducing the size of the labor force, and the ensuing upward pressure on local wages could in turn create a "substitution effect" away from leisure, with a consequent increase in labor supply for those living in areas with high migration rates. In the case of Mexico, for instance, Mishra (2007) estimates that emigration raised average wages by 8 percent between 1970 and 2000. In addition to the above factors, in households with recent migrants, the need to replace the income lost due to the migration of wage earners could reinforce the effect of higher market wages, resulting in an increase in the labor participation of those who remain.

Previous papers on the subject suggest that remittances tend to reduce labor force participation in rural Mexico (Hanson 2005) and El Salvador (Acosta 2006), but do not have a significant effect in Nicaragua (Funkhouser 1992). In particular, Hanson finds that in Mexico, receiving remittances from abroad reduces both the likelihood of working outside the home and the hours worked by both males and females. While Hanson interprets the latter result as evidence of increasing intrahousehold specialization—for example, remittances income allows families to "buy back" some of the labor time of the women who stayed in Mexico—he implies that caution should be used when interpreting the results of a lower

Table 5.6 Remittances and Health Outcomes

Country	*Guatemala*				*Nicaragua*			
Dependent variable	*Weight-for-age z-score*	*Height-for-age z-score*	*Received all vaccines*	*Child delivered by doctor*	*Weight-for-age z-score*	*Height-for-age z-score*	*Received all vaccines*	*Child delivered by doctor*
2nd income quintile	0.117**	0.141**	0.011	0.006	0.154*	0.230**	–0.028	0.104*
	(0.058)	(0.060)	(0.011)	(0.015)	(0.085)	(0.091)	(0.047)	(0.060)
3rd income quintile	0.233***	0.385**	0.016	0.054***	0.077	0.327***	–0.011	0.085
	(0.060)	(0.067)	(0.013)	(0.025)	(0.099)	(0.109)	(0.054)	(0.070)
4th income quintile	0.325***	0.479**	0.010	0.023	0.263**	0.594***	–0.126	0.168*
	(0.073)	(0.076)	(0.016)	(0.023)	(0.117)	(0.113)	(0.062)	(0.079)
5th income quintile	0.594***	0.686**	0.026	0.013	0.352**	0.594***	–0.102	0.263**
	(0.091)	(0.098)	(0.018)	(0.025)	(0.138)	(0.136)	(0.078)	(0.082)
Remittances	0.211**	0.213	0.065**	0.255***	0.306	0.289	0.119	0.297**
	(0.089)	(0.228)	(0.021)	(0.160)	(0.394)	(0.347)	(0.225)	(0.090)
Remittances* Q2	–0.327	0.084	–0.082	–0.034*	–0.370	–0.079	0.034	–0.463*
	(0.283)	(0.264)	(0.079)	(0.007)	(0.457)	(0.421)	(0.275)	(0.225)
Remittances*	–0.423	0.004	–0.041	–0.036***	–0.252	–0.148	0.071	–0.623***
Q3-Q4-Q5	(0.272)	(0.253)	(0.071)	(0.006)	(0.418)	(0.385)	(0.252)	(0.114)

Source: Author's calculations based on household surveys.
Note: *** significant at 1% level; ** significant at 5% level; * significant at 10% level.
Standard errors in parentheses.

male labor supply in households with migrants. Indeed, despite Hanson's efforts to control for self-selection into migration, individual unobserved characteristics could still be driving both the decisions to stay in Mexico and to supply less labor outside the home.

In order to determine whether previous evidence can be generalized to other LAC countries, we explore household survey data for 11 LAC countries. In our sample, 88 percent of adult males ages 20 to 59, and 52 percent of females in that age group are either working or actively looking for a job. Labor force participation among males varies considerably across countries, from around 93 percent in Guatemala and Paraguay, to about 78 percent in Jamaica and Haiti. Among females, the largest rates are found in Haiti and Peru (about 62 percent), and the lowest in Honduras, Guatemala, and Mexico (44 percent). As shown in figure 5.10, in almost all cases, labor force participation is lower for individuals living in households with access to remittances, with the only exceptions found for females in Haiti and Nicaragua. The largest differences are obtained for Mexico, where nearly 90 percent of nonrecipient males are working or looking for a job, while only 60 percent of their recipient counterparts are doing so. The corresponding rates for females are 45 percent and 34 percent, respectively. Differences by remittances-recipient status in other countries are much smaller than in Mexico, but they still average 8 percent for males and 3 percent for females.

While these differences are considerable, they could be driven by individual and household characteristics associated with access to remittances, and also with labor force participation decisions. To investigate whether this is indeed the case, we estimate regression models for hours worked outside the home, as well as for individuals' decisions to participate in the labor market, including access to remittances, among other determinants. In the case of hours, we employ a tobit specification that takes into account the fact that many individuals do not participate in the labor market and thus report zero hours worked. In the case of the labor participation decision, we employ a probit model that controls for the possible endogeneity of remittances using instrumental variables. When possible, we estimate separate regressions for males and females, in urban and rural areas—the only exception being Peru, where recipients are almost absent in rural areas.[16] The estimated models are of the following form:

$$L_i = \alpha + \beta X_i + \gamma H_i + \delta R_i + \varepsilon_i \tag{3}$$

where L_i represents either the number of hours worked by individual i or a dummy variable that takes the value one if the person is active in the labor market (is either working or looking for a job), X_i is a vector of personal characteristics (a quartic in age, indicators for educational attainment, marital status), H_i is a set of household characteristics (household size and composition, home ownership, and state and province indicators), R_i is a

Figure 5.10 Labor Force Participation of Adults (20–59 Years Old), by Gender and Remittances-Recipient Status

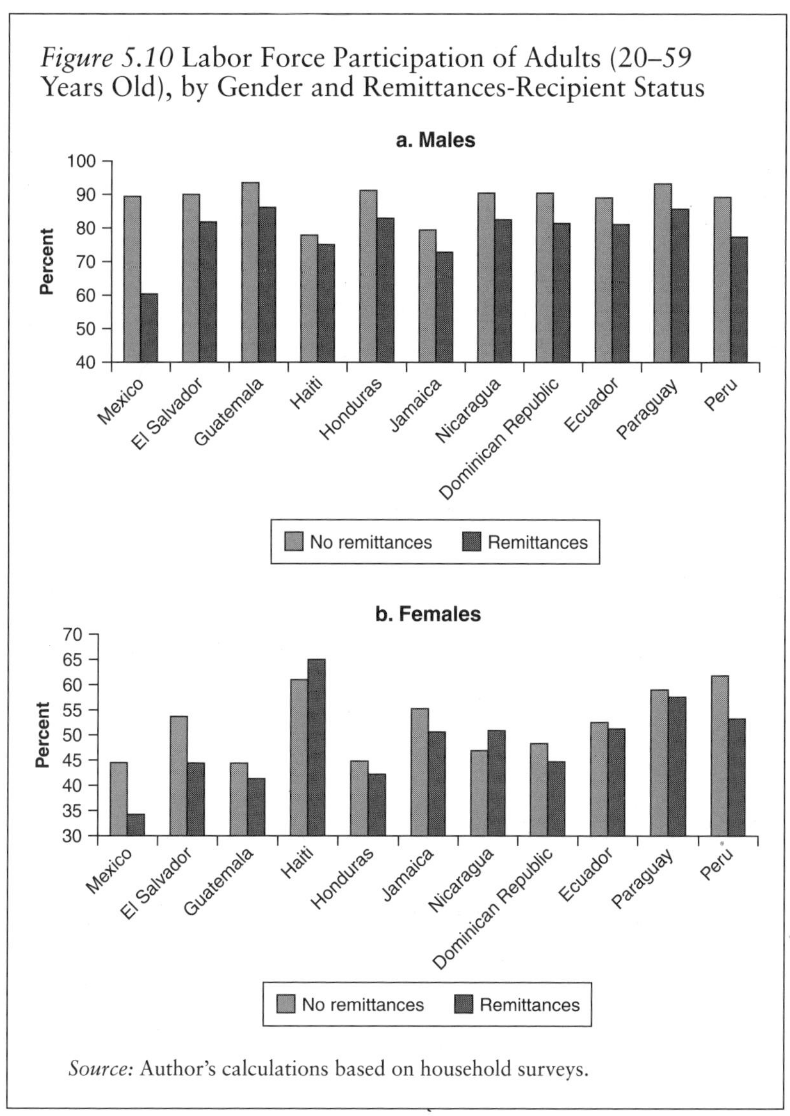

Source: Author's calculations based on household surveys.

"dummy" variable for households that receive remittances, and ε_i is a random error term. Results are presented in tables 5.7 and 5.8, respectively.

Confirming previous evidence, our results suggest that in all 10 countries for which data are available, remittances have the effect of reducing the number of hours worked per week. This negative effect is present both in urban and rural areas, the only exceptions being Paraguay and Haiti, where hours worked are reduced in rural areas only, and Nicaragua, where the estimated effect is significant in urban areas only.

Table 5.7 Access to Remittances and Hours Worked

Age group	*20–59 years old*			
Dependent variable	*Hours worked last week*			
	Rural		*Urban*	
Sample	*Males*	*Females*	*Males*	*Females*
Mexico	−15.473***	−13.187***	−12.686***	−7.561***
	(1.022)	(1.979)	(1.473)	(2.175)
El Salvador	−4.498***	−12.257***	−5.546***	−8.580***
	(0.986)	(2.089)	(0.847)	(1.115)
Guatemala	−0.969	−15.253***	−6.180***	−7.228***
	(1.426)	(3.418)	(1.601)	(2.427)
Honduras	−3.052***	−12.813***	−6.307***	−10.067***
	(0.704)	(2.046)	(0.816)	(1.152)
Ecuador	−2.186*	−4.399**	−3.391***	−5.622***
	(1.264)	(1.723)	(1.117)	(1.621)
Paraguay	−15.395**	−5.583	10.865	7.506
	(7.247)	(13.027)	(11.680)	(10.789)
Haiti	−8.410***	−2.925	−1.221	2.308
	(2.831)	(3.069)	(1.170)	(1.412)
Peru			−12.711***	−7.455***
			(1.870)	(2.306)
Nicaragua	−3.096	−0.701	−7.216***	−7.776***
	(1.889)	(5.208)	(1.643)	(2.134)
Dominican Republic	−5.278***	−8.844***	−7.240***	−10.245***
	(1.301)	(2.828)	(1.031)	(1.514)

Source: Author's calculations based on household surveys.

Note: *** significant at 1% level; ** significant at 5% level; * significant at 10% level.

Standard errors in parentheses.

As for differences by gender, no clear generalizations are possible, with five countries showing larger effects among females and four exhibiting the opposite pattern.

Similar results are obtained for the decision to participate in the labor market using a probit model and assuming remittances to be exogenous. Indeed, such a model yields negative effects in 10 of 11 countries—data is now available also for Jamaica—and the weakest results are obtained for

Table 5.8 Remittances and Labor Force Participation (with Instrumental Variables)

Age group	*20–59 years old*			
Dependent variable	*Labor force participation*			
	Rural		*Urban*	
Sample	*Males*	*Females*	*Males*	*Females*
Mexico	−0.329***	−0.245***	−0.097	0.023
	(0.048)	(0.049)	(0.135)	(0.146)
El Salvador	−0.087	−0.598***	−0.032	0.309***
	(0.070)	(0.083)	(0.101)	(0.100)
Guatemala	0.007	−0.095	−0.228	0.261
	(0.170)	(0.221)	(0.140)	(0.206)
Honduras	−0.006	−0.135**	−0.096	0.095
	(0.068)	(0.067)	(0.094)	(0.095)
Ecuador	−0.228**	−0.154*	−0.310**	0.211
	(0.090)	(0.085)	(0.134)	(0.203)
Paraguay	−0.009	0.052	−0.530*	0.908**
	(0.092)	(0.174)	(0.321)	(0.380)
Haiti	0.254	0.338**	0.114**	0.263***
	(0.164)	(0.165)	(0.051)	(0.088)
Peru			−0.334***	0.284**
			(0.099)	(0.123)
Nicaragua	−0.181*	0.337	−0.211*	0.008
	(0.099)	(0.208)	(0.127)	(0.140)
Jamaica	−0.047	−0.027	−0.128**	0.056
	(0.051)	(0.051)	(0.064)	(0.061)
Dominican Republic	−0.222***	−0.010	−0.108	0.131
	(0.092)	(0.126)	(0.071)	(0.082)

Source: Author's calculations based on household surveys.

Note: *** significant at 1% level; ** significant at 5% level; * significant at 10% level.

Standard errors in parentheses.

Paraguay and Nicaragua (where significant results are restricted to urban areas), as well as for Haiti (where the effects are nonsignificant). However, when remittances are allowed to be endogenous and are appropriately instrumented, their negative impact on labor force participation ceases to be significant in a number of cases (table 5.8)—for example, their impact on labor supply becomes nonsignificant in Guatemala, as well as in urban areas in Mexico, Honduras, and the Dominican Republic. Moreover, in both Paraguay and Haiti, females living in urban areas are found to be more likely to participate in the labor force when receiving remittances, suggesting that the latter may be having a social disruption type of effect that in those cases dominates possible changes in reservation wages.

One possible concern with the above results is that remittances may be expected to have very different effects on the labor supply decisions of individuals with different levels of skills. Indeed, for those with higher levels of schooling, remittances income is likely to represent a smaller fraction of total income, so that income effects derived from remittances may be relatively less important than substitution effects associated with changes in labor market conditions, such as increases in wages as a result of out-migration. To test for this possibility, we have reestimated the model underlying table 5.8, introducing an interactive between remittances and a dummy variable for individuals that have at least four years of schooling (table 5.9).

The findings reported in table 5.9 suggest that the reductions in labor supply caused by remittances tend to be much smaller among individuals with higher levels of schooling. Evidence in this regard is found in 8 of 11 countries, with the exceptions of El Salvador, the Dominican Republic,

Table 5.9 Remittances and Labor Force Participation, by Educational Levels (with Instrumental Variables)

Age group		*20–59 years old*			
Dependent variable		*Labor force participation*			
		Rural		*Urban*	
Country	*Variable*	*Males*	*Females*	*Males*	*Females*
Mexico	Receive remittances	–0.434*** (0.055)	–0.283*** (0.066)	–0.250 (0.153)	0.188 (0.204)
	Receive remittances* education 4+	0.214*** (0.073)	0.059 (0.069)	0.233 (0.186)	–0.223 (0.203)
El Salvador	Receive remittances	–0.108 (0.076)	–0.623*** (0.087)	–0.045 (0.120)	–0.376*** (0.108)
	Receive remittances* education 4+	0.050 (0.059)	–0.072 (0.067)	0.018 (0.074)	0.118 (0.072)
Guatemala	Receive remittances	–0.037 (0.183)	–0.119 (0.223)	–0.164 (0.191)	–0.407* (0.224)
	Receive remittances* education 4+	0.214 (0.168)	0.417* (0.248)	–0.091 (0.175)	0.328 (0.223)

(continued)

Table 5.9 Remittances and Labor Force Participation, by Educational Levels (with Instrumental Variables) *(continued)*

Age group		*20–59 years old*			
Dependent variable		*Labor force participation*			
		Rural		*Urban*	
Country	*Variable*	*Males*	*Females*	*Males*	*Females*
Honduras	Receive remittances	0.032 (0.084)	−0.148** (0.097)	−0.257** (0.130)	−0.326** (0.129)
	Receive remittances* education 4+	−0.067 (0.076)	0.022 (0.086)	0.212** (0.093)	0.315*** (0.102)
Ecuador	Receive remittances	−0.256 (0.158)	−0.158 (0.127)	−1.161** (0.454)	0.241 (0.368)
	Receive remittances* education 4+	0.035 (0.160)	0.006 (0.120)	0.870** (0.432)	−0.033 (0.300)
Paraguay	Receive remittances	−0.125 (0.138)	−0.231 (0.203)	−0.296 (0.587)	0.461 (0.498)
	Receive remittances* education 4+	0.167 (0.148)	0.469* (0.260)	−0.269 (0.579)	0.537 (0.460)
Haiti	Receive remittances	0.029 (0.215)	0.463** (0.191)	0.029 (0.074)	0.241** (0.099)
	Receive remittances* education 4+	0.288* (0.175)	−0.204 (0.148)	0.109 (0.081)	0.056 (0.082)
Peru	Receive remittances			−3.458* (1.780)	−0.748* (0.410)
	Receive remittances* education 4+			3.190* (1.757)	0.522 (0.417)
Nicaragua	Receive remittances	−0.366** (0.161)	0.380 (0.232)	−0.215 (0.163)	0.038 (0.212)
	Receive remittances* education 4+	0.298** (0.152)	−0.093 (0.227)	0.007 (0.141)	−0.054 (0.171)
Jamaica	Receive remittances	−0.133 (0.129)	−0.075 (0.115)	0.125 (0.169)	−0.100 (0.144)
	Receive remittances* education 4+	0.092 (0.128)	0.053 (0.118)	−0.289* (0.176)	0.050 (0.151)
Dominican Republic	Receive remittances	−0.220* (0.122)	−0.075 (0.158)	−0.194* (0.103)	−0.222* (0.121)
	Receive remittances* education 4+	0.001 (0.093)	0.104 (0.120)	0.096 (0.083)	0.108 (0.102)

Source: Author's calculations based on household surveys.

Note: *** significant at 1% level; ** significant at 5% level; * significant at 10% level.

Standard errors in parentheses.

and Jamaica. Moreover, in the cases of rural females in Guatemala and Paraguay, and rural males in Haiti, for those with at least four years of schooling, the effect of remittances appears to be that of increasing labor supply, which is consistent with either social disruption effects or with changing labor market conditions that affect remittances recipients to a larger extent. However, although depending on the country the effects can be quite different across genders, between rural and urban areas, and by levels of schooling, the overall conclusion from this section is that remittances are more likely to reduce and not increase labor supply.

Conclusions

The econometric results presented in this chapter suggest that the effects of remittances on household behavior vary considerably across countries and between different socioeconomic groups. In particular, savings rates tend to increase for poorer recipient households, but the opposite effect is obtained for richer ones. The composition of household expenditures, on the other hand, is altered in the direction of increasing human capital investments, but except for Mexico, this effect is restricted to households located in the middle to upper segments of the income distribution. Moreover, while there is evidence that for some specific groups—defined by country, gender, and urban status—remittances increase children's educational attainment, the impact is often restricted to children with low levels of parental schooling. In the case of health outcomes, the results are restricted to two countries, Nicaragua and Guatemala, but in both cases they suggest that remittances improve children's health, particularly among low-income households. Finally, a negative link is found between remittances and labor supply, but the effects are often restricted to individuals with low levels of schooling.

Notes

1. As in our analysis of the impact of remittances on poverty and inequality in chapter 4, our main purpose is moving beyond simple correlations and—to the extent that it is possible with the existing data—analyzing the existence of a potential causal relationship from remittances to the respective indicator. In this regard, to correct for the potential biases associated with the likely reverse causality in many of the exercises, we rely on instrument sets constructed from the household surveys. Yet we also have to acknowledge that our instruments have limitations, and hence some caution is needed when interpreting the results through the causal lens.

2. These countries are Mexico, El Salvador, Guatemala, Peru, Nicaragua, and the Dominican Republic.

3. See Butelmann and Gallego (2001) and the references therein.

4. The set of household and head characteristics includes dummies for income quintiles, age of household head, average education of adults, number of male and female children ages 6 to 17, number of children under age 5, number of males and females ages 18 to 65, a dummy variable for rural households, the proportion of households with sanitary services in the county of residence, the proportion of household heads working in agricultural activities in the county of residence, and state and province indicators.

5. We have also estimated two-stage least squares regressions in which remittances are instrumented with the share of households in the country interacted with household characteristics that affect their likelihood to migrate. The results are qualitatively similar to those reported in figure 5.1, in the sense that the sign and significance of the differences between the savings rates of recipients and nonrecipients remain.

6. It must be noted that the calculation of savings rates is plagued by problems of underreporting of both expenditures and income. The fact that the gravity of these problems varies across the household surveys of different countries is reflected in the large variance of savings rates across countries—for example, in the case of El Salvador, the underreporting of expenditures is likely to be more serious than that of income, which is reflected in excessively high savings rates. For this reason, we focus on within-country comparisons, both across income quintiles and between recipients and nonrecipients.

7. See Attanasio and Székely (2000).

8. The controls are the same as in equation (1).

9. The only exceptions are given by the lower expenditures for durable goods of remittances recipients in Peru (compared with nonrecipients), the lower share of housing expenditures in urban Mexico, and the lower share of educational expenses among remittances recipients in Mexico and rural Jamaica.

10. In the case of Mexico, food expenses cannot be separated from those for other nondurable goods, which are lower among recipients. The regressions for Jamaica control for quintiles in expenditure rather than income per capita.

11. The following instrumental variables are used for remittances: the percentage of households that receive remittances in the respective country of residence (a proxy for the presence of migrant networks), and its interaction with household-level characteristics that affects the decision to migrate, including an indicator for the presence of newborn to 5-year-old children in the household, the number of adult males in the household, and the average educational level among adults.

12. A potential methodological concern associated with the above results is that unobserved household characteristics that affect the propensity to have migrants and receive remittances could also be driving the decisions to keep children in school. We have attempted the use of instrumental variables to address this simultaneity bias, but have failed to find appropriate instruments that are sufficiently correlated with the migration status of households but do not otherwise affect the educational attainment of children. While the instruments used in other sections of this chapter—the fraction of households that receive remittances in the county and its interaction with household characteristics—have passed standard specification tests, the fact that the size of the sample of children ages 10 to 15 is much smaller than in other sections has led coefficient and standard errors to increase considerably in comparison with ordinary least squares, leading us to focus on the latter.

13. In the case of Peru, the sample includes both urban and rural children.

14. Reference tables can be found at www.cdc.gov/nchs/about/major/nhanes/growthcharts/datafiles.htm. For WAZ, the original tables used are the "weight-for-age charts, birth to 36 months." For older children, values were extrapolated using the "weight-for-age charts, 2 to 20 years." Similarly, for HAZ, the reference tables

used are "length-for-age charts, birth to 36 months," and "stature-for-age charts, 2 to 20 years."

15. We group the third through fifth quintiles due to the relatively small sample size for some of the estimations.

16. Control variables include a quartic in age, indicators for years of education, marital status, indicators for the number of children of different ages in the household, presence of a 0- to 5-year-old child, number of adult males and females in the household, family home ownership, and state and province indicators. The sample is restricted to individuals ages 20 to 59. The instruments for remittances include the incidence of households with remittances in the county and its interaction with household-level characteristics that affect the decision to migrate. The validity of the instruments is confirmed both in the first stage regressions and by means of Sargan's overidentification tests.

References

Acosta, P. 2006. "Labor Supply, School Attendance, and Remittances from International Migration: The Case of El Salvador." Policy Research Working Paper 3903, World Bank, Washington, DC.

Adams, R. 2005. "Remittances, Household Expenditure and Investment in Guatemala." Policy Research Working Paper No. 3532, World Bank, Washington, DC.

Attanasio, O., and M. Székely. 2000. "Saving in Developing Countries: Inequality, Demographics and All That." Unpublished, University College London, London.

Brockerhoff, M. 1990. "Rural-to-Urban Migration and Child Survival in Senegal." *Demography* 27: 601–16

Butelmann, A., and F. Gallego. 2001. "*Estimaciones de los Determinantes del Ahorro de los Hogares en Chile (1988–1997).*" In *Análisis Empírico del Ahorro en Chile*, ed. F. Morandé and R. Vergara, Banco Central de Chile and Centro de Estudios Públicos, Santiago, Chile.

Cox-Edwards, A., and M. Ureta. 2003. "International Migration, Remittances, and Schooling: Evidence from El Salvador." *Journal of Development Economics* 72: 429–61.

Funkhouser, E. 1992. "Migration from Nicaragua: Some Recent Evidence." *World Development* 20: 1209–18.

Hanson, G. 2005. "Emigration, Remittances, and Labor Force Participation in Mexico." Unpublished, University of California, San Diego, CA.

Hanson, G.H., and C. Woodruff. 2003. "Emigration and Educational Attainment in Mexico." Unpublished, University of California, San Diego, CA.

Hildebrandt, N., and D. McKenzie. 2005. "The Effects of Migration on Child Health in Mexico." *Economia, Journal of the Latin American and Caribbean Economic Association* 6 (1): 257–89.

Hoddinott, J., and B. Kinsey. 2001. "Child Growth in the Time of Drought." *Oxford Bulletin of Economics and Statistics* 63 (4): 409–36.

Kanaiaupuni, S., and K. Donato. 1999. "Migradollars and Mortality: The Effects of Migration on Infant Survival in Mexico." *Demography* 36: 339–53.

Kuczmarski, R., C. Ogden, L. Grummer-Strawn, K.M. Flegal, S.S. Guo, W.R. Wei, Z. Mei, L.R. Curtin, A.F. Roche, and C.L. Johnson. 2000. "CDC Growth Charts: United States." U.S. Department of Health and Human Services, Centers for Disease Control and Prevention, National Center for Health Statistics. Advance Data (Revised) 314: 1–28. Atlanta, GA.

López Córdova, E. 2005. "Globalization, Migration and Development: The Role of Mexican Migrant Remittances." *Economia, Journal of the Latin American and Caribbean Economic Association* 6 (1): 217–47.

McKenzie, D., and H. Rapoport. 2005. "Migration and Education Inequality in Mexico." Unpublished, Inter-American Development Bank, Washington, DC.

Mishra, P. 2007. "Emigration and Wages in Source Countries: Evidence from Mexico." *Journal of Development Economics* 82 (1): 180–99.

Ssengonzi, R., G. De Jong, and C. Stokes. 2002. "The Effect of Female Migration on Infant and Child Survival in Uganda." *Population Research and Policy Review* 21: 403–31.

Taylor, J. 1992. "Remittances and Inequality Reconsidered: Direct, Indirect, and Intertemporal Effects." *Journal of Policy Modeling* 14: 187–208.

Thomas, D., and J. Strauss. 1997. "Health and Wages: Evidence on Men and Women in Urban Brazil." *Journal of Econometrics* 77 (1): 159–85.

6

Do Remittances Affect Recipient Countries' Financial Development?

*María Soledad Martínez Pería, Yira Mascaró, and Florencia Moizeszowicz**

As researchers and policy makers have come to notice the increasing volume and stable nature of remittances to developing countries, a growing interest has emerged regarding their development impact along various dimensions. Surprisingly little attention has been given to the question of whether remittances promote financial development in recipient countries. Yet this issue is important because financial systems perform a number of key economic functions and their development has been shown to foster growth and reduce poverty. Furthermore, this question is relevant because many argue that banking remittances recipients will help multiply the development impact of remittances.

Introduction

Whether and how remittances might affect financial development is a priori unclear. The notion that remittances can lead to financial development

* The authors of this chapter received extensive support from Paola Granata for annexes A and B. The chapter is based on research conducted with Asli Demirgüç-Kunt, Chris Woodruff, and Ernesto López Córdova. We are grateful to Ernesto López Córdova, Jose de Luna Martínez, Manuel Orozco, and Anna Paulson for providing us data and information used in this chapter.

in developing countries is based on the concept that money transferred through financial institutions paves the way for recipients to demand and gain access to other financial products and services that they might not have otherwise (Orozco 2005). At the same time, providing remittances transfer services allows banks to "get to know" and reach out to unbanked recipients or recipients with limited financial intermediation. For example, remittances might have a positive impact on credit market development if, as individuals receive stable, sizeable transfers from abroad, banks become more willing to extend credit to remittances recipients. Moreover, even if increased bank lending to remittances recipients does not materialize, overall credit in the economy might increase if banks' loanable funds surge as a result of deposits linked to remittances flows.

Similarly, because remittances are typically lumpy, recipients might have a need for financial products that allow for the safe storage of these funds. In the case of households that receive their remittances through banks, the potential to learn about and to demand other financial products is even larger. On the other hand, because remittances can also help relax individuals' financing constraints, they might lead to a lower demand for credit and have a dampening effect on credit market development. Also, a rise in remittances might not translate into an increase in credit to the private sector if these flows are instead channeled to finance the government. Finally, remittances might not increase bank deposits if they are immediately consumed or if remittances recipients distrust financial institutions and prefer other ways of saving these flows.

Recent accounts of financial institutions' attempts to "bank" remittances recipients—by lowering remittances fees and offering specially designed products—suggest that financial institutions perceive the likely impact of remittances on financial development to be positive.[1] However, empirical research on the impact of remittances on financial development is largely lacking. One exception is a recently completed study by Aggarwal, Demirgüç-Kunt, and Martínez Pería (2006). Using balance of payments (BOP) statistics for over 90 countries during the period 1975–2003, the study uncovers a positive relationship between remittances and financial development. However, this study looks at all developing countries combined and does not test whether this relationship holds across regions and, in particular, for Latin America and the Caribbean (LAC).

This chapter investigates the association between remittances and financial development for Latin American countries both at the macro and micro levels. At the macro level, using the data and empirical approach pursued by Aggarwal, Demirgüç-Kunt, and Martínez Pería (2005), we compare the impact of remittances on financial development for countries in Latin America and outside the region. We try to correct for the potential endogeneity of remittances by using economic conditions in migrant-receiving (or remittances-source) countries as instruments. At the micro level, the chapter presents research on the association between remittances and the use of banking services in Latin America. With data from 19 household surveys for 11 Latin American countries, we test whether the proportion of households that use financial services is different between remittances recipients and nonrecipients in Latin America. Furthermore, we present results from detailed case studies on El Salvador (see Demirgüç-Kunt and Martínez Pería 2006) and Mexico (see Demirgüç-Kunt et al. 2007), two of the largest remittances recipients in the region. These case studies investigate the association between remittances and financial development more rigorously, attempting to correct for potential endogeneity biases. Finally, we complement the micro-level results with findings from interviews with officials of selected banks in the Latin American region (primarily from Colombia and Guatemala). These less rigorous case studies help to illustrate the increasing interest of banks in the remittances business, report on key contributing or limiting factors for the "bancarization" of recipients and senders, and showcase incipient efforts to develop specialized products for cross-selling of services to remittances recipients (see annexes A and B).

The findings from this chapter can be summarized as follows. The macro-level analysis suggests that remittances have a positive impact on the financial development of developing countries overall, but this effect is smaller for Latin American countries. The micro-level analysis reveals that while there is evidence that the likelihood of using deposit accounts is higher among remittances recipients, and deposit markets are more developed in areas where a larger percentage of the population receives remittances, no such effects are present thus far when it comes to bank loan use and credit market development.

Though more research is required to understand what is driving these results, the chapter endorses a number of measures to enhance the impact of remittances on financial development. First, the chapter highlights the importance of policies that facilitate migrants' access to banking services, such as initiatives that provide illegal migrants with valid forms of identification in migrant-recipient countries, promote financial literacy, reduce the costs of sending remittances through banks, and promote the overall use of formal financial institutions. Second, the chapter supports policies that allow financial institutions from Latin America to market their services directly to their diasporas. Third, the chapter underlines the need for governments in Latin America to promote greater outreach by reducing the regulatory burden of opening branches and by allowing banks to provide services through alternative means of delivery like mobile banking and by entering into partnership with nonfinancial firms that offer greater geographical coverage (e.g., post offices, retail stores, and cooperatives). Fourth, the chapter advocates policies that stimulate competition in the financial sector as a way to guarantee greater outreach to both remittances senders and recipients, at lower costs. Finally, the chapter argues that in order to foster a link from remittances flows to loan use and credit market development, issues such as weak creditor rights, inefficient contract enforcement mechanisms, lack of collateral, and government crowding out will have to be considered and tackled by governments as areas in need of reform.

The rest of the chapter is organized as follows. The next section explores the macro-level association between remittances and financial development for Latin America. The third section presents results from the micro-level analysis of the relationship between remittances and financial development. The final section concludes and offers some policy implications. Based on interviews of officials with selected banks in Colombia and Guatemala (complemented by other descriptive documents), annex A discusses the increasing interest of banks in the remittances business and reports key contributing or limiting factors for the "bancarization" of recipients and senders. Annex B describes incipient efforts from banks in Latin America to develop specialized products for cross-selling of services to remittances recipients.[2]

Macro-Level Analysis of the Association between Remittances and Financial Development

Basic Correlations

We begin our analysis of the association between remittances and financial development in Latin America by plotting country-level data on bank deposits and bank credit to the private sector,[3] along with balance of payments statistics on remittances over the period 1975–2003 (see figure 6.1). All three series are expressed as a share of GDP.

For 18 of 25 countries in the region for which we have data on financial development and remittances, we observe that both remittances and financial development have tended to move together in an increasing fashion.[4] This was particularly the case during the 1990s. On the other hand, in five countries—Belize, Dominica, St. Kitts and Nevis, St. Lucia, St. Vincent and the Grenadines—remittances and financial development appear to have moved in opposite directions, with financial development rising over the period and remittances falling consistently throughout the sample.

From the graphs, it is hard to discern a clear pattern between financial development and remittances in the cases of Argentina and Mexico. For these two countries, periods of positive association between these variables have alternated with periods where remittances increase as financial development collapses. This last type of episode—when remittances and financial development appear to be negatively correlated—seems to correspond to periods of financial banking crises in these countries. It is apparent that during such periods both countries underwent recessions, and remittances increased in response to crises, producing the negative association.

Figure 6.1 Remittances and Financial Development in Latin American Countries

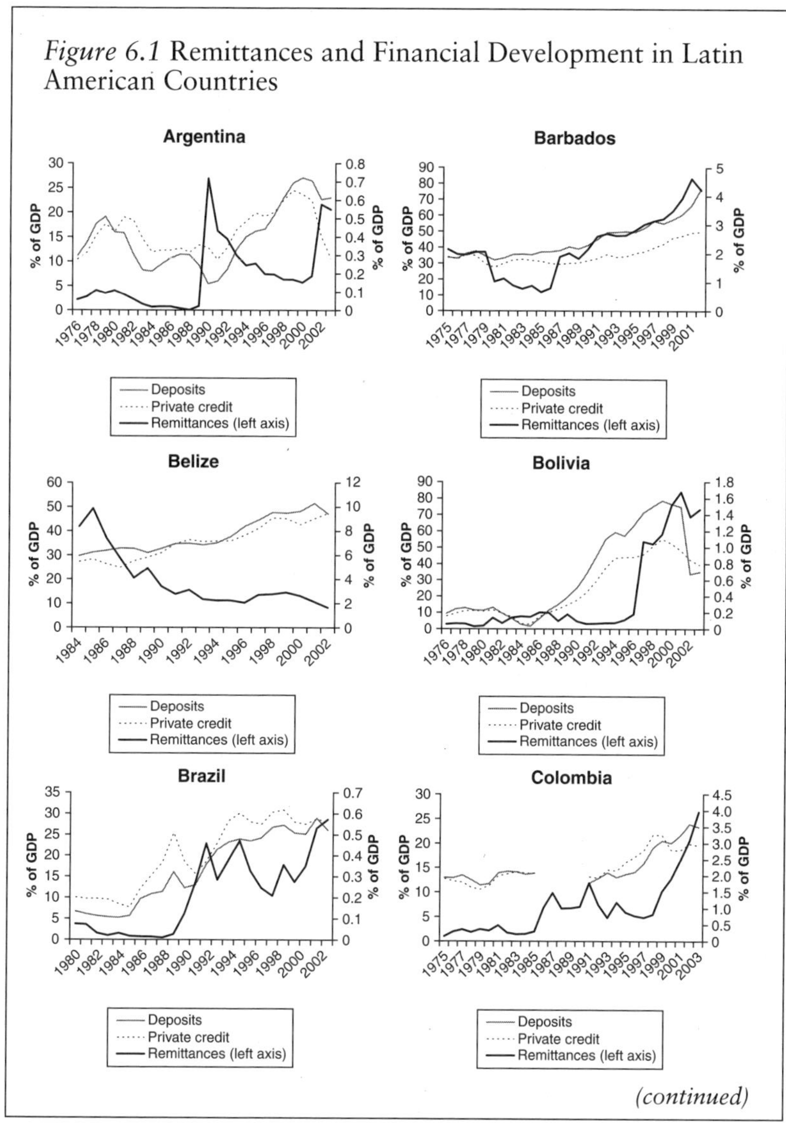

(continued)

Table 6.1 shows country-by-country correlations between remittances and each of the measures of financial development. These results largely confirm the patterns highlighted in figure 6.1. For Belize, Dominica, St. Kitts and Nevis, St. Lucia, and St. Vincent and the Grenadines, we observe a negative correlation between remittances and both measures of financial development. Consistent with what figure 6.1 shows, no clear macro-level relationship appears to exist between financial development and

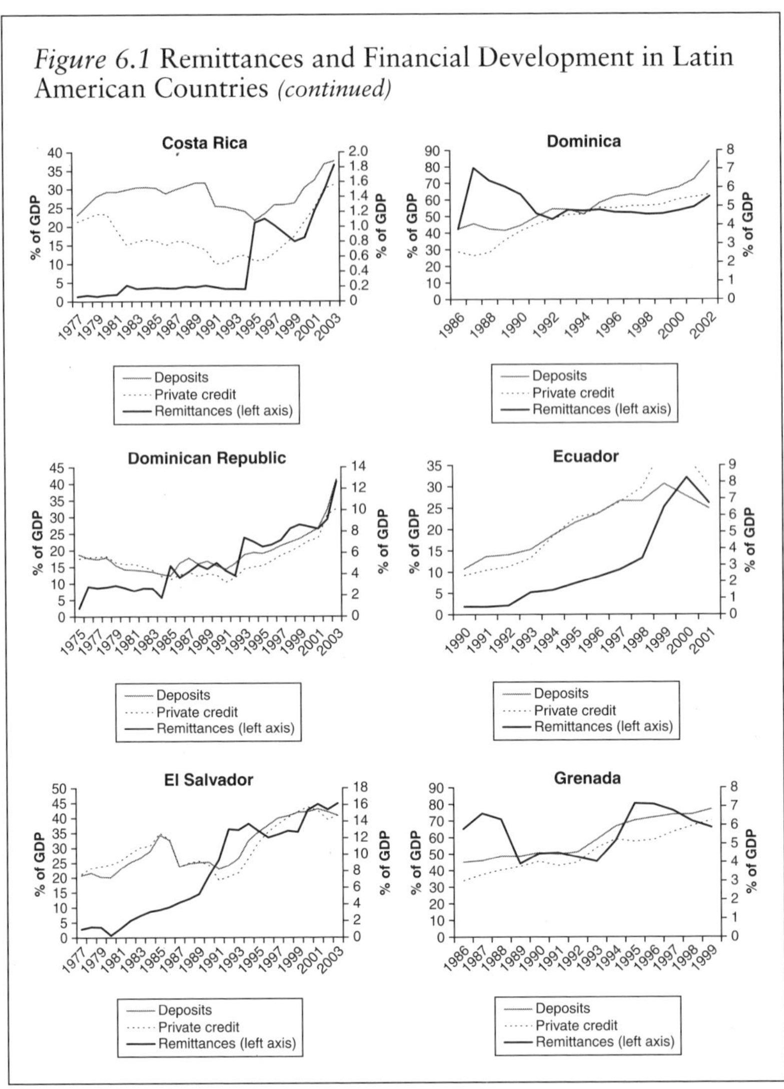

Figure 6.1 Remittances and Financial Development in Latin American Countries *(continued)*

remittances for Argentina and Mexico. Similar results are found for Haiti and Panama. On the other hand, for the remaining 16 countries, the correlations confirm the positive association between financial development and remittances.

Empirical Estimations

While figure 6.1 and table 6.1 are helpful in describing the association between remittances and financial development, a more rigorous empirical

Figure 6.1 Remittances and Financial Development in Latin American Countries *(continued)*

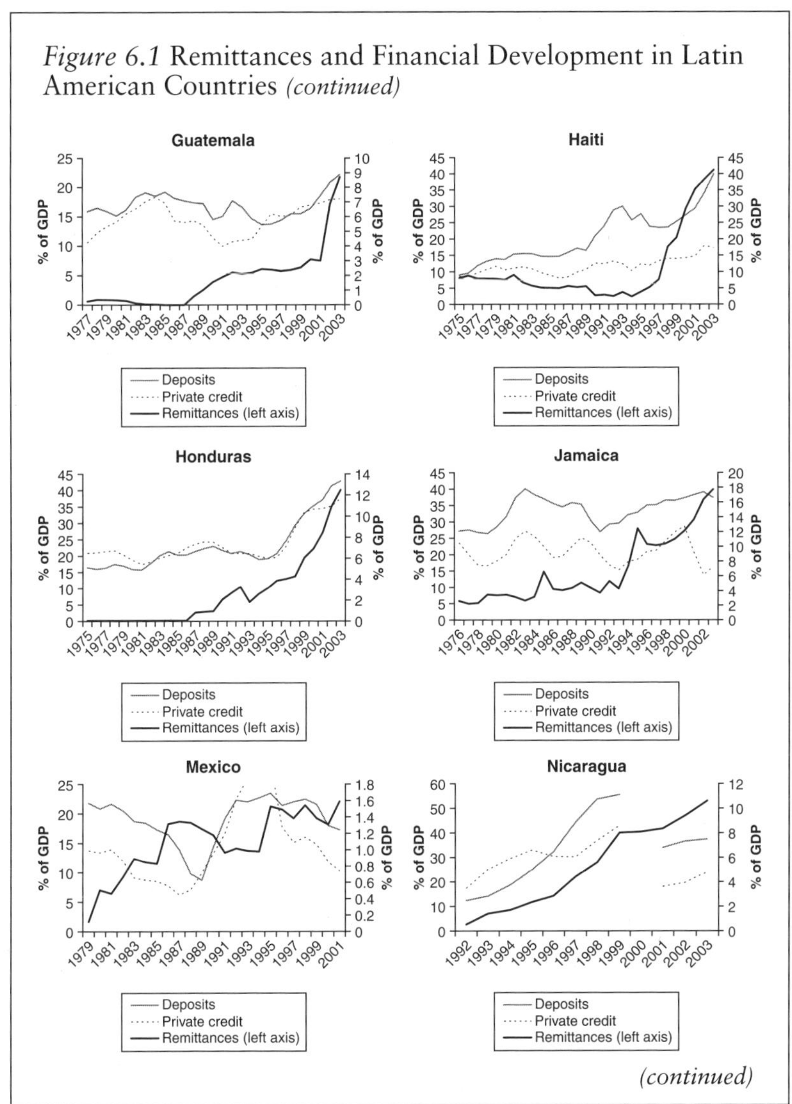

(continued)

approach is required to obtain a more definitive answer regarding the link between these variables. In particular, it is important to consider other factors that might affect both remittances and financial development and to try to correct for biases that might arise as a result of measurement error, reverse causation, and omitted country characteristics.

We empirically examine the relationship between financial development and remittances by regressing two measures of financial development—the share of bank deposits to GDP and the ratio of bank credit to the private

Figure 6.1 Remittances and Financial Development in Latin American Countries *(continued)*

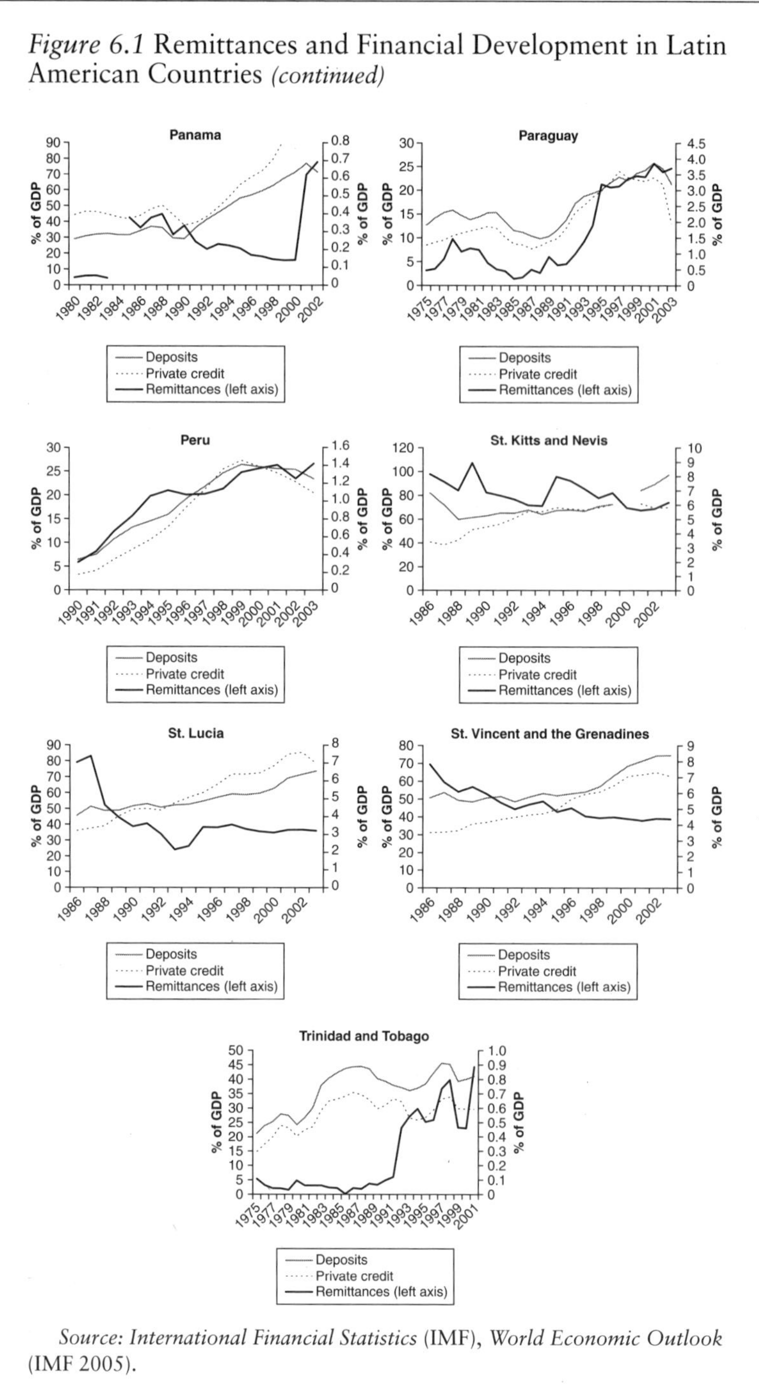

Source: International Financial Statistics (IMF), *World Economic Outlook* (IMF 2005).

sector to GDP—on the ratio of remittances to GDP, while controlling for a number of country characteristics. First, we analyze this relationship for all developing countries combined, allowing for individual country fixed effects. Second, we allow the relationship between remittances and financial development to be different for countries in LAC vis-à-vis other developing countries by including an interaction term between a dummy for LAC and the measures of financial development. Finally, and because figure 6.1 and table 6.1 suggest that there are differences across countries within LAC when it comes to the link between remittances and financial development, we estimate a third model that separates Latin American countries into three groups: countries for which a positive correlation was found between financial development and remittances (identified with the dummy LAC16), countries for which remittances and financial development seemed to be negatively correlated (captured by the LAC5 dummy), and economies for which no significant association was found (reflected in the LAC4 dummy). Finally, in each regression, we control for country size, the level of economic development (as measured by GDP per capita),

Table 6.1 Correlations between Remittances and Indicators of Financial Development

Country	*Remittances and bank deposits*	*Remittances and bank credit*
Argentina	0.0861	–0.0728
Barbados	0.8969***	0.8703***
Belize	–0.6227***	–0.7265***
Bolivia	0.6298***	0.7099***
Brazil	0.8279***	0.7390***
Colombia	0.8074***	0.6256***
Costa Rica	0.3151*	0.4129**
Dominica	–0.2699	–0.4757*
Dominican Republic	0.8415***	0.6779***
Ecuador	0.8279***	0.9183***
El Salvador	0.7791***	0.5756***
Grenada	0.4880*	0.3213
Guatemala	0.3501*	0.278
Haiti	–0.3318	0.1037
Honduras	0.9408***	0.8753***
Jamaica	0.5255***	–0.1291

(continued)

Table 6.1 Correlations between Remittances and Indicators of Financial Development *(continued)*

Country	*Remittances and bank deposits*	*Remittances and bank credit*
Mexico	−0.2216	0.0415
Nicaragua	0.7547***	−0.0628
Panama	0.3181	0.2859
Paraguay	0.9357***	0.8867***
Peru	0.9334***	0.8939***
St. Kitts and Nevis	−0.3610	−0.5200**
St. Lucia	−0.3952	−0.5752**
St. Vincent and the Grenadines	−0.6263***	−0.8606***
Trinidad and Tobago	0.3808**	0.2113

Source: Authors' calculations using data from the following sources:
– Balance of Payments Statistics (IMF). Data reported in WEO (2005)—for remittances
– International Financial Statistics (IMF)—for credit and deposits

Note: The table reports pairwise correlation coefficients between remittances (as a share of GDP) and two indicators of financial development, for the period 1975–2003. *, **, and *** denote significance at 10, 5, and 1 percent, respectively. Countries shaded in dark grey are those for which there appears to be no link between remittances and financial development. Countries shaded in light grey are those for which the correlation between remittances and financial development is mostly negative. The countries that are not shaded are those for which the correlation between remittances and financial development is positive.

the inflation rate, capital and current account openness, and individual country fixed effects.[5]

An important complication in empirically studying the impact of remittances on financial development is the potential for endogeneity biases as a result of measurement error, reverse causation, and omitted variables. Officially recorded remittances are known to be measured with error. In a recent paper based on a survey of central banks, De Luna Martinez (2005) reports that balance of payments statistics produced by developing countries often neglect remittances received via money transfer operators and almost always exclude those transferred via informal means such as hawala operators, friends, and family members.[6] Furthermore, estimates of the size of informal remittances range from 20 percent to 200 percent of official balance of payments statistics, suggesting that the room for measurement error is very large (Freund and Spatafora 2005).

The possibility that remittances affect financial development, giving rise to estimation biases due to reverse causality, is also justified. Better financial development might lead to larger measured remittances, either because financial development enables remittances flows, or because a larger percentage of remittances are measured when those remittances are channeled through formal financial institutions. In addition, financial development might lower the cost of transmitting remittances, leading to an increase in such flows. Finally, omitted factors can explain both the evolution of remittances and financial development, also leading to biases in the estimated impact of remittances on financial development.

To deal with endogeneity biases, following the approach pursued by Aggarwal, Demirgüç-Kunt, and Martínez Pería (2006), we present instrumental variable (IV) estimations where we use economic conditions—GDP per capita, real GDP growth, and the unemployment rate—in the top remittances-source countries (i.e., the countries from which migrants send money) as instruments for the remittances flows received by the countries in our sample. Arguably, economic conditions in the remittances-source countries are likely to affect the volume of remittances flows that migrants are able to send, but are not expected to affect financial development in the remittances-receiving countries in ways other than through their impact on remittances or through the effect on other variables we already control for, such as exports or capital flows. Because bilateral remittances data are largely unavailable, we identify the top remittances-source countries for each country in our sample, using bilateral migration data from the OECD's *Database on Immigrants and Expatriates*. This data set identifies the top five OECD countries that receive the most migrants from each remittances-recipient country. Here we assume that these OECD countries receive the bulk of the migrants from the countries in our sample and account for the majority of the remittances flows sent to the countries in our sample. We construct three instruments by multiplying, respectively, the GDP per capita, the real GDP growth, and the unemployment rate in each of the top five remittances-source countries by the share of migration to each of these five OECD countries.[7]

Results from IV estimations are presented in table 6.2. The estimations include fixed effects and time dummies to mitigate concerns about omitted variables. When we consider the impact of remittances on financial development for all developing countries combined (i.e., without distinguishing Latin American countries from others), we find that remittances have a positive and significant impact on both bank deposits and bank credit. In particular, a 1 percentage point increase in the share of remittances to GDP results in approximately a 5 percentage point rise in bank deposits and credit to GDP. However, this effect is smaller for Latin American countries, where a 1 percentage point rise in remittances leads to at most a 4 percentage point increase in deposits and credit to GDP.[8] Among Latin American countries, we find that remittances have a positive

Table 6.2 Panel Estimates of the Impact of Remittances on Financial Development with Interactions for Different Latin American Country Groupings

	Bank deposits to GDP			*Bank credit to GDP*		
Remittances to GDP	5.244	16.703	15.367	5.055	14.556	13.074
	[5.29]***	[2.31]**	[2.39]**	[5.33]***	[2.34]**	[2.42]**
LAC × remittances to GDP		−12.809			−10.339	
		[1.98]**			[1.86]*	
LAC16 × remittances to GDP			−12.233			−9.618
			[2.08]**			[1.95]*
LAC5 × remittances to GDP			−28.898			−27.900
			[1.97]**			[2.22]**
LAC4 × remittances to GDP			−13.251			−10.599
			[2.27]**			[2.17]**
Log of GDP	30.293	49.860	42.388	35.086	52.418	44.650
	[4.41]***	[2.41]**	[2.33]**	[5.30]***	[2.88]***	[2.88]***
GDP per capita	5.457	6.507	6.038	6.652	7.480	6.940
	[2.61]***	[1.55]	[1.54]	[3.33]***	[2.01]**	[2.06]**
Inflation	−0.002	−0.002	−0.002	−0.002	−0.001	−0.001
	[2.54]**	[1.19]	[1.27]	[1.69]*	[0.84]	[0.92]
Dual exchange rate	0.562	−0.091	−0.484	−1.767	−2.218	−2.658
	[0.35]	[0.03]	[0.16]	[1.16]	[0.79]	[1.03]
Other flows to GDP	−0.022	−0.087	−0.076	−0.014	−0.065	−0.054
	[0.60]	[1.02]	[0.99]	[0.39]	[0.89]	[0.82]

(continued)

Table 6.2 Panel Estimates of the Impact of Remittances on Financial Development with Interactions for Different Latin American Country Groupings *(continued)*

	Bank deposits to GDP			*Bank credit to GDP*		
Exports to GDP	0.055	−0.135	−0.104	−0.069	−0.227	−0.192
	[0.84]	[0.78]	[0.67]	[1.11]	[1.49]	[1.44]
Remittances in LAC		3.894			4.217	
H0: Remittances for LAC = 0		5.51			8.23	
p-value		0.02			0.00	
Remittances LAC16			3.134			3.456
H0: Remittances for LAC16 = 0			3.190			5.210
p-value			0.070			0.020
Remittances LAC5			−13.531			−14.826
H0: Remittances for LAC5 = 0			1.220			1.980
p-value			0.270			0.160
Remittances LAC4			2.116			2.475
H0: Remittances for LAC4 = 0			2.710			5.030
p-value			0.100			0.030
Observations	1,150	1,150	1,150	1,143	1,143	1,143
Country dummies	Yes	Yes	Yes	Yes	Yes	Yes
Time dummies	Yes	Yes	Yes	Yes	Yes	Yes

(continued)

Table 6.2 Panel Estimates of the Impact of Remittances on Financial Development with Interactions for Different Latin American Country Groupings *(continued)*

	Bank deposits to GDP			*Bank credit to GDP*		
Sargan test of overidentifying restrictions	0.18	0.52	3.08	2.54	0.32	3.47
p-value for Sargan test	0.91	0.97	0.93	0.28	0.99	0.90

Sources: Authors' calculations using data from the following sources:

Variable name	*Source*
Remittances to GDP	Balance of Payments Statistics (IMF); (IMF 2005)
Bank credit to GDP	*International Financial Statistics* (IMF)
Bank deposit to GDP	*International Financial Statistics* (IMF)
GDP per capita (World Bank)	World Bank 2005b
Log of GDP	World Bank 2005b
Inflation	World Bank 2005b
Dual exchange rate	*Annual Report on Exchange Arrangement and Exchange Restrictions* (IMF)

Note: Economic conditions in the remittances-source countries are used as instrument for remittances.

The regression equation estimated is of the form $FD_{i,t} = \delta_1 Rem_{i,t} + \delta_2 Rem_{i,t} \times LACDs + \delta_3' X_{i,t} + \alpha_i + u_{i,t}$ where *FD* refers to financial development measured as the ratio of bank deposits and, separately, bank credit to GDP. *Remittances to GDP* is the share of remittances to GDP. *LACDs* is either one or a combination of the following dummy variables: LAC equals 1 for all 25 Latin American countries in our sample, LAC16 is 1 for the countries in Latin America for which the correlation between remittances and financial development was found to be positive, LAC5 is 1 for countries in the region for which the correlation between remittances and financial development was found to be negative, and LAC4 is 1 for countries in the region for which the correlation between remittances and financial development was found to be insignificant. *X* is a matrix of controls including the following: *GDP per capita*, measured in constant dollars; *log of GDP*, stated in constant dollars; inflation, defined as the percentage change in the GDP deflator; *dual exchange rates*, which is a dummy capturing periods when multiple exchange rates were in effect; *other flows to GDP*, defined as foreign direct investment + non-FDI private inflows + aid to GDP; and *exports to GDP* is the ratio of total exports to GDP. GDP per capita, real GDP growth, and unemployment rates in remittances-source countries weighted by migration are used as instruments. Time dummies and fixed effects are included but not shown. Absolute value of *t* statistics in brackets, *, **, and *** denote significance at 10, 5, and 1 percent.

impact on credit and deposits among LAC16 and LAC4 countries, but no significant effect among LAC5 countries. Among LAC16 countries, a 1 percentage point increase in remittances results in approximately a 3 percentage point rise in bank deposit or credit, while for LAC4 countries, this effect is closer to 2 percentage points.

In sum, all the estimations presented so far indicate that remittances have a positive impact on financial development, but the effect is smaller for Latin American countries relative to other developing economies. What explains this finding? This is a hard question to tackle and one for which a definitive answer is not possible given the data available. Nevertheless, below we discuss some possible explanations.

First, the impact of remittances on financial development might be smaller for Latin American countries if remittances recipients in these countries relative to recipients in other countries are generally less likely to use financial institutions. This could be because of greater distrust of banks in LAC. Though there is no formal way of testing this hypothesis, the fact that crises have been more recurrent and severe in Latin America (as shown in table 6.3) is consistent with this possibility.[9] Also, IDB (2006b) indicates that a very small percentage of the remittances paid by banks actually enter the financial system through existing or new accounts, with banks thus operating primarily as payment agents.[10]

Second, the impact of remittances on financial development in Latin America might be smaller if remittances recipients in these countries are less likely to receive remittances via banks. Presumably, in countries where remittances are more frequently received via banks, recipients are more likely to open bank accounts and use other financial services. Also, in countries where banks play a large role in the remittances business, banks are in a better position to learn about remittances recipients and are more likely to seek them out as clients for other products. While good data for evaluating this possibility is lacking, statistics obtained from Osili and Paulson (2004) on the percentage of migrants in the United States who have bank accounts are consistent with this speculation. Their numbers, shown in table 6.3, indicate that Latin American migrants residing in the United States are less likely to have bank accounts when compared to migrants from other regions. One possible explanation might be related to the fact that migrants from Latin America tend to be less educated, as shown in chapter 2. Overall, the lower usage of bank accounts by migrants in the United States is noteworthy because it suggests that Latin American migrants are less likely to send money back home through direct deposits in banks. Recent surveys of remittances senders performed by the IDB indicate that banks account for only 7 percent of all remittances sent to Latin America, compared to 78 percent for money transfer operators and 11 percent for transfers made through people traveling to home countries (see chapter 9).

Third, remittances might not spur as much deposit or credit growth in Latin America if access to physical banking outlets is more limited in this

Table 6.3 Factors that Might Affect the Impact of Remittances on Financial Development

	Latin America	*Europe and Central Asia*	*East Asia and the Pacific*	*South Asia*	*Middle East and North Africa*	*Sub-Saharan Africa*
Use of banking services by migrants in the U.S.						
% migrants with a savings account in the U.S.[a]	30.0	38.0	47.9	48.4	33.1	62.6
Crises frequency and severity						
Episodes per number of countries[b]	0.8	0.9	0.4	0.4	0.4	0.8
Average fiscal costs of crises (% of GDP)[b]	20.1	8.1	16.7	–	–	12.5
Average duration of crises episodes (years)[c]	3.5	1.9	4.2	–	–	1.5
Average output loss (% of GDP)[c]	20.7	6.5	22.4	–	–	3.3
Physical bank presence						
Branches per 1,000 square km[d]	4.78	7.46	15.51	19.98	33.78	6.28
Number of branches per 100,000 people[d]	9.31	8.57	6.82	4.45	9.46	2.89
ATMs per 1,000 square km[d]	10.29	16.08	71.59	3.17	50.81	14.28
Number of ATMs per 100,000 people[d]	18.96	19.89	21.42	1.08	12.49	6.68
Cost of using banking services						
Fees associated with checking accounts[e] (as a percentage of GDP per capita)	0.90	0.20	0	5.50	0.46	10.40
Fees associated with savings accounts[e] (as a percentage of GDP per capita)	0.57	0.05	0.05	3.04	0	1.77

(continued)

Table 6.3 Factors that Might Affect the Impact of Remittances on Financial Development *(continued)*

	Latin America	*Europe and Central Asia*	*East Asia and the Pacific*	*South Asia*	*Middle East and North Africa*	*Sub-Saharan Africa*
Average fees on loans[e]						
(as a percentage of GDP per capita)	1.62	1.23	1.30	4.54	0.80	1.30
Legal rights and contract enforcement						
Legal Rights Index[f]	3.8	5.6	5.3	3.8	4.1	4.4
Time to enforce contracts (days)[f]	461.3	393.0	406.8	385.5	432.1	438.5

Sources: a. Osili and Paulson (2005); b. Caprio and Klingebiel (2003); c. Honohan and Klingebiel (2003); d. Beck, Demirgüç-Kunt, and Martínez Pería (2005); e. Beck, Demirgüç-Kunt, and Martínez Pería (2006); f. Doing Business: Legal Rights Index, which reflects the legal rights of borrowers and lenders and measures the degree to which collateral and bankruptcy laws facilitate lending. The index ranges from 0 to 10, with higher scores indicating that collateral and bankruptcy laws are better designed to expand access to credit. Time to enforce contracts measures the efficiency of the judicial (or administrative) system in the collection of overdue debt. The time required for dispute resolution is recorded in calendar days, counted from the moment the plaintiff files the lawsuit in court until settlement or payment.

Note: – = not available. ATM = automated teller machine.

region than in other countries. Table 6.3 shows data reported in Beck, Demirgüç-Kunt, and Martínez Pería (2005) on the average number of branches and ATMs per square kilometer and per 100,000 inhabitants across regions. While the presence of physical banking outlets per capita is not consistently lower for Latin American countries relative to other regions, there is some evidence that geographic penetration is low in Latin America. In particular, the number of branches per area is the lowest among all regions, suggesting that perhaps distance to the nearest branch is an obstacle for remittances recipients to demand and use financial services in Latin America.

Fourth, the impact of remittances on financial development in Latin America might be smaller than that observed for other countries if the costs of banking are larger in the region. Recently collected data from Beck, Demirgüç-Kunt, and Martínez Pería (2006) suggest that the costs of maintaining a bank account and the fees associated with loans are higher in Latin America than in most countries, with the exception of some in South Asia and Sub-Saharan Africa.

Finally, even if the supply of loanable funds increases with remittances, credit might not rise in Latin America due to weaker creditor protection and poorer contract enforcement. Legal rights rankings and statistics on the number of days to enforce a contract from the World Bank's *Doing Business* (2005a) data set shown in table 6.3 reveal that Latin America ranks below all other regions along these dimensions.

The data presented in table 6.3 offer some support for the validity of the factors discussed above in explaining why remittances might have a smaller impact on financial development in Latin America vis-à-vis other regions. However, further research is required to validate this tentative evidence and to establish the degree to which each of these factors is important.

Micro-Level Analysis of the Association between Remittances and Financial Development

While it is useful to investigate the relationship between remittances and financial development using macro-level data, cross-country analyses have important limitations. In what follows, we use household-level survey data to investigate the association between remittances and financial development. Here we equate financial development with greater use of financial services. First, we compare some simple statistics on the proportion of households with deposit accounts and loans among remittances recipients and nonrecipients in Latin America. Second, we look deeper into the link between remittances and the use of financial services in the region, and report results from case studies on El Salvador and Mexico. Both countries are among the largest recipients of remittances in Latin America and the data available in both cases is detailed enough to allow us to attempt to correct for biases resulting from omitted variables and reverse causation.

Evidence from Household-Level Tests

Using household surveys for 11 Latin American countries—Bolivia, the Dominican Republic, Ecuador, El Salvador, Guatemala, Haiti, Honduras, Jamaica, Nicaragua, Peru, and Suriname—we investigate whether the use of financial services differs between households that receive remittances and those that do not. In particular, we examine the proportion of households that have a deposit account and the share of those that have outstanding bank credit. For comparison, we also report on the share of households with nonbank credit among remittances recipients and nonrecipients.

Table 6.4 shows summary statistics for a total of 19 surveys conducted in the 11 countries mentioned above. The proportion of households with bank accounts for remittances recipients exceeds that for nonrecipients in 12 of the 14 surveys for which deposit information is available. However, these differences are statistically significant in only six surveys and five countries.[11] For the proportion of households that receive credit, we find that ratios are higher among remittances recipients in 9 of 16 surveys. Differences are statistically significant in the right direction in only three cases. Finally, the proportion of remittances-recipient households with credit outstanding from nonbank sources exceeds that for nonrecipients in 7 of the 13 surveys. However, these differences are only significant in the right direction in one case.

All in all, household-level data provides some preliminary evidence consistent with the hypothesis that the use of financial services is more prevalent among remittances-recipient households. This is particularly the case for deposit holdings and less so for credit. However, this evidence needs to be taken with a grain of salt for at least two important reasons. First, the tests conducted do not control for other household characteristics that might account for differences in the use of financial services. Second, these simple statistics suggest a correlation between remittances and the use of financial services, but are in no way proof of causality. Hence, to complement the results reported above we present evidence from case studies involving two of the largest remittances recipients in Latin America, El Salvador and Mexico. In both cases, IV estimations are reported to try to tackle the concern that remittances might be endogenous.

Evidence from Two Case Studies: El Salvador and Mexico

El Salvador. El Salvador is Latin America's fifth-largest recipient of remittances in dollar terms and the third largest as a share of GDP. During the last decade, remittances have averaged almost US$1.4 billion annually, or 14 percent of GDP. El Salvador is also among the most financially developed countries in the region. In 2003, deposits and private bank credit in this country reached 42 percent and 39 percent of GDP, respectively.

Table 6.4 Testing for Differences in the Use of Banking Services by Remittances Recipients and Nonrecipients

Country	Year	Households with bank deposits (%)	Households with bank credit (%)	Households with nonbanking credit (%)	Households receiving remittances (%)	Number of households in survey	Bank deposits: Nonrecipients (%)	Bank deposits: Recipients (%)	Bank deposits: P-value test of differences
Bolivia	2000	9.92	5.47	5.60	3.38	4,994	9.81	13.01	0.319
	2001	—	2.44	17.10	5.43	5,999	—	—	—
	2002	—	2.15	14.90	3.43	5,746	—	—	—
Dominican Republic	1996	—	4.94	—	19.51	5,548	—	—	—
	1997	—	4.64	—	13.44	3,757	—	—	—
	2004	23.46	13.23	12.00	21.57	9,642	19.92	36.35	0.000***
Ecuador	2003	—	12.87	—	6.42	18,959	—	—	—
El Salvador	1995	5.83	11.25	10.43	15.03	738	4.96	9.35	0.139
	1997	14.13	6.58	26.32	13.48	623	13.54	17.86	0.333
	1999	24.57	3.01	23.67	22.83	697	22.70	31.01	0.044**
	2001	24.64	2.03	37.97	26.74	690	19.44	39.13	0.000***
Guatemala	2000	15.43	2.80	8.28	3.41	7,276	14.89	30.70	0.001***
Honduras	2003	—	—	—	—	—	16.00	34.00	—
Haiti	2001	11.74	0.05	9.03	25.25	7,147	7.48	24.60	0.000***
Jamaica	1997	67.82	9.59	86.45	30.85	2,029	65.23	73.59	0.000***
Nicaragua	2000	1.69	6.09	10.49	41.95	4,191	1.40	2.10	0.281
Peru	2001	2.13	—	—	26.86	16,515	2.21	1.89	0.34
	2002	1.68	—	—	28.41	18,598	1.69	1.66	0.92
Suriname	2001	17.32	19.95	6.17	10.73	410	16.67	22.73	0.365

(continued)

Table 6.4 Testing for Differences in the Use of Banking Services by Remittances Recipients and Nonrecipients *(continued)*

		Bank credit			Nonbanking credit		
Country	Year	Nonrecipients (%)	Recipients (%)	P-value test of differences	Nonrecipients (%)	Recipients (%)	P-value test of differences
Bolivia	2000	5.34	9.34	0.198	5.34	9.34	0.198
	2001	2.43	2.60	0.887	17.25	14.44	0.318
	2002	2.17	1.48	0.459	14.74	19.36	0.213
Dominican Republic	1996	4.86	5.24	0.607	—	—	—
	1997	4.33	6.63	0.058*	—	—	—
	2004	12.99	14.13	0.171	12.36	10.67	0.036**
Ecuador	2003	12.71	15.25	0.076*	—	—	—
El Salvador	1995	10.41	14.95	0.218	9.91	12.24	0.435
	1997	6.68	5.95	0.796	27.13	23.26	0.361
	1999	3.18	1.90	0.334	22.75	25.82	0.411
	2001	2.38	1.09	0.207	38.36	36.79	0.694
Guatemala	2000	2.88	0.57	0.000***	8.25	9.30	0.722
Honduras	2003	—	—	—	—	—	—
Haiti	2001	0.06	0.04	0.727	9.86	6.58	0.000***
Jamaica	1997	10.53	7.67	0.098*	86.27	86.67	0.940
Nicaragua	2000	4.89	7.78	0.098*	4.89	7.78	0.098*
Peru	2001	—	—	—	—	—	—
	2002	—	—	—	—	—	—
Suriname	2001	19.56	23.26	0.589	6.37	4.55	0.595

Sources: Bolivia: Encuesta de Hogares—Programa MECOVI; Dominican Republic: Encuesta Nacional de Fuerza de Trabajo—CEPAL; Ecuador: Sistema Integrado de Encuestas de Hogares—ENEMDU; El Salvador: Encuesta a Familias Salvadoreñas—FUSADES; Guatemala: Encuesta Nacional sobre condiciones de vida—MECOVI; Honduras: Orozco and Fedewa (2005); Haiti: Living Condition Survey—IHSI/FAFO/PNUD; Jamaica: Jamaica Survey of Living Conditions; Nicaragua: Encuesta Nacional de Estadísticas y Censos INEC—Proyecto MECOVI; Peru: Encuesta Nacional de Hogares; and Suriname: Expenditure Household Survey - General Bureau of Statistics of Suriname.

Note: – = not available. The table shows tests of differences in the use of bank deposits, bank, and nonbank credit by remittances recipients and nonrecipients in 11 Latin American countries. *, **, and *** denote significance at 10, 5; and 1 percent, respectively.

In this section, we report results from an ongoing study by Demirgüç-Kunt and Martínez Pería (2006), which analyzes whether households that receive remittances are more likely to use financial services, using data from a nationally representative rural panel survey Fundación Salvadoreña para el Desarrollo Económico y Social (FUSADES).[12] This case study examines the effect of remittances on (i) the probability that a household has a bank deposit account, (ii) the likelihood that the household has an outstanding loan, and (iii) the probability that it has applied for a loan in a given period. Because all the dependent variables are discrete, three probit models are estimated, including household-level controls such as household income, educational level of the head of household, the number of rooms in the house, and a dummy for whether at least one member of the household is employed in agricultural activities.

Panel A in table 6.5 shows the results for the likelihood that a household has a bank account. These estimations provide evidence that households receiving remittances have a higher likelihood (between 13 percentage points and 14 percentage points higher) of owning a deposit account, regardless of which household characteristics are included as controls and independently of whether the results focus on households that appear in at least two or in all four years of the survey. Panel B presents the results for the likelihood of having outstanding debt. Across all estimations, the likelihood of having outstanding debt does not seem to be affected by whether households receive remittances.[13] Finally, panel C reports the results for the likelihood of applying for a bank loan in the year of the survey. Once again, the dummy for remittances recipients is never significant, which means that remittances recipients are as likely to apply for a loan as those who do not receive remittances.

The estimates reported so far on whether households that receive remittances are more likely to use financial services might be biased if relevant household characteristics are omitted, or if the likelihood that a household receives remittances is endogenous. To try to address these concerns, table 6.6 presents estimations including household fixed effects and, separately, instrumenting for remittances. Including household fixed effects should help mitigate the concern that the association between remittances and the use of banking services is driven by omitted household characteristics. However, because for many households there is no variation in their status as remittances recipients or as users of banking services, the number of observations when we include fixed effects is smaller, since those households for which there is no change are dropped from the estimations. Fixed effects estimations yield very similar results to those reported above. We find that remittances-recipient households are more likely than nonrecipients to have a bank account, but are no different when it comes to the likelihood of having outstanding debt or applying for a loan.

The IV estimations use the number of years migrants have resided abroad and the number of years squared (to allow for a nonlinear relationship

Table 6.5 Likelihood That Remittances Recipients Will Use Banking Services: Probit Estimations for El Salvador

	Panel A: Likelihood of having a bank account			
	Results for households surveyed two or more times		*Results for households surveyed four or more times*	
International remittances recipient	0.133 6.60***	0.147 6.91***	0.143 5.73***	0.142 4.98***
Household income		0.003		0.002
		4.93***		3.80***
Agricultural employment		0.018		0.027
		1.17		1.33
Rooms in household		0.041		0.040
		5.02***		3.79***
Household schooling		0.022		0.023
		9.30***		7.40***
Observations	2,497	2,396	1,700	1,452
	Panel B: Likelihood of having outstanding debt			
	Results for households surveyed two or more times		*Results for households surveyed four or more times*	
International remittances recipient	–0.004 0.25	0.002 0.16	0.006 0.30	0.011 0.53
Household income		0.000		0.000
		1.25		0.58
Agricultural employment		–0.009		–0.006
		0.71		0.36
Rooms in household		0.007		0.001
		1.10		0.14
Household schooling		0.005		0.007
		2.73***		2.71***
Observations	2,499	2,398	1,700	1,452

(continued)

Table 6.5 Likelihood That Remittances Recipients Will Use Banking Services: Probit Estimations for El Salvador *(continued)*

	Panel C: Likelihood of applying for a loan			
	Results for households surveyed two or more times		*Results for households surveyed four or more times*	
International remittances recipient	−0.015 0.94	−0.010 0.63	−0.002 0.10	−0.003 0.13
Household income		0.000 0.99		0.000 0.21
Agricultural employment		−0.012 0.95		−0.008 0.46
Rooms in household		0.003 0.50		0.000 0.02
Household schooling		0.006 3.00***		0.008 2.90***
Observations	2,499	2,398	1,700	1,452

Sources: Authors' calculations using data from the following sources: Encuesta a familias salvadoreñas, Fundación Salvadoreña para el Desarrollo Económico y Social (FUSADES).

Note: The table shows probit results for the likelihood that remittances recipients in El Salvador use banking services. Marginal effects are shown instead of coefficients. *, **, and *** denote significance at 10, 5, and 1 percent, respectively.

Table 6.6 Likelihood That Remittances Recipients Will Use Banking Services: Fixed Effects Probit and Instrumental Variables Probit Estimations for El Salvador

	Panel A: Likelihood of having a bank account			
	Fixed effect estimations		*Instrumental variables estimations*	
International remittances recipient	0.285 5.06***	0.274 4.62***	0.231 6.14***	0.234 5.91***
Household income		0.003 2.25**		0.003 4.95***
Agricultural employment		0.056 1.32		0.020 1.26
Rooms in household		0.042 1.59		0.041 4.87***
Household schooling		0.009 0.74		0.022 9.13***
Observations	905	852	2,460	2,361

(continued)

Table 6.6 Likelihood That Remittances Recipients Will Use Banking Services: Fixed Effects Probit and Instrumental Variables Probit Estimations for El Salvador *(continued)*

	Panel B: Likelihood of having outstanding bank debt			
	Fixed effect estimations		*Instrumental variables estimations*	
International remittances recipient	−0.056 0.83	−0.008 0.11	−0.010 0.39	−0.097 0.59
Household income		0.002		0.003
		1.28		1.20
Agricultural employment		0.033		−0.041
		0.66		0.58
Rooms in household		0.017		0.042
		0.50		1.07
Household schooling		−0.03		0.030
		1.96**		2.74***
Observations	653	603	2,462	2,363

	Panel C: Likelihood of applying for a bank loan			
	Fixed effect estimations		*Instrumental variables estimations*	
International remittances recipient	−0.071 1.08	−0.031 0.44	−0.039 1.41	−0.043 1.54
Household income		0.001		0.000
		1.07		0.87
Agricultural employment		0.035		−0.011
		0.74		0.82
Rooms in household		−0.008		0.004
		0.26		0.54
Household schooling		−0.009		0.006
		0.61		2.94***
Observations	719	662	2,462	2,363

Source: Authors' calculations using data from the following source: Encuesta a familias salvadoreñas, Fundación Salvadoreña para el Desarrollo Económicoy Social (FUSADES).

Note: The table shows fixed effects probit and instrumental variables probit results for the likelihood that remittances recipients in El Salvador use banking services. Marginal effects are shown instead of coefficients. *, **, and *** denote significance at 10, 5, and 1 percent, respectively.

between length of stay overseas and sending remittances) as instruments for the likelihood that a household receives remittances.[14] Results confirm our earlier findings that remittances-recipient households are more likely than nonrecipients to have a bank account, but the probability that recipient households apply for and have outstanding credit is not different for remittances-recipient and nonrecipient households.

Overall, the findings for El Salvador indicate that remittances recipients are more likely to open bank accounts relative to other individuals. However, when it comes to credit, we do not observe any differences in credit application and usage by remittances recipients and nonrecipients. Since the Salvadoran financial system is relatively deeper than that in other LAC countries, more research is needed to explore if there are other limitations to ease the typical constraints and broaden access to credit for segments of the population that have limited credit payment history and insufficient collateral, or if these constraints are different for remittances recipients.

Mexico. Mexico is Latin America's largest recipient of remittances in dollar terms, so the potential for remittances to impact financial development is perhaps largest in this country. Though remittances are 2 percent of GDP, they amount to approximately 10 percent of banking sector deposits and credit. Also, in recent years, both Mexican and foreign banks have taken steps to enter the remittances business and to cross-sell products to remittances senders and recipients, a move that, if successful, should be reflected in greater financial development.[15]

The case study for Mexico is based on ongoing work by Demirgüç-Kunt et al. (2006) analyzing the relationship among remittances, the use of financial services, and financial development, combining information from the 2000 Mexican Census with data from the Comisión Nacional Bancaria y de Valores (CNBV—National Commission of Banks and Securities). The study examines the impact of remittances on four measures of financial development across Mexican municipalities: (i) the amount of commercial bank deposits to GDP, (ii) the number of commercial bank deposit accounts per capita, (iii) the amount of commercial bank loans outstanding to GDP, and (iv) the number of commercial branches per capita. In all estimations, remittances are measured as the percentage of households in the municipality that receive remittances from abroad. Also, a number of municipal-level controls are included in the analysis, such as municipal GDP per capita, the rural or urban nature of the municipality, the level of education, and the degree of access to physical infrastructure (water and telephones).

Table 6.7 presents ordinary least squares (OLS) results for the impact of remittances on financial development and the use of financial services, controlling for municipal-level GDP per capita and for the percentage of the population in each municipality that lives in localities with fewer

Table 6.7 The Impact of Remittances on Bank Deposits, Branches, and Credit across Mexican Municipalities: OLS Estimations Clustered by State

Variable	*Deposits to GDP*	*Number of accounts per capita*	*Branches per capita*	*Credit to GDP*
Households receiving remittances	0.0026	1.8238	0.0081	0.0000
	[3.33]***	[2.96]***	[2.77]***	[0.02]
GDP per capita	0.0056	11.4587	0.0586	0.0029
	[3.03]***	[7.87]***	[9.35]***	[7.08]***
Rural localities	–0.0009	–0.7113	–0.003	–0.0001
	[4.01]***	[3.55]***	[3.23]***	[2.63]**
Constant	0.0652	35.9478	0.1346	0.0066
	[3.30]***	[2.20]**	[1.81]*	[1.59]
Observations	2,238	2,389	2,230	2,358
R-squared	0.21	0.26	0.33	0.18

Source: Authors' calculations using data from the following sources: INEGI, XII Censo General de Población y Vivienda 2000, Cuestionario Ampliado, Comisión Nacional Bancaria y de Valores, CONAPO 2001; López Córdova (2004).

Note: OLS estimates of the impact of the percentage of households receiving remittances on bank branches in Mexico. Robust t-statistics (in brackets) are shown from estimations where standard errors are clustered by Mexican state. *, **, and *** denote significance at 10, 5, and 1 percent, respectively.

than 2,500 people (so-called rural localities).[16] Estimations show that municipalities where a larger percentage of the population receives remittances also tend to have higher ratios of deposit accounts per capita, higher deposit amounts to GDP, and a higher number of branches per capita. Specifically, a one standard deviation increase in the share of households that receive remittances leads to, approximately, a 0.14 standard deviation change in the ratio of deposits per capita, a 0.20 standard deviation change in the share of deposits to GDP, and a 0.15 standard deviation change in the ratio of branches per capita. Contrary to these findings, there does not appear to be a significant association between remittances and credit to GDP across municipalities.

The estimations reported so far would be biased and inconsistent in the event that remittances are endogenous or there are unobserved municipal characteristics. To try to correct for this possibility, table 6.8 reports results from IV estimations. Two different variables are used as instruments: (i) short-run deviations in rainfall (measured as rainfall for 1999 minus the average historical rainfall for most of the 20th century relative to the standard deviation of rainfall during the last century); and (ii) the sum of the distance of each municipality to the railroad network in existence during the 1920s, plus the distance from that point to the U.S.-Mexico border. The rationale for including short-run deviations in rainfall lies in the fact that variations in rainfall can have a negative impact on households' income and increase the need for remittances. On the other hand, it is less likely that short-run shocks to municipal income will affect financial development directly and immediately. The sum of the distance to the border plus distance to the 1920s railroad is used as an instrument for remittances because previous studies have found that in large part, the migration patterns we observe today that give rise to remittances flows are driven by historical migration patterns that were themselves affected by the location of the railroad (see Woodruff and Zenteno 2001; Hanson and Woodruff 2003; McKenzie and Rapoport 2005; and López Córdova 2004, among others). By using distance as an instrument, the estimations are implicitly assuming that this variable does not affect financial development other than through its effects on remittances. Since it is possible that the establishment of the railroad or proximity to the United States may have fostered economic growth in some municipalities, causing them to be more financially developed today, we present estimations eliminating municipalities in close proximity to the railroad or the border—those within 40 or 50 kilometers.

IV results are shown in table 6.8.[17] In particular, we report results controlling both for GDP per capita and the urban/rural character of the municipality.[18] The IV results are generally consistent with what was reported above. In particular, the share of households that receive remittances has a positive impact on bank deposits (both in numbers and amounts) and bank branches across municipalities, but in two out of three specifications, it does not appear to influence the extent of credit market development—the exception being the specification without excluding municipalities close to the border or the railroad, for which the quality of the instruments based on distance to the railroad may be more questionable.

Conclusions and Policy Recommendations

Using both macro and micro data, this chapter investigated the impact of remittances on the development of the banking sector and the use of banking services. At the macro level, the results indicate that remittances have a positive impact on financial development (considering both deposit and credit services) in LAC, but the effect is lower than in other developing regions.

At the micro level, using data from household surveys for 11 countries, we find preliminary evidence consistent with the hypothesis that the use of financial services is more prevalent among remittances-recipient households, particularly for deposits. These results are verified in detailed case studies for El Salvador and Mexico in which we try to address concerns

Table 6.8 The Impact of Remittances on Bank Deposits, Branches, and Credit across Mexican Municipalities: Instrumental Variables Estimations

	Using distance and rain deviation as instruments (no exclusion on distance)				*Using distance and rain deviation as instruments (excluding municipalities where distance < 40 kilometers)*				*Using distance and rain deviation as instruments (excluding municipalities where distance < 50 kilometers)*			
	Deposits to GDP	*Accounts per capita*	*Branches per capita*	*Bank credit to GDP*	*Deposits to GDP*	*Accounts per capita*	*Branches per capita*	*Bank credit to GDP*	*Deposits to GDP*	*Accounts per capita*	*Branches per capita*	*Bank credit to GDP*
Households receiving remittances	0.0072	6.2966	0.0286	0.0007	0.0141	8.2249	0.039	0.0029	0.0133	7.6359	0.0375	0.0006
	[4.02]***	[3.52]***	[3.91]***	[1.87]*	[2.76]***	[3.76]***	[3.94]***	[1.23]	[2.70]***	[3.85]***	[3.94]***	[1.33]
GDP per capita	0.0057	12.0086	0.0604	0.0029	0.0011	11.4894	0.0553	0.0038	0.0014	11.0017	0.0561	0.0046
	[3.59]***	[10.09]***	[10.95]***	[8.04]***	[0.44]	[7.03]***	[7.80]***	[2.42]**	[0.55]	[8.00]***	[8.01]***	[3.19]***
Rural localities	–0.001	–0.8472	–0.0035	–0.0001	–0.001	–1.0371	–0.0043	–0.0002	–0.001	–0.9874	–0.0042	0
	[5.11]***	[4.87]***	[4.39]***	[3.28]***	[4.17]***	[4.93]***	[4.74]***	[0.91]	[4.22]***	[4.93]***	[4.61]***	[0.32]
Constant	0.042	11.119	0.0163	0.0029	0.0322	19.4692	0.0479	–0.0041	0.0317	20.7659	0.0448	–0.0053
	[1.72]*	[0.54]	[0.18]	[0.69]	[1.02]	[0.90]	[0.46]	[0.38]	[1.04]	[1.02]	[0.44]	[0.57]
Observations	2,000	2,140	1,993	2,108	2,006	2,149	2,001	2,112	1,998	2,141	1,995	2,105
Adjusted R-squared	0.08	0.13	0.18	0.14	–0.02	0.03	0.02	–0.02	–0.02	0.04	0.03	0.01
Craig Donald F-statistic	79.08	84.03	81.13	81.26	82.02	86.4	82.47	82.38	82.51	87.94	83.98	83.84
Hansen test of overidentifying restrictions	2.39	0.08	0.23	0.58	0.99	1.29	0.49	0.23	0.85	0.91	0.32	0.42
P-value	0.12	0.78	0.63	0.45	0.32	0.26	0.49	0.63	0.36	0.34	0.57	0.52

Source: Authors' calculations using data from the following sources: INEGI, XII Censo General de Población y Vivienda (2000), Cuestionario Ampliado, Comisión Nacional Bancaria y de Valores, CONAPO (2001); López Córdova (2004).

Note: Robust t-statistics are shown (in brackets) from estimations where standard errors are clustered by Mexican state. *, **, and *** denote significance at 10, 5, and 1 percent, respectively.

about endogeneity biases. For the case of El Salvador, the results indicate that remittances recipients are more likely—relative to other individuals—to open bank accounts, but are no different in terms of the probability of applying for loans and using credit. For the case of Mexico, results indicate that municipalities where a larger percentage of the population receives remittances also tend to have higher ratios of deposit accounts per capita, deposit amounts to GDP, and branches per capita, but do not show evidence of having higher ratios of credit to GDP.[19]

Though more research is required to further verify the findings in this chapter and better understand what drives them, the results available so far suggest some initial policy implications.[20] First, banks should step up their efforts to "bank" migrants because such efforts will increase the likelihood that migrants send their remittances through bank accounts. In the last couple of years, some Latin American banks have started to look into ways to enter the remittances origination market, including placing agencies in migrant-recipient countries (see annex A). In addition, U.S. banks and credit unions have made significant inroads in providing remittances and other services to migrants.[21] For this trend to continue, banks need to further facilitate access to their services by lowering costs and tailoring products to meet migrants' needs.[22]

Second, governments in migrant-recipient, remittances-sending countries, in partnership with those in Latin America, need to continue to work on programs to foster financial access for migrants. In this context, the ongoing collaboration between Mexico and the United States, as reflected in the *Matrícula Consular,* the Automated Clearing House (ACH) system, and the initiatives of the Institute for Mexicans Living Abroad, are good examples from which other governments can learn. The *Matrícula Consular*, an alternative form of identification for undocumented migrants endorsed by the U.S. Department of Treasury, now allows illegal Mexican migrants in the United States to apply for banking services. The ACH, established by the Federal Reserve Bank and the Mexican Central Bank, allows banks to originate credit payments by sending them to the Federal Reserve for processing via the same method used for domestic operations. Conceived as an attempt to reduce transaction costs for remittances sent via banks, this is also another form of fruitful collaboration, although its impact has not been as large as anticipated.[23] Finally, to promote financial literacy, the Mexican Foreign Ministry's Institute for Mexicans Living Abroad invites banks like Wells Fargo, Bank of America, and Citibank to discuss remittances and other services with hometown association leaders in the United States. In order to foster the use of banking services by migrants, efforts such as those undertaken by Mexico need to be embraced by more countries in the Latin American region.

Third, initiatives and efforts that directly link migrants with financial institutions from their home countries should be fostered to increase the impact of remittances on local financial development. In this sense, it is important that governments in recipient countries allow financial institutions to operate abroad and offer financial services to migrant communities, since such measures have been shown to increase the amount of remittances flowing into the domestic financial sector in other regions.[24]

Fourth, banks need to increase their efforts to "bank" remittances recipients in LAC. Orozco (2005) documents the strategies currently pursued by nine financial institutions in the region to attract remittances recipients, such as offering special promotions for opening accounts and training on how to use banking services. He finds that these efforts have resulted in one-fifth of recipients becoming bank clients. Clearly, more needs to be done. He points out that banks are most successful when they have a strong presence in both remittances-sending and recipient communities, and when they invest in community outreach and socially oriented product offerings.[25]

Fifth, governments should adopt policies that support efforts to convert remittances recipients into bank clients including: (i) minimizing the regulatory costs to banks of opening branches and other outlets to serve these communities; (ii) fostering greater outreach by allowing nontraditional methods of delivering banking services, such as mobile banking or correspondent arrangements with post offices, retailers, and cooperatives that are better positioned to serve recipient communities; (iii) promoting competition in the financial sector; and (iv) continuing to improve the collection and analysis of information on remittances flows and patterns. Among the measures to promote competition, governments should consider requiring more accurate information about the size and structure of the market to increase banks' interest in developing specialized products for remittances recipients; promoting more clarity in the pricing of remittances transfers (more than half of the remitters report they do not know why their beneficiaries receive less money than they had estimated—see chapter 9 for more details on the opacity of fee structures); and fostering partnerships between formal financial institutions and other financial intermediaries (e.g., microfinance institutions and NGOs) that may have broader outreach to poorer (but bankable) segments of remittances recipients.

While getting remittances recipients to become bank depositors is not simple, channeling remittances flows to increase credit in the economy and among remittances recipients is likely to be harder. Even diagnosing why this is not happening at the moment is not easy.[26] One potential problem may be lack of demand. Remittances recipients may not demand credit because the flows they receive from their relatives overseas relax their credit constraints and substitute for credit. Also, remittances recipients might not have viable productive projects to pursue, or the recipients may be supported by third parties. However, the results presented in this chapter for El Salvador do not support the hypothesis that the demand for credit is lower among remittances recipients. Nor do they suggest that remittances recipients are any different when it comes to obtaining credit.

Supply-side factors, such as banks' insufficient understanding of the credit needs of recipients, and collateral requirements that remittances recipients cannot satisfy, might also be affecting why remittances recipients do not seem to enjoy more access to credit. Also, there may be prudential and regulatory obstacles hindering the use of remittances flows as collateral. To the extent that remittances can increasingly be used to compensate for insufficient credit history or even substitute for traditional types of collateral, the more likely it is that banks will increasingly broaden access to credit to recipients. Furthermore, access to information on the nonbank credit history of remittances recipients might also be a limiting factor on the supply side. Given some anecdotal evidence that many remittances recipients have access to credit from informal sources, governments and banks could support the collection of information on remittances payments and nonbank credit, and enhance the capacity of credit bureaus to consider such information in assessing a potential borrower's credit history. One way or another, more detailed surveys of remittances recipients should be undertaken to better understand why credit does not seem to be increasing as a result of remittances, and to provide more specific policy recommendations.

Finally, institutional and macroeconomic factors might also help explain why credit to remittances recipients in Latin American is not growing. Issues such as weak creditor rights, inefficient contract enforcement mechanisms, crowding out as a result of the government demand for credit due to fiscal pressures, and lingering effects of repeated crises in LAC may also need to be considered and tackled by governments seeking to leverage the impact of remittances on financial development.

Annex A: Remittances and Bancarization—The Experiences of Colombia and Guatemala

This descriptive annex presents more details on banking practices related to remittances in two cases, Colombia and Guatemala,[27] based on ad hoc surveys and follow-up interviews carried out during April and May 2006 (World Bank 2006c) at selected banks that have an important participation in the remittances market in each country.[28] Other descriptive studies have also been incorporated. The objective is to complement the analytical findings of the chapter to: (i) illustrate the increasing interest of banks in the remittances market both on the deposit side and, more recently, on the asset side; (ii) identify potential limitations reported by banks for the development of the banking sector and banking services based on remittances; and (iii) help better understand possible alternatives for overcoming these limitations in the near future.

The Colombian Experience

Survey responses and interviews with bank representatives reflect the increased interest and ongoing efforts to further engage in the remittances market, largely based on the size of the market and perceived potential for banking profitable clients. They report that as a result of these recent efforts, remittances recipients are increasingly opening bank deposit accounts, but banks have been less effective thus far at converting remitters into clients, or at increasing credit (for both remitters and recipients).

In general, a first set of obstacles for deepening the banking system through remittances is related to the nonpredominant share of banks in the remittances distribution market.[29] There are several factors that help explain banks' still secondary role in this market, including: (i) their relatively recent entrance in the market;[30] (ii) image disadvantages as compared with their main competitors, foreign exchange houses;[31] (iii) exclusivity agreements with international counterparts (mostly money transfer operators) that have a given (sometimes small) percentage of the remittances origination market and commit banks not to pay remittances of other businesses; (iv) slower customer service for remittances recipients compared to foreign exchange houses; and (v) to a lesser extent, in the case of smaller banks, inadequate locations of branches for targeting remittances recipients.[32]

More recently, the ability of banks to ease some of these limitations and to develop new competitive advantages and exploit existing ones have allowed them to gain market share in the last few years.[33] Banks have improved their image in the remittances market as their customers have had positive experiences with their services; banks also have signed agreements with nonfinancial businesses with a wide geographic penetration; and, in some cases, banks have provided their clients with ATM cards to minimize payment waiting time. Additionally, banks report that they have gained a competitive edge by offering financial services specially tailored to the market[34] and decreasing exchange rate spreads, as well as exploiting existing advantages such as offering greater security[35] and, for larger banks, a wide branch distribution network.

A second set of reported obstacles is directly related to the actual broadening of access to credit for recipients and senders. These include limitations that are more specific to the remittances market and others that are related to the difficulty in accessing credit, but remittances might be used to help ease these credit constraints. One constraint for the remittances market is the competition from nonsupervised retail businesses as the reported preference for durable consumption goods seems to have provided an opportunity for retailers to provide direct credit. Banks state that the interest rate ceilings they face by regulation have given an advantage to retailers, as the latter are not subject to these, and can compensate for higher risks by charging higher interest rates.[36]

Typical limitations in the credit market that are also relevant in the remittances market include: lack of information (insufficient credit history and payment behavior), inadequate risk and scoring models, low demand, and little collateral. Banks report constraints from low demand for credit because they perceive remittances are mainly used to cover basic needs and purchase durable consumption goods.[37] Although the predominance of consumption can limit credit demand, residual remittances available for savings and investment (and paying off credit) may still be significant compared with the savings capacity of nonrecipient households.[38]

The problem of insufficient collateral in the case of remittances recipients emerges because many of them are unemployed and can only offer these transfers as collateral. In principle, remittances can serve as collateral since they can occur periodically over a sustained period of time and be sufficient to cover credit payments. Although interviewed bank officials were not yet offering credit by taking remittances as guarantee of payment, there are incipient efforts for change as some are tracking remittances and planning on using this information to offer credit to recipients.

Finally, a third group of identified obstacles for developing the financial sector are those related to senders. Banks have found several difficulties converting immigrants into clients and, more specifically, for being able to offer them credit. First, banks found that these activities require building a new infrastructure in external markets with business partners that can absorb a sizable percentage of profits.[39] Also, increased competition for the distribution of remittances and the bancarization of recipients have led banks to focus their energy and resources on the domestic market.

Notwithstanding the limitations to convert senders into clients, banks continue to perceive this group as an attractive business opportunity as many of them have not yet been "bancarized" by foreign competitors and are reported to be interested in saving, investing in their home country, and making sure that their transfers serve to lift the living standards of their families by granting them access to education and housing, or supporting entrepreneurial activities. As a result, banks are increasing their efforts to take advantage of the perceived business opportunity.

The Guatemalan Experience

As in Colombia, in Guatemala the share of commercial banks in the retail remittances distribution market seems to have increased markedly in recent years (World Bank 2006a) and recipients have increasingly been converted into clients, although they participate mostly by holding deposits rather than by receiving credit.[40] On the other hand, the "bancarization" of senders has also been limited by the small participation of banks in the remittances origination market.

Although data on the market structure of the retail distribution of remittances in Guatemala are particularly scarce and incomplete, estimates indicate that once small shops and other retailers are taken into account, Guatemalan banks do not have the largest percentage of the market.[41] However, the relevance of banks in the market has been increasing as limiting factors have eased and banks have exploited competitive advantages.

Among the obstacles, Guatemalan banks report that exclusivity agreements have constrained their expansion in remittances distribution. These agreements have also hindered the bancarization of recipients by prohibiting banks from transferring remittances to recipients' bank accounts (both existing and new). This clause limits the benefits of holding savings accounts, as it forces beneficiaries to go to the bank to receive their remittances payments, even if they already have an account. The prohibition also increases the costs of converting beneficiaries into customers. In this process, banks need to assign an identification number to remittances beneficiaries, track remittances histories, and link this information with the transactions that beneficiaries do as bank clients. This implies developing or purchasing compatible information systems to track information (one for remittances and another for other transactions) and dedicating qualified personnel to analyze trends and explore opportunities for cross-selling of other products. Nevertheless, the relevance of exclusivity features is decreasing as banks are broadening their agreements with other agents.

On the other hand, there are several elements contributing to the growth of banks in the remittances distribution market and deepened bancarization through remittances. A good example is the tailoring of products to the needs of the remittances sector, such as the program *Los Chapines Estamos Unidos* (Guatemalans Are United) of Banco Industrial, the largest commercial bank in Guatemala (see annex B). All bank officials interviewed are also making efforts to collect and analyze information on remittances transactions and beneficiaries, which should put them in a better position to take advantage of existing but underutilized strengths.[42] The reported shift from informal to formal transfers recently prompted by Anti-Money Laundering and Combating the Financing of Terrorism (AML-CFT) regulations that improve recording of official flows; banks' broader range of financial services; and, in some cases, their relatively widespread branch network, work in favor of their growth in remittances distribution (World Bank 2006c). The latter is particularly the case for two large banks in Guatemala with large rural networks in geographic regions that are large remittances recipients, which have only started to explore the potential for banking beneficiaries.

Regarding the potential growth of bank liabilities in the remittances sector, a 2004 survey conducted by the World Council of Credit Unions (WOCCU)[43] shows some encouraging evidence. Even when it is estimated that close to 70 percent of remittances recipients do not have bank accounts in Guatemala, 65 percent of the respondents expressed interest in depositing part of their remittances in financial institutions and saving 22 percent of their remittances (Mesbah-Khavari, Evans, and Klaehn 2005).

When interviewees in the WOCCU survey were asked about their reasons for not having a savings account in a financial institution, they mentioned they did not have enough income, were not used to saving, had other more profitable investments, did not know how to do it, or believed they did not meet the requirements (Mesbah-Khavari, Evans, and Klaehn 2005). These limitations could be minimized by, among other things, further adapting deposit services to remittances beneficiaries' needs (for example, eliminating management costs, offering attractive interest rates, and lowering minimum required balances), and explaining the requirements for opening an account.

Competition from informal credit providers and the lack of demand and collateral have been obstacles for granting credit to Guatemalan remittances recipients. The WOCCU survey found that: (i) at the overall sample level, 35 percent of remittances recipients' households were using credit in 2003; (ii) most loans were provided by informal sources (informal moneylenders, supplier credit, friends, or relatives); and (iii) most remittances' beneficiaries did not apply for credit as they lack collateral and feared their applications would be denied (Mesbah-Khavari, Evans, and Klaehn 2005). Credit demand is also influenced by recipients' preferred distribution of income, as Guatemalans primarily use their remittances to cover basic household expenditures, rather than to invest in business, agriculture, or residential property.[44]

There are, conversely, some elements that can lead to credit growth in the remittances sector. The fact that recipients are already using informal credit raises the opportunity to increase formal credit for beneficiaries by offering better terms, if collateral and lack of sufficient credit history can be addressed through remittances. Guatemalan banks are starting to take advantage of remittances to solve the typical limitations of access to credit for low-income individuals by using proven patterns of stable remittances flows during a given period as a positive factor when assessing the credit risk of potential clients. Finally, even when Guatemalan recipients assign the biggest portion of their remittances to consumption, their ability to save and invest is bigger than that of nonrecipient households, as the effect of remittances on income is considerable.

Annex B: Tailoring Financial Products to the Needs of the Remittances Market

The following provides examples of financial products that have been designed by Latin American financial institutions to satisfy the particular needs of remittances senders and recipients. These examples seek to highlight the distinctive and innovative features of these products, rather than to provide a detailed description.

- *Banco Solidario: Gaining market share through product adaptation*

Banco Solidario is a key player in the Ecuadoran remittances market. Even though it entered the market fairly recently (2002), it has managed to rapidly gain participation in the remittances retail distribution business by providing remittances senders and beneficiaries with savings and credit products tailored to their needs (Orozco and Fedewa 2005) and establishing strategic alliances with international banks in several countries (most important, savings banks in Spain).[45]

Senders who hold savings accounts at Banco Solidario have transfer fees waived (since December 2003) and have the option of designating beneficiaries who can withdraw funds in their home country. Savings accounts have low costs and allow the customer to have funds available upon request and have a savings plan that lets clients decide how much to save each month and for how long.[46]

Banco Solidario also offers mortgages and loans to migrants and their families with several innovative features. Mortgages are sold to migrants through a network of sales offices in Spain and Italy, have low savings requirements,[47] and a minimum down payment of 30 percent (Derham 2005). Relatives of the sender can also apply for a similar mortgage by showing proof of the last three remittances received from Spain (Derham 2005). Beneficiaries who receive their remittances from Spain can also apply for loans of up to US$5,000 by demonstrating that they are receiving remittances, even when they are clients of other financial institutions. Banco Solidario also offers loans to remitters of up to US$10,000 that can be used for several purposes (for example, migration travel costs, improvement of microenterprises, and housing).

- *Banco Salvadoreño: Reaching senders*

Banco Salvadoreño has opened several branches in the United States to reach senders. So far, the institution has seven agencies in the U.S. cities with the highest concentration of Salvadoran migrants.[48] This has allowed the bank to charge competitive fees for transfers, and migrants to transfer funds directly to beneficiaries' savings accounts, capturing 12 percent of El Salvador's remittances market (Orozco and Fedewa 2005).

Financial products have also been adapted to the needs of Salvadoran senders and recipients, who are given preferential treatment to facilitate the establishment of a long-term relationship (Orozco and Fedewa 2005). In particular, the bank has developed a mortgage product line for senders, which offers three products according to the legal status of the migrant (that is, legal residents, work-permit holders, and undocumented).[49] Mortgages to acquire homes in El Salvador (new or existing) use the property as collateral and the senders can finance up to 90 percent of the value of the house, for a maximum term of 15 years. Mortgages to acquire lots also use the property as collateral, and senders can finance up to 70 percent of the value for a maximum term of 10 years.

- *Banco Industrial: Tailoring credit to recipients*

Banco Industrial (BI), the largest Guatemalan bank, has developed the "*Los Chapines] Estamos Unidos*" (Guatemalans Are United) program, which includes money transfers, savings, and credit services tailored to the needs of the remittances market. The program's savings and credit services are mainly sold to remittances recipients.

Credit products consider the recipient's remittances history to assess risk and determine the maximum loan amount (on average, an amount equal to 70 percent of remittances) and are generally short term (maximum of two years). Banco Industrial offers two credit products within its "*Los Chapines Estamos Unidos*" program: *Los Chapines Estamos Unidos* Loan and Remittances in Advance. While the former offers a 2 percent monthly interest rate and a longer term (6 to 24 months), the latter carries higher interest rates (4 percent to 6 percent) and a maximum term of three months.

- *Bansefi: Networking to reach economies of scale and underserved areas*

Bansefi (*Banco de Ahorro Nacional y Servicios Financieros*, or National Savings and Financial Services Bank) is a public development bank created as part of a strategy of the the Mexican government, designed to upgrade the Popular Savings and Credit Sector, which is formed by semi-informal and informal financial intermediaries that serve unbanked areas (De la Torre, Gozzi, and Schmukler 2006).[50] The strategy seeks to support these institutions to increase the depth of the financial sector and promote access to financial services for lower-income individuals through a networking model that links financial intermediaries to support common activities and reach economies of scale (Coutinho 2006).

Bansefi administers "*L@ Red de la Gente*" (The People's Network), a strategic association among the bank and financial institutions belonging to the Popular Savings and Credit Sector, which is facilitating the "bancarization" of underserved sectors (lower- and middle-income individuals). Aside from exploiting operational and commercial economies of scale,[51] *L@ Red de la Gente* performs activities directly related to remittances, including (i) negotiating fees with foreign banks and transfer companies to lower transfer costs, (ii) channeling the transferred funds, and (iii) attracting senders and beneficiaries to open savings accounts that generate financial records (Coutinho 2006).

- *Peru: Mortgages for recipients*

Fondo MIVIVIENDA, a Peruvian public fund that provides housing finance through private institutions, modified one of its products (*Crédito MIVIVIENDA*) to facilitate access for remittances recipients. Currently, close relatives of Peruvian immigrants who meet specified requirements can request a mortgage from the private banks that participate in the program, and their remittances are considered as part of their income to lower their risk profile.

In order to qualify, all recipients must have received and deposited in their accounts a monthly remittance that should not be smaller than the monthly payments of the desired mortgage for a period of six months. In turn, private financial institutions that belong to the program define other requirements for senders and recipients, and can tailor their products to the needs of their clients. For instance, Banco de Crédito has developed the product "*MIVIVIENDA con Remesas*," which offers three different mortgages—two for recipients who have an additional source of income (Plans 1 and 2), and one for direct relatives of senders who have remittances as their sole source of income (Plan 3). Plan 1 requires savings for 12 months and a minimum down payment of 10 percent, Plan 2 requires savings for six months and a minimum down payment of 20 percent. Finally, Plan 3 offers two options: savings for 9 months, with a minimum down payment of 30 percent, or savings for 12 months, with a minimum down payment of 20 percent.

Notes

1. See Orozco and Fedewa (2005) for a summary of recent efforts by banks in Latin America to convert remittances recipients into bank clients.

2. Annex B describes the experiences of banks from Ecuador, El Salvador, Guatemala, Mexico, and Peru.

3. Bank deposits include all demand, savings, and time deposits held at deposit money banks as reported in the IMF's *International Financial Statistics*. Bank credit refers to claims on the private sector held by deposit money banks. These numbers also come from the IMF's *International Financial Statistics*.

4. This is the case for the following countries: Barbados, Bolivia, Brazil, Colombia, Costa Rica, the Dominican Republic, Ecuador, El Salvador, Grenada, Guatemala, Haiti, Honduras, Jamaica, Nicaragua, Panama, Paraguay, Peru, and Trinidad and Tobago.

5. Data on financial development, country size, GDP per capita, and inflation come from the *International Financial Statistics* (IMF) and the *World Development Indicators* (World Bank 2005a). Information on dual exchange rates systems comes from the *Annual Report on Exchange Arrangements and Restrictions* (IMF).

6. There is anecdotal evidence that official estimates of remittances flows in LAC have increased sharply during the last few years, partly due to better reporting. At least for the case of Guatemala, this seems to be the result of recently introduced regulatory changes related to reporting agencies. For more details, see World Bank (2006c).

7. The bilateral migration data is only available for 2000, so the weights we use are constant. The time variation arises from the series on the GDP per capita, real growth rate, and unemployment rate in remittances-source countries. To check the validity of our set of instruments, in all estimations we report the Sargan test of overidentifying restrictions. The joint null hypothesis for this test is that the instruments are uncorrelated with the error term, and that excluded instruments do not belong in the estimated equation.

8. Effect for LAC (shown in table 6.2 as "Remittances in LAC") was calculated summing the coefficient on remittances to GDP with the coefficient on the remittances times LAC interaction term.

9. Another possible reason for mistrust, but which cannot be formally tested either, is the public perception of an excessive focus of banks on profits and lack of commitment to support the needs of poorer clients. This is cited in annex B, as reported by bank officials interviewed in Colombia. However, it is unclear if this is a generalized perception in Colombia, if it is the case in other countries in LAC, or—even if both of these are true—if this is different from perceptions in other regions.

10. At least for the cases analyzed through ad hoc surveys and field interviews, exclusivity agreements of banks with money transfer operators have hindered banks' capacity to convert these recipients into clients (see annex A).

11. In the case of Honduras, the ratios come from Orozco (2005), and he does not report a test for differences across recipients and nonrecipients.

12. For all estimations, we report marginal effects as opposed to coefficients and we include estimations for households that appear at least twice and, separately, four times in the four-year database.

13. These results continue to hold for the case of nonbank credit. In the interest of space, these estimations are available upon request.

14. Based on a survey of Latin American migrants in the United States conducted in November 2001 by Bendixen and Associates, Orozco (2003) reports that there is a nonlinear relationship between remittances sent and length of stay in the United States. In the first years of arrival, migrants are less likely to remit, partly because of their limited income and obligations incurred when arriving in the country. As immigrants settle in over time, they send more, in part because they earn more. However, after an extended period of time, remittances decline, in part because of greater obligations faced by the migrants in the host country and because ties to the country of origin weaken in some cases. Arguably, we assume that migrants' length of stay abroad affects the likelihood of the use of banking services only through its effect on remittances.

15. See Hernandez-Coss (2004) and Orozco (2004) for a description of efforts by U.S. banks to penetrate the remittances business to Latin America.

16. Results do not change when we include other combinations of controls. Additional estimations are available upon request.

17. F-statistics for the significance of the instruments in explaining remittances and Hansen's tests for overidentifying restrictions suggest that our instruments are valid.

18. However, results do not change if we include other municipal-level controls instead of these.

19. Information on the experiences of Guatemalan and Colombian banks, gathered through interviews and described in annex A, also shows that banks have been much more effective at selling savings products than credit to remittances recipients.

20. Arguably, given the wide variety of remittances patterns that appear to exist among LAC countries, which led to the classification of countries into three sets based on plotted flows, more specific recommendations may have to vary depending on the set of countries. However, the following focuses on broad recommendations since further research is needed to undertake such an endeavor, which requires more data than available for this study (e.g., not enough observations to carry out detailed empirical analysis for each group of countries identified based on plotted flows).

21. For example, as reported by Orozco (2004), by 2003, Hispanics represented 20 percent of Bank of America's new accounts and, as of 2004, Wells Fargo had attracted 250,000 new clients since offering Intercuenta Express, an account-to-account service allowing customers at Wells Fargo branches to pay $10 to transfer up to $1,000 directly into their beneficiaries' BBVA-Bancomer account in Mexico.

22. Suro (2005) finds that the cost and lack of flexibility of banking services are among the main reasons why Latin American migrants in the United States are not using banks.

23. In part, the limited success has been due to the relevance of exchange rate differentials for intermediaries, which would be kept as profit by the Mexican Central Bank for transactions under the ACH (see World Bank 2006b, and chapter 9).

24. The 2006 *Global Economic Prospects* (World Bank 2006a) on migration and remittances mentions examples for countries such as China, Eritrea, India, Israel, Lebanon, Pakistan, and the Philippines.

25. An important step for banks to increase credit to remittances market participants is to systematically collect and analyze information on remitters' and beneficiaries' transactions to develop products tailored to their needs. The case studies based on selected bank interviews presented in annexes A and B further illustrate the potential limitations, avenues for improving them, and ongoing efforts pursued by banks for tailoring their products.

26. The obstacles discussed in annex A, as reported by selected banks in Guatemala and Colombia, could be explored further to improve diagnosis and determine how best to ease these limitations. Notwithstanding existing difficulties, the potential for increasing the impact of remittances is perceived to be large, at least as reflected in the increased interest of banks in furthering their role in the market, as reported in annex A, coupled with the incipient development of specialized products, as reported in annex B.

27. In the LAC region, Colombia and Guatemala are, respectively, the third- and fourth-largest remittances recipients in absolute terms. In 2005, Colombia received US$4.12 billion (equivalent to 4.1 percent of GDP), while Guatemala received US$2.99 billion (or 9.3 percent of GDP in relative terms) (IDB 2006b).

28. Although interviewed banks represent an important percentage of the remittances market in each country, due to diversity among banking financial institutions and the informal nature of the surveys, they may not necessarily be representative of the country or the region.

29. Notwithstanding data scarcity, Orozco (2006) estimates that Colombian banks have about 40 percent of this market, while foreign exchange houses represent about 47 percent. In this sense, Colombia differs from the weighted regional average (according to country volume), where banks are estimated to have the greatest percentage of the remittances distribution market (close to 50 percent), followed by retail stores, with approximately 38 percent (IDB 2006a). It is worth noting that these market participation estimates are based on data collected by Orozco from 13 LAC countries and a total of 50 enterprises that offer money transfer services (Orozco 2006).

30. Banks started growing in the remittances retail distribution market after 2001.

31. Banks report the need to improve their own image to gain market share, as they believe the public perceives them to be excessively focused on profits and has some difficulty in trusting them with their funds.

32. This refers to the actual withdrawal of remittances at banks' offices. As banks did not always have separate customer lines to pay remittances, foreign exchange houses have been able to offer faster service in some cases.

33. Although foreign exchange houses traditionally held most of the market, they have been losing ground to other businesses. In 2001, foreign exchange houses paid 95 percent of remittances, but their share declined to 81 percent in 2004 (Banco de la República de Colombia 2004). Moreover, Orozco (2006) estimates that their share declined to 47 percent by 2006.

34. The development of products adapted to the needs of the remittances market was at different stages in interviewed banks, but all report a large focus on this strategy. Some banks were already offering new products and getting positive results, while others were still in the process of designing them.

35. This refers to the confidence that can be generated when a renowned bank is involved in the transaction and the greater personal security that can be enjoyed

receiving the payment. As banks offer several services aside from money transfers, a client leaving one of its branches might not be carrying cash and, therefore, is less likely to be victimized.

36. Nevertheless, the influence of retailers is limited by the fact that they can only provide credit for the products they sell and banks have the ability to further adapt their credit products.

37. This expenditure pattern could be explained, at least in part, by the fact that LAC migration tends to be longer term as compared with other regions (see chapter 2). Therefore, migrants and their families back home might not feel the urge to save in order to invest and lift their living standards in anticipation of the sender's return to the home country.

38. This is the case in Guatemala, where remittances have a considerable impact on household income. Even when consumption goods constitute the main expenditure of recipient households, they still manage to save and invest more than nonrecipient households.

39. In fact, one of the interviewed banks had launched a mortgage credit product for migrants, but later withdrew it because profit margins were insufficient.

40. As table 6.4 shows, while 30.7 percent of beneficiaries hold savings accounts, only 0.57 percent have bank credit.

41. Banks have about 23.5 percent of the remittances distribution market. Most of the market is held by retailers, who account for 72.8 percent of the business, according to the IDB (2006a).

42. Larger banks with wide distribution networks that already target lower-income individuals will probably be in a particularly good position to increase their participation by taking advantage of these features once they adapt their products and marketing to the remittances sector based on this information.

43. The World Council of Credit Unions, Inc. (WOCCU) conducted a survey of users of its International Remittance Network (IR*net*) services at the five Guatemalan credit unions during the spring of 2004, covering 502 individuals (Mesbah-Khavari, Evans, and Klaehn 2005).

44. According to a recent USAID survey, remittances recipients spend 56 percent of remittances on covering basic needs, while the remaining 44 percent is distributed among health and home investments and debt repayment.

45. These alliances with saving banks (*cajas de ahorro*) have formed a network, called "*Red de Servicios Financieros a Emigrantes* (Network of Financial Services for Immigrants)," that includes more than 9,000 outlets in Spain (see http://www.banco-solidario.com/noticia.php?notID=5). Through these network, migrants in Spain transferred US$120.4 million in the three years through July 2005, and deposited US$7.8 million, or 6 percent of that figure, into savings accounts (Derham 2005).

46. Administrative costs are $1.50 for accounts if the average balance is smaller than US$300.

47. Initial savings for mortgages can start at US$40.

48. These are Los Angeles, Santa Ana, San Francisco, and Van Nuys in California; Houston, Texas; and Las Vegas, Nevada.

49. Undocumented migrants are offered shorter-term mortgages and are not required to present documentation to prove their legal status in the United States, remittances history, or tax declarations.

50. Bansefi was established through an organic law, sanctioned by the Mexican Congress in April 2001, which mandated the transformation of the existent *Patronato del Ahorro Nacional* (PAHNAL).

51. Economies of scale are sought by providing an Internet-based financial services network and a trademark for the products of the Internet members.

References

Aggarwal, R., A. Demirgüç-Kunt, and M.S. Martínez Pería. 2005. "Do Workers' Remittances Promote Financial Development?" Unpublished, World Bank, Washington, DC.

Beck, T., A. Demirgüç-Kunt, and M.S. Martínez Pería. 2005. "Reaching Out: Access to and Use of Banking Services Across Countries." Policy Research Working Paper No. 3754, World Bank, Washington, DC.

———. 2006. "Banking Services for Everyone? Barriers to Bank Access Around the World." Unpublished, World Bank, Washington, DC.

Bendixen & Associates. 2001. "Survey of Remittance Senders: U.S to Latin America." Bendixen & Associates, Coral Gables, FL.

Caprio, G., and D. Klingebiel. 2003. *Episodes of Systemic and Borderline Financial Crises 1970s-2002*. Washington, DC: World Bank.

Coutinho, L. 2006. "Networking: The Case of Bansefi." Unpublished, World Bank, Washington, DC.

De la Torre, A., J. Gozzi, and S. Schmukler. 2006. *Innovative Experiences in Access to Finance: Market Friendly Roles for the Visible Hand?* Washington, DC: World Bank.

De Luna Martinez, J. 2005. "Workers' Remittances to Developing Countries: A Survey of Central Banks on Selected Public Policy Issues." Policy Research Working Paper No. 3638, World Bank,Washington, DC.

Demirgüç-Kunt, A., and M.S. Martínez Pería. 2006. "Remittances and the Use of Banking Services. Evidence from El Salvador." Unpublished, World Bank, Washington, DC.

Demirgüç-Kunt, A., E. López Córdova, M.S. Martínez Pería, and C. Woodruff. 2006. "Remittances and Financial Development. Evidence from Mexican Municipalities." Unpublished, World Bank, Washington, DC.

Derham, M. 2005. "Every Dollar Counts." *Latin Finance* 173: 34–6.

Freund, C., and N. Spatafora. 2005. "Remittances: Transaction Costs, Determinants and Informal Flows." Policy Research Working Paper 3704, World Bank, Washington, DC.

FUSADES. 1995. *Uso productivo de las remesas familiares*. La Libertad, El Salvador: Fundación Salvadoreña para el Desarrollo Económico y Social.

Hanson, G.H., and C. Woodruff. 2003. "Emigration and Educational Attainment in Mexico." Unpublished, University of California, San Diego, CA.

Hernandez-Coss, R. 2004. *Lessons from the United States-Mexico Remittances Corridor on Shifting from Informal to Formal Transfer Systems*. Washington, DC: World Bank.

Honohan, P. and D. Klingebiel. 2003. "The Fiscal Cost Implications of an Accommodating Approach to Banking Crises." *Journal of Banking and Finance* 27 (8): 1539–60.

Inter-American Development Bank. 2006a. *Enviando Dinero a Casa: Marcador de la Industria de Remesas*. Washington, DC: Inter-American Development Bank.

———. 2006b. *Remittances 2005: Promoting Financial Democracy*. Washington, DC: Inter-American Development Bank.

IMF (International Monetary Fund). 2005. *World Economic Outlook 2005*. Washington, DC: International Monetary Fund.

———. Various issues. *Annual Report on Exchange Arrangements and Exchange Restriction*. Washington, DC: International Monetary Fund.

———. Various issues. *International Financial Statistics*. Washington, DC: International Monetary Fund.

López Córdova, E. 2004. "Globalization, Migration and Development: The Role of Mexican Migrant Remittances." *Economia, Journal of the Latin American and Caribbean Economic Association* 6(1): 217–47.

Mesbah-Khavari, D., A. Evans, and J. Klaehn. 2005. "Credit Union Remittance Services in Guatemala: Expanding the Access of Low-Income Remittance Recipients to Financial Institutions." United States Agency for International Development (USAID), Washington, DC.

McKenzie, D. and H. Rapoport. 2005. "Migration and Education Inequality in Mexico." Unpublished, Inter-American Development Bank, Washington, DC.

OECD (Organisation for Economic Co-Operation and Development). 2005. "Database on Immigrants and Expatriates." OECD, Paris, France. http://www.oecd.org/document/51/0,2340,en_2825_494553_34063091_1_1_1_1,00.html.

Orozco, M. 2003. *Changes in the Atmosphere? Increase in Remittances, Price Decline and New Challenges*. Washington, DC: Inter-American Dialogue.

———. 2004. "The Remittance Marketplace: Prices, Policy and Financial Institutions." Pew Hispanic Center Report, Georgetown University and Institute for the Study of International Migration, Washington, DC.

———. 2005. "Markets and Financial Democracy: The Case for Remittance Transfers." *Journal of Payment Systems Law* 2: 166–215.

———. 2006. "International Financial Flows and Workers' Remittances: Best Practices." Unpublished, Inter-American Dialogue.

Orozco, M. and R. Fedewa. 2005. "Leveraging Efforts on Remittances and Financial Intermediation." Report commissioned by the Inter-American Development Bank, Washington, DC.

Osili, U. O., and A. Paulson. 2004. "Prospects for Immigrant-Native Wealth Assimilation: Evidence from Financial Market Participation." Working Paper No. 18, Federal Reserve Bank of Chicago, Chicago, IL.

———. 2005. "Institutions and Financial Development: Evidence from International Migrants in the U.S." Working Paper 2004-19, Federal Reserve Bank of Chicago, Chicago, IL.

Suro, R. 2005. "Survey of Mexican Migrants: Attitudes about Immigration and Major Demographic Characteristics." Research & Publications, Pew Hispanic Center, Washington, DC.

WOCCU. 2004. *A Technical Guide to Remittances*. Washington, DC: World Council of Credit Unions, Inc.

———. 2006. *How to Serve Undocumented Individuals*. Washington, DC: World Council of Credit Unions, Inc.

Woodruff, C., and R. Zenteno. 2004. "Remittances and Microenterprises in Mexico." Unpublished, University of California, San Diego.

World Bank. 2005a. *Doing Business*. Washington, DC: World Bank.

———. 2005b. *World Development Indicators Database*. Washington, DC: World Bank.

———. 2006a. *Global Economic Prospects: Economic Implications of Remittances and Migration.* Washington, DC: World Bank.

———. 2006b. "The Development Impact of Workers' Remittances in Latin America." Report No. 37026, World Bank, Washington, DC.

———. 2006c. "The U.S.-Guatemala Remittances Corridor Analysis." World Bank, Washington, DC.

7

Remittances, the Real Exchange Rate, and the Dutch Disease Phenomenon

J. Humberto López, Luis Molina, and Maurizio Bussolo

Even though remittances appear to have a positive impact on recipient countries, when flows are too large relative to the size of the receiving economies, as those observed in a number of Latin American countries, they may also bring a number of undesired problems. Among those, probably the most feared in this context is Dutch disease. This chapter explores the empirical evidence regarding the impact of remittances on the real exchange rate. Do countries with high remittances flows experience losses of competitiveness due to real exchange rate appreciation? Should policy makers react to this potential phenomenon? If so, what options do they have to address this concern?

Introduction

In the previous chapters, we have argued that remittances may have a number of beneficial effects for the welfare of the receiving countries. The evidence presented so far in this book suggests that at the country level, higher remittances inflows tend to be associated with lower poverty indicators and higher growth rates. Beyond these typical income dimensions of welfare, remittances seem to reduce output volatility (a measure of risk faced by countries[1]), and at least in some countries and for some socioeconomic groups, lead to improvements in social indicators. Yet the magnitude of these flows relative to the size of the receiving economies[2] implies that remittances may also pose an important number of challenges. For while these inflows may ease external financing constraints and therefore hold the potential for higher investment by developing countries, in many circumstances remittances are so large that they can impact macroeconomic stability and more specifically carry the potential for a Dutch disease type of phenomena (see the International Monetary Fund's *World Economic Outlook 2005* [IMF 2005], and the *Work Bank's Global Economic Prospects 2006* [World Bank 2006]).

Workers' remittances can be viewed as a capital inflow, and therefore the theory of the Dutch disease phenomenon associated with a surge in inflows (perhaps because of the discovery of new natural resources) can also be applied in this context. In order to isolate the specific channels transmitting remittances shocks through the economy, consider first a small open economy model with no leisure-consumption trade-off. In this setup, an increase in remittances is equivalent to a (permanent) increase in incomes of the households.

Assuming that nontradables are normal goods, this positive income shock results in extra spending on both tradables and nontradables. Because most Latin American countries are price takers in international markets, growing demand does not raise the prices of tradables. However, because the prices of nontradables are determined in the domestic economy, they increase due to additional demand, or the so-called spending effect. There is also a "resource movement effect." The relative price change between tradables and nontradables makes production of the latter more profitable. Output growth in the nontradable sectors will push up factor demands, especially for those factors used intensively in these sectors. Increased factor demand by the expanding sectors will be accommodated by factors released from other sectors (the resource movement effect) and, depending on the behavior of total supply of the factor, will normally result in higher factor returns in the final equilibrium. The price shift and resource reallocation in favor of nontradables erode the competitiveness of export-oriented sectors and hurt import-competing sectors. The final result of this real exchange rate appreciation is normally increased import flows and lower export sales. When the above assumption of no consumption-leisure trade-off in the household utility function is removed, the above effects are exacerbated. Without this assumption, an increase in nonlabor income, as is the case with remittances, influences household decisions to supply labor—namely, individuals can now consume more of both goods and leisure (that is, the income effect dominates), and thus their labor supply is reduced. In turn, reduced labor supply implies rising wages, and this additional pressure on wages intensifies the effects of real exchange rate appreciation described earlier.

Obviously, the pressure on the real exchange rate will be somewhat mitigated if (i) there are productivity gains, particularly in the nontradable sector, that offset the effects of the increasing demand; (ii) governments implement policies that aim at stimulating labor demand by reducing labor costs[3]; and (iii) a large share of the remittances are channeled to the external sector via additional imports so that the price effect on nontradable goods is limited. Yet, in principle it seems difficult to justify that these effects are enough to mitigate appreciating pressures.

In turn, there are a number of connected macroeconomic effects that can result from a real exchange rate appreciation associated with remittances flows. They include:

- Adverse effects on the tradable sector of the economy. Although remittances flows are likely to lead to an expansion of the nontradable sector (as a result of the increase experienced in domestic demand), both export- and import-competing industries (that is, the tradable sector of the economy) would be adversely affected by real exchange rate appreciation and the associated loss of international competitiveness. The negative impact of remittances on the tradable sector may be reinforced if they also fuel inflation and higher prices result in higher economywide wages.[4] As mentioned above and as was documented in chapter 5, this effect would be further magnified if remittances also reduce the labor supply. In these circumstances, the nontradable sector may be in the position of passing some of the wage pressures on to prices, but this is likely to be much more difficult for a tradable sector facing international competition, which, as a result, will lose competitiveness.
- Widening of the current account deficit. In principle, it is difficult to justify that an increase in domestic demand will be passed in full to the nontradable sector. So, to the extent that some of the remittances-induced consumption is directed toward tradable goods, there will be an increase in the demand for imports. This, coupled with the loss of international competitiveness for domestic firms mentioned in the previous paragraph, would likely result in deteriorations of the external position. For example, according to the World Bank (2003), the surge in remittances observed in El Salvador during the 1990s was the most likely factor behind the worsening of the country's trade deficit, which over the 1990s deteriorated from less than 7 percent of GDP to almost 14 percent of GDP.
- Weaker monetary control, inflationary pressures, and the sectoral allocation of investment. If remittances flows do not leave the country (at least in full) through a widening of the current account, large flows will push up monetary aggregates, potentially derailing inflation targets. Experience also indicates that prices of financial assets, and particularly of real estate, can rise rapidly following a surge in

remittances, something that in turn may introduce significant distortions in the economy and affect the sectoral allocation of investment and lead to overinvestment in some sectors (for example, real estate).

On the whole, the previous discussion highlights a number of problems that policy makers may have to face in the context of a surge in remittances. True, to the extent that these Dutch disease phenomena are part of the natural adjustment process toward a new equilibrium, they should not be a matter of particular concern for policy makers. Indeed, if we view remittances as a positive shock to the economy, then the real appreciation and related effects experienced by the receiving country would simply be part of the inevitable relative price adjustment process that goes with favorable shocks. Yet if this real appreciation is very dramatic, or the adjustment process toward the new equilibrium is uneven (that is, not fully consistent with the change in economic fundamentals at each point in time) policy makers may wish to mitigate—to the extent possible—its adverse effects on export industries.

In principle, one could also mention two additional reasons for concern for policy makers that are usually mentioned in the context of surges of capital inflows. One is the potential for a flow reversal over the medium run. This is important because if there is hysteresis in the real sector, a real exchange rate appreciation may wipe out important sectors of the economy that would not reappear even if the currency subsequently depreciates. The other potential concern is a very sudden appreciation that cannot be accommodated and therefore brings a very painful adjustment. However, it must be noted that the documented stability[5] and countercyclicality of remittances would lead one to assume that the probability of short-run reversals or sudden adjustments is quite low, leaving as the main concern the magnitude of the real appreciation associated with the remittances inflows.

Against this backdrop, what does the economics literature have to say about the evolution of the exchange rate in countries that have experienced important increases in remittances? The truth is that the existing empirical literature is very limited and less than unanimous. For example, Amuedo-Dorantes and Pozo (2004) rely on cross-country econometrics techniques and find that in a sample of 13 Latin American countries,[6] a doubling of workers' remittances would lead on average to a real exchange rate overvaluation of about 22 percent. This estimate would be robust to the presence of fixed effects in the data, and to the use of instrumental variable (IV) estimation techniques to account for reverse causality from the exchange rate to remittances.

However, Rajan and Subramanian (2005), who rely on a cross-national data set of three-digit industry value added growth data to explore whether remittances have a differential impact depending on the labor intensity of the different industries, find that unlike other types of capital flows (particularly aid flows), remittances do not seem to have a negative impact on external competitiveness. Rajan and Subramanian (2005) argue that this could be the result of remittances being directed to a large extent toward unskilled labor–intensive activities—for example, goods and services provided by microenterprises—or tradable sectors such as manufacturing, and thus having limited effects on the prices of skilled labor and other relatively scarce resources.

This chapter addresses these issues and contributes to the existing limited literature along several dimensions. First, it discusses the different channels through which remittances can affect the real exchange rate using a framework where the equilibrium exchange rate is characterized by an external equilibrium similar to those analyzed in asset market models (Mussa 1984; Frenkel and Mussa 1985) and an internal equilibrium based on a productivity differential model such as those in Balassa (1964) and Samuelson (1964).

Second, it provides estimates of the impact of remittances flows on the real exchange rate using a large cross-national data set rather than information for a limited number of countries. Our approach allows testing of whether there are regional differences and, more specifically, whether Latin America is different in this context. Note that one of the main differences between the work of Amuedo-Dorantes and Pozo (2004) and Rajan and Subramanian (2005) is the coverage of the data. Thus, if the impact of remittances on the real exchange rate is different in Latin America than in the rest of the world, then the different findings of Amuedo-Dorantes and Pozo (2004) and Rajan and Subramanian (2005) should not be surprising. In fact, to preview some of the results in the Results section, this chapter argues that remittances flows appear to affect the real exchange rate at a global level, and that Latin American countries do not appear to be an exception. These results are robust to the presence of fixed effects in the data, potential reverse causality from the exchange rate to remittances, and variations in the set of control variables.

Third, the chapter also explores the extent to which the estimated appreciation in Latin America is consistent with the change in economic fundamentals implied by the increase in remittances, or instead whether it can be attributed to changes in the misalignment component of the real exchange rate (that is, changes in the underlying real overvaluation or undervaluation of the currency). To also preview our results on this, we find that the evolution of the Latin American real exchange rate seems to be driven by a combination of changes in the equilibrium real exchange rate and changes in the degree of misalignment.

Finally, on the basis of its empirical results, the chapter discusses a number of options for policy makers who are concerned with the impact that a surge in remittances may have on the external competitiveness of a country. In particular, we discuss the possibility that a revenue-neutral policy of a partial switch from direct to indirect taxation may reduce labor costs and thus (at least to a degree) sterilize the negative labor supply effect as well as the real exchange rate appreciation caused by rising remittances—an encouraging outcome for countries under budget constraint pressure. The rest of the chapter is organized as follows. In the next section we consider an additional number of theoretical considerations that may explain why remittances may lead to real exchange rate appreciation and review the evolution of remittances, the real exchange rate, and exports and imports for the eight largest receivers of remittances (as a percentage of GDP) in Latin America. The Empirical Strategy section reviews the empirical strategy used to assess the impact of remittances on the real exchange rate. In the Results section, we present the results of estimating two econometric models. One relates changes in the real effective exchange rate to the ratio of remittances to GDP. The second uses as an explanatory variable the changes in a measure of real exchange rate overvaluation. The basic idea is to try to disentangle how much of the observed changes in the real exchange rate are due to changes in the equilibrium exchange rate, and hence consistent with the evolution of economic fundamentals. The section on Tax Structure and Competitiveness discusses whether one specific policy option (shifting the tax structure from direct toward indirect taxation) can contribute to somewhat alleviating the losses in competitiveness that seem to be associated with a surge in remittances. Note that this intervention would aim at expanding the labor supply. The final section closes with some conclusions and a review of policy options.

Remittances and the Real Exchange Rate

Theoretical Considerations

Remittances can potentially affect the real exchange rate through three main channels (see annex A for a formal discussion). First, remittances may affect the external equilibrium of the economy by raising the net foreign asset position of the country. For example, the theoretical models of Mussa (1984), Frenkel and Mussa (1985), Alberola and López (2001), and Aberola et al. (2002) imply that the external equilibrium of the economy will be reached when any current account imbalance is compensated for by a sustainable flow of international capital. In turn, the rate of sustainable capital flows will be a function of the stock of foreign assets and liabilities of the economy, so that changes to the net foreign asset position of the country will lead to changes in the real equilibrium exchange rate.

Given that international remittances are transfers of foreign currency that—unlike other types of international flows—have no obligation associated with them, remittances will have a direct impact on the net financial position of the country vis-à-vis the rest of the world. Note in this regard that the impact of remittances on the stock of net foreign assets differs from the impact of other flows such as loans or foreign direct investment. In the case of a loan, there is an associated liability (the repayment), and therefore the contribution to the net foreign asset position of the country is given by the difference between the proceeds and the net present value of the repayment obligations. In this regard, loans will positively affect net foreign assets to the extent that they have a positive grant component. On the other hand, foreign direct investment flows coming into the home country will increase the foreign liabilities and therefore will lead to a decline of the net foreign asset position.

Second, remittances can also affect the internal equilibrium of the economy, understood as the situation where domestic capital and labor are efficiently utilized. If, as discussed above, remittances lead to an acceleration in the demand for services, inflation will tend to be higher in these sectors, which typically are not tradable (and hence somewhat protected from competition), leading to a real exchange rate appreciation (the traditional Balassa-Samuelson effect). Similarly, market rigidities may result in productivity differentials between sectors.

For example, if remittances raise the reservation wage, then excessive wage pressures in the tradable sector may lead to employment adjustments to maintain competitiveness, whereas in the nontradable sector, employers may cope with these pressures because they can pass them on to prices. As a result, remittances can also lead to higher productivity growth and lower inflation in the tradable sector through their potential impact on the reservation wage. One implication of this discussion is that whether remittances are primarily used for household consumption or investment purposes will have a direct impact on the way they affect the real exchange rate, with remittances that are predominantly consumption oriented having more of an appreciating impact on the real exchange rate.

A third possibility for remittances to affect the real exchange rate is through their impact on growth (see chapter 3 for evidence in this regard), although in this case the impact on the exchange rate is likely to be uncertain. On the one hand, an acceleration in the growth rate would lower the stock of net foreign assets as a percentage of GDP, and hence this would lower the real exchange rate (that is, growth would have the same impact as an increase in the liabilities of the country). If, on the other hand, the net foreign asset position of the country is negative vis-à-vis the rest of the world, the increase in the rate of growth would lower the liabilities to GDP ratio, and hence lead to an appreciation.

On the internal front, faster growth would be associated with a real exchange rate appreciation. Higher growth would lead to higher internal demand, and the mechanism described above in the description of the internal adjustments will apply (the Balassa-Samuelson argument). Thus, on the whole, the impact of growth acceleration could go in either direction, or the effects could cancel each other out and have no impact.

What Do the Data Look Like?

We now move beyond the theoretical considerations just discussed and focus on the data. Table 7.1 reports the annualized change in the (log) real effective exchange rate (REER) between 1990 and 2003 for a number of Latin American countries, together with the initial and final levels of remittances (in percentage of GDP). The remittances data are the same

Table 7.1 Remittances and the Real Exchange Rate

	REER growth (percent)	*Remittances (percent of GDP)*	
		Initial	*Final*
Argentina	−1.6	0.7	0.2
Belize	32.6	3.4	3.4
Bolivia	−0.3	0.1	2.0
Brazil	−5.3	0.1	0.6
Chile	0.1	0	0
Colombia	0.5	1.1	3.9
Costa Rica	0.3	0.2	1.8
Dominican Republic	−0.4	5.0	14.2
Ecuador	3.0	0.5	5.7
El Salvador	3.4	7.4	14.1
Guatemala	3.3	1.6	8.6
Haiti	3.0	2.7	27.6
Honduras	1.1	2.1	12.6
Jamaica	1.0	4.4	17.0
Mexico	1.8	1.2	2.3
Nicaragua[a]	−1.3	0.5	10.7
Panama	−1.2	0.3	0.7
Paraguay	−1.6	0.6	4.8
Peru	−0.6	0.3	1.4
Venezuela, R.B. de[b]	−1.5	0.1	0

Source: Author's calculations.
Note: Initial period is 1990 and final period is 2003.
[a] Nicaragua initial period is 1992.
[b] República Bolivariana de Venezuela initial period is 1997.

that have been used throughout this book. The REER is from the IMF's *International Financial Statistics*, and is defined as the relative price of domestic to foreign goods, so that increases imply a real exchange rate appreciation. Table 7.1 indicates that between 1990 and 2003, the REER appreciated in 11 of the 20 countries under consideration. The countries where it appreciated the most are Belize, Ecuador, El Salvador, Guatemala, and Haiti. Interestingly, Ecuador, El Salvador, Guatemala, and Haiti are among the top receiver countries of remittances in the region (as a percentage of GDP). Other countries where the REER appreciated over the period under consideration by at least 1 percent per year on an annual basis are Honduras, Jamaica, and Mexico. The first two of those are also among the countries of the region with a high remittances to GDP ratio, whereas Mexico is the country with the largest remittances flows in the world.

Figure 7.1 presents similar information, but now restricts the sample to the eight Latin American countries with the largest remittances to GDP ratio in 2002. Even though we should stress that this figure can only provide evidence of unconditional correlations, it is suggestive of a positive relationship between the evolution of the REER and that of remittances (as a percentage of GDP). In fact, in most of the eight countries in the figure, it is possible to observe a real exchange rate appreciation in parallel to an increase in the remittances to GDP ratio. The first apparent exception to this rule is Nicaragua, where the evolution of the real exchange rate over the early 1990s and 2000s appears to move in the opposite direction to what one could expect. The second exceptions are Ecuador and the Dominican Republic, where marked real depreciations followed the crises of 1999 and 2002, respectively, at a time when remittances were increasing substantially. However, in the case of the Dominican Republic, the real exchange rate and the remittances to GDP ratio also moved in parallel before 2002.

Note also that in some of the other countries, the observed real exchange rate appreciations have been quite dramatic. For example, in Ecuador, El Salvador, Guatemala, and Haiti, over the 1990–2003 period, the real exchange rate appreciated by about 40 percent. In the cases of Honduras and Jamaica, the recorded appreciation is more modest, but it would still be in the 20 percent range.

In figure 7.2, we compare the evolution of the real exchange rate and the volume of exports of goods and services. The figure indicates that the only countries where export volumes have significantly increased over the 1990–2003 period are El Salvador, a country where exports increased from about 19 percent of GDP in 1990 to close to 30 percent in 2003, and Ecuador, where exports increased by almost 20 percentage points, to close to 55 percent of GDP. In Honduras and Nicaragua, export volumes were more or less stable over this period, oscillating between 30 percent and 50 percent of GDP in the case of Honduras, and hovering around 20 percent in the case of Nicaragua (although with a large variance). In the rest of the countries under analysis, we observe declines in export volumes,

Figure 7.1 Remittances and the Real Exchange Rate

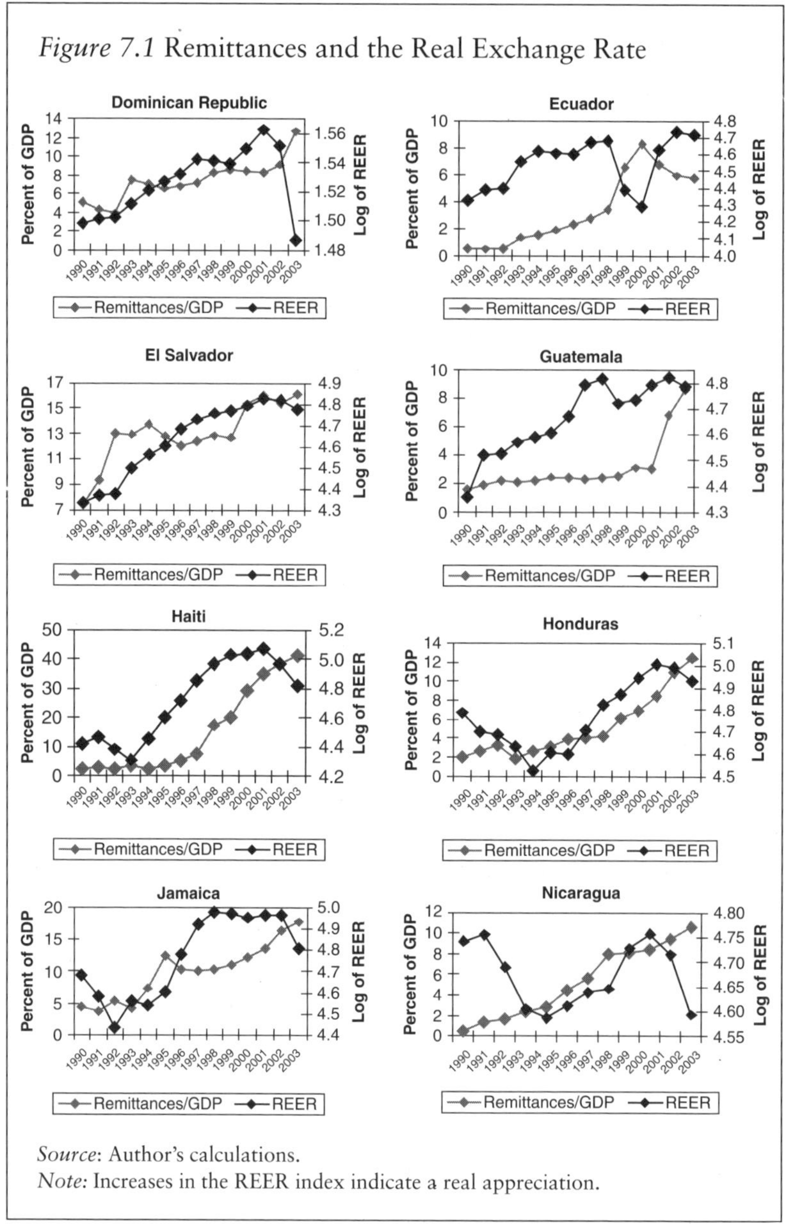

Source: Author's calculations.

Note: Increases in the REER index indicate a real appreciation.

Figure 7.2 Exports and the Real Exchange Rate

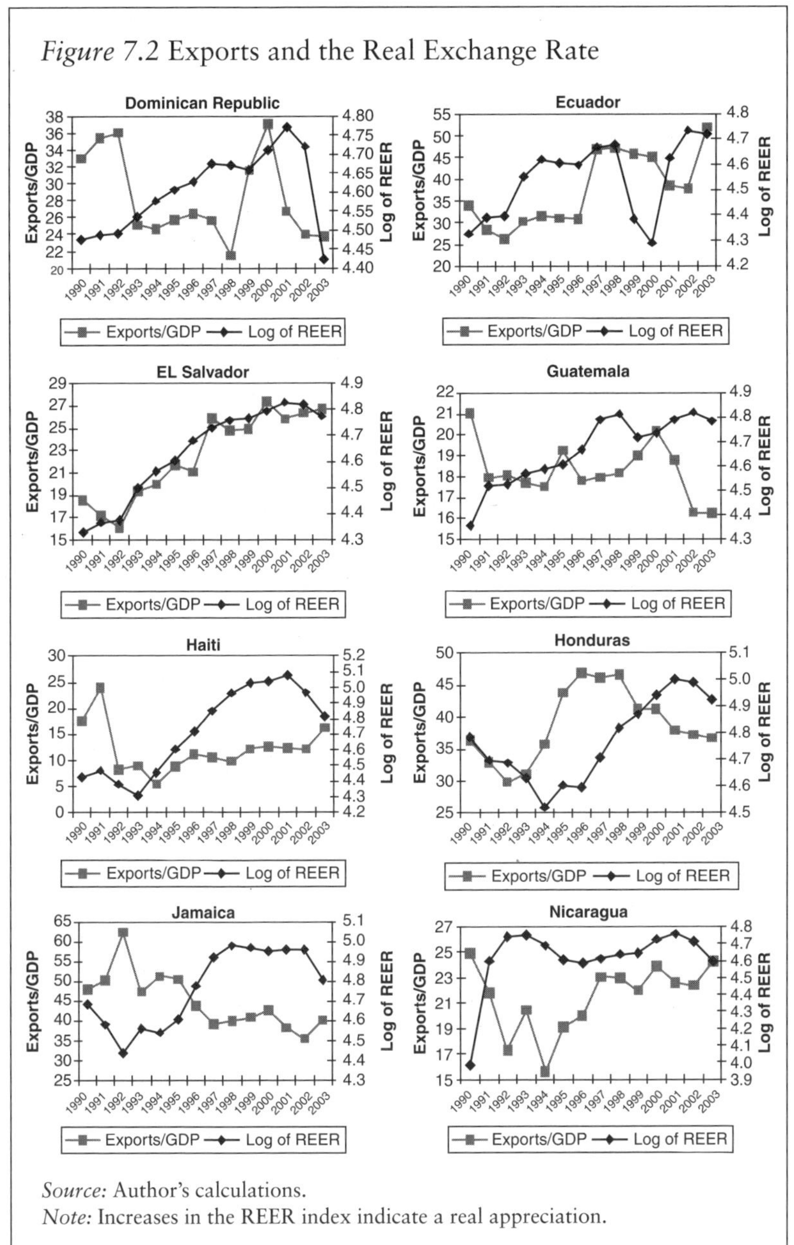

Source: Author's calculations.

Note: Increases in the REER index indicate a real appreciation.

which in some cases have been quite dramatic. For example, in Guatemala and Jamaica, export volumes have fallen over the period under analysis by about 5 percentage points of GDP.

As for the evolution of imports, figure 7.3 indicates that over the 1990 to 2003 period, there is only one country—Ecuador—where the imports to GDP ratio fell. In the other seven countries under analysis, imports increased. True, in some countries like Guatemala, Jamaica, and Nicaragua, they rose only slightly (by less than 10 percentage points of GDP), but in the cases of Honduras and Haiti, the increase has been quite marked: 15 percentage points of GDP in Honduras and close to 30 percentage points of GDP in Haiti.

Overall, the figures would indicate that in general, increases in remittances have been accompanied by real exchange rate appreciations, and these in turn by declines in exports and increases in imports, elements that could be taken as a loss of competitiveness. The next section explores whether the empirical evidence is also supportive of some causality between developments on the remittances front and the evolution of the real exchange rate.

Empirical Strategy

Empirical Model

To explore the existence of causal links between the real exchange rate and remittances in the data, we rely on the following regression model:

$$\Delta\theta_{\iota\tau} = \omega'\xi_{\iota\tau} + \beta\Delta P_{\iota\tau} + \nu_{\iota} + \upsilon_{\iota\tau} \tag{1}$$

where q is the log of the real effective exchange rate,[7] Δ is the first difference operator (such that $\Delta q_t = q_{t-1}$), R is a measure of remittances flows (in this chapter the remittances to GDP ratio[8]), x represents a set of control variables, which we shall discuss shortly, ν_i is a country-specific effect, and υ_{it} is an indgrendent and identically distributed error term. Finally, i and t are a country and a time index, respectively. Note that what drives the evolution of the exchange rate in equation (1) is the evolution of remittances rather than its stock (see annex A for a discussion). In other words, if they are stable, even high remittances flows will be consistent with a stable real exchange rate.

Our primary focus is the estimate of β in equation (1). If an increase in remittances leads to a real exchange rate appreciation, we should find $\beta > 0$. If, however, remittances have no impact on the real exchange rate, then we should find $\beta = 0$. Although it is theoretically possible here, we do not consider the possibility of $\beta < 0$, because this would imply that remittances contribute to real exchange rate depreciation.[9] (See annex A for a discussion.)

Figure 7.3 Imports and the Real Exchange Rate

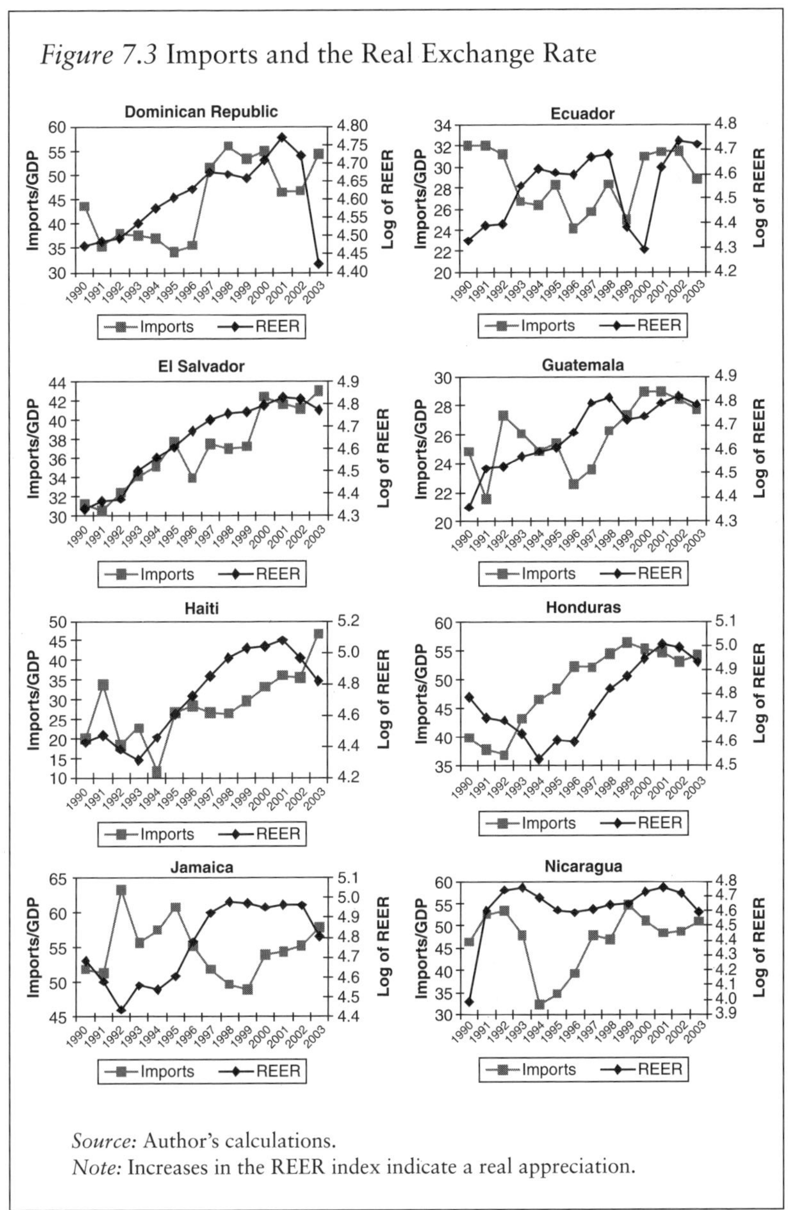

Source: Author's calculations.

Note: Increases in the REER index indicate a real appreciation.

The previous model can easily be extended to allow remittances to have a different impact in Latin America than in the rest of the world by simply adding an additional regressor to the specification in equation (1)[10]:

$$\Delta q_{it} = \omega' x_{it} + \beta_1 \Delta R_{it} + \beta_2 \Delta R_{it} \times lac + \nu_i + \upsilon_{it}, \tag{2}$$

where *lac* is a dummy variable that takes a value of 1 if the country in question is in Latin America and 0 otherwise.

One additional issue that needs attention is the specific set of control variables that are included in x. Here we follow to a large extent the strategy in Amuedo-Dorantes and Pozo (2004) and consider the terms of trade, government expenditure, the world real interest rate, and GDP per capita. These variables would capture, respectively, the effects of potential external shocks, fiscal policy differences, changes in external financial conditions, and productivity gains.[11]

Despite the broad similarities between equations (1) and (2) and those estimated by Dorantes and Pozo (2004), there are a number of important differences. First, our results are based on a large cross-national data set, rather than on a limited number of countries (in the case of the Dorantes and Pozo study, 13 Latin American countries). As argued previously, if Latin American migration patterns are different from those of other regions (see chapter 2 for a discussion of this issue), this could also be reflected in a differentiated effect of remittances on the real exchange rate.

Second, we focus on changes in the exchange rate rather than on its levels. The reason for this is that since the real effective exchange rate variable is an index, it is not possible to make cross-country comparisons on the basis of the levels of the variable.[12] Fixed effects estimation can somewhat mitigate this problem, but it is not likely to fully address it in a satisfactory way. Note that this lack of cross-country comparability also prevents us from estimating dynamic models for the real exchange rate where, for example, the changes in the exchange rate are related to a control set that includes the lagged level of the exchange rate (which would capture mean reverting forces). The need to work with the first difference of the real exchange rate in turn implies that it is probably more appropriate to work with transformations of the original explanatory variable set. For example, rather than working with the levels of the terms of trade, we work with its changes. Similarly, rather than working with GDP per capita, we work with GDP growth rates.

A third difference with respect to Amuedo-Dorantes and Pozo (2004) is that we explore whether the results are robust to excluding GDP growth from the specification. The reason for this is that if remittances affect per-capita growth, and growth, in turn, affects the real exchange rate, either à la Balassa-Samuelson or as in portfolio models, then econometric models that control for the evolution of income levels will not capture the full impact of remittances on the exchange rate (that is, these models will produce results that are biased).

Fourth, our variable of interest is the changes in the remittances to GDP ratio, whereas Amuedo-Dorantes and Pozo (2004) use remittances per capita. We believe that our choice is more appropriate in this context since it is likely to better capture the importance of remittances flows relative to the size of the economy (see annex A). Finally, we also explore the extent to which the results for the real exchange rate are driven by changes in fundamentals and changes in the disequilibrium level. In this regard, we also present the results of a regression model that has as a dependent variable an index of overvaluation based on Dollar (1992). To better understand the idea here, consider the following decomposition of the real exchange rate:

$$q_{it} = \bar{q}_{it} + \hat{q}_{it} \tag{3}$$

where the bar on top of the variable indicates an equilibrium value and the hat indicates a disequilibrium value. Then our strategy is based on the following regression:

$$\Delta\hat{q}_{it} = \kappa' x_{it} + \delta\Delta R_{it} + \eta_i + u_{it} \tag{4}$$

Note that some simple manipulations of (1), (3), and (4) yield

$$\Delta\bar{q}_{it} = \Delta q_{it} - \Delta\hat{q}_{it} = (\kappa - \omega)' x_{it} + (\beta - \delta)\Delta R_{it} + error$$

so that from those regressions it is possible to recover the impact of remittances on the real equilibrium exchange rate.

Econometric Issues

There are two problems that have to be faced before proceeding with the results of the estimation. First, there is the potential reverse causality from the real exchange rate to the remittances. Rajan and Subramanian (2005) note that countries that had overvalued exchange rates in the early 1990s received significantly lower remittances during the rest of the decade, and argue that it is plausible that if emigrants perceive an overvalued exchange rate, they may switch to sending goods directly. Similarly, following a devaluation emigrants can have incentives to send home more remittances. In this regard, the expected positive causal relationship from remittances to the real exchange rate can be contaminated by a possible negative causal relation from changes in the real exchange rate to remittances. To somewhat address the potential reverse causality, one can resort to IV estimation techniques and follow Aggarwal, Demirgüç-Kunt, and Martínez Pería (2005), who propose two instruments for remittances: the level of output per capita of the host countries of migrant workers, weighted by (i) distance between sending and receiving country and (ii) share of migrants of the receiving country in the sending country. In the results section we use as instruments the (logged) levels and first differences of these two variables.

Second, there is the issue of measurement error in the remittances data that, if not addressed, will lead to inconsistent results. In fact, a number of development practitioners have argued that part of the observed increase in officially recorded remittances over the past few years is likely to be related to improvements in the statistical capacity of recipient countries. In this context, however, the use of instrumental variables will also correct for this aspect, provided that the measurement error in the data is uncorrelated with the levels of output per capita of the host countries of migrant workers, something that at least a priori, seems reasonable.

Results

Remittances and the Real Exchange Rate

We start this section by presenting results corresponding to equation (1) under the restriction that the GDP growth rate does not enter into the equation, so that if remittances affect the exchange rate though their impact on growth, this specification should capture their full impact. Column (I) of table 7.2 suggests that indeed remittances would lead to a real exchange rate appreciation. Judging from point estimates, this basic model indicates that a 1 percentage point increase in the remittances to GDP ratio would lead to a real effective exchange rate appreciation of about 2.5 percent. Thus a doubling of the remittances to GDP ratio would lead to a real exchange rate appreciation of 5 percent. This estimate is much lower than the estimate of Amuedo-Dorantes and Pozo (2004), which, as noted above, would be slightly above 22 percent.

The estimates for the rest of the variables in this specification carry the expected signs, although they are not always statistically different from zero. As discussed above, higher interest rates and improvements in the terms of trade would, in principle, be associated with a higher real exchange rate. Regarding government consumption, if it falls disproportionately on nontradable goods, (which is not very unreasonable) Balassa-Samuelson considerations would also suggest that it contributes to an appreciation. As for the impact of including GDP growth among the explanatory variables, column (II) indicates only a modest impact. In fact, even if the point estimate of the parameter of GDP growth is negative, it is never significantly different from zero.

Could these results be biased by reverse causality considerations? As discussed above, in principle one would expect that a potential causal relationship from the real exchange rate to remittances would introduce a negative bias in the previous results. However, missing variables considerations could make the sign of the bias go in any direction. Columns (III), (IV), and (V) explore whether the findings in columns (I) and (II) are robust to the use of IV estimation techniques, using as instruments the variables described in the

Table 7.2 The Impact of Remittances on the Real Exchange Rate

Variable	*(I)* FE	*(II)* FE	*(III)* FE/IV1	*(IV)* FE/IV1	*(V)* FE/IV2	*(VI)* FE	*(VII)* FE	*(VIII)* FE/IV1	*(IX)* FE/IV1	*(X)* FE/IV2
Change remittances	2.44	2.42	17.78	18.04	24.06	2.04	2.06	21.43	20.07	29.39
(% of GDP)	*3.26*	*3.22*	*2.93*	*2.85*	*2.35*	*1.95*	*1.96*	*2.31*	*2.31*	*1.96*
Change remittances × LAC						0.83	0.75	–7.87	–4.78	–10.53
(% of GDP)						*0.55*	*0.49*	*–0.54*	*–0.34*	*–0.52*
Interest rates	0.01	0.01	0.02	0.02	0.02	0.01	0.01	0.01	0.01	0.01
(U.S. 6-month rate)	*1.27*	*1.24*	*1.01*	*1.00*	*1.00*	*1.32*	*1.29*	*0.43*	*0.56*	*0.44*
Terms of trade	0.28	0.27	0.24	0.24	0.33	0.28	0.27	0.28	0.26	0.39
(change, %)	*2.96*	*2.81*	*1.38*	*1.37*	*1.32*	*2.91*	*2.77*	*1.42*	*1.39*	*1.34*
Government consumption	0.62	0.69	1.32	1.31	1.03	0.61	0.68	1.26	1.29	0.93
(% of GDP)	*1.43*	*1.54*	*1.52*	*1.50*	*0.85*	*1.40*	*1.51*	*1.38*	*1.44*	*0.71*
Growth		0.10		–0.03	–1.00		0.09		0.00	–1.07
(%)		*0.86*		*–0.13*	*–1.03*		*0.83*		*0.02*	*–1.01*
Number of observations	250	250	221	221	221	250	250	221	221	221
Anderson canon. correlation (p-val)			0.05	0.07	0.17			0.07	0.05	0.10
Sargan test of overidentification (p-val)			0.47	0.48	0.85			0.37	0.31	0.89

Source: Author's calculations.

Note: FE = fixed effects. The table reports the results of regressing the changes in the logged real effective exchange rate on the variables in the first column, allowing for fixed effects. IV1 indicates that remittances are treated as endogenous; IV2 indicates that remittances and growth are treated as endogenous. Instruments are in both cases the level and first differences of (logged) output per capita of the host countries of migrant workers weighted by (i) distance between sending and receiving country and (ii) share of migrants of the receiving country in the sending country. The t-statistics are in italics.

section on Econometric Issues. These specifications indicate that, if anything, the impact of remittances on the real exchange rate would be much larger than in the models that treat remittances as an exogenous variable (that is, the ordinary least squares estimates seem to be affected by a negative bias). In fact, while the estimates in column (I) suggested an impact parameter of about 2.5, with the IV specification, the estimated parameter is more than sevenfold (between 18 and 24, depending on the instrument set used).

Table 7.2 includes two specification tests accompanying our IV models. The first is the Anderson canonical correlations likelihood ratio test, and it assesses the relevance of the instruments. A rejection of the null hypothesis in this test indicates that the model is identified and that the instruments are relevant. The second test assesses the validity of the instruments by means of a Sargan test of overidentifying restrictions. The null hypothesis is that the excluded instruments are not correlated with the error term, and rejection of the null hypothesis points to the presence of invalid instruments. Although column (V) might indicate some problems with the Anderson test, the results do not appear to indicate serious concerns with these tests. Columns (VI) to (X) of table 7.2 report the results of extending the previous basic model as in equation (2); that is, it reports the results of a model that allows remittances to have different impacts on the real effective exchange rate in Latin America and in the rest of the world (using the variable "change remittances × LAC"). The estimates of these exercises indicate that the null hypothesis that the impact of remittances on the exchange rate of the Latin American countries is not different from their impact in the rest of the world cannot be rejected in any case. In fact, the t-statistic of the interaction of remittances and a dummy for the Latin American countries hovers around 0.5 (in absolute value), not coming close to rejection of the null.

Remittances and Real Exchange Rate Misalignment

What is the driver behind the observed real exchange rate appreciation? Is it a reaction of the real equilibrium exchange rate to a positive shock and hence a natural adjustment to a new equilibrium? Or instead, is it a temporary deviation from the equilibrium? We now empirically assess this issue and proceed to regress a measure of real exchange rate misalignment (the cyclical component that results from filtering the real exchange rate using the Hodrick-Prescott filter [with λ=100] on the explanatory variables). That is, we now estimate equation (3), using $\hat{q}_{it}$ rather than q_{it}. The results of this exercise are presented in table 7.3. Inspection of this table indicates that the parameter of remittances continues to be significant. That is, it would be difficult to defend that all the changes in the real exchange rate would be driven by an adjustment toward the new equilibrium. As in table 7.2, the interaction of remittances with a Latin American dummy continues to be not significantly different from zero, and hence we cannot reject the null hypothesis that Latin America is not different from the rest of the world in this case. On the other hand, the point estimates of the

Table 7.3 The Impact of Remittances on Real Exchange Rate Misalignment

Variable	*(I)* FE	*(II)* FE	*(III)* FE/IV1	*(IV)* FE/IV1	*(V)* FE/IV2	*(VI)* FE	*(VII)* FE	*(VIII)* FE/IV1	*(IX)* FE/IV1	*(X)* FE/IV2
Change remittances	1.29	1.31	10.28	11.14	14.19	1.33	1.33	14.87	14.62	19.83
(% of GDP)	*2.30*	*2.31*	*2.66*	*2.65*	*2.27*	*1.69*	*1.68*	*2.36*	*2.42*	*2.05*
Change remittances × LAC						–0.08	–0.04	–9.89	–8.23	–11.31
(% of GDP)						*–0.07*	*–0.03*	*–1.00*	*–0.85*	*–0.86*
Interest rates	0.02	0.02	0.02	0.02	0.02	0.02	0.02	0.01	0.01	0.01
(U.S. 6-month rate)	*2.65*	*2.65*	*1.97*	*1.92*	*1.69*	*2.62*	*2.62*	*0.77*	*0.89*	*0.67*
Terms of trade	0.26	0.26	0.24	0.24	0.26	0.26	0.26	0.28	0.27	0.31
(change, %)	*4.04*	*4.07*	*2.40*	*2.31*	*1.98*	*4.03*	*4.05*	*2.36*	*2.34*	*1.93*
Government consumption	0.29	0.26	0.67	0.64	0.50	0.29	0.26	0.60	0.59	0.41
(% of GDP)	*0.87*	*0.77*	*1.22*	*1.10*	*0.69*	*0.87*	*0.77*	*0.97*	*0.96*	*0.48*
Growth		–0.05		–0.13	–0.61		–0.05		–0.07	–0.67
(%)		*–0.58*		*–0.89*	*–1.05*		*–0.58*		*–0.44*	*–1.01*
Number of observations	250	250	221	221	221	250	250	221	221	221
Anderson canon. correlation (p-val)			0.05	0.06	0.15			0.06	0.05	0.09
Sargan test of overidentification (p-val)			0.31	0.44	0.60			0.39	0.44	0.85

Source: Author's calculations.

Note: FE = fixed effects. The table reports the results of regressing the changes in the estimated real effective exchange rate misalignment on the variables in the first column, allowing for fixed effects. IV1 indicates that remittances are treated as endogenous; IV2 indicates that remittances and growth are treated as endogenous. Instruments are in both cases the level and first differences of (logged) output per capita of the host countries of migrant workers weighted by (i) distance between sending and receiving country and (ii) share of migrants of the receiving country in the sending country. The t–statistics are in italics.

impact of remittances on the degree of real exchange rate misalignment are always smaller than the point estimates of the impact of remittances on the observed real exchange rate, an indication that the observed changes in the real exchange rate are a combination of adjustment toward the new equilibrium and some apparent overshooting.

For example, the basic models in columns (I), (II), (VI), and (VII) would suggest that about one-half of the observed change in the real exchange rate would be due to adjustments in the real equilibrium exchange rate (that is, an estimated impact of remittances on the real exchange rate of 2.1 to 2.5 against an estimated impact of about 1.3 on the measure of misalignment change). On the other hand, the IV-based estimates would suggest that less than one-third of the fluctuations in the real exchange rate would be due to equilibrium adjustments (estimates of β in the 17 to 30 range in table 7.2 and of 10 to 20 in table 7.3).

Tax Structure and Competitiveness

As mentioned earlier the Dutch disease effects are exacerbated by the domestic supply response. Inflationary pressure for domestic nontradables (and thus real exchange rate appreciation) is directly linked to what happens to factors supply, and in particular to labor supply. Econometric evidence shows that labor supply tends to shrink in response to rising remittances. Within the margins of narrow fiscal spaces, can governments implement policies that counteract this negative labor supply and thus mitigate wage and real exchange rate increases?[13]

A policy response considered here consists of a contemporary reduction of payroll taxes and an increase in sales taxes, that is, a partial switch from direct taxes to indirect taxes. Taxing remittances directly is not a viable policy option for at least two reasons: the income generating the remittances has already been taxed at the origin, and the double taxation would increase the agents' incentives to transfer money through the black market; and remittances are an important source of household income, and taxing them could increase the vulnerability of households to income shocks. A reduction in payroll taxes is a better alternative policy tool to limit the negative labor supply response following a remittances shock. From the workers' point of view, lower payroll taxes directly provide greater incentives to work through higher wages. This policy also reduces the wages paid by the employers, and thereby increases their labor demand. Payroll tax (or other direct tax) cuts should be considered as illustrative for any set of policies aimed at stimulating labor supply.[14]

With the help of a computable general equilibrium (CGE) model, we have tested this policy for Jamaica, a country that during the 1990s witnessed, on the one hand, a combination of lagging participation rates (especially for women) and rising real wages and, on the other hand, a remarkable increase in international remittances inflows, reaching almost 20 percent of GDP in 2003.

Using data for Jamaica, we test whether a 25 percent cut in payroll tax is a viable policy to sterilize the reduction in labor supply induced by a 10 percent increase in remittances.[15] The main results are shown in table 7.4. Consider initially the effect of higher remittances in the first column. Total labor income change comprises two components: on the one hand, labor income falls because more nonlabor income encourages households to consume more leisure, but on the other hand, reduced labor supply is accompanied by increased labor demand (given the increased demand for goods) and wages rise. The change in wages adds a set of second-order effects to the change in labor supply, since an increase in the wage rate raises the opportunity cost of leisure and, as long as the substitution effect dominates the income effect, encourages households to supply more labor. Given that skilled and unskilled workers are employed with different intensities across sectors, and that final demand does not increase equally for all goods and services, the general equilibrium effects will differ across the types of workers. In this specific case for Jamaica, the relative wage of unskilled workers increases slightly.

Overall, total labor supply declines by 8,000 workers, which represents about 1 percent of the overall employment. Greater household income generates more demand for consumption goods and services, which is satisfied by a combination of increased domestic supply and import flows. International prices are not affected by this surge in Jamaican imports, whereas prices of domestically produced goods rise in response to domestic market conditions. The erosion of Jamaican competitiveness is summarized in a real exchange rate appreciation of almost 1 percent.

Consider now the effects of the 25 percent cut in the payroll tax. The starting point is the equilibrium attained after the 10 percent remittances shock, and the results, as percentage changes from that previous simulation, are presented in the second column of table 7.4. The third column contains the cumulative change from the initial equilibrium (that is, the total effect of the remittances shock and the policy response). The reduction in payroll taxes increases after-tax wages. In this new situation, households choose to reduce their consumption of more expensive leisure and increase their labor supply. This increase does not fully neutralize the negative withdrawal due to the remittances shock, yet it significantly corrects its initial effect: 72 percent and 47 percent of the remittances-induced reduction in labor supply for unskilled and skilled labor, respectively, is offset by the payroll tax change.

As a result of increased labor force participation and higher wages, household labor income rises by 2.2 percent, with a cumulative increase of 3.7 percent after both simulations. Total household income increases at a slower pace because labor is not their only income source. The reduction in payroll taxes benefits employers by reducing their labor costs. This

Table 7.4 Macroeconomic Results of a Remittances Shock and a Payroll Tax for Jamaica

	Remittances effect, percent change from initial equilibrium	*Tax effect, percent change from remittances shock*	*Total effect, percent change from initial equilibrium*
Remittances	10	0	10
Total household income	2.04	1.16	3.22
Household labor income	1.43	2.20	3.67
CPI	0.54	-0.03	0.50
Real exchange rate	0.88	-0.08	0.80
Real GDP	-0.37	0.10	-0.26
Private consumption	150	1.19	2.71
Investment	-0.06	-2.58	-2.63
Exports	-2.70	0.05	-2.66
Imports	0.81	-0.06	0.75
Unskilled labor supply	-0.76	0.55	-0.21
Skilled labor supply	-0.84	0.40	-0.45
Unskilled wage	2.31	2.08	4.45
Skilled wage	2.26	1.99	4.29
Memo			
Absolute change in unskilled labor supply	-3,822	2,761	-1,061
Absolute change in skilled labor supply	-4,563	2,139	-2,424

Source: Author's calculations using Computable General Equilibrium (CGE) model for Jamaica.

Note: CPI = consumer price index.

counterbalances the remittances-induced appreciation of the real exchange rate by lowering domestic prices, and exports rise and imports fall.

These basic results are unaffected when revenue losses from payroll taxes are compensated for by increasing sales taxes. Sales taxes affect consumption choices and should be preferred to direct increases of income taxes, which could potentially deter future or even current flows of remittances. Increasing taxes on international trade is not recommendable, since protectionism is likely to reduce welfare at home.

In sum, a reduction in payroll taxes compensated for by an increase in sales taxes appears to counteract many of the undesirable effects of increased remittances inflows: lower rates of labor force participation and reduced export competitiveness. However, this switch from direct to indirect taxation can have relevant income distribution consequences, which need to be taken into consideration. Although in principle indirect taxes tend to be regressive and their increase should have worse consequences for poorer individuals, for the case of Latin America, Goñi, López, and Servén (2006) have shown that the impact of taxes overall (direct and indirect) on the distribution of income is minimal.

Conclusions

In this chapter we have reviewed the impact of workers' remittances on the real exchange rate and concluded that surges in workers' remittances are typically accompanied by real exchange rate appreciations. Moreover, our analysis does not detect any differential impact for the Latin American region. We have also explored whether the estimated appreciation would be consistent with the natural appreciation that one would expect in the real equilibrium exchange rate following a positive shock, or instead whether the observed changes are more likely to be driven by changes in the misalignment component. The findings of the chapter would indicate that not all of the observed changes are consistent with the equilibrium changing according to the new fundamentals.

Against this backdrop, a natural question arises: What can policy makers do about that real appreciation, and therefore about the potential losses in international competitiveness that may come with large remittances flows to the region? We now discuss these issues.

- Rein in fiscal policy. Fiscal restraint is probably one of the only tools that governments have to prevent overheating and avoid a real exchange rate appreciation in the context of a surge in international workers' remittances. Beyond the theoretical reasoning in support of this tool,[16] the estimates presented in this paper indicate that increases in the government consumption to GDP ratio would be associated with real appreciations. Yet it must also be noted that our estimates indicate that the impact of this variable tends to be much lower than the impact of remittances. In other words, the adjustment needed to stabilize the real exchange rate may be quite large and therefore constrained by political economy considerations.
- Limit the use of sterilizing operations. One natural question in this context is the extent to which countries should try to sterilize the remittances inflows. Sterilization can be defined as the exchange of government paper for foreign exchange so that the monetary base is insulated from the remittances flows (other sterilization-type policies would include increases in reserve requirements on all or selected

parts of bank deposits). Sterilizing operations could be effective if used over the short run, but may prove infeasible if needed on a sustained basis for two main reasons. First, the magnitude of the remittances would make the quasi-fiscal costs of sterilizing these flows untenable. Large remittances inflows, coupled with Latin American spreads that for the 10 top receiving countries range from 141 basis points (bp) in Mexico to almost 300 bp in Jamaica would in fact make this alternative extremely expensive (to the point that even assuming no pressure on the domestic interest rate, in a number of countries the cost of sterilizing the inflows in full would be measured in tenths of percentage points). Second, sterilization would possibly put pressure on the domestic interest rates—something that may attract other types of inflows in search of high returns, and this in turn would put more pressure on the exchange rate. In this regard, if sterilization is implemented without fiscal adjustment (that is, tight money plus loose fiscal policies) it would not be unlikely to observe a further appreciation.

- Microeconomic interventions. Although the thrust of responses to surges of capital inflows of any type (including remittances) may be expected to be in the macro policy arena, there are a number of microeconomic interventions that governments can implement. The discussion in the Remittances and the Real Exchange Rate section suggested that rigidities in labor and product markets could contribute to a real appreciation in this context because of Balassa-Samuelson types of arguments. Thus, efforts aimed at making domestic markets more efficient could also ease exchange rate pressures. More generally, microeconomic interventions that make the economy more competitive could somewhat offset the real exchange rate pressures.
- Consider a shift from payroll taxes to value added taxes (VAT) or sales taxes. As documented in chapter 5 of this book, remittances appear to have a negative impact on labor supply, something that in turn may exacerbate the real exchange rate appreciation and the loss in competitiveness of the economy. Yet as discussed above, a reduction in payroll taxes, compensated for by an increase in VAT or sales taxes, appears to counteract many of the undesirable effects of increased remittances inflows.
- Accept some appreciation. Taking together all the elements in the chapter, and to the extent that fiscal adjustment and microeconomic interventions may not be enough to correct the upward pressures in the real exchange rate, it is possible that Latin American policy makers will have to accept some real appreciation, especially in those countries with substantial flows. This loss of competitiveness, however, should not be viewed as a cost associated with remittances, but rather as a reflection of the changing conditions brought by the significant remittances flows.

Annex A

The argument that a real exchange rate appreciation is a natural outcome in the presence of remittances can be illustrated with a simple model of exchange rate determination. Here, we follow Alberola et al. (1999) and assume that there are two countries in the world, each producing two goods: one tradable (subscript T, in what follows) and one nontradable (N). The real exchange rate (q) is defined as the relative price of domestic to foreign goods in the consumption basket, p and p^*, respectively,[17] expressed in domestic currency:

$$q = p - (s + p^*), \tag{A1}$$

where s is the (log) nominal exchange rate, defined as the price of foreign currency in terms of domestic currency. Thus, an increase in q represents an appreciation of the real exchange rate.

The consumer price index for each country is a weighted average of the tradable, nontradable, and imported (tradable) prices, all expressed in their own currencies:

$$\begin{aligned} p &= (1-\alpha_N-\alpha_T)p_T+\alpha_N p_N+\alpha_T(s+p_T^*) \\ p^* &= (1-\alpha_N^*-\alpha_T^*)p_T^*+\alpha_N^* p_N^*+\alpha_T^*(p_T-s) \end{aligned} \tag{A2}$$

where the α's are the weights of the respective goods in the consumer basket. Substituting these expressions in (A1), assuming that $\alpha_N = \alpha_N^*$ and rearranging terms, we obtain

$$q = (1-\alpha_T-\alpha_T^*)q_X+\alpha_N q_I \tag{A3}$$

where:

- $q_X = \left[p_T-(s+p_T^*)\right]$ is the relative price of domestic to foreign tradables and
- $q_I = \left[(p_N-p_T)-(p_N^*-p_T^*)\right]$ is the price of nontradables relative to tradables across countries.

The first component of (A3) ($(1-\alpha_T-\alpha_T^*)q_X$), captures the competitiveness of the economy and determines the evolution of the foreign asset position, while the second ($\alpha_N q_I$) plays a central role in adjusting excess demand across sectors in the economy. Each relative price adjusts to achieve equilibrium in one of the markets, and hence we will denote q_X and q_I as the internal and the external relative prices, respectively. The equilibrium exchange rate ($\bar{q}$, where the bar denotes equilibrium values) will require simultaneous equilibrium in both markets, and thus it will be a combination of the equilibrium internal and external relative prices.

We next characterize the external and internal equilibrium of the economy.

External Equilibrium

Portfolio models of real exchange rate determination (Mussa 1984) focus on asset equilibrium, as defined by the attainment of agents' desired foreign asset stock. Over time, the accumulation of net foreign assets (F) is given by the current account balance (CA), which equals the trade balance (XN), plus the net income that residents receive (or pay) on F, plus net current transfers from abroad (T). For simplicity, we will assume that the only transfers in this economy are international remittances (R), so that we can write

$$\Delta F = CA = XN + i^{*}F + T = XN + i^{*}F + R \tag{A4}$$

where i^{*} is the international interest rate, which is assumed given. It will be more convenient to focus on the trajectory of the foreign asset stock relative to GDP, which can be written

$$\Delta f = ca = xn + (i^{*} - g)f + r \tag{A5}$$

where f, xn, and r denote the ratios to GDP of the respective uppercase variables, and g is the rate of GDP growth. If the Marshall-Lerner condition holds, an increase in the relative price of domestic tradables q_X shifts consumption toward foreign tradables and worsens the trade balance. Consistent with this interpretation, it is plausible to assume that the trade balance as a percentage of GNP (xn) is given by

$$xn = -\gamma q_x, \quad \gamma > 0. \tag{A6}$$

The capital account deficit reflects the desired rate of accumulation of net foreign assets by the home country, which is assumed to depend on the divergence between the current level of assets as a percentage of GDP (f) and the desired equilibrium level ($\bar{f}$), itself determined by exogenous factors such as savings preferences and demographics, which will not be modelled here:

$$\Delta f = ca = a(\bar{f} - f) \quad a > 0. \tag{A7}$$

Equation (A7) indicates that if the actual net foreign asset position is below its desired level, agents will accumulate assets to reach the target, Conversely, if f is greater than $\bar{f}$, agents will reduce their asset holdings until they reach $\bar{f}$.

Equating (A7) and (A5) after using (A6), and solving for q_x we get

$$q_x = a\gamma(f - \bar{f}) + (i^* - g)/\gamma f + 1/\gamma r. \tag{A8}$$

Equation (A8) shows that the external real exchange rate depends on (i) the divergence between current and equilibrium asset holdings; (ii) the current stock of net foreign assets f; and (iii) the ratio of remittances to GDP. Defining the equilibrium external real exchange rate $\bar{q}_X$ as that consistent with $f = \bar{f}$ (the exchange rate consistent with asset holdings at their equilibrium level) it follows that

$$\bar{q}_X = (i^* - g)/\gamma \bar{f} + 1/\gamma r, \tag{A9}$$

From equation (A9) it follows that (i) improvements in the equilibrium net foreign asset position $\bar{f}$ would lead to a real exchange rate appreciation; (ii) increases in the international interest rate i^* would also lead to a real exchange rate appreciation; (iii) a higher growth rate would be associated with a lower equilibrium real exchange rate; and (iv) increases in the remittances to GDP ratio would be associated with a real exchange rate appreciation.

Internal Equilibrium

The differential behavior of sectoral relative prices between countries determines the evolution of the internal real exchange rate. Sectoral prices are in turn related to the evolution of sectoral productivity. These notions can be illustrated using a simple model with two production factors, labor (L) and capital (K). Output Y in each sector is determined by a Cobb-Douglas production technology:

$$\begin{aligned} Y_N &= A_N L_N{}^{\delta} K_N{}^{1-\delta} \\ Y_T &= A_T L_T{}^{\theta} K_T{}^{1-\theta} \end{aligned} \tag{A10}$$

where $0 < \theta,\ \delta < 1$ represent the intensity of labor in each sector. Labor is perfectly mobile among sectors (but not across countries), implying nominal wage equalization:

$$W_T = W_N = W. \tag{A11}$$

Labor is paid the value of its marginal product $\partial Y_i / \partial L_i = W/P_i$. Under Cobb-Douglas technology, the ratio of marginal productivities is proportional to the ratio of average productivities:

$$\frac{\partial Y_T / \partial L_T}{\partial Y_N / \partial L_N} = \frac{\theta Y_T / L_T}{\delta Y_N / L_N}. \tag{A12}$$

From (A12) it follows that the (log) sectoral price differential is equal to the labor productivity differentials plus a drift capturing the relative intensity of labor. Expressing with lower case the natural logarithms of sectoral labor productivities, (A12) reduces to

$$\bar{p}_N - \bar{p}_T = \log(\theta/\delta) + [(y_T - y_N)] \tag{A13}$$

Neglecting constant terms and denoting $n = [(y_T - y_N) - (y_T^* - y_N^*)]$, the internal equilibrium exchange rate is just

$$\bar{q}_I = \bar{n}. \tag{A14}$$

Thus, in line with the argument put forward by Balassa (1964) and Samuelson (1964), productivity differentials between the tradable and nontradable sectors relative to the foreign country will also affect the evolution of the real exchange rate. In particular, productivity gains in the domestic tradable sector relative to the domestic nontradable sector would result in a real exchange rate appreciation.

How do remittances operate in this context? If the home country spends part of the remittances on nontraded goods, this additional demand will draw labor out of the export sector. Since from (A10) $\partial \gamma / \partial L < 0$, it follows that the productivity of the nontradable sector (y_N) will decline and the productivity of the tradable sector (y_T) will increase. That is, we would expect that

$$(y_T - y_N) = \eta r \tag{A15}$$

with $\eta > 0$. As a result, remittances would also lead to a real exchange rate appreciation in the internal real exchange rate.

On the whole, the previous discussion indicates that remittances can be expected to affect both the internal and the external equilibrium of the economy, and that higher remittances would be associated with real exchange rate appreciations.

Annex B

Initial Benchmark Data: The 2002 Jamaica Social Accounting Matrix (SAM)

The 2002 SAM has been assembled from various sources and includes 22 sectors, 22 commodities, three factors (skilled and unskilled labor, and composite capital), an aggregate household account, government, savings-investment, taxes, tariffs, and the rest of the world (see table 7B.1). In order to construct this SAM, we relied on published STATIN data (national

Table 7B.1 List of Accounts for Jamaica SAM (2002)

Production sectors and commodities	*Factors of production*
1 Export crops	23 Skilled labor
2 Food crops	24 Unskilled labor
3 Livestock	25 Capital and land
4 Forestry fishing	
5 Mining	*Institutions and other accounts*
6 Food products	26 Household
7 Processed sugar	27 Government
8 Beverages and tobacco	28 Investment and savings
9 Textiles and clothing	29 Indirect taxes
10 Wood products	30 Tariffs
11 Paper and print	31 United States
12 Refined oil	32 European Union
13 Chemicals	33 Rest of the world
14 Capital goods	34 Balance of payment
15 Electricity and water	
16 Construction	
17 Commerce	
18 Transport	
19 Financial and insurance services	
20 Real estate & business services	
21 Government services	
22 Other services	

Source: Constructed by authors.

accounts and disaggregated GDP by sector), a 2000 SAM for Jamaica constructed by the International Food Policy Research Institute (IFPRI), the 2002 National Labor Force Survey, the 2002 National Survey of Living Conditions, and the UN Commodity Trade Statistics Database (Comtrade) and UN Trade Analysis and Information System (TRAINS) database.

Macro SAM. In order to build the macroeconomic SAM, we relied mainly on the national accounts data from STATIN. We have followed this sectoral detail with one exception: we have aggregated "other manufacturing"—a very small sector—with "metal products and machinery." Since the VAT are applied equally to domestically produced goods and imports, we impose the VAT on commodities rather than activities for simplicity. STATIN data combines taxes on international trade (tariffs) with other indirect taxes, and therefore we need additional information to separate indirect taxes from tariffs. We collect these data from UN Comtrade and TRAINS databases. We use Comtrade for trade flows (imports and exports) at a disaggregated level, and TRAINS for applied tariff rates in the same commodity groups. This allows us to calculate the overall tariff revenue, and subtract it from other taxes.

Value added. The disaggregation of total value added by sector is available from STATIN. We combine this information with the earlier IFPRI SAM to disaggregate total value added into capital, labor, and indirect tax components. We also take advantage of the information in the Labor Force Survey to ensure that the labor value added by sector is consistent with the aggregate survey results. In order to ensure that all of these constraints are satisfied, we use the RAS technique to estimate the shares of labor, capital, and indirect taxes.

Taxes. We use the VAT rates reported in the IFPRI SAM and apply them to the value added calculated in the previous step. We then adjust tax collection by sector to get the VAT total consistent with the macro SAM. Payroll taxes are not explicitly identified in the SAM—they are calculated within the model using a universal payroll tax rate.

Intermediate and final demand. We use the shares of intermediate consumption to total value added from the IFPRI SAM to obtain a table of input coefficients, which are then applied to our data. Household consumption shares by commodity are calculated from the Survey of Living Conditions, and are quite close to those reported in the IFPRI SAM. We assume that the government consumes only its own services. Aggregate investment (net of stock changes) is split into sectoral investments using coefficients from the IFPRI SAM.

International trade. Data on merchandise imports, exports, and tariffs is obtained from UN Comtrade and UN TRAINS. In order to impute service imports and exports (which include tourism), we use the IFPRI SAM to disaggregate total service exports and imports.

The resulting social accounting matrix is quite unbalanced, although the imbalances are limited to the commodity rows and columns. We balance this SAM using a cross-entropy approach that allows only the input-output coefficients to move (the input-output coefficients from the IFPRI SAM serve as a starting point). This implies that we trust our final demand estimates (which come from the survey and Comtrade data) and allow the production structure to change slightly.

A Brief Description of the CGE Model

Production. Output results from nested constant elasticity of substitution (CES) functions that, at the top level, combine intermediate and value added aggregates. At the second level, the intermediate aggregates are obtained combining all products in fixed proportions (Leontief structure), and total value added is obtained by aggregating the primary factors. The full structure of production nests is shown in figure 7B.1.

Income distribution and absorption. Labor income and capital revenues are allocated to households according to a fixed coefficient distribution matrix derived from the original SAM. Private consumption demand, as well as labor supply decisions, are obtained through maximization of household specific utility function following the linear expenditure system (LES). Household utility is a function of consumption of different goods and leisure. Once total value of private consumption is determined, government and investment demand are disaggregated into sectoral demands according to fixed coefficient functions.

Figure 7B.1 Production Structure of the Jamaica CGE Model

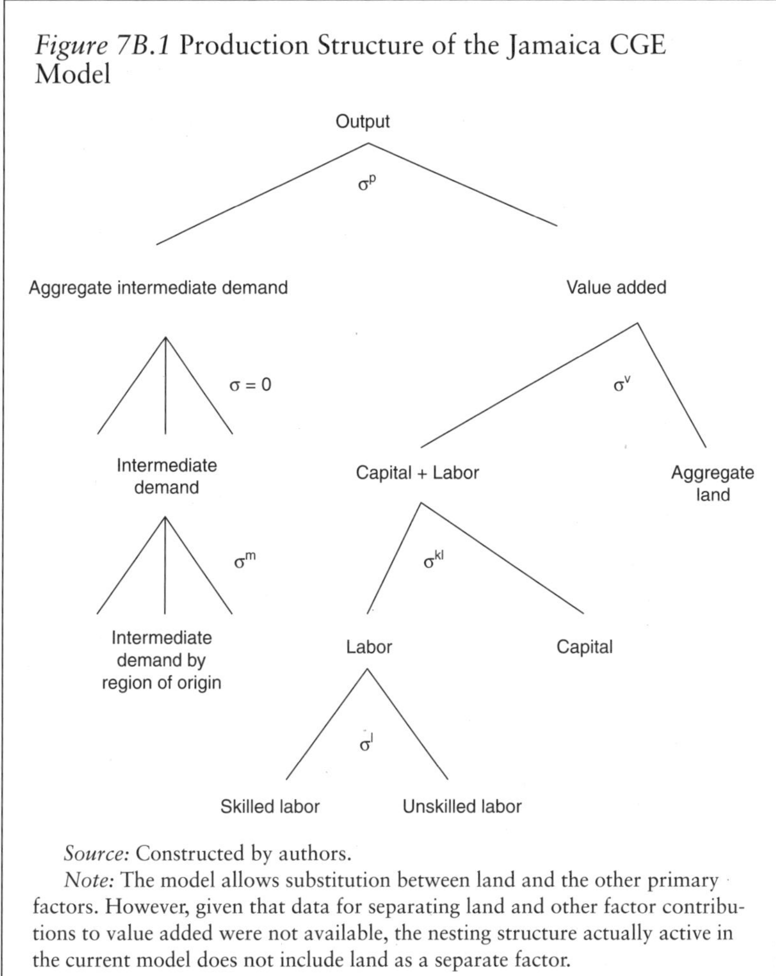

Source: Constructed by authors.

Note: The model allows substitution between land and the other primary factors. However, given that data for separating land and other factor contributions to value added were not available, the nesting structure actually active in the current model does not include land as a separate factor.

International trade. The model assumes imperfect substitution among goods originating in different geographical areas.[18] Import demand results from a CES aggregation function of domestic and imported goods. Export supply is symmetrically modeled as a constant elasticity of transformation (CET) function. Producers allocate their output to domestic or foreign markets, according to relative prices. Under the small country assumption, Jamaica is unable to influence world prices and its import and export prices are treated as exogenous. Assumptions of imperfect substitution and imperfect transformability grant a certain degree of autonomy to domestic prices with respect to foreign prices and prevent the model from generating corner solutions. Furthermore, they permit cross-hauling—a feature normally observed in real economies. The balance of payments equilibrium is determined by the equality of foreign savings (which are exogenous) to the value of the current account. With fixed world prices and capital inflows, all adjustments are accommodated by changes in the real exchange rates. Increased import demand due, for instance, to trade liberalization, must be financed by increased exports, and these can expand due to improved resource allocation. Import price decreases drive resources toward export sectors and contribute to falling domestic resource costs (or real exchange rate depreciation).

Factor markets. Labor is divided into two categories: skilled and unskilled. These categories are considered imperfectly substitutable inputs in the production process. The labor market skill segmentation[19] has become a standard assumption in CGE modeling and is easily justifiable for the case of Jamaica, where inequalities in educational endowments and access to education support this assumption. Skilled and unskilled labor types are then aggregated into a composite labor bundle, which is then combined with composite capital (see production nest in figure 7B.1). In the standard version, composite capital and labor types are fully mobile across sectors; however, in a variant version, we assume that labor markets are segmented between agriculture and nonagriculture, with labor fully mobile within each of the two broad sectors, but fully immobile across them. The restrictive conditions of this second version are imposed on the modeling framework so that it mimics more closely the behavior of the economy in the short term when factors are less mobile across sectors. Capital supply is fixed. Labor supply, for both the skilled and unskilled categories, is derived from utility maximization, where individuals choose the optimal consumption level for both commodities and leisure time under their budget constraints.

In order to allow changes in remittances inflows to influence the household decision to supply labor, a consumption-leisure trade-off in the household utility function—similar to the approach of Barzel and McDonald (1973), de Melo and Tarr (1992), and Annabi (2003)—is introduced.

Consider a Stone-Geary utility function and a budget constraint of the following form:

$$u = \sum_{i=0}^{N} \mu_i \ln(C_i - \theta_i) \text{ s.t } \sum_{i=0}^{N} P_i C_i = Y = WT + y \tag{A16}$$

In the utility function, C_i denotes the consumption of good i, with leisure (C_0) being a normal good, θ_i are usually interpreted as consumption minima,[20] and the share parameters μ_i (including μ_0) must sum to unity. T denotes the total time a household has available for work and leisure activities, and the amount of resources available for nonleisure consumption is limited by nonlabor income (y) and total wage income (ignoring savings and taxes for simplicity).[21] Constrained maximization gives rise to the familiar LES demand functions:

$$C_i = \theta_i + \frac{\mu_i}{P_i}(Y - \sum_{i=0}^{N} P_i \theta_i) \tag{A17}$$

The household labor supply is the difference between total time available and the time allocated to consumption of leisure, and substituting the budget constraint into the demand function yields

$$LS = (1 - \mu_0)(T - \theta_0) - \frac{\mu_0}{W}(y - \sum_{i=1}^{N} P_i \theta_i) \tag{A18}$$

Partially differentiating the labor supply equation with respect to disposable income and the wage rate yields the following elasticities:

$$\varepsilon_y = \frac{\partial LS}{\partial y}\frac{y}{LS} = -\frac{\mu_0}{W}\frac{y}{LS} < 0 \tag{A19}$$

$$\varepsilon_W = \frac{\partial LS}{\partial W}\frac{W}{LS} = \frac{\mu_0}{W * LS}(y - \sum_{i=1}^{N} P_i \theta_i) \tag{A20}$$

While the labor supply is decreasing in nonlabor income, the sign of the wage elasticity depends on the ratio of nonlabor income to the total "committed" consumption expenditures.[22]

Model closures. The equilibrium condition on the balance of payments is combined with other closure conditions so that the model can be solved. First, aggregate government expenditures are fixed at the base year value. Government surplus is exogenous, and the household income tax schedule shifts in order to achieve this predetermined net government position. Second, aggregate investment is set equal to aggregate savings. The volume of available savings is determined by a fixed level of foreign savings, exogenous government savings, and households that save a fixed share of their post-tax income (i.e., the marginal propensity to save is fixed).

Notes

1. See Perry et al. (2006) for a discussion of nonmonetary dimensions (including risk considerations) of welfare.

2. Recall that as discussed in chapter 1, there are a number of Latin American countries where remittances are above 10 percent of GDP, and in the case of Haiti they reach almost 40 percent.

3. A reduction of payroll (or other direct) taxes (compensated for by an increase in indirect taxes) is the most straightforward of such policies; however, one can also think of other polices that increase labor market flexibility and ultimately reduce wage pressure (and support labor demand).

4. This is a typical result of economic models with labor mobility.

5. The stability of remittances over time is one of the most important differences between remittances and other types of capital inflows. In fact, as noted by IMF (2005), non-FDI private capital flows, exports, FDI, and even official aid all show greater volatility than remittances.

6. The countries in their sample are Argentina, Belize, Bolivia, Colombia, the Dominican Republic, El Salvador, Guatemala, Honduras, Jamaica, Mexico, Nicaragua, Peru, and Trinidad and Tobago.

7. Recall that as argued above, increases in q correspond to a real exchange rate appreciation.

8. In this context, it seems more appropriate to work with the remittances to GDP ratio than with, for example, remittances per capita. The reason is that in principle one would expect that the real exchange rate is more affected when remittances are large relative to the size of the economy than when they are large relative to the population.

9. This, however, would require that the main effect of remittances on the exchange rate is through the growth channel described above and that the country has a positive net foreign asset position.

10. This can occur if regional migration flow patterns are different, and as a result, migrants remit for different purposes. Once again, remittances that result in higher consumption will likely lead to an appreciation of the real exchange rate, whereas remittances that lead to higher investment may have less of an effect.

11. The remittances data are as in Aggarwal, Demirgüç-Kunt, and Martínez Pería (2005), and the data come from the IMF's *World Economic Outlook 2005* database. As for the rest of the variables, the terms of trade and per-capita growth variables come from the *World Development Indicators* database, government consumption is from the *World Economic Outlook 2005* database, and the world real interest rate is computed using the U.S. interest rate (six month) and U.S. producer price index from the *International Financial Statistics*.

12. For example, the base year of all the countries in the sample will have the same value, say 100. Clearly, this does not imply that the real exchange rate level is comparable among them.

13. The following discussion draws heavily on Bussolo and Medvedev (2007).

14. Here we assume that the government, through a cut in the payroll tax, is directly able to stimulate supply by reducing the wedge between wages paid by the employers and those received by the workers; however, the actual fiscal instruments at the government's disposal may be less direct, and revenues from payroll taxes

may not be easily substituted by revenues from other taxes. Less direct ways of affecting labor market outcomes may consist of a set of microeconomic interventions aimed at increasing market flexibility and labor productivity (see below).

15. This increase in remittances inflows is not very large considering the rapid pace of remittances growth over the last decade. Since remittances represent approximately one-fifth of Jamaican total household income, a 10 percent remittances shock raises total household income by 2 percent.

16. That fiscal expansions (contractions) lead to a real exchange rate appreciation (depreciation) in the presence of perfect capital mobility is a typical result of the basic IS-LM model.

17. An asterisk denotes foreign variables.

18. See Armington (1969) for details.

19. See Taubman and Wachter (1986) for a general discussion of labor market segmentation.

20. Note that there is no theoretical requirement for any of the θ_i to be positive.

21. Note that the price of leisure is the economywide wage rate W ($P_0 = W$).

22. This sign ambiguity allows for a backward-bending labor supply curve.

References

Aggarwal, R., A. Demirgüç-Kunt, and M.S. Martínez Pería. 2005. "Do Workers' Remittances Promote Financial Development?" Unpublished, World Bank, Washington, DC.

Alberola, E., S.G. Cervero, H. López, and A. Ubide. 1999. "Global Equilibrium Exchange Rates: Euro, Dollar, 'Ins,' 'Outs' and Other Major Currencies in a Panel Cointegration Framework." Working Paper No. 175, International Monetary Fund, Washington, DC.

———. 2002. "Quo vadis euro?" *European Journal of Finance* 8 (4): 352–70.

Alberola, E., and H. López. 2001. "Internal and External Exchange Rate Equilibrium in a Cointegration Framework. An Application to the Spanish Peseta." *Spanish Economic Review* 3 (1): 23–40.

Amuedo-Dorantes, C., and S. Pozo. 2004. "Workers' Real Exchange Rate: A Paradox of Gifts." *World Development* 32: 1407–17.

Annabi, N. 2003. "Modeling Labor Markets in CGE Models: Endogenous Labor Supply, Unions, and Efficiency Wages." Poverty and Economic Policy (PEP) Network working paper.

Armington P.S. 1969. "A Theory of Demand for Products Distinguished by Place of Production." *IMF Staff Papers* 16: 159–78.

Balassa, B. 1964. "The Purchasing Power Parity Doctrine: A Reappraisal." *Journal of Political Economy* 72: 584–96.

Barzel, Y., and R. McDonald. 1973. "Assets, Subsistence, and the Supply Curve of Labor." *American Economic Review* 63 (4): 621–33.

Bussolo, M., and D. Medvedev. 2007. "Do Remittances Have a Flip Side? A General Equilibrium Analysis of Remittances, Labor Supply Responses and Policy Options for Jamaica." Policy Research Working Paper No. 4143, World Bank, Washington, DC.

De Melo, J., and D. Tarr. 1992. *General Equilibrium Analysis of US Foreign Trade Policy*. Cambridge, MA: MIT Press.

Dollar, D. 1992. "Outward-Oriented Developing Economies Really Do Grow More Rapidly: Evidence from 95 LDCs, 1976–1985." *Economic Development and Cultural Change* 40 (3): 523–44.

Frenkel, J., and M. Mussa. 1985. "Asset Markets, Exchange Rates, and the Balance of Payments." In *Handbook of International Economics, Vol. 2*, ed. R.W. Jones and P.B. Kenen. Amsterdam: North-Holland.

Goñi, E., H. López, and L. Servén. 2006. "Fiscal Reform for Social Equity in Latin America." Unpublished, World Bank, Washington, DC.

IMF (International Monetary Fund). 2005. *World Economic Outlook*. Washington, DC: International Monetary Fund.

———. Various years. *International Financial Statistics*. Washington, DC: International Monetary Fund.

Mussa, M. 1984. "The Theory of Exchange Rate Determination." In *Exchange Rate Theory and Practice, NBER Conference Report,* ed. J. Bilson, and R. Marston, Chicago, IL: University of Chicago Press.

Perry, G., O. Arias, H. López, W. Maloney, and L. Servén. 2006. *Poverty Reduction and Growth: Virtuous and Vicious Circles.* Washington, DC: World Bank.

Rajan, R., and A. Subramanian. 2005. "What Undermines Aid's Impact on Growth?" Unpublished, International Monetary Fund, Washington, DC.

Samuelson, P.A. 1964. "Theoretical Notes on Trade Problems." *Review of Economics and Statistics* 46: 145–54.

Taubman, P., and M. Wachter. 1986. "Segmented Labor Market." In *Handbook of Labor Economics, Vol. 2,* ed. O. Ashenfelter and P.R.G. Layard. Amsterdam: North-Holland.

World Bank. 2003. *World Development Report 2003: Sustainable Development in a Dynamic World.* Washington, DC: World Bank.

———. 2006. *Global Economic Prospects: Economic Implications of Remittances and Migration.* Washington, DC: World Bank.

8

Do Conditional Cash Transfer Programs Crowd Out Private Transfers?

*Pedro Olinto and Mette E. Nielsen**

There is extensive economics literature, both theoretical and empirical, that focuses on whether public spending crowds out private spending and on the implications for policy design of this potential crowding. Could it be also possible that public transfers affect remittances, which in essence are private transfers, and that increases in the former result in at least a partial decline in the latter?

Introduction

The effectiveness of public assistance programs for families who receive remittances may be weakened to the extent that private income transfers, motivated by altruism, are crowded out by public transfers. Interhousehold transfers are an important source of income for many families, particularly those who live in poverty. Thus, testing for crowding out of private transfers by public transfers is an important part of assessing the effectiveness of welfare programs.

There is extensive economics literature that has focused on whether public spending crowds out private spending. Martin Bailey (1971) first

* This chapter is based on the paper "Do Conditional Cash Transfers Crowd Out Private Transfers? Evidence from Randomized Trials in Honduras and Nicaragua," by Mette E. Nielsen and Pedro Olinto (2007).

proposed that increases in some public spending categories, like school lunches, would likely substitute for private consumption and therefore, as the government spends more on that item, individual households would likely cut their consumption. True, government consumption does not need to always substitute for private consumption, and in fact there are spending categories, such as transportation, that probably act as a complement rather than as a substitute. In those cases, public spending will crowd in private spending.

At the aggregate level then, one would expect to find public spending categories that substitute for private spending coexisting with others that complement them. What does the empirical evidence have to say in this regard? Earlier works on the topic (see, for example, Kormendi [1983] and Aschauer [1985] for the United States and Ahmed [1986] for the United Kingdom) found evidence of the substitutability argument. Yet Evans and Karras (1996) analyzed the evidence in 54 countries and found that at standard significance levels, in a large majority of cases they could not reject the null hypothesis that public and private consumption are independent. Interestingly, the results reported by Evans and Karras also indicate significant heterogeneity between developed and developing countries: In fact, public consumption would appear to substitute for private consumption in developing countries and to complement it in developed countries. This result is also found by López, Schmidt-Hebbel, and Servén (2000), who estimate a private consumption function derived from first principles using a cross-national panel database. In this case, however, the hypotheses that public consumption complements in richer countries and substitutes in poorer countries cannot be rejected at standard levels.

A similar line of reasoning can be put forward for a potential relationship between public and private investment. If public investment drives down the rate of return of private investment, perhaps because the public sector is involved in activities that could be carried out by the private sector, or because deficit financing of the investment raises domestic interest rates, then it is likely that public investment will crowd out, at least in part, private investment. On the other hand, governments also invest in activities that raise the rate of return of private projects (for example, infrastructure projects). In those cases, it is likely that public investment will have a net positive effect on private investment.

Once again, what does the empirical evidence have to say on this issue? Easterly, Rodriguez, and Schmidt-Hebbel (1994) argue that there are a large number of developing countries where public investment is found to have a negative and statistically significant effect on private investment. Other studies for developing countries (Blejer and Khan 1984; Khan and Reinhart 1990) also found that public investment has, at best, ambiguous results on private investment.

In this chapter we add to the literature exploring the degree of substitutability between public and private spending, and focus on whether a particular type of public transfers, conditional cash transfers, or CCTs, substitute for a particular type of private transfers, remittances. CCT programs have become pervasive in Latin American and the Caribbean. They currently reach more than 60 million people, representing approximately 60 percent of the extremely poor in the region (Lindert, Skoufias, and Shapiro 2005). In Mexico and Brazil alone, OPORTUNIDADES (Opportunities) and Bolsa Familia, respectively, take approximately 0.4 percent of these countries' GDPs. A natural concern of policy makers and academics alike is whether these programs are in fact crowding out private transfers, particularly remittances, which represent an important source of foreign exchange for most countries in Latin America. This would be the case if, for example, recipients of remittances are in the same income range targeted by CCTs. If private transfers do play a role in fighting poverty, policy makers may fear that public transfers substitute for private transfers, and thus do not have the expected impacts on the welfare of the poor. It is therefore crucial to establish whether CCTs tend to crowd out private transfers before prescribing these programs to developing nations.

The problem of public cash transfers crowding out private ones has been examined before by several authors. Schoeni (1996) finds that private assistance in the form of both cash and time-help were crowded out by Aid to Families with Dependent Children (AFDC) benefits in the United States. Also, Schoeni (2002) concludes that unemployment insurance crowds out interfamilial transfers. However, the empirical robustness of the estimated effects in both studies is questionable.[1] Beneficiaries of social programs are known to move to states that offer better benefits. Thus, beneficiaries who have less access to interfamilial transfers may in fact choose to live in states in which the rules for enrollment in social insurance programs are favorable to them.

Similarly, Cutler and Gruber (1996) find that the extension of Medicaid to pregnant women and children in the United States crowds out private insurance coverage. But like the Schoeni studies, one may question the validity of the empirical methods employed.[2] If states expand coverage of public insurance schemes to respond to a reduction in private coverage, the estimators utilized will be biased. Cox, Eser, and Jimenez (1998) also find that social security benefits crowd out the incidence of private transfers in Peru. However, their estimator may also be biased downward because those who are more likely to receive social security may also be less likely to receive private transfers because of unobserved household characteristics, such as, for instance, access to savings and to credit markets. That is, in developing countries like Peru, it is well known that formal workers who have access to social security also tend to have more access to credit and savings mechanisms, and are better able to mitigate shocks and less likely to need private transfers.

The recent availability of data from social experiments of CCTs have allowed for more robust estimation of the hypothesized crowding out effects of public transfers. Attanasio and Rios-Rull (2000) find some weak evidence supporting the crowing out hypothesis for the Mexican CCT program Programa de Educación, Salud y Alimentación (PROGRESA, or Program for Education, Health, and Nutrition), which was implemented in randomly selected communities. However, that study only used one ex post sample survey, ignoring possible baseline imbalances, which further weakened their results. In a more thorough analysis that employs two rounds of the PROGRESA evaluation data, Teruel and Davis (2000) more convincingly reject the crowding out impact of PROGRESA on private transfers.

In this chapter, we address the crowding out question by estimating the impact of CCT programs similar to PROGRESA on private transfers in Honduras and Nicaragua. These countries were chosen because, like Mexico, they implemented experimental CCT pilots to robustly estimate the impact of these programs on a series of outcome variables, including remittances. However, to the best of our knowledge, the data on remittances have not yet been analyzed. This is a policy-relevant question because if remittances react negatively to public transfer programs, then unless the crowding effect is fully incorporated into the analysis, the actual impact of those programs will likely be well below expectations.

The rest of the chapter is organized as follows: In the next section, we describe the *Red de Protección Social* (RPS or Social Protection Network) and *Programa de Asignación Familiar* (PRAF-II or Family Allowance Program) pilot projects and their evaluation designs. We also present some summary statistics for the data that is later used in the econometric analysis. The following section discusses the econometric estimation results. Finally, the chapter closes with some conclusions.

CCT Pilots in Honduras and Nicaragua and Their Evaluation Data

As in the case of PROGRESA in Mexico, both Honduras and Nicaragua implemented experimental CCT pilots in poor rural areas. In Honduras, the inhabitants of the 70 poorest municipalities in the country were selected to participate in the PRAF experiment. Of these 70 municipalities, 40 were randomly assigned to participate in the program, while 30 were randomly assigned to a control group.[3] For the RPS in Nicaragua, 42 rural communities (*comarcas*) were included in the experiment. Half were randomly assigned to the program, while the other half were selected for the control group.[4] In both pilots, baseline and follow-up surveys of a sample of beneficiary and control households were conducted before and after the start of the interventions to allow researchers to measure the impact of the interventions on several socioeconomic indicators of interest. Below, we describe each pilot in detail.

Box 8.1 Conditional Cash Transfers in Colombia

Familias en Acción is a conditional cash transfer program that has successfully increased human capital accumulation in low-density, high-poverty regions of Colombia. The program was initiated in 2001, in a context of high unemployment, slow economic growth, increasing armed conflict, and increased poverty rates. Although impact evaluations from Mexico's *Oportunidades* suggested that this program design could be effective, the Colombian doubters argued that *Familias en Acción* would create a culture of dependency and crowd out adult labor; the cash would be diverted to adult consumption; fertility rates would increase; and the human capital impacts observed in Mexico were an anomaly that would not be replicated in Colombia. A well-designed and implemented program, coupled with carefully designed impact evaluations, showed the critics to be wrong and showed the potential of such a program in poor, rural zones. The objectives of the *Familias en Acción* program were as follows:

- complement the income of extremely poor families with children ages 0–18
- reduce the nonattendance and desertion rates of students
- improve health outcomes of children younger than seven years old
- improve health care practices and conditions for children, including aspects such as nutrition, early stimulation, and intrafamily violence

Familias en Acción was implemented in 631 municipalities, covering 58 percent of all low-density areas, and benefited nearly a million children in 340,000 families. Before the program began, the target population had monthly household expenditures below US$30 per capita, 10 percent of the children were severely malnourished, nearly 50 percent of the children age 0–6 were ill, and 9 percent of primary school children and 37 percent of secondary school children were not attending school. Eligible families were the indigent poor living in the target municipality. Families with children younger than age 7 were eligible for a bimonthly transfer equivalent to US$17 if they complied with the growth and development control appointments for their children over the two-month period. Mothers of school-age children received the equivalent of US$5.50 monthly for each child who met the primary school attendance requirements and US$10 monthly for each child who met the secondary enrollment requirements.

An impact evaluation using a randomized sample design showed that after two years, the *Familias en Acción* program had significant impacts on health and education, including the following:

- increased consumption of food, especially proteins and dairy
- increased vaccinations by 7–12 percentage points

(continued)

Box 8.1 Conditional Cash Transfers in Colombia *(continued)*

- increased height of children by 0.62–0.75 centimeters and increased weight by 0.32–0.48 kilograms
- reduced illness by 11 percentage points
- increased secondary school attendance by 4.6–10.1 percentage points
- increased primary school attendance by 3 percentage points, and without generation of the feared adverse incentives
- reduced child labor by an average of 80 hours monthly
- increased adult labor by 3.6–6.5 percentage points
- reduced likelihood of participant migration by 2.5 percentage points
- reduced birth rates by 9–13 percentage points
- static alcohol, tobacco, and other adult consumption

Given these positive results, the future of the program looks bright. The government has been implementing the program in pilot urban areas to determine its effectiveness in high-density, high-poverty zones and, depending on the results from future impact evaluations, the government plans to expand coverage to the entire poor population by 2019. On a larger scale, Familias en Acción shows that a successful conditional cash transfer program is not specific to the Mexico Oportunidades context or Brazil's Bolsa Escola program, both programs that have been well evaluated. Careful evaluation has provided a new data point that supports the human capital accumulation power of conditional cash transfers, with few of the efficiency losses predicted.

Source: Perry et al. 2007.

The PRAF-II Program in Honduras

The *Programa de Asignación Familiar* (PRAF) is one of the largest social welfare programs in Honduras. PRAF was initiated in 1990 as a social safety net to compensate the poor for lost purchasing power brought about by macroeconomic adjustments. It was restructured in 1998, and now includes a reformulated CCT pilot project known as PRAF—Phase II (henceforth referred to as PRAF-II). The objective of this project is to encourage poor households to invest in family education and health by providing monetary incentives to increase primary school enrollment and use of preventive health care services.

PRAF-II was launched in October 2000. It has the following specific objectives: (i) boost the demand for education services; (ii) encourage the "education community" to take part in children's learning development; (iii) instruct mothers of young children in feeding and hygiene practices;

(iv) ensure that sufficient money is available for a proper diet; (v) promote demand for, and access to, health services for pregnant women, nursing mothers, and children under age 3; and (vi) ensure timely and suitable health care for PRAF beneficiaries.

PRAF-II was piloted in 40 municipalities selected randomly from a set of 70 similarly poor municipalities in western Honduras. The municipalities were selected in October 1999, and the interventions began in late 2000. Among the 30 control municipalities, 10 were supposed to receive supply-side block grants, to be invested in health centers and schools. But by the final round of data collection of the evaluation study, these block grants had not been delivered.

PRAF-II has two CCT components: one for health and nutrition, and another for education. The CCT for health and nutrition consists of monetary transfers to pregnant women and mothers of children less than 3 years old. The monetary voucher is provided only for women who have visited health clinics every month, as required by the program. Each family may receive up to two vouchers per month (one woman and one child, or two children), each worth approximately US$4.

The CCT component for education consists of monetary payments to families for each child ages 6 to 12 who is enrolled in the first four years of primary school and attends regularly. A maximum of three children per family are eligible (this is in addition to any monetary payments received from the transfer for health and nutrition). The family receives approximately US$5 per month for each eligible child. To be eligible for a payment, the child needs to be enrolled by the end of March (the school year in Honduras begins in March and ends in December) and to maintain an attendance rate of at least 85 percent. In fact, although the enrollment requirement was supposed to be strictly enforced, there were serious problems monitoring attendance, so for most families the 85 percent attendance requirement was not enforced.

The RPS in Nicaragua

The *Red de Protección Social* (RPS) is a CCT program comprising two phases over five years, starting in 2000. The pilot phase lasted three years. For this pilot, the government of Nicaragua selected the departments of Madriz and Matagalpa from the northern part of the central region, on the basis of poverty as well as on their capacity to implement the program. Approximately 80 percent of the rural population in Madriz and Matagalpa were poor, and half of those were extremely poor (IFPRI 2002). From these two departments, 42 *comarcas* were selected to participate in the pilot, with half to receive the intervention, and the other half to serve as control communities.[5]

The RPS has two core components. A food security, health, and nutrition component gives each eligible household a conditional cash transfer known as the *bono alimentario*, or food security transfer, every other month, contingent on attendance at educational workshops held every other month, and on bringing children under age 5 for scheduled preventive (or well child) health care appointments. Second, an education component is given to each eligible household as a cash transfer known as the *bono escolar*, or school attendance transfer, every other month, contingent on enrollment and regular school attendance of children ages 7 to 13 who have not completed the fourth grade of primary school. Additionally, for each eligible child, the household receives an annual cash transfer intended for school supplies (including uniforms and shoes) known as the *mochila escolar*, or school supplies transfer, which is contingent on enrollment. The amounts for each transfer were initially determined in U.S. dollars and then converted into Nicaraguan córdobas (C$) in September 2000. The food security transfer was US$224 a year, and the school attendance transfer was US$112. Both were delivered to beneficiaries every two months.

The Evaluation Data

In Honduras, a representative sample from the 70 municipalities of approximately 5,600 households was surveyed in 2000 and again in 2002, which was before and after the PRAF-II pilot was launched. In Nicaragua, a representative sample from the 42 *comarcas* of approximately 1,500 households were surveyed in 2000, just before the program began, and then again in 2001 and 2002. The household questionnaires applied in both countries collected data on (i) housing, education, and employment of all household members; (ii) education (very detailed) of all children ages 6 to 16; (iii) the health of all women who were pregnant in the past 12 months; (iv) the health of all children below 3 years of age (and height, weight, and hemoglobin information for all children under 5 years); (v) consumption expenditures on food and nonfood items; (vi) access to credit; (vii) remittances received from household members who have moved away; (viii) receipt of assistance from various government and private agencies; (ix) ownership of livestock and durable goods; (x) time spent by the "woman of the house" and by children ages 6 to 12 doing various activities; and (xi) households' evaluation of the quality of local health centers and primary schools.

As seen by the figures in table 8.1, households are about evenly divided between intervention and control groups, indicating that at least the level of attrition was not significantly different between them (see Maluccio and Flores (2004), for a more detailed analysis of the attrition in this sample, which concludes that attrition is not correlated to treatment or control status). Table 8.1 also shows that very few households in this sample received remittances during the years covered by the survey (between 4 percent in 2000 and 6 percent in 2002). Differences between the treatment and control samples suggest, at first glance, that there is no impact of RPS on the

Table 8.1 Summary Statistics of Eligible Households Surveyed in Nicaragua in 2000, 2001, and 2002

		2000			*2001*			*2002*		
		C	*T*	*Total*	*C*	*T*	*Total*	*C*	*T*	*Total*
ALL	Number of households (HH)	771	810	1,581	687	766	1,453	675	722	1,397
	% of HH that participated in the program	n.a.	n.a.	n.a.	0	94.9	50.0	0	94.5	48.8
	Average annual HH expenditure (US$)	1,512	1,527	1,520	1,315	1,637	1,485	1,364	1,588	1,480
	% of HH that received remittances	5	3	4	6	4	5	6	7	6
	Remittances as % of HH expenditure*	4	4	4	5	4	5	3	3	3
	Average remittances received (US$)*	46	61	52	57	45	52	31	47	40

(continued)

Table 8.1 Summary Statistics of Eligible Households Surveyed in Nicaragua in 2000, 2001, and 2002 *(continued)*

		2000			*2001*			*2002*		
		C	*T*	*Total*	*C*	*T*	*Total*	*C*	*T*	*Total*
EXTREME POOR	Number of households (HH)	338	299	637	300	283	583	291	260	551
	% of HH that participated in the program	n.a.	n.a.	n.a.	0	97.5	47.3	0	97.7	46.1
	Average annual HH expenditure (US$)	952	943	948	1,121	1,527	1,318	1,142	1,408	1,267
	% of HH that received remittances	4	2	3	7	2	5	4	3	4
	Remittances as % of HH expenditure*	4	2	4	3	3	3	2	5	3
	Average remittances received (US$)*	20	16	19	32	34	33	24	41	32

(continued)

Table 8.1 Summary Statistics of Eligible Households Surveyed in Nicaragua in 2000, 2001, and 2002 *(continued)*

		2000			*2001*			*2002*		
		C	*T*	*Total*	*C*	*T*	*Total*	*C*	*T*	*Total*
MODERATE POOR	Number of households (HH)	264	311	575	238	292	530	236	278	514
	% of HH that participated in the program	n.a.	n.a.	n.a.	0	96.2	53.0	0	95.0	51.0
	Average annual HH expenditure (US$)	1,615	1,672	1,646	1,343	1,734	1,558	1,409	1,706	1,569
	% of HH that received remittances	5	5	5	6	5	5	8	9	9
	Remittances as % of HH expenditure*	4	7	5	7	3	5	4	3	4
	Average remittances received (US$)*	55	73	65	55	33	44	34	65	51

(continued)

Table 8.1 Summary Statistics of Eligible Households Surveyed in Nicaragua in 2000, 2001, and 2002 *(continued)*

		2000			*2001*			*2002*		
		C	*T*	*Total*	*C*	*T*	*Total*	*C*	*T*	*Total*
NONPOOR	Number of households (HH)	169	200	369	149	191	340	148	184	332
	% of HH that participated in the program	n.a.	n.a.	n.a.	0	89.0	50.0	0	89.1	49.4
	Average annual HH expenditure (US$)	2,472	2,175	2,311	1,662	1,653	1,657	1,731	1,666	1,695
	% of HH that received remittances	6	5	5	5	4	4	5	8	7
	Remittances as % of HH expenditure*	2	3	2	6	9	7	3	2	2
	Average remittances received (US$)*	71	67	69	133	80	107	35	20	25

Source: Nielsen and Olinto (2007) and authors' calculations, from RPS program in Nicaragua.

Note: The column with the heading C reports statistics for the control group, whereas that with the heading T reports statistics for the treatment group.

* = receiving households only.

n.a. = not available.

incidence of remittances. If anything, remittances prevalence appears to grow more for treatment than for control households, suggesting, counterintuitively, a positive impact of CCTs on remittances. The average amount received per year is also very low, ranging from US$16 per household per year for the extreme poor to US$107 for nonpoor households. As a share of household expenditures, these transfers range from 2 percent to 9 percent of total annual expenditures for receiving households.

Table 8.2 presents some descriptive statistics for the sample in Honduras. As can be seen, approximately 20 percent of households in the sample received remittances in 2000 and 2002. This figure is slightly higher for the nonpoor and the moderate poor (21 percent in 2000 and 24 percent in 2002), than for the extremely poor (19 percent in 2000 and 18 percent in 2002). There seems to be no substantial differences in the incidence of remittances between the treatment and control households, except perhaps for the extreme poor. But since this difference was present before the program started (baseline difference), the difference in the 2002 data seems to be a consequence of the original difference. The average remittances amount received by a household in 2000 was about US$191 dollars per year. In 2002, the average had increased to approximately U$298 per receiving household per year. For these receiving households, this amount represented approximately 9 percent of annual household expenditures in 2000, and 14 percent in 2002. Also note from table 8.2 that not all eligible (treatment) households participated in the program. About 86 percent of the eligible households living in treatment municipalities took up the program. In the control municipalities, it appears that the program leaks to approximately 4 percent of the "would be" eligible households.

Do CCTs Crowd Out Remittances in Nicaragua and Honduras? Econometric Results

In annex A to this chapter, we discuss the empirical strategy adopted for estimating the crowding out effects of CCTs on private transfers. Here we present and discuss the estimation results. In the next section we offer concluding remarks.

Tables 8.3 through 8.13 contain the results of estimating the instrumental variable (IV) and panel data models specified in annex A. We look at the impact of CCTs on six different measures of private transfers: the incidence of receiving a private food transfer; household daily consumption of donated foods (Honduras only); the probability of receiving remittances; the amount of remittances received in the preceding year (measured in local currency); the probability of receiving food or money from a nongovernmental organization; and the incidence of receiving any of the above types of transfers. The reduced form estimates yield similar results and are presented here, but can be found in Olinto and Nielsen (2007).

Table 8.2 Summary Statistics of Eligible Households Surveyed in Honduras in 2000 and 2002

		2000			*2002*		
		C	*T*	*Total*	C	*T*	*Total*
ALL	Number of households (HH)	1,872	2,554	4,426	1,719	2,381	4,100
	% of HH that participated in the program	n.a.	n.a.	n.a.	4.0	85.7	51.4
	Average annual HH expenditure (US$)	2,296	2,663	2,508	2,060	2,250	2,170
	% of HH that received remittances	20	19	19	21	20	20
	Remittances as % of HH expenditure*	10	9	9	14	14	14
	Average remittances received (US$)*	176	204	191	286	308	298
EXTREME POOR	Number of households (HH)	1,386	1,734	3,120	1,289	1,621	2,910
	% of HH that participated in the program	n.a.	n.a.	n.a.	4.8	87.4	50.8
	Average annual HH expenditure (US$)	1,623	1,715	1,674	1,615	1,725	1,677
	% of HH that received remittances	20	17	19	20	17	18
	Remittances as % of HH expenditure*	10	8	9	14	12	13
	Average remittances received (US$)*	139	111	125	219	215	217
MODERATE POOR	Number of households (HH)	151	233	384	137	217	354
	% of HH that participated in the program	n.a.	n.a.	n.a.	2.9	86.2	54.0
	Average annual HH expenditure (US$)	2,720	2,855	2,802	2,187	2,403	2,319
	% of HH that received remittances	23	20	21	26	24	24
	Remittances as % of HH expenditure*	7	9	8	10	14	12
	Average remittances received (US$)*	154	221	192	213	314	273

(continued)

Table 8.2 Summary Statistics of Eligible Households Surveyed in Honduras in 2000 and 2002 *(continued)*

		2000			*2002*		
		C	*T*	*Total*	C	*T*	*Total*
NONPOOR	Number of households (HH)	335	587	922	293	543	836
	% of HH that participated in the program	n.a.	n.a.	n.a.	1.0	80.3	52.5
	Average annual HH expenditure (US$)	4,891	5,390	5,209	3,955	3,754	3,824
	% of HH that received remittances	19	22	21	24	25	24
	Remittances as % of HH expenditure*	10	9	9	15	17	17
	Average remittances received (US$)*	348	422	396	569	501	524

Source: Nielsen and Olinto (2007) and authors' calculations.

Note: The column with the heading C reports statistics for the control group, whereas that with the heading T reports statistics for the treatment group.

* = receiving households only.

n.a. = not available.

Table 8.3 The Impact of RPS on the Incidence of Receiving at Least One of the Following Transfers: Private Food Transfer, Remittances, and Food or Money Donation from Nongovernmental Organizations

	(1)	*(2)*	*(3)*	*(4)*	*(5)*
	IV	*IV*	*IV*	*RE-IV*	*RE*
Constant	0.2231***	0.2254***	0.2245***	0.2231***	0.2231***
	[0.0149]	[0.0149]	[0.0150]	[0.0151]	[0.0151]
Participation dummy	0.0268	0.0221	0.0235	0.0268	
	[0.0227]	[0.0225]	[0.0227]	[0.0226]	
2001 dummy	0.0418*	0.0399*	0.0410*	0.0423**	0.0423**
	[0.0224]	[0.0224]	[0.0225]	[0.0210]	[0.0210]
2002 dummy	–0.0009	–0.0018	–0.0011	0.0002	0.0003
	[0.0219]	[0.0219]	[0.0219]	[0.0211]	[0.0211]
Participation × 2001 dummy	–0.1024***	–0.0984***	–0.1000***	–0.1019***	
	[0.0324]	[0.0323]	[0.0325]	[0.0309]	
Participation × 2002 dummy	–0.0319	–0.0303	–0.0315	–0.0328	
	[0.0326]	[0.0324]	[0.0326]	[0.0313]	
Ln baseline pc exp. (lnpcx)		0.0385***	0.0235		
		[0.0105]	[0.0147]		
2001 × lnpcx		–0.0334**	–0.0152		
		[0.0150]	[0.0222]		
2002 × lnpcx		–0.0147	–0.0028		
		[0.0151]	[0.0218]		

(continued)

Table 8.3 The Impact of RPS on the Incidence of Receiving at Least One of the Following Transfers: Private Food Transfer, Remittances, and Food or Money Donation from Nongovernmental Organizations *(continued)*

	(1) IV	*(2)* IV	*(3)* IV	*(4)* RE-IV	*(5)* RE
Participation × lnpcx			0.0328		
			[0.0236]		
2001 × participate × lnpcx			–0.0395		
			[0.0335]		
2002 × participate × lnpcx			–0.0262		
			[0.0336]		
Treatment dummy					0.0251
					[0.0211]
2001 × treat dummy					–0.0963***
					[0.0291]
2002 × treat dummy					–0.0308
					[0.0294]
Observations	4,431	4,431	4,431	4,431	4,431
Number of i_var				1,581	1,581

Source: Nielsen and Olinto 2007.

Note: Standard errors in brackets; * significant at 10%; ** significant at 5%; *** significant at 1%. Columns (1)–(3) are IV regressions where actual participation (and its interactions) are instrumented by originally being assigned to treatment, and the stratification of the data are taken into account. Columns (4)–(5) are random effects estimations that ignore stratification; (4) is an IV regression while (5) gives the reduced form for comparison to the results from Honduras.

lnpcx = log baseline per capita household expenditure.

Table 8.4 The Impact of PRAF-II on the Incidence of Receiving at Least One of the Following Transfers: Private Food Transfer, Remittances, and Food or Money Donation from Nongovernmental Organizations

	(1)	*(2)*	*(3)*	*(4)*	*(5)*	*(6)*	*(7)*	*(8)*
	All	*2002*	*All*	*2002*	*All*	*2002*	*RE*	*1st diff*
Constant	0.7207***	0.7235***	0.7224***	0.7237***	0.7213***	0.7240***	0.7169***	0.0041
	[0.0147]	[0.0132]	[0.0147]	[0.0132]	[0.0147]	[0.0132]	[0.0148]	[0.0170]
Participation dummy	–0.1036***	0.0036	–0.1073***	0.0033	–0.1044***	0.0027		
	[0.0232]	[0.0197]	[0.0231]	[0.0197]	[0.0231]	[0.0198]		
2002 dummy	0.0028		0.0013		0.0027		0.0063	
	[0.0177]		[0.0177]		[0.0177]		[0.0186]	
2002 × participation	0.1071***		0.1106***		0.1070***			
Dummy	[0.0275]		[0.0275]		[0.0276]			
Ln baseline pc exp. (lnpcx)			0.0230*** [0.0075]	0.0015 [0.0072]	–0.0040 [0.0122]	0.0069 [0.0117]		
2002 × lnpcx			–0.0215**		0.0109			
			[0.0101]		[0.0166]			
Participation × lnpcx					0.0575*** [0.0209]	–0.0105 [0.0186]		

(continued)

Table 8.4 The Impact of PRAF-II on the Incidence of Receiving at Least One of the Following Transfers: Private Food Transfer, Remittances, and Food or Money Donation from Nongovernmental Organizations *(continued)*

	(1)	*(2)*	*(3)*	*(4)*	*(5)*	*(6)*	*(7)*	*(8)*
	All	*2002*	*All*	*2002*	*All*	*2002*	*RE*	*1st diff*
2002 × participate × lnpcx					–0.0680**			
					[0.0274]			
Treatment dummy							–0.0791***	0.0908***
							[0.0198]	[0.0219]
2002 × treat dummy							0.0835***	
							[0.0237]	
Observations	8,526	4,100	8,526	4,100	8,526	4,100	8,526	4,426

Source: Nielsen and Olinto 2007.

Note: Standard errors in brackets; * significant at 10%; ** significant at 5%; *** significant at 1%. "All" uses data from both years; "2002" uses data from 2002 only. Columns (1)–(6) are IV regressions where actual participation (and its interactions) are instrumented by originally being assigned to treatment, and the stratification and clustering of the data are taken into account. Column (7) is a reduced form random effects estimation, taking into account clustering but not stratification. Column (8) is a regression of first differenced data on the treatment dummy, taking into account the complete survey structure of the data.

Table 8.5 The Impact of RPS on the Incidence of Receiving Remittances

	(1)	*(2)*	*(3)*	*(4)*	*(5)*
	IV	*IV*	*IV*	*RE-IV*	*RE*
Constant	0.0467***	0.0475***	0.0473***	0.0467***	0.0467***
	[0.0076]	[0.0076]	[0.0077]	[0.0078]	[0.0078]
Participation dummy	–0.0130	–0.0146	–0.0144	–0.0130	
	[0.0106]	[0.0106]	[0.0107]	[0.0117]	
2001 dummy	0.0144	0.0139	0.0135	0.0143	0.0143
	[0.0119]	[0.0119]	[0.0119]	[0.0110]	[0.0110]
2002 dummy	0.0111	0.0113	0.0112	0.0111	0.0111
	[0.0117]	[0.0118]	[0.0119]	[0.0111]	[0.0110]
Participation × 2001 dummy	–0.0143	–0.0131	–0.0126	–0.0142	
	[0.0159]	[0.0158]	[0.0160]	[0.0162]	
Participation × 2002 dummy	0.0237	0.0231	0.0231	0.0241	
	[0.0173]	[0.0172]	[0.0174]	[0.0164]	
Ln baseline pc exp. (lnpcx)		0.0130**	0.0110		
		[0.0052]	[0.0081]		
2001 × lnpcx		–0.0099	–0.0156		
		[0.0077]	[0.0114]		
2002 × lnpcx		0.0037	0.0017		
		[0.0078]	[0.0106]		

(continued)

Table 8.5 The Impact of RPS on the Incidence of Receiving Remittances *(continued)*

	(1)	*(2)*	*(3)*	*(4)*	*(5)*
	IV	*IV*	*IV*	*RE-IV*	*RE*
Participation × lnpcx			0.0045		
			[0.0119]		
2001 × participate × lnpcx			0.0116		
			[0.0172]		
2002 × participate × lnpcx			0.0043		
			[0.0174]		
Treatment dummy					–0.0121
					[0.0109]
2001 × treat dummy					–0.0137
					[0.0152]
2002 × treat dummy					0.0227
					[0.0154]
Observations	4,431	4,431	4,431	4,431	4,431
Number of i_var				1,581	1,581

Source: Nielsen and Olinto 2007.

Note: Standard errors in brackets; * significant at 10%; ** significant at 5%; *** significant at 1%. Columns (1)–(3) are IV regressions where actual participation (and its interactions) are instrumented by originally being assigned to treatment, and the stratification of the data are taken into account. Columns (4)–(5) are random effects estimations that ignore stratification; (4) is an IV regression while (5) gives the reduced form for comparison to the results from Honduras.

Table 8.6 The Impact of PRAF-II on the Incidence of Receiving Remittances

	(1)	*(2)*	*(3)*	*(4)*	*(5)*	*(6)*	*(7)*	*(8)*
	All	*2002*	*All*	*2002*	*All*	*2002*	*RE*	*1st diff*
Constant	0.2032***	0.2088***	0.2042***	0.2119***	0.2038***	0.2117***	0.2025***	–0.0041
	[0.0106]	[0.0122]	[0.0106]	[0.0118]	[0.0106]	[0.0119]	[0.0107]	[0.0120]
Participation dummy	–0.0211	–0.0138	–0.0231	–0.0193	–0.022	–0.0189		
	[0.0176]	[0.0179]	[0.0174]	[0.0174]	[0.0175]	[0.0175]		
2002 dummy	0.0056		0.0077		0.0079		0.0028	
	[0.0122]		[0.0121]		[0.0121]		[0.0119]	
2002 × participation dummy	0.0072		0.0038		0.0031			
	[0.0195]		[0.0193]		[0.0195]			
Ln baseline pc exp. (lnpcx)			0.0125**	0.0331***	0.0028	0.0298**		
			[0.0062]	[0.0066]	[0.0105]	[0.0116]		
2002 × lnpcx			0.0206***		0.0270**			
			[0.0077]		[0.0133]			
Participation × lnpcx					0.0206	0.0064		
					[0.0176]	[0.0174]		
2002 × participate × lnpcx					–0.0142			
					[0.0212]			

(continued)

Table 8.6 The Impact of PRAF-II on the Incidence of Receiving Remittances *(continued)*

	(1)	*(2)*	*(3)*	*(4)*	*(5)*	*(6)*	*(7)*	*(8)*
	All	*2002*	*All*	*2002*	*All*	*2002*	*RE*	*1st diff*
Treatment dummy							–0.0161	0.0150
							[0.0143]	[0.0157]
2002 × treat dummy							0.0079	
							[0.0158]	
Observations	8,526	4,100	8,526	4,100	8,526	4,100	8,526	4,426

Source: Nielsen and Olinto 2007.

Note: Standard errors in brackets; * significant at 10%; ** significant at 5%; *** significant at 1%. "All" uses data from both years; "2002" uses data from 2002 only. Columns (1)–(6) are IV regressions where actual participation (and its interactions) are instrumented by originally being assigned to treatment, and the stratification and clustering of the data are taken into account. Column (7) is a reduced-form random effects estimation, taking into account clustering but not stratification. Column (8) is a regression of first-differenced data on the treatment dummy, taking into account the complete survey structure of the data.

Table 8.7 The Impact of RPS on the Amount of Remittances Received

	(1)	*(2)*	*(3)*	*(4)*	*(5)*
	IV	*IV*	*IV*	*RE-IV*	*RE*
Constant	28.5720***	29.5204***	29.3744***	28.5720***	28.5720***
	[9.2299]	[9.3772]	[9.5569]	[9.8321]	[9.8364]
Participation dummy	–0.4760	–2.4382	–2.2093	–0.4760	
	[13.0261]	[13.0660]	[13.4261]	[14.6981]	
2001 dummy	17.9069	17.9756	18.4445	17.9069	17.9069
	[17.1880]	[17.5875]	[18.0938]	[14.3235]	[14.3297]
2002 dummy	–4.4238	–4.8360	–4.8538	–4.4238	–4.4238
	[10.5136]	[10.6599]	[10.8391]	[14.3907]	[14.3969]
Participation × 2001 dummy	–26.0121	–25.9306	–26.5794	–26.0121	
	[21.4693]	[21.8576]	[22.6396]	[21.0831]	
Participation × 2002 dummy	19.7356	20.4808	20.4320	19.7356	
	[20.0645]	[19.7737]	[20.1838]	[21.3420]	
Ln baseline pc exp. (lnpcx)		16.1379***	13.6547*		
		[6.0460]	[7.3974]		
2001 × lnpcx		–1.8157	5.2141		
		[10.5254]	[17.9095]		
2002 × lnpcx		–6.7446	–7.1303		
		[7.6334]	[8.1522]		

(continued)

Table 8.7 The Impact of RPS on the Amount of Remittances Received *(continued)*

	(1)	*(2)*	*(3)*	*(4)*	*(5)*
	IV	*IV*	*IV*	*RE-IV*	*RE*
Participation × lnpcx			5.4332		
			[13.8403]		
2001 × participate × lnpcx			–14.8863		
			[24.5212]		
2002 × participate × lnpcx			0.7123		
			[17.1274]		
Treatment dummy					–0.4448
					[13.7423]
2001 × treat dummy					–24.6946
					[19.8701]
2002 × treat dummy					18.6374
					[20.0671]
Observations	4,431	4,431	4,431	4,431	4,431
Number of i_var				1,581	1,581

Source: Nielsen and Olinto 2007.

Note: Dependent variable is the amount of remittances received in the last 12 months in Cordobas. Standard errors in brackets; * significant at 10%; ** significant at 5%; *** significant at 1%. Columns (1)–(3) are IV regressions where actual participation (and its interactions) are instrumented by originally being assigned to treatment, and the stratification of the data are taken into account. Columns (4)–(5) are random effects estimations that ignore stratification; (4) is an IV regression while (5) gives the reduced form for comparison to the results from Honduras.

Table 8.8 The Impact of PRAF-II on the Amount of Remittances Received

	(1)	*(2)*	*(3)*	*(4)*	*(5)*	*(6)*	*(7)*	*(8)*
	All	*2002*	*All*	*2002*	*All*	*2002*	*RE*	*1st diff*
Constant	584.82***	975.26***	619.87***	1,034.1***	613.25***	1,037.7***	586.01***	363.87***
	[65.3059]	[113.849]	[63.5397]	[111.821]	[65.6771]	[115.009]	[62.5245]	[92.5600]
Participation dummy	32.1651	23.1735	–43.7314	–82.7704	–26.7435	–89.9095		
	[126.969]	[171.115]	[114.352]	[163.544]	[123.624]	[171.835]		
2002 dummy	390.44***		414.18***		424.44***		382.73***	
	[96.871]		[98.639]		[100.981]		[95.079]	
2002 × participation dummy	–8.9915		–39.039		–63.1661			
	[164.114]		[158.164]		[168.074]			
Ln baseline pc exp. lnpcx			470.97***	638.81***	312.60***	699.85***		
			[101.363]	[86.636]	[99.190]	[163.348]		
2002 × lnpcx			167.8404		387.25***			
			[118.428]		[137.742]			
Participation × lnpcx					337.5142	–118.2704		
					[250.088]	[239.313]		
2002 × participate × lnpcx					–455.7847			
					[288.887]			

(continued)

Table 8.8 The Impact of PRAF-II on the Amount of Remittances Received *(continued)*

	(1)	*(2)*	*(3)*	*(4)*	*(5)*	*(6)*	*(7)*	*(8)*
	All	*2002*	*All*	*2002*	*All*	*2002*	*RE*	*1st diff*
Treatment dummy							24.5565	29.8836
							[103.078]	[130.396]
2002 × treat dummy							4.4264	
							[134.224]	
Observations	8,526	4,100	8,526	4,100	8,526	4,100	8,526	4,426

Source: Nielsen and Olinto 2007.

Note: Dependent variable is the amount of remittances received in the last 12 months in Lempiras. Standard errors in brackets; * significant at 10%; ** significant at 5%; *** significant at 1%. "All" uses data from both years; "2002" uses data from 2002 only. Columns (1)–(6) are IV regressions where actual participation (and its interactions) are instrumented by originally being assigned to treatment, and the stratification and clustering of the data are taken into account. Column (7) is a reduced form random effects estimation, taking into account clustering but not stratification. Column (8) is a regression of first differenced data on the treatment dummy, taking into account the complete survey structure of the data.

Table 8.9 The Impact of RPS on the Incidence of Receiving Food

	(1)	*(2)*	*(3)*	*(4)*	*(5)*
	IV	*IV*	*IV*	*RE-IV*	*RE*
Constant	0.1699***	0.1717***	0.1710***	0.1699***	0.1699***
	[0.0134]	[0.0134]	[0.0135]	[0.0137]	[0.0137]
Participation dummy	0.0454**	0.0416**	0.0427**	0.0454**	
	[0.0210]	[0.0209]	[0.0210]	[0.0205]	
2001 dummy	0.0048	0.0029	0.0037	0.0054	0.0055
	[0.0197]	[0.0197]	[0.0198]	[0.0188]	[0.0188]
2002 dummy	0.0005	–0.0003	0.0002	0.0021	0.0023
	[0.0198]	[0.0198]	[0.0199]	[0.0189]	[0.0189]
Participation × 2001 dummy	–0.0603**	–0.0564*	–0.0576*	–0.0594**	
	[0.0295]	[0.0294]	[0.0296]	[0.0277]	
Participation × 2002 dummy	–0.0542*	–0.0529*	–0.0538*	–0.0555**	
	[0.0298]	[0.0296]	[0.0298]	[0.0281].	
Ln baseline pc exp. (lnpcx)		0.0310***	0.0192		
		[0.0099]	[0.0134]		
2001 × lnpcx		–0.0317**	–0.0182		
		[0.0139]	[0.0202]		
2002 × lnpcx		–0.0120	–0.0040		
		[0.0138]	[0.0198]		

(continued)

Table 8.9 The Impact of RPS on the Incidence of Receiving Food *(continued)*

	(1)	*(2)*	*(3)*	*(4)*	*(5)*
	IV	*IV*	*IV*	*RE-IV*	*RE*
Participation × lnpcx			0.0256		
			[0.0222]		
2001 × participate × lnpcx			–0.0292		
			[0.0310]		
2002 × participate × lnpcx			–0.0177		
			[0.0306]		
Treatment dummy					0.0424**
					[0.0192]
2001 × treat dummy					–0.0557**
					[0.0260]
2002 × treat dummy					–0.0521**
					[0.0263]
Observations	4,431	4,431	4,431	4,431	4,431
Number of i_var				1,581	1,581

Source: Nielsen and Olinto 2007.

Note: Standard errors in brackets; * significant at 10%; ** significant at 5%; *** significant at 1%. Columns (1)–(3) are IV regressions where actual participation (and its interactions) are instrumented by originally being assigned to treatment, and the stratification of the data are taken into account. Columns (4)–(5) are random effects estimations that ignore stratification; (4) is an IV regression while (5) gives the reduced form for comparison to the results from Honduras.

Table 8.10 The Impact of PRAF-II on the Incidence of Receiving Food

	(1)	*(2)*	*(3)*	*(4)*	*(5)*	*(6)*	*(7)*	*(8)*
	All	*2002*	*All*	*2002*	*All*	*2002*	*RE*	*1st diff*
Constant	0.6257***	0.6546***	0.6267***	0.6539***	0.6257***	0.6541***	0.6213***	0.0349**
	[0.0166]	[0.0133]	[0.0165]	[0.0133]	[0.0166]	[0.0133]	[0.0166]	[0.0176]
Participation dummy	–0.1199***	–0.0027	–0.1221***	–0.0014	–0.1194***	–0.0019		
	[0.0255]	[0.0204]	[0.0254]	[0.0205]	[0.0255]	[0.0205]		
2002 dummy	0.0289		0.0271		0.0284		0.0335*	
	[0.0185]		[0.0185]		[0.0186]		[0.0197]	
2002 × participation dummy	0.1172***		0.1207***		0.1175***			
	[0.0289]		[0.0289]		[0.0290]			
Ln baseline pc exp. (lnpcx)			0.0142*	–0.0076	–0.0109	–0.0036		
			[0.0082]	[0.0075]	[0.0131]	[0.0120]		
2002 × lnpcx			–0.0218**		0.0073			
			[0.0110]		[0.0169]			
Participation × lnpcx					0.0536**	–0.0078		
					[0.0229]	[0.0193]		
2002 × participate × lnpcx					–0.0614**			
					[0.0292]			

(continued)

Table 8.10 The Impact of PRAF-II on the Incidence of Receiving Food *(continued)*

	(1)	*(2)*	*(3)*	*(4)*	*(5)*	*(6)*	*(7)*	*(8)*
	All	*2002*	*All*	*2002*	*All*	*2002*	*RE*	*1st diff*
Treatment dummy							–0.0915***	0.0953***
							[0.0216]	[0.0229]
2002 × treat dummy							0.0903***	
							[0.0253]	
Observations	8,526	4,100	8,526	4,100	8,526	4,100	8,526	4,426

Source: Nielsen and Olinto 2007.

Note: Standard errors in brackets; * significant at 10%; ** significant at 5%; *** significant at 1%. "All" uses data from both years; "2002" uses data from 2002 only. Columns (1)–(6) are IV regressions where actual participation (and its interactions) are instrumented by originally being assigned to treatment, and the stratification and clustering of the data are taken into account. Column (7) is a reduced form random effects estimation, taking into account clustering but not stratification. Column (8) is a regression of first differenced data on the treatment dummy, taking into account the complete survey structure of the data.

Table 8.11 The Impact of PRAF-II on the Amount of Food Received

	(1)	*(2)*	*(3)*	*(4)*	*(5)*	*(6)*	*(7)*	*(8)*
	All	*2002*	*All*	*2002*	*All*	*2002*	*RE*	*1st diff*
Constant	2.0547***	2.7596***	2.1573***	2.7628***	2.1266***	2.7601***	2.1086***	0.7385***
	[0.1155]	[0.1611]	[0.1109]	[0.1612]	[0.1147]	[0.1616]	[0.1151]	[0.1785]
Participation dummy	1.4611***	0.6484**	1.2375***	0.6427**	1.3174***	0.6479**		
	[0.3099]	[0.2721]	[0.2844]	[0.2723]	[0.3020]	[0.2729]		
2002 dummy	0.7050***		0.6054***		0.6335***		0.6836***	
	[0.1880]		[0.1835]		[0.1861]		[0.2107]	
2002 × participation dummy	–0.8127**		–0.5948		–0.6695*			
	[0.3991]		[0.3781]		[0.3921]			
Ln baseline pc exp. (lnpcx)			1.3978***	0.0341	0.6444***	–0.0105		
			[0.1805]	[0.1153]	[0.1773]	[0.1760]		
2002 × lnpcx			–1.3638***		–0.6549***			
			[0.2146]		[0.2416]			
Participation × lnpcx					1.6045***	0.0863		
					[0.4462]	[0.2907]		
2002 × participate × lnpcx					–1.5182***			
					[0.5262]			

(continued)

Table 8.11 The Impact of PRAF-II on the Amount of Food Received *(continued)*

	(1)	*(2)*	*(3)*	*(4)*	*(5)*	*(6)*	*(7)*	*(8)*
	All	*2002*	*All*	*2002*	*All*	*2002*	*RE*	*1st diff*
Treatment dummy							1.1154***	–0.5842*
							[0.2562]	[0.3187]
2002 × treat dummy							–0.5857*	
							[0.3553]	
Observations	8,526	4,100	8,526	4,100	8,526	4,100	8,525	4,426

Source: Nielsen and Olinto 2007.

Note: Dependent variable is household daily consumption of donated foods in Lempiras at current prices. Standard errors in brackets; * significant at 10%; ** significant at 5%; *** significant at 1%. "All" uses data from both years; "2002" uses data from 2002 only. Columns (1)–(6) are IV regressions where actual participation (and its interactions) are instrumented by originally being assigned to treatment, and the stratification and clustering of the data are taken into account. Column (7) is a reduced form random effects estimation, taking into account clustering but not stratification. Column (8) is a regression of first differenced data on the treatment dummy, taking into account the complete survey structure of the data.

Table 8.12 The Impact of RPS on the Incidence of Receiving Food, Money Transfer, or Both from Nongovernmental Organizations

	(1)	*(2)*	*(3)*	*(4)*	*(5)*
	IV	*IV*	*IV*	*RE-IV*	*RE*
Constant	0.0402***	0.0406***	0.0407***	0.0402***	0.0402***
	[0.0070]	[0.0070]	[0.0071]	[0.0066]	[0.0066]
Participation dummy	–0.0153	–0.0161*	–0.0162*	–0.0153	
	[0.0095]	[0.0095]	[0.0097]	[0.0099]	
2001 dummy	0.0311***	0.0306**	0.0310**	0.0309***	0.0311***
	[0.0120]	[0.0120]	[0.0121]	[0.0094]	[0.0096]
2002 dummy	–0.0047	–0.0050	–0.0050	–0.0047	–0.0047
	[0.0100]	[0.0100]	[0.0101]	[0.0095]	[0.0096]
Participation × 2001 dummy	–0.0475***	–0.0465***	–0.0470***	–0.0472***	
	[0.0146]	[0.0147]	[0.0148]	[0.0139]	
Participation × 2002 dummy	0.0084	0.0092	0.0092	0.0084	
	[0.0138]	[0.0139]	[0.0139]	[0.0140]	
Ln baseline pc exp. (lnpcx)		0.0067	0.0082		
		[0.0043]	[0.0068]		
2001 × lnpcx		–0.0081	–0.0031		
		[0.0061]	[0.0110]		
2002 × lnpcx		–0.0067	–0.0051		
		[0.0068]	[0.0109]		

(continued)

Table 8.12 The Impact of RPS on the Incidence of Receiving Food, Money Transfer, or Both from Nongovernmental Organizations *(continued)*

	(1)	*(2)*	*(3)*	*(4)*	*(5)*
	IV	*IV*	*IV*	*RE-IV*	*RE*
Participation × lnpcx			–0.0034		
			[0.0099]		
2001 × participate × lnpcx			–0.0102		
			[0.0140]		
2002 × participate × lnpcx			–0.0032		
			[0.0153]		
Treatment dummy					–0.0143
					[0.0092]
2001 × treat dummy					–0.0453***
					[0.0133]
2002 × treat dummy					0.0078
					[0.0134]
Observations	4,431	4,431	4,431	4,431	4,431
Number of i_var				1,581	1,581

Source: Nielsen and Olinto 2007.

Note: Standard errors in brackets; * significant at 10%; ** significant at 5%; *** significant at 1%. Columns (1)–(3) are IV regressions where actual participation (and its interactions) are instrumented by originally being assigned to treatment, and the stratification of the data are taken into account. Columns (4)–(5) are random effects estimations that ignore stratification; (4) is an IV regression while (5) gives the reduced form for comparison to the results from Honduras.

Table 8.13 The Impact of PRAF-II on the Incidence of Receiving Food, Money Transfer, or Both from Nongovernmental Organizations

	(1)	*(2)*	*(3)*	*(4)*	*(5)*	*(6)*	*(7)*	*(8)*
	All	*2002*	*All*	*2002*	*All*	*2002*	*RE*	*1st diff*
Constant	0.0964***	0.1358***	0.0962***	0.1338***	0.0961***	0.1330***	0.0962***	0.0367***
	[0.0099]	[0.0129]	[0.0098]	[0.0126]	[0.0098]	[0.0125]	[0.0123]	[0.0125]
Participation dummy	–0.0074	0.0111	–0.0070	0.0148	–0.0066	0.0162		
	[0.0161]	[0.0188]	[0.0160]	[0.0186]	[0.0160]	[0.0183]		
2002 dummy	0.0394***		0.0375***		0.0370***		0.0394***	
	[0.0130]		[0.0127]		[0.0126]		[0.0136]	
2002 × participation dummy	0.0185		0.0218		0.0228			
	[0.0194]		[0.0192]		[0.0189]			
Ln baseline pc exp. (lnpcx)			–0.0025	–0.0223***	–0.0069	–0.0348***		
			[0.0047]	[0.0063]	[0.0080]	[0.0110]		
2002 × lnpcx			–0.0198***		–0.0280**			
			[0.0066]		[0.0121]			
Participation × lnpcx					0.0094	0.0243		
					[0.0133]	[0.0165]		
2002 × participate × lnpcx					0.0149			
					[0.0180]			
Treatment dummy							–0.0056	0.0129
							[0.0154]	[0.0157]

(continued)

Table 8.13 The Impact of PRAF-II on the Incidence of Receiving Food, Money Transfer, or Both from Nongovernmental Organizations *(continued)*

	(1)	*(2)*	*(3)*	*(4)*	*(5)*	*(6)*	*(7)*	*(8)*
	All	*2002*	*All*	*2002*	*All*	*2002*	*RE*	*1st diff*
2002 × treat dummy							0.0143	
							[0.0180]	
Observations	8,526	4,100	8,526	4,100	8,526	4,100	8,523	4,426

Source: Nielsen and Olinto 2007.

Note: Standard errors in brackets; * significant at 10%; ** significant at 5%; *** significant at 1%. "All" uses data from both years; "2002" uses data from 2002 only. Columns (1)–(6) are IV regressions where actual participation (and its interactions) are instrumented by originally being assigned to treatment, and the stratification and clustering of the data are taken into account. Column (7) is a reduced form random effects estimation, taking into account clustering but not stratification. Column (8) is a regression of first differenced data on the treatment dummy, taking into account the complete survey structure of the data.

Looking first at the incidence of receiving any of the above types of private transfers in Nicaragua (table 8.3), the estimates for 2001 suggest some crowding out of private transfers; the difference-in-difference estimate is –0.1024 (significant at the 1 percent level) for the simplest specification, implying that participation in the CCT program reduces the probability of receiving a private transfer by 10.24 percentage points. The results for 2002 look different, however, with an insignificant effect of much smaller magnitude. Using random effects estimation (reduced form or IV) yields the 2001 result significant at the 1 percent level, while the 2002 result is still insignificant and negative.

Note that there seems to be a positive relationship between socioeconomic status, as measured by the log of initial per-capita expenditures, and the incidence of private transfers. This is a common finding in the literature, which suggests that recipient households are less likely to find themselves in extreme poverty.

In Honduras (table 8.4), we see a very different and surprising pattern: program participation increases the probability of receiving a private transfer by approximately 10 percentage points. However, the strongly significant and negative coefficient on the participation variable indicates a baseline imbalance between the two samples. As explained above, the likely reason for this baseline difference is seasonality, combined with different interview times for treatment and control groups. More confidence should therefore be given to the estimates based on the 2002 sample alone. Though the estimate remains positive, it is now insignificant and of negligible magnitude (0.3 percentage points). Random effect estimation yields similar results.

The main reason for the results for private transfers seems to stem from its food component: recall from tables 8.1 and 8.2 that food transfers account for the largest share of transfers. Indeed, for both countries, estimating the program impact on the incidence of receiving food, we see a pattern of coefficients similar to the one above for overall transfers. For Honduras (table 8.10), program participation increases the probability of receiving food according to the difference-in-difference estimate, and program participants are initially less likely to receive food than are nonparticipants. Furthermore, the random effects and first difference estimates indicate an insignificant negative effect on the likelihood of receiving food. If the explanation for this pattern is indeed the combination of seasonality and differences in timing of surveys for control and treatment groups, it is reasonable that the effect stems mainly from the food component, since this is measured for a shorter interval of time and is more likely to exhibit seasonality. This hypothesis is supported by the fact that there were substantial differences in production and consumption of food for treatment and control groups in 2000, but not in 2002 (results not shown).

For Nicaragua (table 8.9), program participation has an intuitive significant negative impact on the incidence of households receiving food transfers. Though the Nicaragua sample does display initial sample imbalances in the likelihood of receiving food, as evident from the significant coefficient on the participation dummy, there is no obvious source of this baseline difference as in the Honduras sample: treatment and control groups were interviewed simultaneously. Our preferred specification is therefore to exploit all data, as in table 8.9, and we conclude that there was crowding out of private food transfers in Nicaragua in both 2001 and 2002. Program participation results in a 5 percentage point to 6 percentage point reduction in the probability of receiving food.

The amount of food received in Honduras (table 8.11) is positively related to living in a treatment area when looking at the simple difference estimate (that is, estimating using 2002 data only). Looking at data from both years, the impact is positive, but significance varies with the specification, and the coefficient of program participation is of the opposite sign and of larger magnitude. Taken together, these point toward the 2002 data estimates being more reliable, though the positive value is difficult to explain.

Turning to remittances, the difference-in-difference results indicate that there seems to be no impact whatsoever of RPS or PRAF-II on the incidence of remittances for either 2001 or 2002 (tables 8.5 and 8.6). Random effects and first difference estimation takes us to a similar conclusion, as does looking at the amount of remittances instead of their incidence (tables 8.7 and 8.8). This is comforting as remittances represent an important source of foreign exchange for most countries in LAC.

While program participation did not affect money or food transfers from nongovernmental organizations in Honduras and Nicaragua in 2002 (tables 8.12 and 8.13), the impact in Nicaragua is significant at the 1 percent level for 2001. This points toward the possibility of private organizations focusing their aid in areas not already covered by a government program. That is, CCTs may crowd out private-organization and nongovernmental organization transfers.

Conclusions

In this chapter we explored the degree of substitutability between public and private transfers. If senders target a certain minimum income level for the recipient household, remittances would likely behave countercyclically with respect to fluctuations in the income of the recipient households. This is of policy relevance because if private transfers respond negatively to public transfer programs like CCTs, then unless the crowding out effect is fully incorporated into the ex ante analysis of CCT programs, the actual impact of those programs will likely be well below expectations.

With few exceptions, previous empirical evidence suggesting that public transfer programs have important crowding out effects may have been biased since they did not utilize experimental data. In this chapter we have used experimental data from the evaluations of two CCTs in Central America, the RPS in Nicaragua and PRAF-II in Honduras, to assess the link between the access to CCTs and the incidence and volume of private transfers. That is, we try to answer the question: Do CCTs crowd out private transfers?

Overall, the evidence is mixed. In line with the findings of Teruel and Davis (2000) for the PROGRESA CCT program in Mexico, we find no evidence that CCTs crowd out remittances in either Nicaragua or Honduras. However, there is a reduction in the incidence of food transfers in treatment areas compared to control areas in Nicaragua, along with some evidence pointing toward crowding out of nongovernmental organizations' food or money transfers. In Honduras, though food donations exhibit a baseline imbalance causing a significant difference-in-difference estimate of the causal effect of program participation on the likelihood of receiving food, this effect seems to be an artifact due to a combination of seasonality in food consumption and production and different timing of surveys for control and treatment groups. Interestingly, program participation significantly increases the amount of food received in Honduras.

The reason we find crowding out in Nicaragua but not in Honduras could be that the CCTs given in Honduras are too low to actually crowd out private transfers, while the larger amounts given out in Nicaragua do affect private networks and informal insurance schemes. As discussed in Glewwe and Olinto (2004), PRAF-II transfers amount on average to only 4 percent of household annual expenditures, while other CCTs like PROGRESA, Bolsa Familia, and RPS range from 15 percent to 20 percent of household expenditures (Lindert, Skoufias, and Shapiro 2006). These results suggest that as long as CCTs continue to be well-targeted and transfer relatively small amounts that are just enough to encourage families to bring their children to health monitoring appointments and keep them in school, CCTs are unlikely to crowd out private transfers.

Annex A

The Data

In Honduras, a representative sample from the 70 municipalities of approximately 5,600 households was surveyed in 2000 and then again in 2002—before and after the PRAF-II pilot was launched. In Nicaragua, a representative sample from the 42 *comarcas* of approximately 1,500 households were surveyed in 2000, just before the program began, and then again in 2001 and 2002. The household questionnaires applied in both countries collected data on (i) housing, education, and employment of all household members; (ii) education (very detailed) of all children ages 6 to 16; (iii) the health of all women who were pregnant in the past

12 months; (iv) the health of all children below 3 years of age (and height, weight, and hemoglobin information for all children under 5 years); (v) consumption expenditures on food and nonfood items; (vi) access to credit; (vii) remittances received from household members who have moved away; (viii) receipt of assistance from various government and private agencies; (ix) ownership of livestock and durable goods; (x) time spent by the "woman of the house" and by children ages 6 to 12 doing various activities; and (xi) households' evaluation of the quality of local health centers and primary schools.

For the RPS in Nicaragua, the questionnaire was a comprehensive household questionnaire based on the 1998 Nicaraguan Living Standards Measurement Study (LSMS), conducted by the World Bank. The survey sample is a stratified random sample at the *comarca* level for all 42 *comarcas* described above. Forty-two households were randomly selected in each *comarca* using a census carried out by RPS three months prior to the survey as the sample frame, yielding an initial target sample of 1,764 households. The first wave of fieldwork was carried out in late August and early September 2000. The education CCT started to be distributed at the end of September 2000, and the health care CCT component was not initiated until June 2001. In October 2001, when beneficiaries had been receiving education CCT transfers for 13 months, the second round of data collection was conducted. The 2002 survey was also carried out in October. Overall, 90 percent (1,581) of the intended sample were interviewed in the first round in 2000. For the follow-up surveys in October 2001 and October 2002, the target sample was limited to these 1,581 first-round interviews. In 2001, just over 91 percent (1,453) of these were reinterviewed. In 2002, 88 percent (1,397) of the original 1,581 were found and interviewed. Because the same target sample was used in 2002 as in 2001, regardless of whether the household was interviewed in 2001, some households that were not interviewed in 2001 were successfully interviewed in 2002.

In Honduras, after the 70 municipalities were chosen, baseline data were collected from all before the CCTs were given out in the 40 municipalities selected to receive the program. The baseline data were collected from mid-August to mid-December 2000. One follow-up survey was conducted approximately two years later, from mid-May to mid-August 2002. From each of the 70 municipalities, eight communities ("clusters") were randomly selected, and from each cluster, 10 dwellings were randomly selected (see IFPRI 2000 for details of the sampling methodology). Assuming one household per dwelling, this implies a total sample of 5,600 households. However, some of the dwellings had more than one household, so the total number of households selected was 5,748. In most cases, each group of 10 dwellings is found within a different village (*aldea*) of the municipality, but in some cases two or more groups of 10 are from the same village. Of these 5,748 households, 5,546 were interviewed in 2000. The remaining households were either unavailable or refused to talk to interviewers. Of the 5,546 households interviewed, 30 refused to complete the consumption module of the questionnaire, and 40 completed it with unusable data. Of the 5,476 remaining households, 1,050 were not eligible for the PRAF-II pilot because they did not have pregnant women, or children between the ages of 0 and 3, or 6 and 13. Therefore, 4,426 valid baseline interviews with eligible households were conducted in 2000. In the 2002 follow-up survey, about 93 percent of the 4,426 households in the 2000 survey were reinterviewed. This high reinterview rate reflects attempts made to follow households that moved (more specifically, all children ages 0 to 13 years and all woman ages 15 to 49 who still lived in one of the seven departments from which the 70 municipalities were drawn were targeted to be followed in 2002). In addition, household members who left the household they belonged to in 2000, either to form a new household or to join an existing household, were followed if they were part of PRAF-II's target population: pregnant women, lactating mothers, and children ages 0 to 16 years.

The Empirical Strategy

We use the randomized design of the PRAF-II and RPS programs to estimate the impact of CCTs on private transfers, remittances, food transfers, and food and money donations from nongovernmental organizations. We use a difference-in-difference approach, estimating the following equations for dependent variable Y_{it}:

$$Y_{it} = \alpha_0 + \alpha_1 D_s + \alpha_2 P_i + \alpha_{3s} D_s P_i + \varepsilon_{it} \tag{1}$$

$$Y_{it} = \alpha_0 + \alpha_1 D_s + \alpha_2 P_i + \alpha_{3s} D_s P_i + \alpha_4 I_{i;2000} + \alpha_{5s} I_{i;2000} D_s + \varepsilon_{it} \tag{2}$$

$$Y_{it} = \alpha_0 + \alpha_1 D_s + \alpha_2 P_i + \alpha_{3s} D_s P_i + \alpha_4 I_{i;2000} + \alpha_{5s} I_{i;2000} D_s + \alpha_6 P_i I_{i;2000} + \alpha_{7s} D_s P_i I_{i;2000} + \varepsilon_{it} \tag{3}$$

In the equations, Ds are dummy variables for years s = 2001 and 2002, P_i denotes actual program participation, and $I_{i;2000}$ is log baseline per capita expenditure of household i, which is standardize to mean zero and unit variance. The subscript t refers to the year of the observation. The estimates of main interest are α_{3s} and α_{7s}, which can be interpreted as the difference-in-difference estimates of the impact of the programs. While the α_{3s} give the estimate of impact for the household with average baseline consumption per capita, the α_{7s} give the differential impact for each standard deviation above the average.

The identifying assumption behind the difference-in-difference estimates is that absent the program, the private transfers received by eligible households (that is, those satisfying the criteria for participation in the program) would have evolved similarly for participants and nonparticipants. Because actual participation may not be random (since not all persons living in treatment areas participate, while some households in control areas do), this will not necessarily hold. We therefore use an instrumental variables approach, instrumenting actual participation (*P*) and its relevant interactions by the randomized assignment to treatment (*T*) and its corresponding interactions. Because *T* is random, all estimates of the program effect are valid, but the latter equations add log baseline income as an explanatory variable to absorb residual variation.

For Honduras, we find that the program has a significant impact on some outcome variables only because it cancels out baseline sample imbalances. Because of the special way the sample was collected, with the treatment group sampled first, we suspect that baseline sample seasonality issues are driving the results. We therefore reestimate the effect of program participation using the 2002 follow-up sample only:

$$Y_{it} = \alpha_0 + \alpha_2 P_i + \varepsilon_{it} \tag{4}$$

$$Y_{it} = \alpha_0 + \alpha_2 P_i + \alpha_4 I_{i;2000} + \varepsilon_{it} \tag{5}$$

$$Y_{it} = \alpha_0 + \alpha_2 P_i + \alpha_4 I_{i;2000} + \alpha_6 P_i I_{i;2000} + \varepsilon_{it} \tag{6}$$

where *P* is again instrumented for by *T*.

It is important to make clear that though the randomization of *T* ensures that the relationship between *Y* and *T* is causal, it does not guarantee that actual program participation is the only channel through which *T* works. For instance, belonging to a community selected for treatment could increase awareness of the importance of health and schooling so that these measures develop differently than they would absent the program, even for families that are not actually participating. This again could have an impact on private transfers. In addition to the IV estimates, we estimate reduced form equations, regressing the dependent variable directly on an indicator variable for belonging to a treatment community. Because not all eligible households in treatment areas participate, and some from control areas in Honduras do participate, this will tend to attenuate the estimate compared to IV. The estimate thus obtained is the so-called "intent to treat" effect, namely, the average effect of living in an area selected for treatment.

Notes

1. The estimators employed in both studies utilize state program design characteristics as instrumental variables for participation in social programs (unemployment insurance and Aid to Families with Dependent Children), and the identification assumption that state program characteristics are exogenous may not be believable.

2. The identification of the effects of public-provided insurance relies on the assumption that state legislation is exogenous.

3. See Morris, Duncan, and Rodriguez (2004) and Glewwe and Olinto (2005) for detailed descriptions of the experimental design of PRAF.

4. Maluccio and Flores 2004.

5. For more details on the criteria for selecting these 42 municipalities, see Maluccio and Flores 2004.

References

Ahmed, S. 1986. "Temporary and Permanent Government Spending in an Open Economy: Some Evidence for the United Kingdom." *Journal of Monetary Economics* 17: 197–224.

Aschauer, D. 1985. "Fiscal Policy and Aggregate Demand." *American Economic Review* 75: 117–27.

Attanasio, O., and V. Rios-Rull. 2000. "Consumption Smoothing in Island Economies: Can Public Insurance Reduce Welfare?" *European Economic Review* 44: 1225–58.

Bailey, M.J. 1972. "The Optimal Full Employment Surplus." *Journal of Political Economy* 80: 649–61.

Blejer, M.I., and M.S. Khan. 1984. "Government Policy and Private Investment in Developing Countries." *IMF Staff Papers* 31 (2): 379–403.

Cox, D., Z. Eser, and E. Jimenez. 1998. "Motives for Private Transfers Over the Life Cycle: An Analytical Framework and Evidence for Peru." *Journal of Development Economics* 55 (1): 57–80.

Cutler, D.M., and J. Gruber. 1996. "Does Public Insurance Crowd our Private Insurance?" *Quarterly Journal of Economics* 112 (2): 391–430.

Easterly, W., C.A. Rodriguez, and K. Schmidt-Hebbel. 1994. *Public Sector Deficits and Macroeconomic Performance*. New York, NY: Oxford University Press.

Evans, P., and G. Karras. 1996. "Convergence Revisited." *Journal of Monetary Economics* 37: 249–65.

Glewwe, P., and P. Olinto. 2004. "Evaluating the Impact of Conditional Cash Transfers on Schooling: An Experimental Analysis of Honduras' PRAF Program." Final report for USAID, International Food Policy Research Institute, Washington, DC.

IFPRI (International Food Policy Research Institute). 2000. *Honduras: IFAD Technical Assistance Grant*. Washington, DC: International Food Policy Research Institute.

Khan, M.S. and C.M. Reinhart. 1990. "Private Investment and Economic Growth in Developing Countries." *World Development* 18: 19–27.

Kormendi, R. 1983. "Government Debt, Government Spending, and Private Sector Behavior." *American Economic Review* 73: 994–1010.

Lindert, K., E. Skoufias, and J. Shapiro. 2005. "Redistributing Income to the Poor and the Rich: Public Transfers in Latin America and the Caribbean." Regional Study Working Paper, World Bank, Washington, DC.

———. 2006. "How Effectively Do Public Transfers in Latin America Redistribute Income?" Regional Study Working Paper, World Bank, Washington, DC.

López, H., K. Schmidt-Hebbel, and L. Servén. 2000. "How Effective is Fiscal Policy in Raising National Saving?" *The Review of Economics and Statistics* LXXXII (2): 226–38.

Maluccio, J.A., and R. Flores. 2004. "Impact Evaluation of a Conditional Cash Transfer Program: The Nicaraguan *Red de Protección Social.*" Food Consumption and Nutrition Division Discussion Paper No.184, International Food Policy Research Institute, Washington, DC.

Morris, P., G. Duncan, and C. Rodrigues. 2004. "Does Money Really Matter? Estimating Impacts of Family Income on Children's Achievement with Data from Random Assignment Experiments." Paper prepared for the "Next Generation" project, MDRC, New York.

Nielsen, Mette E., and P. Olinto. 2007. "Do Conditional Cash Transfers Crowd Out Private Transfers? Evidence from Randomized Trials in Honduras and Nicaragua." Policy Research Working Paper, World Bank, Washington, DC.

Perry, G., O. Arias, H. López, W. Maloney, and L. Servén. 2007. "Poverty Reduction and Growth: Virtuous and Vicious Circles." World Bank, Washington, DC.

Schoeni, R.F. 1996. "Does Aid to Families with Dependent Children Displace Familial Assistance?" Rand Corporation Working Paper, DRU-1453-RC.

———. 2002. "Does Unemployment Insurance Displace Familial Assistance?" *Public Choice* 110: 99–119.

Teruel, G., and B. Davis. 2000. *Final Report: An Evaluation of the Impact of PROGRESA Cash Payments on Private Inter-Household Transfers*. Washington, DC: International Food Policy Research Institute.

9

Facilitating Remittances Flows and Security in the System

Massimo Cirasino, Mario Guadamillas, and Emanuel Salinas

Remittances should be welcomed, encouraged, and facilitated, and one critical area in this regard relates to the costs that migrants sending money home have to face and absorb. But what specific actions could governments take to facilitate these flows while guaranteeing the security of the payments systems? What can be done to increase competition and transparency in the systems? What type of security regulations should be considered to avoid criminal misuse of remittances channels?

Introduction: The Scope of Regulation of Remittances Services

Remittances transactions are inherently private operations and, as such, regulation does not address in any way the allocation of remittances funds, which receivers clearly have the freedom to spend or invest as they choose. Within this scope, regulatory concerns should be aimed at facilitating the provision of formal[1] remittances services at the lowest cost possible to as many users as possible, while maintaining high levels of security in the system.

By nature, remittances involve operations in various jurisdictions, under different regulatory frameworks. There have been significant multilateral efforts to address regulation of remittances and provide guidance to local regulators and authorities (see box 9.1). However, the reconciliation of the overall objectives of high security with low costs remains a major challenge.

The first objective of regulation is enforcing security in remittances services. Remittances channels are subject to the risk of misuse for illegal transactions, including money laundering and financing of terrorism. While other financial sector activities face similar risk of misuse, the nature and volume of remittances operations make remittances systems attractive vehicles for illicit activities.[2] Accordingly, authorities worldwide have strived to reduce this risk through regulations aimed at ensuring the legality of funds transferred and of the operations of senders and receivers. While necessary, these regulations—commonly known as Anti-Money Laundering and Combating the Financing of Terrorism (AML/CFT)—can have a major negative impact on the accessibility and price of remittances services.

First, AML/CFT regulation usually requires service providers to positively identify their clients and assess the legality of their transactions. This can be a significant deterrent for immigrants lacking legal status, who may prefer informal or higher-cost channels that preserve their anonymity. Second, compliance with these regulations is costly, increasing the price of the service for users, and posing barriers to entry of new remittances service providers (RSPs) or creating incentives for informality. Third, these regulations have made many financial institutions reluctant to service sectors of the population that cannot demonstrate lawful residency in the host country; this, by some accounts, could be as many as 12 million people in the case of the United States.[3]

The second broad objective of regulation refers to facilitating the reduction of the price of remittances. For immigrants sending money home, remittances services have traditionally been expensive, with fees of up to 20 percent of the principal sent, depending on the size and type of the transfer and the destination.[4] By some accounts, reducing the cost of remittances to 5 percent of the amount remitted would free up more than US$1 billion per year for migrants and their relatives.[5]

Authorities have shied away from imposing direct price controls on remittances services, favoring mechanisms aimed at increasing transparency, enhancing competition in the system, and, in some cases, reducing barriers for users to access a wider range of service providers. Prices for some remittances services have indeed decreased in high-volume corridors in Latin America where competition is highest, but remittances fees remain opaque (with hidden charges and poor exchange rates), and penalize small transfer amounts of the type commonly sent by immigrants. At the same time, cost savings achieved through technological advances in payments systems have not necessarily translated into lower prices for remittances services,[6] as most immigrants sending money home still do not have access to banking services, especially in the United States.

The Challenge of Regulation

The main challenge for authorities is to ensure the integrity of the system by reducing the opportunities for misuse, while also aiming at minimizing the disruption and cost of the service for bona fide participants.

Box 9.1 The General Principles for International Remittances Services

In March 2006, a task force including the World Bank and the Committee on Payments and Settlement Systems (CPSS) released a set of "General Principles for International Remittance Services" (hereinafter the General Principles) describing key features and functions that should be satisfied by remittances systems, providers, and financial intermediaries. These principles are intended as universally applicable international standards and aim at improving the conditions in the remittances markets. The General Principles cover areas such as transparency and consumer protection, payments system infrastructure, legal and regulatory environment, market structure and competition, and governance and risk management.

The General Principles and related roles of the authorities and remittances service providers are summarized below and are discussed in detail throughout the chapter.

Transparency and consumer protection
General Principle 1. The market for remittance services should be transparent and have adequate consumer protection.

Payments system infrastructure
General Principle 2. Improvements to payments system infrastructure that have the potential to increase the efficiency of remittance services should be encouraged.

Legal and regulatory environment
General Principle 3. Remittance services should be supported by a sound, predictable, nondiscriminatory, and proportionate legal and regulatory framework in relevant jurisdictions.

Market structure and competition
General Principle 4. Competitive market conditions, including appropriate access to domestic payments infrastructures, should be fostered in the remittance industry.

Governance and risk management
General Principle 5. Remittance services should be supported by appropriate governance and risk management practices.

Roles of remittance service providers and public authorities

A. *The role of remittance service providers.* Remittance service providers should participate actively in the implementation of the General Principles.

B. *The role of public authorities.* Public authorities should evaluate what action to take to achieve the public policy objectives through implementation of the General Principles.

Source: World Bank and CPSS 2006.

Overcoming this challenge requires the active participation and coordination of authorities in different locations. Without the clear engagement and active participation of regulators in the United States—the country of origin of most of these remittances and thus the place where remittances services are contracted by users—the impact of regulatory efforts in destination countries will likely continue to have only a limited impact.

Organization of the Chapter

The first section of this chapter addresses regulatory measures to ensure security in remittances services. The second section focuses on accessibility considerations, reviewing the obstacles for remittances senders and receivers to use all formal channels. The third addresses competition in remittances services in light of regulatory requirements and access to payments systems. The final section includes recommendations and areas for further action.

Security Considerations in Remittances' Regulation

Remittances channels, as any other mechanism to transfer money across jurisdictions, are subject to the risk of misuse for illicit purposes. In order to reduce this risk, authorities across the world have introduced anti-money laundering (AML)[7] and combating the financing of terrorism (CFT)[8] measures and regulations (see box 9.2). Many of these measures have been in place since the 1990s, although they had been applied primarily to banks. However, since the events of September 11, 2001, AML and CFT regulations have taken on new urgency, and their applicability has been extended to all participants in the financial system, including remittances operators.

However, while AML/CFT regulations address an important issue for the security of the system, their implementation has the potential to create adverse effects on the remittances channels. First, AML/CFT regulations can lead to considerable upfront investment in compliance systems, which in turn can be a significant barrier to entry to new remittances service providers. Similarly, ongoing compliance costs can increase the overall costs of operations for remittances service providers, thus pushing up the prices of the remittances services. Second, strict AML/CFT regulations can restrict access to formal channels for many bona fide users who may not have the means to prove the origin or purpose of remittances. These factors can generate incentives for senders, receivers, and even remittances operators, to use informal channels that, by definition, are unregulated and thus have the highest risk of misuse.

The role of authorities is to devise and implement an effective AML/CFT regime that balances the security of the system with the need to

Box 9.2 The AML/CFT Regulations

The AML/CFT regulations are measures intended to curtail the risk of misuse of the financial system. These regulations can be summarized on four main types of requirements for all providers of financial services:

- Create internal controls to deal with the risk of money laundering and financing of terrorism. Train staff on these controls.
- Perform due diligence on all clients in order to obtain reasonable certainty on the legality of their proceeds and activities.
- Undertake monitoring of all operations in order to identify suspicious transactions. Maintain records of all operations (suspicious or not) to be provided to authorities at request.
- Report suspicious transactions to authorities.

The overall guidelines of the AML/CFT regulations are defined by the Financial Action Task Force (FATF), an intergovernmental, policy-making body.[a] Currently, there are 40 FATF recommendations on anti-money laundering and 9 special recommendations on combating the financing of terrorism.[b] It is the responsibility of each country to adapt the international AML/CFT standards developed by FATF in designing its national regulation.

Source: Financial Action Task Force: www.fatf-gafi.org/document/28/ 0,2340, en_32250379_32236930_33658140_1_1_1_1,00.html#40recs.

a. The Financial Action Task Force on Money Laundering (FATF) was established following agreement in the G-7 Summit in Paris in 1989. Initially the task force included representatives of the G-7 member states, the European Commission, and eight other countries. At the present time it has 32 member countries and territories and 2 regional organizations.

b. The full list of recommendations is available at www.fatf-gafi.org/document/28/ 0,2340,en_32250379_33658140_1_1_1_1,00.html#40recs.

minimize hurdles and unnecessary costs to users. Moreover, such a regime must aim at broadening access to formal financial services for all bona fide users, as the only effective mechanism to broaden the outreach and effectiveness of regulation.

Formalization of RSPs

By definition, informal markets cannot be subject to oversight from authorities; thus, the first step for effective regulation of the remittances channels is the formalization of RSPs' operations. Formalization refers to the process of authorization of activities of new RSPs, and can be done through either licensing or registration of service providers. These mechanisms imply different levels of oversight, entry prerequisites, and compliance requirements, and thus can have implications for the accessibility of the market for new entrants and on the responsibilities for regulators.

Licensing implies a fairly rigorous formalization process, with significant qualification requirements usually addressing the financial and technical capabilities of prospective new operators, as well as fit-and-proper tests on management and owners. Licensing provides authorities with the power to perform a prequalification due diligence on the RSP's operational and basic security systems, including AML and CFT.

Accordingly, in general terms, licensing of remittances operators can translate into high levels of security in the system. On the other hand, high entry requirements can pose a significant barrier to entry to new remittances operators. Similarly, licensing requires national regulatory bodies to have significant resources in order to perform the due diligence process required on all new prospective operators.

Registration, on the other hand, poses significantly lower entry barriers to new RSPs, and its main objective is to encourage all RSPs to identify themselves and commit to comply with AML/CFT requirements in the course of their operations. However, since registered RSPs are not required upfront to have systems or procedures in place for basic security, authorities are required to set up monitoring mechanisms to ensure compliance throughout RSPs' ongoing operations.

Formalization as a Regulatory Barrier to Entry

Inadequate formalization processes can create distortions in the market by limiting competition. At the present time, the most common regulatory barrier to entry for prospective operators is related to the process for authorization for new RSPs to set up business.[9] Moreover, these barriers appear higher at countries of origin of remittances than in recipient countries, which has helped to enhance and maintain the market position of incumbent RSPs.

Since remittance services, by definition, imply operations in multiple jurisdictions, RSPs are subject to different regulatory frameworks at the same time, which increases the complexity and costs of regulatory compliance. While international homologation may be difficult to achieve, authorities should strive to ensure standardization of entry requirements at a national level. In practice, formalization requirements are far from consistent even within the same country (see box 9.3), which demonstrates that they still are not based on objective security considerations.

Box 9.3 Regulatory Requirements in the United States as Barriers to Entry

A recent survey[a] of RSPs operating in corridors between various states of the United States and different world regions showed that the single most important barrier regions faced when trying to enter the remittances market was obtaining a license to operate. By the same token, surety bonds required to operate were seen as a constraint by one in four of these firms (see figure below).

Barriers to Entry as Reported by Surveyed RSPs in the United States

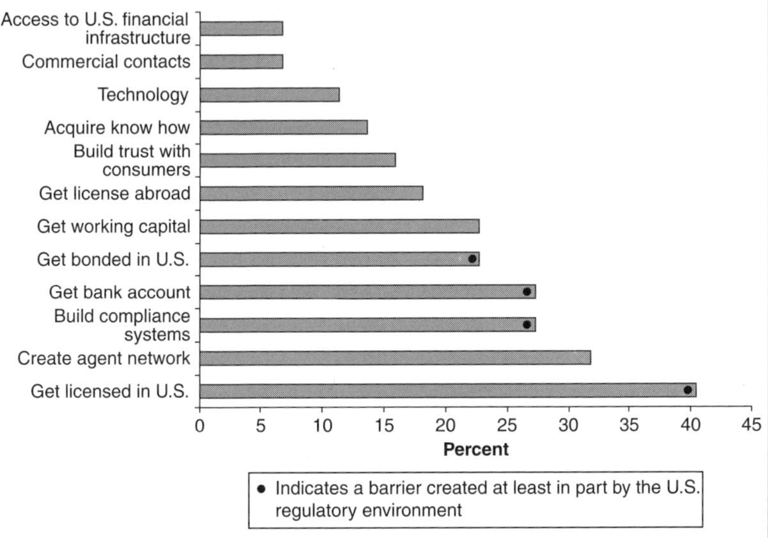

Source: Andreassen 2006.

There is significant lack of consistency in regulatory requirements among different jurisdictions within the United States. Indeed, the minimum amount required by regulation to set up a new RSP (including net worth and bonding) varies drastically across states, from a low of US$15,000 in Alabama to US$1.5 million in Pennsylvania (figure below). Surety bonds requirements also differ significantly. Moreover, the fact that bonding requirements in many states are fixed regardless of the operational volume of RSPs creates a cost bias against smaller RSPs and diminishes the prudential merit of this requirement. There is no evident rationale for these divergences in regulatory requirements across states, as they do appear

(continued)

Box 9.3 Regulatory Requirements in the United States as Barriers to Entry *(continued)*

to be proportionate to the overall volume of remittances in each state (see "Range in Bonding Requirements" figure) or each operator. In turn, this fragmented and inconsistent regulation within the United States has acted as a significant constraint to new operators, limiting competition and thus helping to maintain the preponderant situation of incumbent RSPs.

Minimum Amount Required to Set Up a New RSP

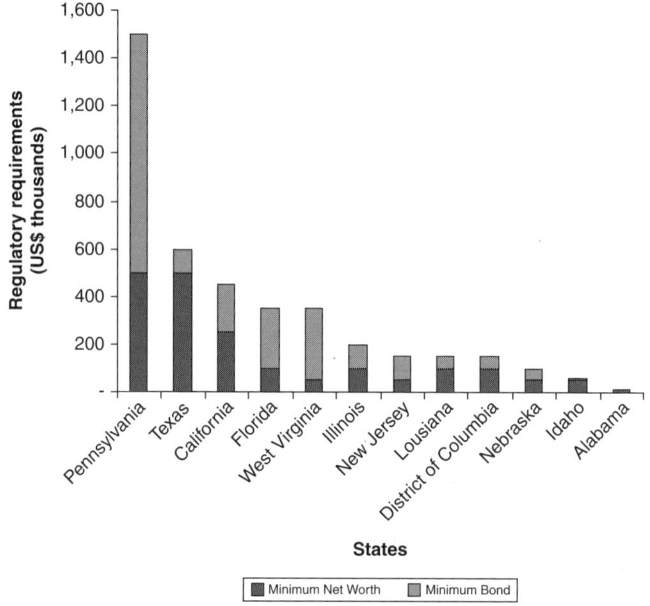

Source: Ratha and Riedberg 2005.

Besides the initial costs of setting up AML/CFT systems, RSPs also incur high compliance costs. In a recent survey of RSPs in North America, respondents considered the compliance with AML/CFT as the third highest operating expense, immediately after salaries and rent (see "Largest Expenses" figure).

Compliance costs include the overhead expenses of compliance officers, operating expenses of monitoring and reporting systems, costs associated with enforcement of internal procedures, constant training of personnel, and often external audits to these systems. Moreover, RSPs must report to multiple authorities and, in the United States, are subject to state-level regulation.

(continued)

Box 9.3 Regulatory Requirements in the United States as Barriers to Entry *(continued)*

Range in Bonding Requirements and Level of Remittances by State

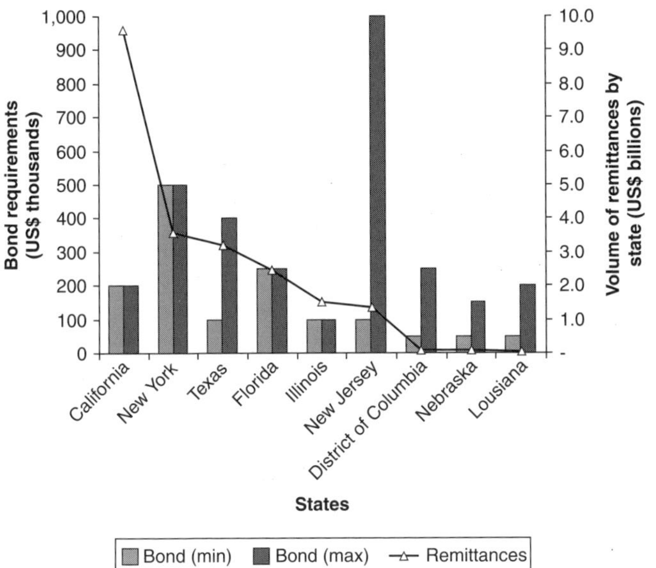

Source: Ratha and Riedberg 2005; IADB 2004.

Largest Expenses Reported by RSPs

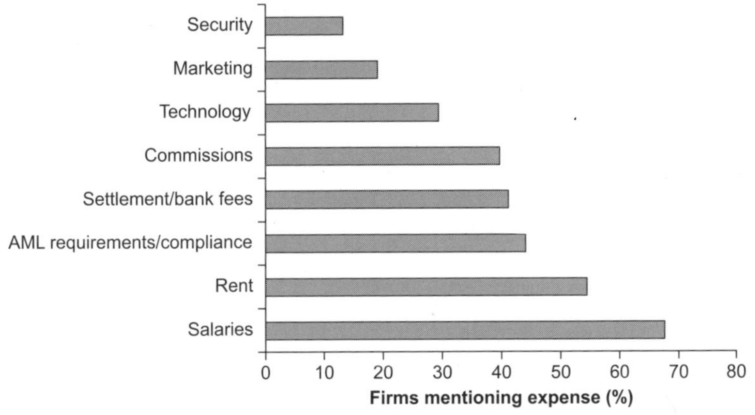

Source: Andreassen (2006) based on a survey of 73 remittances firms in six U.S. states.

Box 9.3 Regulatory Requirements in the United States as Barriers to Entry *(continued)*

Ongoing compliance costs can have two major negative impacts on the formal remittances channels. First, the costs of compliance with AML/CFT are transferred to remittances users as higher fees for the services. Second, increased costs of operation can create incentives for proliferation of informal RSPs. Because formality usually entails observance of specific operational requirements, formal RSPs face compliance costs and rigidity in their processes. Consequently, informal remittance systems can be attractive to users because of their speed, low cost, convenience, versatility, and potential for anonymity.[b]

A major challenge for authorities seeking to strengthen the integrity of remittances systems is to create a regulatory framework that brings the informal remittances providers into the formal arena. However, this framework should not impede the flows of remittances nor drive remittances systems underground through excessive regulatory requirements.[c]

a. This case study draws on data and conclusions from Andreassen (2006). All figures are taken from the aforementioned document unless otherwise stated.
b. See Orozco (2005) for further information on creation of incentives for informality through inadequate regulation.
c. See World Bank and CPSS (2006) for general principles on proportionality in the implementation of local regulatory requirements.

The Role of Authorities

The determination of the most adequate mechanism to formalize remittances operations depends on a number of factors, which are not limited only to the security of the system, but also to the circumstances of the local markets and the capabilities of participants. In determining whether a license or registration is required from new RSPs, authorities must ensure that the process of formalization complies with three major conditions:

- *Consistency*. The process for formalization of RSPs must be clear and consistent to create even and certain entry conditions for different operators.
- *Proportionality*. The formalization requirements must be in line with the reality of the local markets, proportional to the relative risk of the operations, and commensurate with the type and size of the operations of the RSP. The proportionality of regulation is essential to ensure a fair and competitive market. Overregulation or unduly high requirements to entry in the remittances market increase costs, which are passed on to users through price increases, while realistic

and adequate rules are expected to encourage entities currently in the informal sector to come under the regulatory regime.[10]

- *Realistic.* The institutional capacity of local regulators must be in line with their responsibilities—including due diligence, surveillance, and monitoring of RSPs—under the chosen formalization mechanism. Regulatory requirements should be set up in a realistic way, comparing benefits of security in the system with the consequent costs for authorities.

Accessibility to Formal Remittances Services

The existence of numerous providers of remittances services in a given corridor does not ensure the efficiency of the market. The wide divergence in prices still observed among RSPs can be explained in part by the lack of transparency. However, this divergence can also be caused by differentiated access to specific service providers, at both the countries of origin and at the destinations of the transactions.

Over the past two decades, the market has evolved from one dominated by labor-intensive physical transmission and courier services to one dominated by cash-to-cash wire transfers through money transfer operators (MTOs) (see figure 9.1). The entrance of financial institutions into the remittances market has made available more cost-efficient transactions such as account-to-cash and account-to-account remittances, which are slowly gaining market share.

However, constraints to accessibility appear to be inversely related to the level of efficiency of each channel. In other words, informal remittances channels may be the most easily accessible for users, but they can be highly inefficient and risky. On the flip side, remittances services can be cheapest and most secure through bank services (see table 9.1), but a large percentage of migrants do not have access to banking facilities.[11]

Historically, migrants' access to bank accounts in the United States has been constrained by their legal status (figure 9.2). Other constraining factors appear to be related to expectations of costs, level of income, and, to a lesser extent, distrust of financial institutions. In these cases, lack of information, rather than regulation, may be the source of constraints. These factors are analyzed below.

Regulatory Constraints to Accessibility at the Country of Origin[12]

AML/CFT regulations can create severe hurdles for remittances senders using formal providers such as banks.[13] Moreover, these regulations

Figure 9.1 Channels for Remittances (2004)

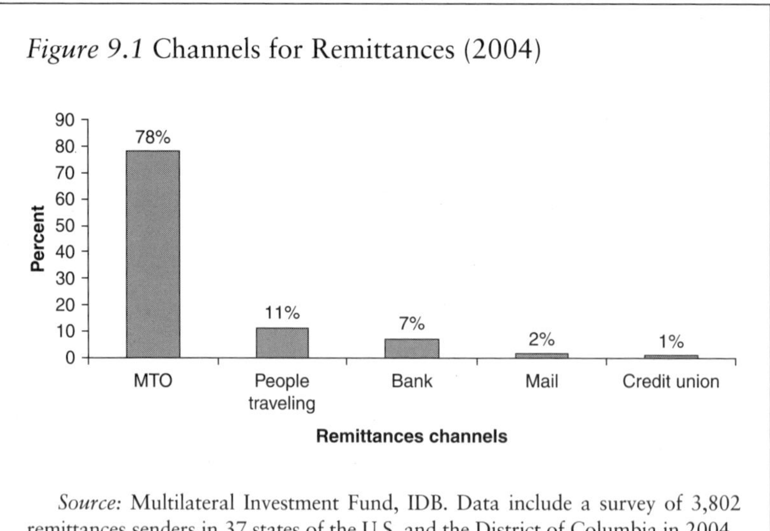

Source: Multilateral Investment Fund, IDB. Data include a survey of 3,802 remittances senders in 37 states of the U.S. and the District of Columbia in 2004.

can prevent access to these services to potential users who cannot comply with regulatory requirements. For example, regulation in the United States requires that, for security purposes, financial institutions verify the identity of applicants when opening up new bank accounts. While federal regulation does not expressly forbid the provision of financial services to undocumented applicants, in reality, most financial institutions service only clients who can demonstrate their legal presence in the United States. By some accounts, this constraint may prevent access to banking services to as many as two-fifths of the Latin American community in the United States.[14] This appears to be largely due to seemingly unfounded concerns among many banks that provision of financial services to undocumented migrants or specific ethnic groups could subject them to more stringent regulatory oversight, with the consequent increased costs and loss of efficiency (Bair 2005).

There have been significant efforts both from the private and the public sectors to reduce accessibility constraints to migrants. The U.S. Treasury Department opened access to bank accounts to undocumented individuals of Mexican nationality,[15] but it is not clear whether migrants of other nationalities would receive similar treatment. Similarly, in 2002, the Treasury Department advised Congress that, under the terms of the regulation to ensure security in the system (USA PATRIOT Act), an official identification issued by the Mexican government (consular identity card or *Matricula Consular*) can be used as a valid form of identification to open an account with a financial institution. However, this has not been reflected in the requirements of most financial institutions, especially large commercial banks (see table 9.2).

Table 9.1 Types of Remittances Service and Accessibility Considerations

Type of service	*Provider*	*Price*	*Accessibility constraints*
Physical delivery	Informal providers and courier services	Difficult to monitor and quantify due to informal nature of the service	Lowest: No identification or reporting requirements and arguably few constraints to amounts.
Cash-to-cash	MTOs	Usually highest among formal RSPs	Low: Identification usually required only for transactions above US$300. Foreign IDs accepted.
Account-to-cash	Financial institution with disbursing agent	Usually cheaper than many MTOs	High: Requires that sender has a bank account.
Account-to-account	Financial institutions only	Cheapest—can be zero due to cross-selling of other financial services	Highest: Requires that both sender and recipient have bank accounts.

Source: Prepared by authors.

Some smaller financial institutions are increasingly providing services to undocumented migrants in a simplified way. For example,

- The World Council of Credit Unions (WOCCU) has issued a recommendations document[16] to member credit unions in the United States clarifying that (i) official documents issued by foreign governments are acceptable forms of identification for opening up an account and (ii) federal regulation does not prohibit providing services to undocumented individuals. However, it highlights that state-specific regulations may do so.
- The *Coalición Internacional de Mexicanos en el Extranjero* (CIME—Mexicans Living Abroad) has reached agreements with various banks

Figure 9.2 Reasons for Not Having a Bank Account

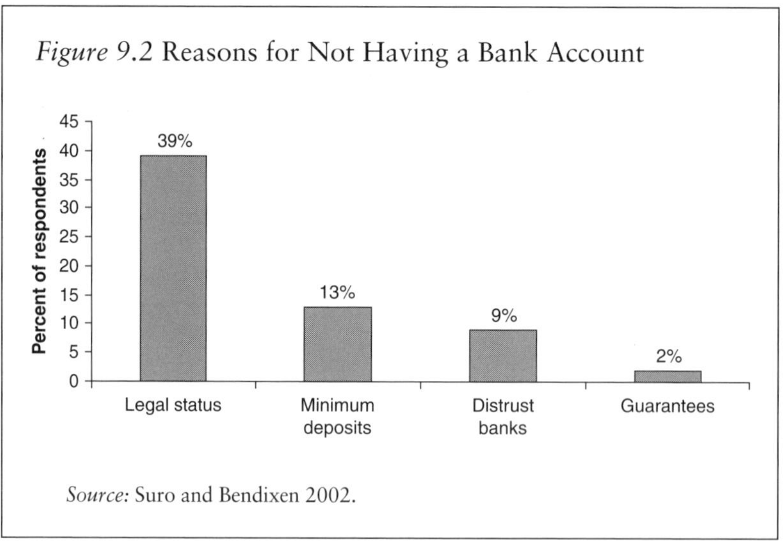

Source: Suro and Bendixen 2002.

in Illinois to reduce requirement for opening new bank accounts and to provide these services to undocumented migrants. However, this initiative is limited to banks in Chicago but has recently been expanded to Indianapolis.

While these initiatives are positive, many of them have been based on bilateral efforts and hence their benefits may not reach immigrants of different nationalities. Authorities from other recipient countries should seek to implement similar programs to facilitate the access of their nationals to banking facilities in the United States.

Consumer Protection and Transparency in the Provision of Remittances Services

The pricing of remittances services has usually been notoriously opaque, limiting the positive effects of competition and helping to preserve products that may have unduly high profit margins for operators. Remittances senders are often unaware of the different direct and indirect costs and fees charged by RSPs, and therefore ignore the total price of their remittances transactions until the money is delivered to their relatives (see figure 9.3).

Calculating the Total Price of Remittances

The calculation of the total price of remittances services is complex and requires the collection of various explicit and implicit components (see box 9.4). The components of the price of remittances include fees, exchange

Table 9.2 Requirements to Open a Bank Account in the United States (March 2006)

Bank	*Requirements to open an account*
Citibank	• Be a U.S. citizen or resident alien • Have a U.S. address • Have a Social Security number or tax ID
Bank of America	• Social Security numbers • Home addresses for the last 12 months • Driver's license, U.S. passport, or state ID numbers • Credit card or bank account number for funding the new account • Current e-mail address
U.S. Bank	• Social Security number • Driver's license, state or military ID number and expiration date • E-mail address
Harris Bank	• Social Security number • Employment information (company name, address, and phone number) • Driver's license or other ID numbers

Source: Information provided in the Web site of each institution. Compiled by author.

rate differentials, and other less transparent implicit costs such as float and fees charged by disbursing agents. Accordingly, senders are often unaware of the prices that other providers would charge for the same type of service (figure 9.4).[17]

Direct fees. These are the most explicit component of the price, and are charged on a transaction basis. Frequently these are flat fees with little or no variation, regardless of the amount of the transaction, which works to the detriment of smaller remittances as it can represent a large percentage of the money sent (figure 9.5).

Exchange rate differential. RSPs usually obtain additional revenues from the differential between the exchange rate in the market and the rate set by the RSP for disbursement of the remittances in local currency. It is often the case that the RSP with the lowest fees charges a high exchange rate differential (see figure 9.6). Given the fact that many users are not

Figure 9.3 Perceptions on Why the Total Cost of Remittances Transfers Are Higher than the Flat Commissions Paid by Senders

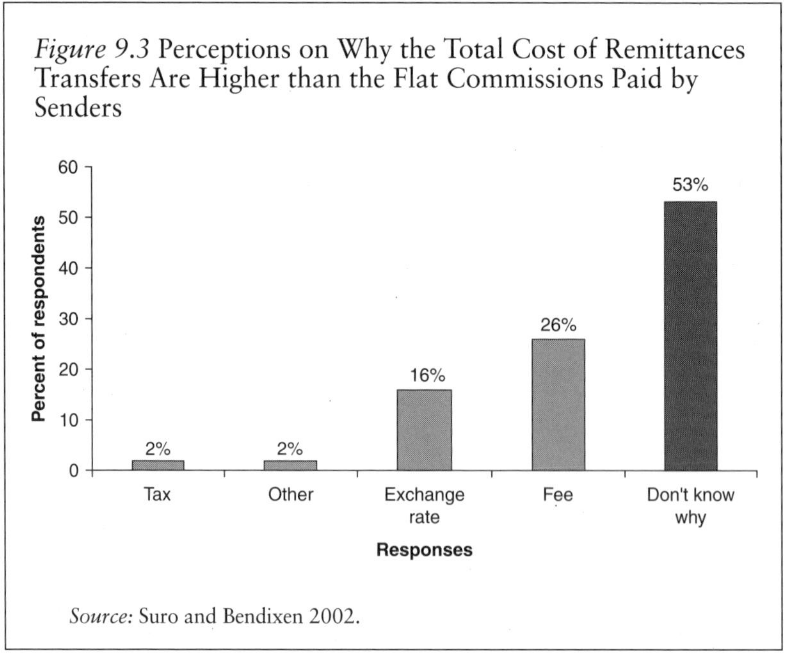

Source: Suro and Bendixen 2002.

aware of this additional cost, advertisement of fees by RSPs provides incomplete information and can be misleading.

Float. RSPs can also make money by holding the remittances funds for a period longer than needed and investing them in overnight transactions. Accordingly, the speed of the service is also a factor in determining the overall cost of the remittances.

Additional fees may be charged at disbursement, especially when this is done by agents rather than through branches of the capturing RSP.

The problem of transparency is exacerbated when a given RSP offers various remittances services with similar features but significantly different prices (see box 9.4).

Authorities' Role in Enhancing Transparency in the Market

Given the difficulty for typical remittances users to adequately quantify the price of services from different RSPs, the role of the authorities is to actively facilitate transparency in remittances markets.

So far, multilateral regulatory efforts such as those outlined in the "General Principles for International Remittances Services"[18] have not called for direct regulation of RSPs regarding disclosure of price information. Rather, they suggest that other mechanisms, such as self-regulatory

Figure 9.4 Cost of Sending a US$300 Remittance from Chicago to Mexico (March 2006)

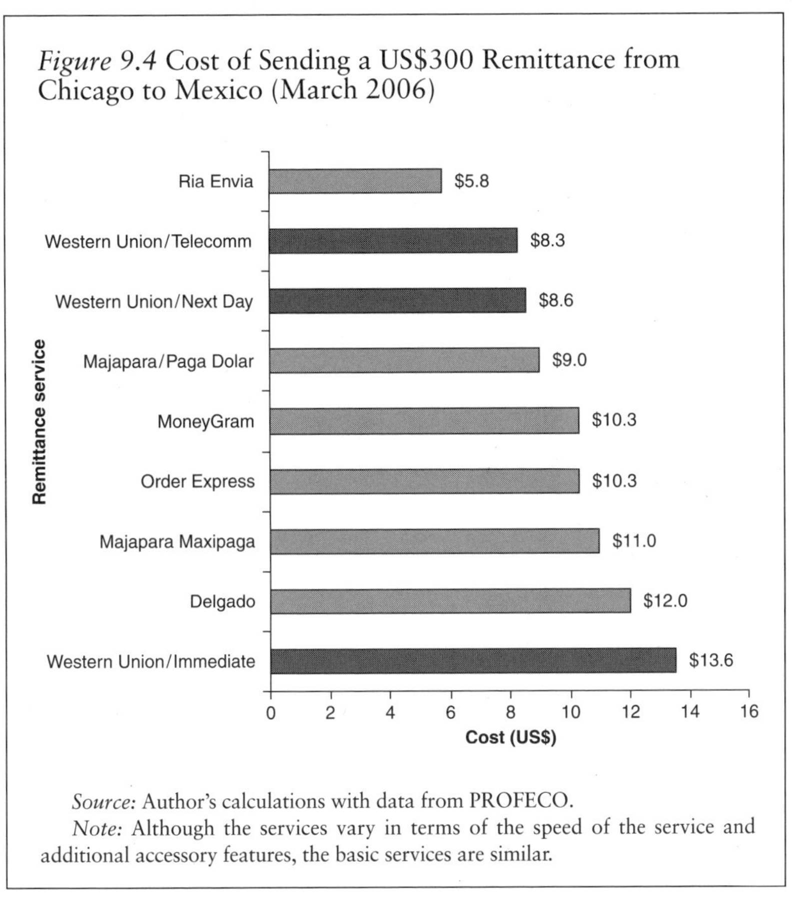

Source: Author's calculations with data from PROFECO.

Note: Although the services vary in terms of the speed of the service and additional accessory features, the basic services are similar.

efforts or definition of best practices at the industry level may prove more efficient in enhancing transparency.[19] In this context, a "name-and-shame" approach through the publication of comparative prices can create public awareness and consequently pressure RSPs to lower prices.

In some corridors in Latin America, the active involvement of consumer protection authorities in increasing transparency in the market has had a positive impact through the collection and publication of comparative prices and conditions of service among different RSPs (see box 9.5). However, transparency in origin countries is likely to have a higher impact, as it is senders who ultimately decide on the choice of service provider.

Authorities' efforts to foster transparency can be complemented with the provision of basic financial literacy to users in order to create awareness of the different service options available to them.

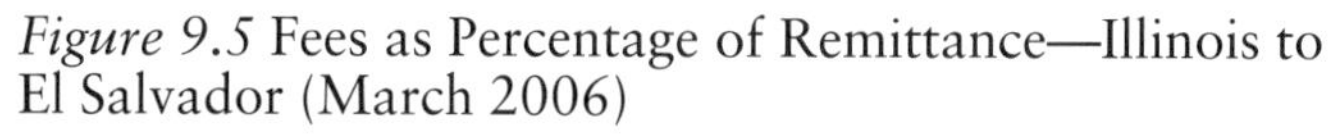
Figure 9.5 Fees as Percentage of Remittance—Illinois to El Salvador (March 2006)

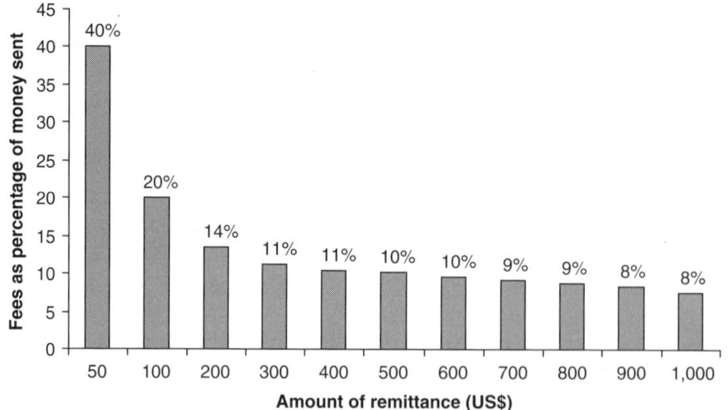

Source: Author's calculations based on information from RSP.

Note: Data is based on the service "Money in Minutes" from Illinois to El Salvador, March 31, 2006.

Figure 9.6 Fees and Exchange Rate Costs

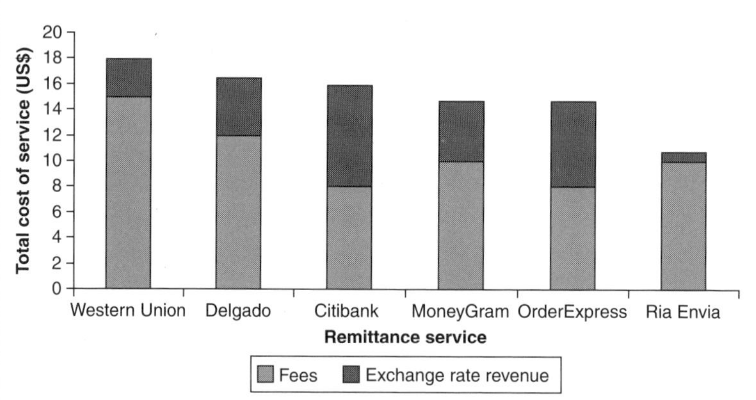

Source: Author's calculations based on data from PROFECO and Oanda Currency Exchange.

Note: Data is a based on a US$300 remittance from New York to Mexico as of March 6, 2006. The exchange rate cost was calculated using the differential between the exchange rate applied by each RSP and the average interbank exchange rate of the same date (Mex$10.5958 per US$1).

Box 9.4 Money in Minutes or Next Day

Western Union is the largest RSP in the U.S.-Mexico corridor, with the largest market share. In this corridor Western Union offers six different remittances services, which are mainly differentiated by the speed of the service and the disbursing agent locations.

Information on total pricing (including fees and the exchange rate differential) is available publicly only for one of the six services. Furthermore, this limited information was obtained through the Internet, which is arguably a medium seldom used by most remittances clients.

Information on total pricing can be disclosed on an ad hoc basis to users by capturing agents. However, comparative pricing of the same transaction under different types of services is not directly provided. The total price of the service is usually disclosed to the users in the receipt of the transaction, issued after the operation has been processed.

As shown in the table below, immediate availability of the remittance at destination can be priced almost 60 percent higher than next-day service. Considering that the same capturing and disbursing agents (and presumably same network and infrastructure) are used in both cases, it is not clear that the incremental costs incurred by the RSP for immediate delivery of the remittance can justify the high price differential.

Often users cannot easily differentiate among the different services offered by a given RSP or do not know that cheaper options are also provided by the same operator.

Cost of a US$300 Remittance from Chicago to Mexico

Service	*Speed*	*Disbursing agent*	*Total price of remittance (US$)*[a]
Dinero en minutos	Immediate	Partner banks, stores, Telecomm[b]	13.6
Dinero dia siguiente	Next day	Partner banks, stores, Telecomm	8.6
Dinero a domicilio	3–7 days	Home delivery	Depends on location of recipient
Giro Paisano	Immediate	Telecomm	10.6
Giro Telegrafico	Next day	Telecomm	8.3
Giro Telegrafico con Aviso	Next day	Telecomm (includes a home-delivered telegram notification)	15.5

Source: Based on author's calculations with information from Western Union's Web site and capturing agent as of October 2005.

a. Includes fees, commissions and exchange rates differential.

b. Telecomm is the state-owned telegraph service, still widely used in Mexico.

Payments Systems and Their Role in Competition in Remittances Corridors

Prices for remittances have decreased in the last few years in some Latin American corridors. This has been especially the case in those markets that are served by multiple RSPs, such as is the case in Mexico (see figure 9.7), while prices in corridors with less competition have remained stable or even increased,[20] These figures suggest that pricing of remittances services is largely determined by the level of competition faced by operators, and does not necessarily reflect the actual costs of the services.

Transaction costs for RSPs are relatively low compared to the fees charged to users, and there is room for decrease in both costs and prices.[21] However, the incentives for incumbent RSPs to realize cost savings and reduce prices are limited in smaller corridors, where the limited volume of operations represents a natural barrier to entry for new operators.

Box 9.5 Official Efforts for Transparency in the U.S.-Mexico Remittances Market

In 1998 PROFECO, the consumer protection agency in Mexico, created a unilateral program to increase transparency in the U.S.-Mexico remittances corridor.

Although initially the program relied on Mexican consulates in the United States to collect the information on cost of transactions, eventually many RSPs provided the information themselves.

Currently, PROFECO monitors and reports weekly comparative statistics of the prices charged by 24 RSPs. Although the program has expanded geographically over time, it currently monitors prices in only the nine wwcities with the largest concentration of Mexican migrants. Since RSPs' prices vary by state in the United States, there may be significant differences between the states monitored and those not covered by the program.

Both commissions and exchange rate differentials have decreased significantly in the states where this program operates. At the same time, price differentials across different states of origin have also decreased (see box figure). However, several other factors may have also supported this improvement.

A significant constraint to the program is the limited dissemination of the information collected. At the present time, the main dissemination channels are postings in Mexican consulates, a dedicated information hotline (within Mexico), and PROFECO's Web site. Diffusion of this information, and overall transparency in the market could be further enhanced by the participation of a counterpart in the United States, such as the Bureau of Consumer Protection.

(continued)

Box 9.5 Official Efforts for Transparency in the U.S.-Mexico Remittance Market *(continued)*

Total Cost of Sending a US$300 Remittance from Various U.S. Cities to Mexico, 1998–2004 (Average of All RSPs Monitored)

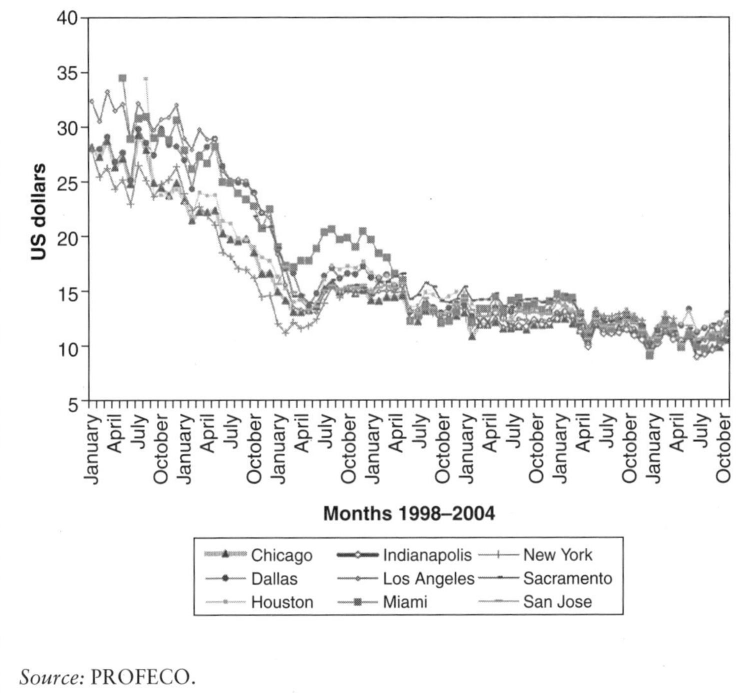

Source: PROFECO.

Even in the absence of regulatory or infrastructure barriers to entry, competition can be limited by the size of the corridor, as the volume of operations in small remittances corridors may not afford the existence of multiple RSPs. In these cases, many of the benefits of competition can be achieved if there is contestability in the market. A contestable market is one where transparency and absence of barriers to entry create incentives for incumbents to provide high-quality services at fair prices, as new entrants could easily start up and enter the market.

Fostering contestability is arguably one of the most important responsibilities of authorities in low-volume corridors. In this context, enabling the entry of new RSPs into the market requires the definition of a clear legal framework governing the national payments system in order to clearly

Figure 9.7 Range of Prices of Remittance Services in the U.S.-Mexico Corridor, 1999–2005 (Percent of Amount Sent)

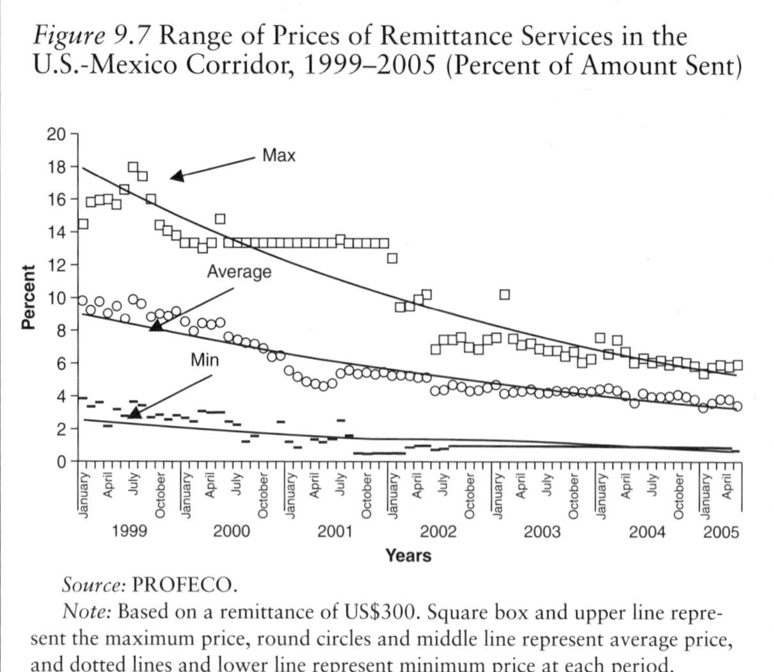

Source: PROFECO.

Note: Based on a remittance of US$300. Square box and upper line represent the maximum price, round circles and middle line represent average price, and dotted lines and lower line represent minimum price at each period.

define the conditions for appropriate access to domestic payment infrastructures under fair conditions.

The Role of Payments Systems in Facilitating Competition

RSPs require constant access to payment and settlement systems in the course of their operations. The degree of development of those systems and the extent to which new RSPs can access them largely determines the potential for competition in the market. Indeed, remittances services depend to a great extent on the domestic payment infrastructure for settlement.[22] Even though from a technological perspective access of new RSPs to existing payments systems should be relatively easy to achieve either directly or indirectly (through a bank), many RSPs face formal restrictions in accessing these systems.

Direct access to national payments systems is normally granted to well-capitalized and established banking institutions. A recent survey found that 35 of 40 authorities in different countries were not favorable to opening the clearing and settlement systems to smaller institutions, which are perceived as lacking the required technology platform, and hence would arguably pose a risk to the systems.[23]

RSPs can have indirect access to payment and settlement systems through banks. In theory, this should not create unfair competitive disadvantages to RSPs, as regulation of payment and settlement systems should ensure that indirect access to RSPs is provided under fair conditions. However, there are concerns that indirect access could be unduly constrained due to competition (when both the standalone RSP and the bank provide remittances services), or regulatory concerns.

For nonbank RSPs operating in the United States, accounts with commercial banks are the only way to access the official payment and settlement systems, and hence an essential component in their operations. However, more than 40 percent of RSPs recently surveyed[24] considered that limited access to the bank settlement system was an obstacle for their ongoing operations. More important, 65 percent of respondent RSPs in the same survey reported problems opening and maintaining accounts with U.S. banks. This may be linked to the fact that many banks are concerned that participation in remittances activities could make them subject to heightened regulatory oversight and costs, even though authorities have expressed that this is not the case.[25]

Multilateral Efforts to Create Cross-Border Settlement Systems

The problem of accessibility to payments systems, as well as the challenges for cross-border settlement, can be addressed through bilateral or multilateral efforts linking existing networks in sending and receiving countries.[26]

In Latin America, efforts to develop cross-border payment and settlement systems have been conducted through private or public initiatives with different degrees of success. For example, official efforts to link U.S. payments and settlement systems to Mexican banks[27] for elimination of costly wire transfers have failed to raise significant interest from commercial banks, largely due to revenue expectations.[28] Conversely, private efforts to link networks of credit unions appear to be successful at attracting new entrants and providing remittances services at a significantly lower cost (see box 9.6).

However, these arrangements can create barriers to new competitors if they require exclusivity. This is especially the case when the disbursing RSP has a large network such as the postal system, telecommunications companies, or large store chains. While exclusivity agreements between private businesses are difficult to prevent, local governments should ensure that public networks are open to different RSPs, rather than being limited by exclusivity agreements.

Box 9.6 Linking Credit Unions through the International Remittance Network (IRnet)

IRnet is a platform created by the World Council of Credit Unions (WOCCU), a multinational trade organization, creating a direct link for remittances between credit unions in origin and destination countries worldwide. The coverage of IRnet includes Latin America, Asia, Africa, Europe, and Australia.

The stated objective of IRnet is offering inexpensive remittances services. Savings to users appear significant: fees for a US$1,000 remittance from the United States to Mexico are US$10[a] versus US$30[b] for a similar service with a leading MTO.

Access to IRnet for new participants appears fairly simple and exceptionally affordable, with sign-up fees between US$300 and US$750 (depending on the size of the credit union) and maximum quarterly fees of US$150. But most important, transaction fees are between US$0.25 and US$0.75.

Even though IRnet is primarily a network for credit unions, it is open to affiliated MTOs (including MoneyGram, Travelex, and Vigo Remittance Corporation[c]), which can act as capturing or disbursing agents. An essential element for the development of this service is its accessibility. To this end, after legal consultation, WOCCU issued clear guidelines to member credit unions in the United States aimed at facilitating the access of undocumented migrants to financial services provided by these entities.[d]

Source: WOCCU Web site (http://www.woccu.org) unless otherwise stated.
a. WOCCU 2006.
b. Author's calculation based on "Money in Minutes" service from Western Union. This figure does not include the exchange rate implicit fee.
c. Vigo Remittance Corporation was recently acquired by Western Union. The scope of Vigo's participation on IRnet going forward is not clear.
d. The guidelines also clarify that identification requirements to open an account can be met with a foreign government document such as passport or consular identity card (commonly known as Matricula Consular).

Conclusions and Policy Recommendations

Summing up, the main messages that emerge from the previous discussion are the following.

Security

- Regulatory requirements for new RSPs should balance the need to maintain security in the system with eliminating unnecessary hurdles to bona fide entrants. Entry requirements must be clear, transparent, and uniformly applicable to all entrants with similar characteristics. These requirements should also be proportional to the risk and volume of operations. While homogeneity across countries is hard to achieve, these requirements should be homogenized within the same country.

- The definition and implementation of regulatory measures to ensure security in the system must be based on authorities' efforts to collect information and fully understand the characteristics of the remittances markets.
- Basic security regulations to avoid criminal misuse of remittances channels should be applicable to all RSPs. Uneven application of these regulations can hamper the security of the system by creating loopholes than can be exploited for illegal purposes. Similarly, uneven regulation can create market disruptions through unfair competitive advantages in favor of less-regulated entities. However, the even application of security regulations may pose significant challenges to authorities in countries where the regulatory framework is different for RSPs that are financial institutions and those that are commercial companies.

Transparency

- Authorities should take an active role in the collection and dissemination of information on comparative prices of remittances services under different providers. This information should be disseminated through adequate channels in a form that is clear and easily understandable. Bilateral efforts should be made so that this information is disseminated at countries of both origin and destination of remittances.
- Many authorities have avoided direct regulation and enforcement of transparency for RSPs. However, the experience in some countries shows that RSPs have found it in their best interest to cooperate with official efforts for transparency on a voluntary basis. Similarly, establishment of best practices at an industry level can be encouraged as a form of self-regulation on this matter. The price information disclosed by RSPs should be clear, easily understandable, and provided in the languages of the corresponding corridor. This information should also be presented using an industrywide format to facilitate users' comparisons across RSPs.

Accessibility

- Accessibility to financial services at the country of origin of remittances can be limited by unnecessarily high documentation requirements that particularly affect illegal immigrants.
    - In cases where this is due to actual regulation, authorities should review the merit and need for such constraints.

- In other cases this is not a direct regulatory requirement, but appears to be derived from misinterpretation of regulations or unfounded bank expectations of stronger oversight by regulators if they provide services to undocumented migrants. Authorities should ensure clarity in regulatory requirements and transparency in their oversight processes in order to avoid misinterpretations that can translate into artificial constraints to accessibility.
- Financial services may also be underutilized by immigrants, based on perceptions of high costs or distrust of financial institutions. Financial services such as bank accounts can indeed pose significant transaction costs and administrative fees, especially to users who cannot maintain a minimum balance. While it is unlikely that this is an issue that can be addressed by authorities, there is room for provision of basic financial literacy that can lower mistrust of banks while helping migrants to understand the costs and benefits of using financial institutions for remittances and other services. Joint efforts by authorities and financial institutions should be considered.
- Accessibility to financial services at the country of destination of remittances can be improved by permitting access to remittances services to smaller financial institutions such as credit unions, savings and loans, and microfinance companies. Because of their focus, these institutions may be closer to the recipients of remittances than mainstream commercial banks.
- Given the fact that compliance with regulatory requirements is costly and can create operational inefficiencies, regulation to ensure security of the system should be proportionate to the risk of misuse and the volume of operations of the RSPs.

Competition

- Unwarranted regulatory barriers to access payment and settlement systems (either directly or indirectly) should be removed. While direct access may not be strictly necessary, indirect access through financial institutions should not translate into competitive disadvantages for RSPs.
- Exclusivity agreements between capturing and disbursing RSPs can limit competition in the market, especially when they involve wide networks. While these may be difficult to prevent when both RSPs are private entities, local authorities at destination countries should maintain public networks, such as the postal systems, that are open to different service providers.
- Authorities in low-volume corridors should ensure contestability in their local markets as a way to create incentives for efficiency of incumbent RSPs.

Annex A. AML and CFT Regulations

FATF Recommendations[29]

Extracts from "The Forty Recommendations," Financial Action Task Force on Money Laundering (FATF), revised October 22, 2004. See http://www.fatf-gafi.org/document/28/0,3343,en_32250379_32236930_33658140_1_1_1_1,00.html#40recs.

Recommendation 5: Financial institutions should undertake customer due diligence measures, including identifying and verifying the identity of their customers, when carrying out occasional transactions that are wire transfers.

Recommendation 7: Financial institutions should, in relation to cross-border correspondent banking and other similar relationships, in addition to performing normal due diligence measures: (a) Gather sufficient information about a respondent institution to understand fully the nature of the respondent's business and to determine from publicly available information the reputation of the institution and the quality of supervision, including whether it has been subject to a money laundering or terrorist financing investigation or regulatory action. (b) Assess the respondent institution's anti-money laundering and terrorist financing controls. (c) Obtain approval from senior management before establishing new correspondent relationships. (d) Document the respective responsibilities of each institution. (e) With respect to "payable-through accounts," be satisfied that the respondent bank has verified the identity of and performed ongoing due diligence on the customers having direct access to accounts of the correspondent and that it is able to provide relevant customer identification data upon request to the correspondent bank.

Recommendation 8: Financial institutions should pay special attention to any money laundering threats that may arise from new or developing technologies that might favor anonymity and take measures, if needed, to prevent their use in money laundering schemes. In particular, financial institutions should have policies and procedures in place to address any specific risks associated with non-face to face business relationships or transactions.

Recommendation 23: . . . Other financial institutions should be licensed or registered and appropriately regulated, and subject to supervision or oversight for anti-money laundering purposes, having regard to the risk of money laundering or terrorist financing in that sector. At a minimum, businesses providing a service of money or value transfer, or of money or currency changing, should be licensed or registered, and subject to effective systems for monitoring and ensuring compliance with national requirements to combat money laundering and terrorist financing.

Extracts from "Special Recommendations on Terrorist Financing," FATF, revised October 22, 2004.

VI. Alternative remittance: Each country should take measures to ensure that persons or legal entities, including agents, that provide a service for the transmission of money or value, including transmission through an informal money or value transfer system or network, should be licensed or registered and subject to all the FATF Recommendations that apply to banks and non-bank financial institutions. Each country should ensure that persons or legal entities that carry out this service illegally are subject to administrative, civil or criminal sanctions.

VII. Wire transfers: Countries should take measures to require financial institutions, including money remitters, to include accurate and meaningful originator information (name, address, and account number) on funds transfers and related messages that are sent, and the information should remain with the transfer or related message through the payment chain.

Countries should take measures to ensure that financial institutions, including money remitters, conduct enhanced scrutiny of and monitor for suspicious activity funds transfers which do not contain complete originator information (name, address, and account number).

USA PATRIOT Act[30]

The USA PATRIOT Act required that all RSPs adopt a written anti-money laundering program that is designed to ensure monitoring and reporting of suspicious transactions. This program must include:

- Internal policies, procedures, and controls to verify customers' identification, filing of reports, keeping of records, and responding to law enforcement requests
- Designation of a compliance officer responsible for ensuring that procedures are followed
- Provision of ongoing training to employees on compliance to procedures
- Independent review of the anti-money laundering program

Record-keeping requirements follow:

- Transactions below US$1,000 require presentation of identification of sender that includes name and address (identification cards issued by a foreign government can be accepted). Identification of the receiver is not required.
- Transactions (both sending and receiving) above US$3,000 require collecting information on identification, address, and occupation of sender and receiver.
- Transactions above US$10,000 require filing of a standard Currency Transaction Report (CTR). CTRs must be filed with the Internal Revenue Service.

- Records of transactions above US$3,000 must be retained for five years.

Similarly, RSPs must report "suspicious activity," such as structuring (splitting remittances into small transactions to avoid reporting) through a Suspicious Activity Report. However, there are no clear guidelines for the definition of "suspicious," and this is left to the individual agent or operator to identify and report.

Reporting to the Office of Foreign Assets Control (OFAC)

The Office of Foreign Assets Control (OFAC) is the unit of the U.S. Department of the Treasury in charge of enforcing economic and trade sanctions against targeted foreign countries, terrorists, and drug cartels. OFAC issues a list of governments, terrorists, drug traffickers, and those engaged in the proliferation of weapons of mass destruction. This list is known as Specially Designated Nationals (SDN).

Any transaction with individuals or entities included on the SDN list is prohibited by OFAC regulation, and businesses are required to identify and freeze assets of organizations or individuals included in the list and report to the Department of Treasury.

Criminal Penalties

Noncompliance with the anti-money laundering regulations derived from the Bank Secrecy Act, USA PATRIOIT Act, and OFAC can be punished by high fines and prison terms. Businesses can be held criminally liable for the acts of employees.

Annex B. Legal Framework, Transparency, Oversight, and Cooperation in Payments Systems

A sound and appropriate legal framework is generally considered the basis for a sound and efficient payments system. The legal environment should include the following:

- Laws and regulations of broad applicability that address issues such as insolvency and contractual relations between parties
- Laws and regulations that have specific applicability to payments systems (such as legislation on electronic signatures, validation of netting, settlement finality)
- Rules, standards, and procedures agreed to by the participants of a payments system

The legal infrastructure should also cover other activities carried out by both public and private sector entities. For example, the legislative framework may establish clear responsibilities for the central bank or other regulatory bodies, such as oversight of the payments system or the provision of liquidity to participants in these systems. Finally, relevant pieces of legislation that have an impact on the soundness of the legal framework of the payments system include laws on transparency and security of payment instruments, terms, and conditions; antitrust legislation for the supply of payments services; and legislation on privacy. While laws are normally the appropriate means to enforce a general objective in the payments field, in some cases regulation by the overseers might be an efficient way to react to a rapidly changing environment. In other cases, specific agreements among participants might be adequate—in this case, an appropriate professional assessment of the enforceability of these arrangements is usually required. Finally, since the payments systems typically include participants incorporated in foreign jurisdictions, or the payments systems might operate with multiple currencies or across borders, in some cases it may be necessary to address issues associated with foreign jurisdictions.

The oversight role of the central bank is currently at the heart of the international debate and the function is emerging as key in central bank activity.[31] Direct involvement of the central bank in managing clearing and settlement systems has been, in all countries, the first step to governing the overall structure and operation of a country's payments system and ensuring that the desire to limit systemic risk, especially in the area of large-value payments systems, is adequately taken into account. In many cases, this role stems from the need to ensure a widespread adoption of more advanced technology in fund transfer mechanisms, and to avoid possible discrimination in access to payment services. In all cases, in order to pursue the public interest in the payments system, central banks should ensure that the systems they operate comply with the principles and guidelines they establish, and as overseers, ensure the (financial and operational) reliability and efficiency of the clearing and settlement systems they do not operate. The importance of the oversight role of the central bank is more likely to emerge when payments reform is complete and the central bank is called to ensure proper monitoring of the reliability and efficiency of the domestic system on an ongoing basis.

In recent years, in an increasing number of countries, payments system oversight has been explicitly entrusted to central banks by law. Specifying the objectives in relevant legislation may be the most direct way for providing a well-founded legal basis for the central bank to implement its policies and make it accountable in pursuing its goal and mandate regarding the payments system. For countries facing the implementation of reforms in the payments system, it is of utmost importance for the central bank to have a well-founded legal framework that clearly defines its payments system role and objectives.

Scope of the Oversight Function

As for the scope of the oversight function, at the international level there is consensus on the fact that systems posing systemic risks should fall under the direct control of the overseer. Typical examples of these systems are those that handle transactions of a high value at both the individual and aggregate levels. For example, the CPSS Task Force on Core Principles identified four responsibilities of the central bank in applying the core principles for systemically important payment systems. However, a broader scope including retail payment systems is common in many countries, especially developing ones.

"Central banks have different roles in retail payments, including remittance services, depending on their responsibilities, policies, and powers. It may be desirable that central banks monitor developments in the market for remittances to assess their significance for safety and efficiency. In some cases, central banks' responsibilities may also make it appropriate for them to oversee certain remittance services. To the extent that central banks provide payment services, they may be able, where appropriate, to enhance these services to support the smooth functioning of international remittance services. Examples might include the development of new services that support cross-border payments, or enhancing existing services to make them more useful for supporting cross-border payments. The central bank should cooperate with other public authorities to address significant policy issues arising from remittance market structures and performance. Central banks may wish to enter into discussions with the private sector and other central banks to facilitate the achievement of public policy objectives regarding remittance services and to foster international cooperation" (World Bank and CPSS 2006, p. 22).

In May 2005, the CPSS published a report totally devoted to payments systems' oversight in G-10 countries.

Effective cooperation among market participants, between regulators and market participants, and among regulators is essential for the development of a sound and efficient payment system. On one hand, the use of payment instruments generates significant externalities on the demand side, since the usefulness of an instrument is strictly linked to the degree of its acceptance and use for transaction purposes. Consequently, widespread use of new payment instruments and services relies heavily on public confidence in them. On the other hand, within the payments system, the supply of services can be affected by coordination failures due to the existence of conflicts of interest (and information costs), as well as the intermediaries' unwillingness to cooperate. This can lead to "suboptimal" equilibria in the organizational arrangements regarding the system's reliability and efficiency. The payments system overseer is therefore entrusted with making up for a specific type of failure in the market for payment services, that is, the coordination failures. Cooperation problems may be especially relevant within interbank clearing and settlement systems. In fact, in these systems the risk profiles—both at the system level and at the level of the individual intermediary—may not be fully assessed by participants. In addition, the concern of having to support less reliable intermediaries may lead larger participants to discriminate against smaller ones, even when these are technically eligible to participate in the system. Finally, the payments system industry also depends on agreements between producers to ensure that different components of the system are compatible. Most recently, the emergence of new types of nonbank intermediaries and payment instruments has strengthened the need for a comprehensive level of cooperation in the payment system.

With regard to the cooperation among regulators, the safety and efficiency objectives of payment and securities settlement systems may be pursued by a variety of public sector authorities, in addition to the central bank and the securities commission. Examples of these regulators include legislative authorities, ministries of finance, and competition authorities. There are also complementary relationships among oversight, bank supervision, and market surveillance authorities. Appropriate cooperation among supervisors can be achieved in a variety of ways. For example, exchanges of views and information between relevant authorities may be conducted by holding regular or ad hoc meetings. Agreements on the sharing of information may be useful for such exchanges.

Notes

1. For the purpose of this chapter, a "formal" provider is one registered or licensed by government agencies. Formal service providers are usually—but not necessarily—regulated or overseen by financial sector regulators. "Informal" providers of remittances services operate without license or registration by authorities. However, informal providers are not necessarily illegal, as many countries have not yet issued the regulations necessary to formalize remittances services.

2. IMF (2005).

3. According to Passel (2006), the Current Population Survey indicates that there were 11.1 million unauthorized migrants in the United States in March 2006. Based on other data sources, the Pew Hispanic Center developed an estimate of 11.5 million to 12 million for the unauthorized population as of March 2006.

4. Frias (2004).

5. Suro and Bendixen (2002)

6. *Global Economic Prospects 2006: International Remittances and Migration*, World Bank, Washington, DC.

7. Remittances providers have been associated with facilitating tax evasion, capital flight, circumventing excise requirements, and smuggling (El Qorchi, Maimbo, and Wilson 2003).

8. Examples of remittances being used to fund terrorism, civil wars, and liberation struggles include remittances being used to acquire arms for guerrillas in Somalia, remittances originated in Sweden to fund the Free Aceh Movement, in Canada for the Liberation Tigers of Tamil Eelam, and from the United Kingdom for the Kashmiri cause (Kapur 2004).

9. World Bank (2006).

10. While regulatory hurdles can deter RSPs from formalizing their operations, they do not necessarily impede the operations of informal RSPs, which can operate without proper authorization. In turn, this can create an environment of unfair competition (where informal RSPs can offer lower prices by not being subject to regulatory costs), and where the system is more open to misuse. According to Andreassen (2006), around 55 percent of RSPs surveyed in the United States considered informal competitors to be a considerable or major obstacle

11. A survey of remittances senders in 2002 (IDB 2002) showed that in only 26 percent of the cases both sender and recipient of the remittances had bank accounts.

12. This section focuses on the situation in the United States, as the country of origin of most of the remittances to Latin America.

13. According to recent remarks by Citibank officials, the process of sending remittances through commercial banks is "expensive, challenging, and time consuming," both for the customer and the bank, [largely due to regulatory requirements] (Annibale 2005).

14. According to some estimates (Lowell and Suro 2002), at least two-fifths of the adult Latino immigrant population is made up of individuals not authorized to be in the country.

15. Orozco (2005).

16. "How to Serve Undocumented Individuals," World Council of Credit Unions, Inc., Washington, DC.

17. A survey of remittances senders conducted by *Procuraduría Federal del Consumidor* (PROFECO), the consumer protection agency in Mexico, found that 61 percent of respondents did not know how much would be charged by a different provider for the same remittances transaction (PROFECO 1998).

18. Henceforth referred to as "the General Principles." The World Bank and the Committee on Payments and Settlement Systems (CPSS) convened a task force in November 2004 to address the need for international policy coordination for remittances systems. Following its mandate, in March 2006 the task force produced a report on "General Principles for International Remittances Services," describing key features and functions that should be satisfied by remittances systems, providers, and financial intermediaries.

19. According to World Bank and CPSS (2006), RSPs should disclose the total price of their remittances services, the conditions, and the characteristics of the service in a way that is clear and easy to understand by their common users. Arguably, the way in which this information is presented should be standardized, in order to facilitate the comparison across different MTOs.

20. Orozco (2004).

21. World Bank (2006).

22. CPSS-WB Consultative Report: "General Principles for International Remittance Services," March 2006, pages 16–17.

23. De Luna and Martinez (2005).

24. Andreassen (2006).

25. Bair (2005).

26. CPSS-WB Consultative Report: "General Principles for International Remittance Services," March 2006, pages 16–17.

27. Through the Federal Reserve Bank's Automated Clearing House (FedACH) system for Mexico.

28. Exchange rate differentials in operations through the FedACH facility are kept by the Mexican Central Bank. At the same time, many large commercial banks in Mexico can achieve higher profitability in remittances transactions when

they use their own internal cross-border systems (because many are subsidiaries of foreign banks) or closed agreements with capturing agents in the United States.

29. Extract from World Bank (2006).

30. This section draws from MoneyGram (2006a).

31. Recent examples are the focus on central banks' responsibilities in the CPSS Core Principles report and the Bank for International Settlements/International Organisation of Securities Commission (BIS/IOSCO) recommendations for securities settlement systems and the paper on payment system oversight of the Bank of England. See also Bossone and Cirasino (2001).

References

Andreassen, O. 2006. *Remittance Service Providers in the United States: How Remittance Firms Operate and How They Perceive Their Business Environment.* Washington, DC: World Bank.

Annibale, B. 2005. "Balancing Competition and Regulation in the Remittance Market." Remarks at the IDB International Forum on Remittances, Washington, DC.

Bair, S.C. 2005. *Improving Access to the U.S. Banking System among Recent Latin American Immigrants.* Washington, DC: Center for Public Policy and Administration, University of Massachusetts and The Multilateral Investment Fund.

Bossone, B., and M. Cinasino. 2001. "The Oversight of the Payments Systems: A framework for the Development and Governance of Payment Systems in Emerging Economies." Payments and Securities Clearance and Settlement Research Series No. 1, CEMLA and World Bank, Washington, DC.

De Luna Martinez, J. 2005. "Workers' Remittances to Developing Countries: A Survey of Central Banks on Selected Public Policy Issues." Policy Research Working Paper No. 3638, World Bank, Washington, DC.

El Qorchi, M., S. Maimbo, and J. Wilson. 2003. "Informal Funds Transfer Systems: An Analysis of the Informal Hawala System." IMF Occasional Paper No. 222, International Monetary Fund, Washington, DC.

Frias, M. 2004. "Linking International Remittance Flows to Financial Services: Tapping the Latino Immigrant Market." *Supervisory Insights Winter 2004*, Federal Deposit Insurance Corporation.

IDB (Inter-American Development Bank). 2002. *Survey of Remittance Senders: U.S. to Latin America.* Washington, DC: Inter-American Development Bank.

———. 2004. *State by State Survey of Remittance Senders: United States to Latin America.* Washington, DC: Inter-American Development Bank.

Kapur, Davesh. 2004. "Remittances: The New Development Mantra?" G-24 Discussion Paper No. 29, UN Conference on Trade and Development, Geneva, Switzerland.

Lee, Chee Sung, M. Boekkerink, and R. Hernandez-Coss.2005. *Approaches to a Regulatory Framework for Formal and Informal Remittance Systems: Experiences and Lessons.* Washington, DC: International Montetary Fund.

Lowell, B.L., and R. Suro. 2002. "How Many Undocumented: The Numbers Behind the United States-Mexico Migration Talks." Pew Hispanic Center, Washington, DC.

MoneyGram. 2006a. *Agent Compliance Manual.* St. Louis Park, MN: MoneyGram.

———. 2006b. *Anti-Money Laundering Compliance Guide*. St. Louis Park, MN: MoneyGram.

Orozco, M. 2004. "The Remittance Marketplace: Prices, Policy and Financial Institutions." Pew Hispanic Center Report, Georgetown University and Institute for the Study of International Migration, Washington, DC.

———. 2005. "Markets and Financial Democracy: The Case for Remittance Transfers." *Journal of Payment Systems Law* 1 (2): 166–215.

Passel, J. 2006. *The Size and Characteristics of the Unauthorized Migrant Population in the United States*. Washington, DC: Pew Hispanic Center.

PROFECO. 1998. "El Mercado de envio de dinero de Estados Unidos a Mexico." Procuraduría Federal del Consumidor, Mexico City.

———. 2004."Programa quien es quien en el envio de dinero de Estados Unidos a Mexico, origen y evolucion." Procuraduría Federal del Consumidor, Mexico City.

Ratha, D. and J. Riedberg. 2005. *On Reducing Remittance Costs*. Washington, DC: World Bank.

Suro, R., and S. Bendixen. 2002. *The Remittance Process and the Unbanked*. Washington, DC: Pew Hispanic Center and Multilateral Investment Fund.

World Bank. 2006. *Global Economic Prospects: Economic Implications of Remittances and Migration*. Washington, DC: World Bank.

World Bank and Committee on Payment and Settlement Systems. 2006. "General Principles for International Remittance Services." Consultative report, Bank for International Settlements and World Bank, Washington, DC.

WOCCU. 2004. "A Technical Guide to Remittances." World Council of Credit Unions, Inc, Washington, DC.

———. 2006. "How to Serve Undocumented Individuals." World Council of Credit Unions, Inc, Washington, DC.

10

Remittances and Growth: The Role of Complementary Policies

Cesar Calderón, Pablo Fajnzylber, and J. Humberto López

Despite some potential policy challenges, remittances have a number of beneficial effects for the welfare of the receiving countries. However, beyond facilitating remittances flows by, for example, reducing the cost of transfers or improving the payments system, what can policy makers do to enhance the positive impact of remittances? Is it possible that remittances flows, when complemented with appropriate policies, can have a larger impact on growth and poverty reduction? If so, which policy areas deserve particular attention?

Introduction

One typical concern that development practitioners have with studies on workers' remittances is that even when they present good descriptions of the nature (magnitude, cyclicality, profile of receivers, etc.) and impact (on, for example, poverty, growth, financial development, etc.) of these flows, policy recommendations are often restricted to suggesting (either implicitly or explicitly) that countries should try to improve their payments systems and reduce the costs of sending international remittances (see chapter 9). That is, in many cases the main recommendation of these studies is that policy makers should aim only at facilitating and increasing those flows.[1]

In fact, we have to admit that the concern mentioned in the previous paragraph is to a large extent understandable if one considers that remittances are transfers between private parties and that it is difficult to imagine government policies that could enhance their positive impact. For example, if recipients and senders jointly decide that given the country's existing economic environment and their specific personal situation, remittances should be directed toward consumption[2] rather than toward savings or investment (a typical concern of policy makers in recipient countries), then it is difficult to imagine which type of *direct* policy interventions may induce those individuals to do otherwise, other than forcing recipients to save, as a number of countries have done at some point—for example, Lesotho or Mozambique[3] in Africa, and Mexico in Latin America (see box 10.1). And indeed this is probably the type of policy recommendation to avoid because, as argued by Maimbo and Ratha (2005), forcing remittances recipients to save more and consume less tends to reduce consumer welfare.

Yet this is not to say that governments cannot do anything to increase the development impact of remittances, especially if we open the door to consider *indirect* policy interventions; that is, policies that try to change the incentives of remittances recipients to use their resources in one or another way. For example, as noted by Burnside and Dollar (2000), if one considers a modified neoclassical model with imperfect international capital markets, the impact of an international income transfer (such as a remittances flow) on the growth rate of the recipient economy will depend on whether the transfer is invested or consumed. Whenever the income transfer is invested it will positively affect growth, whereas if consumed it will have no impact.

Box 10.1 Remittances and Forced Savings: The Bracero Program

On June 23, 1942, the United States signed a bilateral guest worker agreement with Mexico, the *Bracero* program. Over the next 22 years, some 4.6 million Mexicans were admitted to the United States as *braceros*, or guest workers, to fill jobs in U.S. farms.

During the first phase of the Bracero program, the U.S. government guaranteed bracero contracts, meaning that the U.S. government would pay wages owed to Mexican workers if American farmers failed to do so. A second feature of the program was forced savings. The 256,000 Mexicans who received contracts to work as braceros in the United States between 1942 and 1949 had 10 percent of their U.S. wages withheld by U.S. employers and forwarded via the Wells Fargo Bank and Union Trust Company of San Francisco to the Bank of Mexico and then to the Banco de Credito Agricola in Mexico.

The theory was that, because of these forced savings, braceros would arrive home with at least some savings. In 1948, a new agreement had U.S. employers issuing the bracero a check for money withheld when the work contract expired, and the check was to be validated when the bracero returned to Mexico. The 10 percent deductions stopped in 1950.

Source: Based on *Migration News* 8(2)(April), 2001.

The critical link, however, is that in this context the incentive to invest and its subsequent productivity will depend on the policy environment. Good policy environments will increase the return on investment and hence will raise the opportunity cost of consumption. On the contrary, a bad policy environment will drive down the return on investment (or increase the risk associated with a given return) and lower the opportunity cost of consumption. Put in other words, in the context of this simple model, the impact of the international transfer on the growth rate will depend on the policies being implemented by the country. Policy makers, therefore, can potentially affect the impact that an international income transfer has on growth by introducing appropriate changes to the policy environment.

Indeed, at the empirical level, Burnside and Dollar (2000) find that a specific international income transfer—aid—has a more positive impact on growth in good policy environments. Moreover, they also show that this effect goes beyond the direct impact that good policies themselves have on growth. In a follow-up paper, Burnside and Dollar (2004) also conclude that there is far more evidence to support the idea that complementarity between aid and good policies matters for growth more than the competing hypothesis that aid has the same positive effect in all institutional environments.

The idea that a package of policies (or an appropriate combination of policies and exogenous factors) can be more than the sum of its parts is not new in the economics literature (see Perry et al. [2006] for a review). In fact, there is now some evidence that from an economic development point of view that what matters is not only the "quantity" of an implemented policy, but also the overall policy mix. For example, Gallego and Loayza (2002) estimate that good performers that jointly implement a series of growth-promoting measures and eliminate bottlenecks in different areas at the same time might achieve growth rates that exceed by more than 1 percentage point the sum of the contributions of each policy reform if implemented in isolation. Similarly, Calderón and Fuentes (2005) find that, in effect, institutional quality seems to play a significant role in explaining the impact on growth of both financial sector liberalization and openness to trade.

Thus, to gain knowledge about the impact that one policy has on growth, one needs to also know the rest of the policy package. This chapter explores these issues following a similar approach to the one in Burnside and Dollar (2000), but focusing on whether there may be complementarities between a surge of remittances, which we treat as an exogenous factor for policy makers,[4] and the implementation of policies in a number of areas. That is, unlike in chapter 4, where we explore whether remittances in general tend to accelerate growth rates, our concern now is whether developing countries could benefit from an "extra bonus" in terms of growth when remittances are accompanied by progress on a number of policy areas.

The rest of the chapter is structured as follows. In the next section we review a number of areas that are susceptible to being complements to remittances when the objective is achieving a faster growth rate. We also assess whether the Latin American countries have room to make progress in those particular areas. Note that this assessment is critical from a policy-making point of view because it measures the extent to which countries can exploit the potential complementarity in the future. In the third section we review the empirical strategy and present the results for our growth equations. Our main argument is that policy makers can affect the incentives that recipients have to invest their remittances. Thus, in the penultimate section we explore that hypothesis and present the results of empirical models relating the investment rate to remittances. Finally, the chapter presents some concluding remarks.

Policy Areas That May Complement Remittances

In the previous section, we have argued that there may be a number of areas where progress may result in an "extra bonus" in the presence of remittances. Clearly, one natural question that emerges from this discussion regards which policies are likely to be the most critical in this context. Here we explore the potential role of interventions in four areas: education, institutions, the financial sector, and macroeconomic distortions. We next elaborate on our motivation for focusing on these areas.

Policy Complementarities and Education

Education is typically considered an important growth determinant. In addition to participating as an input in the production process, it can also determine the rate of technological innovation and facilitate the absorption of technologies. Moreover, education also appears as an important complement of the growth process. For example, the flagship report of the World Bank's Latin American region, *Closing the Gap in Education and Technology* (de Ferranti et al. 2003), argued that the interaction between technology and skills is critical in determining growth, productivity, and the distribution of earnings across individuals. In fact, when that report explores whether there is evidence suggesting that low levels of skills can be a constraint to technology through trade and foreign direct investment (FDI), the answer is a clear "yes."

The academic literature has also devoted significant attention to the topic recently. For example, Levin and Raut (1997) showed the existence of a high degree of complementarity between human capital and growth in the export sector for a sample of semi-industrial countries. They justify this result by noting that it is likely that the export sector can utilize human capital more efficiently than the rest of the economy. This can be the case if, for example, educated workers are better able to adapt quickly to the more sophisticated technologies and rapid production changes required for maintaining competitiveness in world markets. Similarly, using an analogous approach to Levin and Raut's (1997), Borensztein, Gregorio, and Lee (1998) present evidence of complementarity between FDI and human capital. That is, FDI would contribute to higher productivity and higher economic growth only when sufficient absorptive capacity is available in the host country.

Why is this aspect important in the Latin American context? There are two main reasons. The first is because to the extent that education drives up the returns to physical investment, it will imply that ceteris paribus for a given remittances flow, the higher the educational level of the country in question, the higher the share of remittances devoted to investment and therefore the higher the growth rate associated with those remittances. The second reason is that, as noted in *Closing the Gap in Education and Technology*, even if the Latin American picture regarding net primary enrollment rates is quite encouraging, most Latin American countries have massive deficits in net enrollments in secondary education (see figure 10.1). Moreover, most of these educational deficits are also apparent even after controlling for income levels. In fact, for the region, and controlling for per-capita income levels, the secondary enrollment deficit would be estimated at about 19 percent. For tertiary education, the estimated deficit would be lower, but still above 10 percent.

Policy Complementarities and Institutions

A second area that has received significant attention as a potential policy complement in the growth literature is institutional quality. Institutions, understood as the rules and norms constraining human behavior (North

Figure 10.1 Secondary Net Enrollment Deficit in Selected Latin American Countries

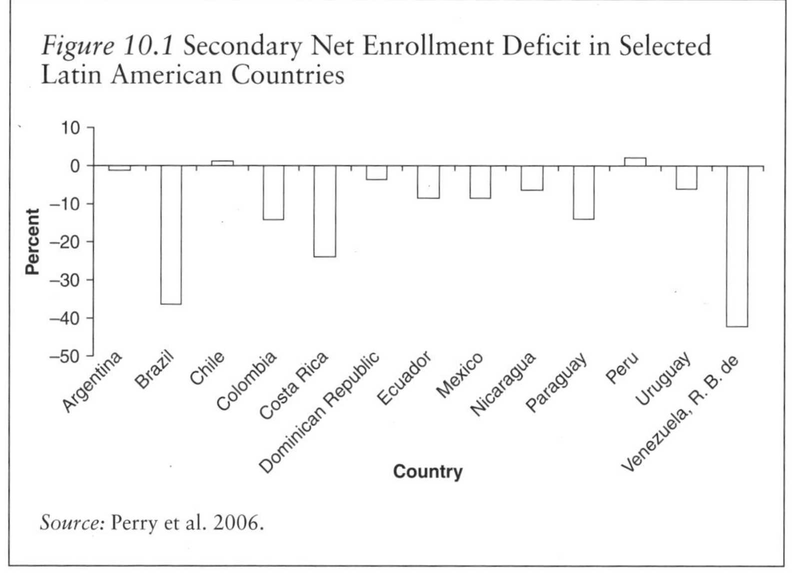

Source: Perry et al. 2006.

Figure 10.2 Institutional and Per Capita Income Levels

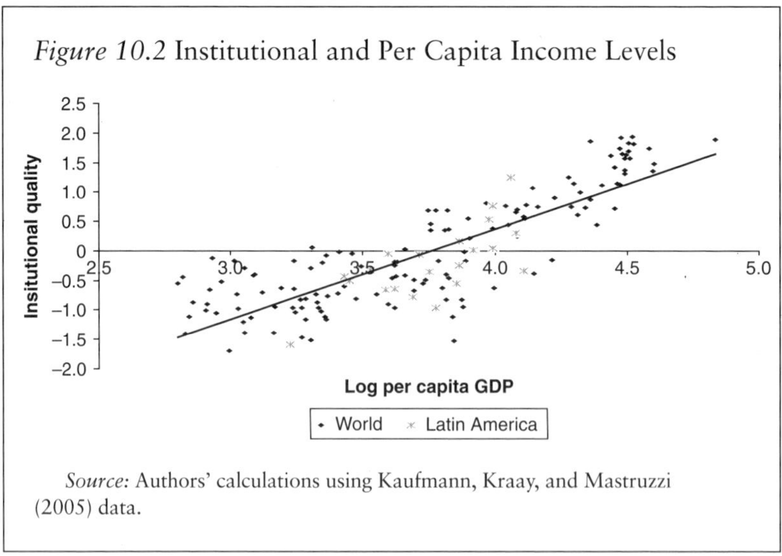

Source: Authors' calculations using Kaufmann, Kraay, and Mastruzzi (2005) data.

1990), establish the rules of the game for a society. The importance of institutions in the process of development has long been understood—going back to the writings of Adam Smith. More recently, however, it has been argued that growth-enhancing policies, including the areas of human capital accumulation and trade openness, are less likely to be effective where political and other institutions are weak. As a result, the adverse effects of weak institutions on economic performance are reinforced by their interaction with other policies.[5] Thus, could it also be the case that because of low institutional quality, recipients of remittances tend to invest less, and therefore remittances have little or no impact on growth?

A second question would be related to the extent to which Latin American countries could made progress on this front. To explore this issue, figure 10.2 plots the average for the six indexes contained in the Kaufmann, Kraay, and Mastruzzi (2005) database of institutional quality against the log per-capita income level of each country. The figure indicates that there is a very close association between per-capita income levels and institutional quality—something that in turn would suggest that a comparison of institutional quality based on absolute indicators may be misleading. Yet it also appears that a large number of the Latin American countries in the sample are below the regression line—an indicator of underperformance on the institutional front and therefore of potential progress.

Policy Complementarities and the Financial Sector

There is now ample evidence form firm-level, industry-level, and cross-country studies that financial development and well-functioning financial systems promote long-run growth. They influence economic efficiency and economic growth through different channels. Financial markets facilitate risk diversification through risk pooling and hedging financial instruments. In this regard, the impact of major economic shocks on the economy, and therefore the risk faced by investors, will be determined in large measure by the role played by domestic financial markets, which together with world financial markets are perhaps the most important absorbers or amplifiers of external shocks.

The financial sector can also be critical for identifying profitable investment projects and mobilizing savings, which in principle could be related to remittances. Thus, even if a remittances recipient does not want to undertake an entrepreneurial activity, but still is willing to save, the financial sector can facilitate the intermediation between that individual and those willing to take investment risks. All things being equal, one could expect that for a given flow of remittances, investment (and therefore growth) would be higher in countries with more developed financial sectors.

However, in this area it is also possible that remittances and financial sector development substitute for each other. In fact, with perfect capital markets, investment decisions in physical or human capital would depend on the expected returns on the investment and on the associated cost. When the returns are higher than the cost of capital, an individual would have the same incentive to invest, regardless of his or her initial income level: poor people could always borrow the capital they need to make the investment and then repay the loan out of the returns on the investment.

However, in real life and especially in less developed countries to which remittances are likely to flow, capital and financial markets are plagued with imperfections. In many economies, large segments of the population may not have access to credit at all. The poor, for instance, may be constrained because of their lack of assets to be used as collateral, which may be required to gain access to credit. This is likely to be a larger issue if the institutional framework is such that financial operators find it difficult to enforce contracts and make individuals' access to credit conditional on their initial wealth (that is, those with low or no initial wealth may be excluded from capital markets). Moreover, even among those with access to credit, there are important differences. Since deposit rates tend to be much lower than borrowing rates, the opportunity cost of capital is lower for those who need to borrow less. This would imply that even if both a rich and a poor person face a similar rate of return on a project, it is likely that the rich will invest much more than the poor. In other words, the opportunities and costs of borrowing can be very different for rich and poor people and play against the latter group.

Imperfect capital markets, coupled with fixed costs, will imply that important segments of the population may get excluded from investing in physical and human capital. For example, Banerjee and Newman (1993) stress the impact that an individual's initial wealth has on the level of physical investment when there are credit constraints. Thus, capital market imperfections coupled with high poverty rates might result in low investment rates and hence in lower growth. A similar point is made by Galor and Zeira (1993), who note that a number of people at the bottom of the distribution may be in a situation where they can neither cover the cost of education nor access the financial sector to borrow for that purpose. As a result, the high poverty rates will result in low educational outcomes because poor individuals will likely opt out of the education sector and work as unskilled, low-return labor.

In this context, increases in remittances flows, particularly if directed toward the poor who are excluded from the financial sector due to market imperfections, would have the effect of making the budget constraints of those individuals less binding and therefore would allow them to undertake investments (both in human and physical capital). Thus, higher remittances would result in higher growth in this case. Yet if one considers the extreme case (and admittedly not very realistic in real life) of an economy without capital market imperfections, it is possible that remittances have no impact on growth because all the profitable investment activities would have already taken place.

Similarly, for given levels of poverty and remittances, increases in financial sector development will lead to faster growth rates. In addition to the direct growth effect of a better developed financial sector, progress on this front would allow more individuals at the bottom of the distribution to participate in the investment and growth processes. Yet going again to an extreme case, if nobody is constrained because the country is awash with remittances, a more developed financial sector will have no impact.

Thus, in principle it is not clear whether remittances will have more or less of an impact on growth in a country with a more or a less developed financial sector. How does Latin America score in this area? The truth is that the region has significant room to improve. Figure 10.3 reports the ratio of domestic credit to the private sector to GDP for the six developing regions of the world. Inspection of this figure indicates that in 2004, Latin America and the Caribbean (LAC) is the region with the lowest ratio: below 26 percent of GDP. This contrasts sharply with what is found for high-income countries where credit to the private sector is around 120 percent of GDP. Note that even Sub-Saharan Africa has a ratio larger than LAC—although it is mostly driven by South Africa, where credit is 141 percent of GDP.

Policy Complementarities and Macroeconomic Distortions

Following the approach in Burnside and Dollar (2000), the final set of policies that we consider as potential complements of remittances in their impact on growth is that associated with macroeconomic policy distortions. As noted above, the larger the distortions, the lower the incentives that recipients of remittances have to invest. As indicators of macroeconomic policies, we compute an index (see figure 10.4) that weights trade openness, inflation, and government consumption as a measure of the government burden on the economy.

Figure 10.3 Domestic Credit to the Private Sector

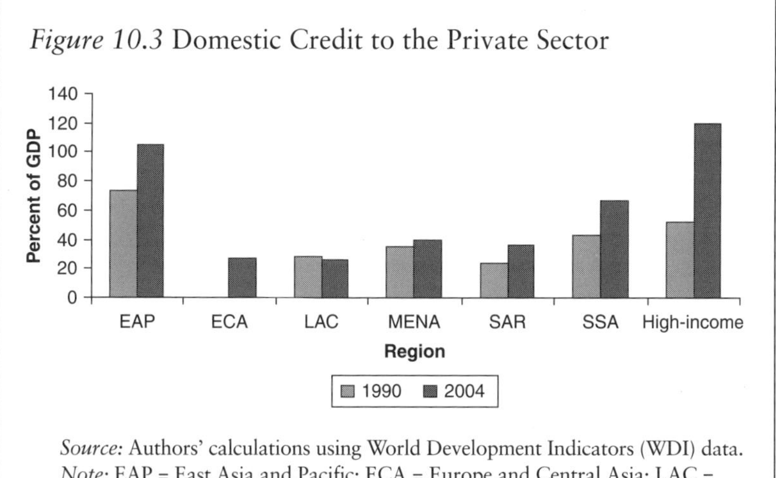

Source: Authors' calculations using World Development Indicators (WDI) data.

Note: EAP = East Asia and Pacific; ECA = Europe and Central Asia; LAC = Latin America and the Caribbean; MENA = the Middle East and North Africa; SAR = South Asia; SSA = Sub-Saharan Africa.

Figure 10.4 Regional Policy Index

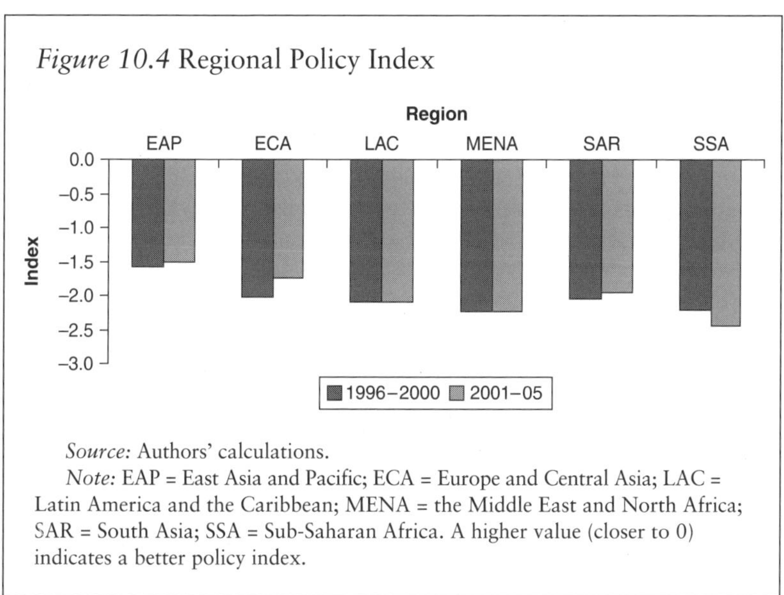

Source: Authors' calculations.

Note: EAP = East Asia and Pacific; ECA = Europe and Central Asia; LAC = Latin America and the Caribbean; MENA = the Middle East and North Africa; SAR = South Asia; SSA = Sub-Saharan Africa. A higher value (closer to 0) indicates a better policy index.

Figure 10.4 plots this policy index by region for the periods 1996–2000 and 2001–05. The index is constructed in such a way that higher values (closer to 0) would imply that the region in question is implementing better policies. This figure indicates once more that Latin America has considerable room to improve in terms of macroeconomic distortions. In fact, in the first half of the present decade, Latin America was, together with the Middle East and Sub-Saharan Africa, the region with the lowest scores. South Asia, East Asia and Pacific, and Europe and Central Asia all present better macroeconomic policy indicators. This should not be a surprise considering LAC's relatively low levels of trade openness, which tend to drive down our macroeconomic policy index.

Empirical Evidence

In order to investigate the questions of interest of this chapter, we rely on variants of the following basic econometric specification:

$$growth_{i,t} = \beta_0'X_{i,t} + \beta_1 R_{i,t} + \beta_2 R_{i,t} \times Complement_{i,t} + \mu_t + \eta_i + \varepsilon_{i,t} \qquad (1)$$

where i and t are a country and time index, respectively; X is a set of control variables (see box 10.2) including lagged income levels; R is the ratio of remittances to GDP; and μ_t and η_i are a time and a country effect, respectively. Finally, $\varepsilon_{i,t}$ is an error term. In equation (1) *growth* is measured in per-capita terms and *Complement* refers generally to each of the four areas under consideration, which may also be included in X. Thus, equation (1) is basically a standard growth equation augmented with remittances, and an interaction of remittances and a policy variable.

In equation (1), our main interest centers on the value of the parameter β_2. Note that with this setup, the marginal impact of a change in remittances on growth is given by $\partial growth / \partial R = \beta_1 + \beta_2 \times Complement$. Thus, when β_2 is positive, this will be an indication that in general the higher the value of the index for the complementary policy in question, the higher the impact of remittances on growth. It is also worth noting that when $\beta_2 \neq 0$, then β_1 can take values smaller than 0, since for remittances to have a positive impact on growth, all that is required is that $\beta_1 + \beta_2 \times Complement > 0$. We next move to explore what the empirical evidence has to say on this issue.

Remittances, Human Capital, and Economic Growth

In our first experiment, we test whether there are complementarities between education and remittances for the growth process. Empirically, we replace *Complement* in equation (1) with our indicators of human capital: enrollment rates in primary and secondary schooling. Table 10.1 presents the estimation results for enrollment rates in each level of education, as well as for three different sets of estimates, depending upon the specific instrument used to control for potential reverse causality from growth to remittances. More specifically, and as done previously in this report, we rely on the *Distance* and *Migration* instruments first introduced by Aggarwal, Demirgüç-Kunt, and Martínez Pería (2005). In all the cases, the models are

Box 10.2 Control Set in the Empirical Model

The set of growth determinants used in the empirical model is selected from Loayza, Fajnzylber, and Calderón (2005). It includes the following variables. *Conditional convergence* is proxied by the initial value of the GDP per capita (in logs). The ratio of total secondary enrollment (regardless of age) to the population of the age group corresponding to that level is the proxy for *human capital.* Our source is Barro and Lee (2001) and World Bank (2005b). *Financial depth* is measured by the stock of claims on the private sector by deposit money banks and other financial institutions, expressed as a ratio to GDP. The data on financial depth was obtained from Beck, Demirgüç-Kunt, and Levine (2000). On the other hand, *trade openness* is the log of the ratio of exports and imports (in 1995 U.S. dollars) to GDP (in 1995 U.S. dollars). *Institutions* are proxied by the International Country Risk Guide (ICRG) index of political risk published by the PRS Group. We also classify the different indexes of institutions according to the following groups as in Bekaert, Campbell, and Lundblad (2006): political institutions (ICRG1 is the sum of the subcomponents military in politics and democratic accountability); quality of institutions (ICRG2 is the sum of corruption, law and order, and bureaucratic quality); socioeconomic environment (ICRG3 is the sum of government stability, socioeconomic conditions, and investment profile); and conflict (ICRG4 comprises internal and external conflict as well as ethnic and religious tensions). In addition to indicators of structural policies and institutions, we include the average annual CPI inflation rate (taken from World Bank [2005b]) as a proxy of lack of price stability, and the real exchange rate overvaluation as a proxy for external imbalances. Finally, the external conditions are captured by terms of trade shocks and period-specific shifts. The first variable is approximated by the log difference of the terms of trade and the data is taken from World Bank (2005b). The second variable is approximated using time-dummy variables, which are not reported in our regression results.

Source: Authors.

estimated using a General Method of Moments–Instrumental Variables (GMM-IV) system estimator. Inspection of this table indicates that in most cases, the coefficient of remittances is negative and significant, whereas that corresponding to the interaction between remittances and education is positive and also significant.[6] This implies that the growth benefits of remittances rise as the level of human capital increases. In other words, education and remittances seem to be complementary factors in the growth process.

The estimates in table 10.1 can also be used to compute the educational threshold for which remittances have no impact on growth. For example, using the estimates corresponding to secondary schooling and the *Distance* instrument, we find this threshold at a low 27 percent (located in the 40th

Table 10.1 Remittances, Education, and Economic Growth

	Primary schooling			*Secondary schooling*		
Variable	*[1] Exogenous remittances*	*[2] Distance instrument*	*[3] Migration instrument*	*[4] Exogenous remittances*	*[5] Distance instrument*	*[6] Migration instrument*
Transitional convergence						
Initial GDP per capita	–0.501**	–0.588**	–0.547**	–0.233**	–0.430**	–0.293**
(in logs)	(0.11)	(0.09)	(0.07)	(0.09)	(0.07)	(0.07)
Macroeconomic policies and institutions						
Education	2.831**	2.032**	2.208**	0.156*	0.329**	0.247*
(in logs)	(0.53)	(0.49)	(0.51)	(0.10)	(0.13)	(0.13)
Financial depth	0.345**	1.072**	0.644**	0.509**	0.779**	0.511**
(private domestic credit to GDP, in logs)	(0.15)	(0.13)	(0.13)	(0.18)	(0.16)	(0.13)
Institutions	3.224**	2.872**	3.195**	3.861**	3.474**	3.627**
(ICRG political risk index, in logs)	(0.31)	(0.27)	(0.25)	0.30)	(0.25)	(0.26)
Trade openness (TO)	0.179	0.022	0.078	0.216*	0.301**	0.453**
(real exports and imports to GDP, in logs)	(0.19)	(0.15)	(0.15)	(0.13)	(0.13)	(0.12)
Lack of price stability	–0.010**	–0.009**	–0.009**	–0.008**	–0.005**	–0.006**
(inflation rate, in log[100 + inf.rate])	(0.00)	(0.00)	(0.00)	(0.00)	(0.00)	(0.00)

(continued)

Table 10.1 Remittances, Education, and Economic Growth *(continued)*

	Primary schooling			*Secondary schooling*		
Variable	*[1] Exogenous remittances*	*[2] Distance instrument*	*[3] Migration instrument*	*[4] Exogenous remittances*	*[5] Distance instrument*	*[6] Migration instrument*
RER overvaluation (proportional index in logs, overvaluation if >0)	–0.014** (0.00)	–0.013** (0.00)	–0.013** (0.00	–0.012** (0.00)	–0.012** (0.00)	–0.011** (0.00)
Government burden (general government consumption in logs)	–0.756** (0.20)	–0.735** (0.19)	–0.807** (0.18)	–0.868** (0.19)	–0.961** (0.20)	–0.925** (0.15)
Workers' remittances						
Remittances (workers remittances to GDP, in logs)	–8.040** (1.69)	–4.164** (1.40)	–4.976** (1.50)	–1.063** (0.39)	–0.536* (0.32)	–0.904** (0.34)
Remittances and development						
Remittances × Education	1.834** (0.38)	0.960** (0.32)	1.139** (0.34)	0.366** (0.12)	0.162* (0.08)	0.277** (0.10)

Source: Authors' calculations.

Note: The table reports the results of regressing per capita growth on the variables in the first column using the GMM system estimator. For all the variables we use internal instruments, except for remittances that can be treated as exogenous or instrumented with the distance or migration instrument of Aggarwal, Demirgüç-Kunt, and Martínez Pería (2005).

* significant at 10%; ** significant at 5%; *** significant at 1%.

percentile of the distribution of secondary enrollment in our developing country sample). Beyond this critical level, remittances-recipient countries would start reaping growth benefits. In fact, the marginal growth impact of remittances for the median countries in the distribution of secondary enrollment rates is 0.04, with a one standard deviation increase in remittances generating an increase in the growth rate of 7 basis points. In contrast, countries with enrollment rates in the 75th percentile of the distribution have a marginal impact of remittances on growth of 0.19 percent per year.

Panel A of figure 10.5 plots the growth response of higher remittances as a function of the level of secondary schooling across all developing

Figure 10.5 Growth and Education: Impact of a One Standard Deviation Increase in Remittances

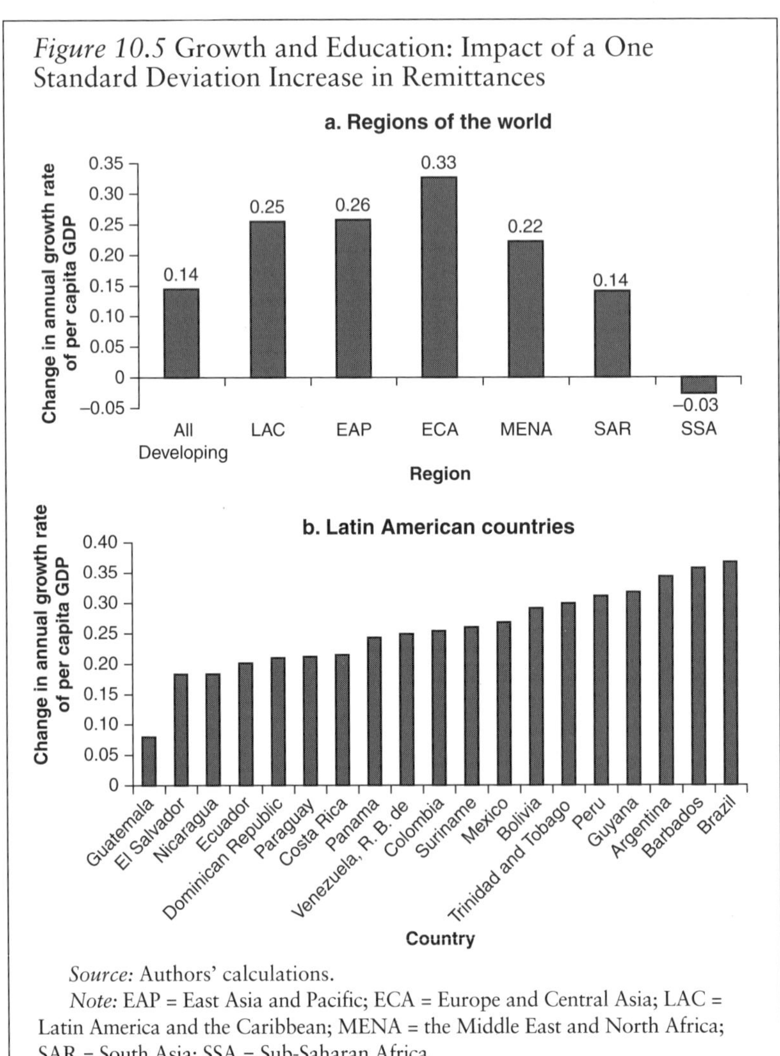

Source: Authors' calculations.

Note: EAP = East Asia and Pacific; ECA = Europe and Central Asia; LAC = Latin America and the Caribbean; MENA = the Middle East and North Africa; SAR = South Asia; SSA = Sub-Saharan Africa.

regions and across individual regions. It shows that, ceteris paribus, regions with higher rates of enrollment in secondary education display the largest potential growth benefits associated with surges in remittances. A one standard deviation increase in the ratio of remittances to GDP would raise the growth rate of Europe and Central Asia by 0.33 percent per year, while, on average, annual growth in East Asia and Pacific and Latin America would be higher by 0.26 percent and 0.25 percent per year, respectively. In panel B of figure 10.5, we repeat the same exercise, but now focusing on Latin American countries. This panel indicates that there is substantial variation in the growth benefits of remittances across countries, a reflection of the significant differences in human capital within the region. For instance, 9 of 19 countries with data on secondary enrollment for 2000 have a growth response to higher remittances below the average response for Latin America. Guatemala is the country with the smallest potential response—an increase in the growth rate of 0.08 percent per year. On the other hand, Brazil and Argentina have the largest potential growth benefits due to higher remittances (between 0.34 percent and 0.37 percent per year), with growth effects slightly larger than the average observed in Europe and Central Asia.

A complementary interpretation of the above results is that the impact of progress on the educational front is amplified when remittances are higher. Thus, the growth effect of increases in secondary enrollment rates in countries that start from low levels would be even larger if remittances flows are considerable. To get an idea, assume that Guatemala, El Salvador, and Nicaragua (which had the lowest levels of secondary enrollment in 2000) reform their educational systems and raise their enrollment rates to the median level in the region (equal to Colombia, with 70 percent enrollment rate in secondary schooling in 2000). The growth benefits of this change, in excess of those attributed to their high remittances (that is, the extra bonus), would range between 0.07 percent per year (El Salvador and Nicaragua) and 0.17 percent (Guatemala).

Remittances, Institutions, and Economic Growth

In our second experiment, we explore the potential complementarity between remittances and institutions, and to this end we rely on the International Country Risk Guide index of political risk published by the Political Risk Service Group to proxy for our *Complement* variable in equation (1). In this subsection we also look at two of the components of this overall index of institutions in order to test the forces behind the impact of institutions and remittances on growth. Specifically, we use the indexes of political institutions and the socioeconomic environment. The former sub-index captures the responsiveness of the government to its people. The latter sub-index, on the other hand, comprises information on the government's ability to carry out its programs and stay in office, the socioeconomic pressures at work in society that could restrain government actions, and factors affecting risk to investment (such as contract expropriation, profits repatriation, and payment delays).

Table 10.2 reports the estimates for this specification for each of the indexes under analysis using once again the *Distance* and *Migration* variables to instrument for remittances.[7] The first three columns of table 10.2 correspond to the *Distance* instrument, whereas the latter three columns use the *Migration* instrument. Inspection of this table indicates that the two groups of estimations show analogous results. The estimates in the table also indicate that the parameter of remittances enters the specification with a negative (and statistically significant) sign. Similarly, the parameter corresponding to the interaction term is always positive and significant, suggesting that the marginal impact of remittances is higher for countries with higher levels of institutional quality.

Figure 10.6 shows the effects of a surge of remittances by region, taking into account their average institutional levels. In each case, we assume a positive shock equivalent to one standard deviation to remittances. The simulations indicate that in Latin America, an increase in remittances would lead to a higher growth rate of 0.5 percent per year, surpassed by Europe and Central Asia (about 0.63 percent) and only slightly by the Middle East and North Africa (0.52 percent). The poor institutional records of Sub-Saharan Africa and South Asia would be reflected in their lower potential growth benefits across regions—0.36 percent and 0.25 percent, respectively.

Across Latin American countries, the growth response to higher remittances also varies significantly. Countries with poorer institutions, such as República Bolivariana de Venezuela, only observe their growth rates increase by approximately 0.2 percent per year following an increase in remittances. On the other hand, countries with better institutions, like Costa Rica, would experience surges in growth rates higher than 0.7 percent per year. Our findings here indicate that if countries improve their overall institutional framework, remittances can be further allocated into productive activities and, hence, foster growth. For instance, if Latin American countries were to improve their institutional frameworks to the levels displayed by the regional leaders, growth gains would range from 0.1 percentage points (Panama) to more than 0.5 percentage points per year (República Bolivariana de Venezuela).

Remittances, Financial Depth, and Economic Growth

As discussed above, from a theoretical point of view it is not clear whether remittances and financial sector development should complement or substitute for each other. To empirically explore this issue, table 10.3 reports the results of a growth regression that includes an interaction term between workers' remittances and measures of financial development, such as domestic credit to the private sector and liquid liabilities, and money as a percentage of GDP. The first three columns of this table present the results for

Table 10.2 Remittances, Institutions, and Economic Growth

	Using the "distance" instrument for remittances			*Using the "migration" instrument for remittances*		
Variable	*[1] ICRG political risk index*	*[2] Political institutions*	*[3] Socioeconomic environment*	*[4] ICRG political risk index*	*[8] Political institutions*	*[9] Socioeconomic environment*
Transitional convergence						
Initial GDP per capita	–0.274**	–0.511**	–0.371**	–0.176*	–0.416**	–0.219*
(in logs)	(0.09)	(0.13)	(0.09)	(0.11)	(0.14)	(0.11)
Macroeconomic policies and institutions						
Education	0.426*	1.106**	0.346**	0.119	0.869**	0.291*
(in logs)	(0.24)	(0.30)	(0.17)	(0.28)	(0.28)	(0.16)
Financial depth	0.254*	0.359	0.565**	0.386**	0.368	0.218
(private domestic credit to GDP, in logs)	(0.13)	(0.28)	(0.16)	(0.19)	(0.26)	(0.15)
Institutions	4.304**	1.241**	4.778**	4.385**	1.254**	4.851**
(ICRG political risk index, in logs)	(0.36)	(0.24)	(0.29)	(0.35)	(0.20)	(0.27)

(continued)

Table 10.2 Remittances, Institutions, and Economic Growth *(continued)*

	Using the "distance" instrument for remittances			*Using the "migration" instrument for remittances*		
Variable	*[1]* ICRG *political risk index*	*[2]* Political *institutions*	*[3]* Socieconomic *environment*	*[4]* ICRG *political risk index*	*[8]* Political *institutions*	*[9]* Socieconomic *environment*
Trade openness (TO) (real exports and imports to GDP, in logs)	0.524** (0.15)	0.386** (0.19)	0.388** (0.16)	0.478** (0.17)	0.394** (0.20)	0.423** (0.19)
Lack of price stability (inflation rate, in log[100+inf.rate])	–0.007** (0.00)	–0.004* (0.00)	–0.003* (0.00)	–0.008** (0.00)	–0.004* (0.00)	–0.003* (0.00)
RER overvaluation (proportional index in logs, overvaluation if >0)	–0.012** (0.00)	–0.009** (0.00)	–0.010** (0.00)	–0.012** (0.00)	–0.009** (0.00)	–0.012** (0.00)
Government burden (general government consumption in logs)	–1.121** (0.17)	–0.768** (0.26)	–0.929** (0.21)	–1.140** (0.18)	–0.793** (0.24)	–1.019** (0.20)

(continued)

Table 10.2 Remittances, Institutions, and Economic Growth *(continued)*

Variable	*Using the "distance" instrument for remittances*			*Using the "migration" instrument for remittances*		
	[1] ICRG political risk index	*[2] Political institutions*	*[3] Socieconomic environment*	*[4] ICRG political risk index*	*[8] Political institutions*	*[9] Socieconomic environment*
Workers' remittances						
Remittances (workers remittances to GDP, in logos)	–2.877** (1.22)	–0.840* (0.50)	–1.729* (0.99)	–2.948** (1.99)	–0.822* (0.46)	–2.572** (1.01)
Remittances and Institutions						
Remittances × Institutions	0.760** (0.30)	0.557** (0.28)	0.563* (0.34)	0.774* 0.29	0.557** 0.26)	0.890** (0.35)

Source: Authors' calculations.

Note: The table reports the results of regressing per capita growth on the variables in the first column using the GMM system estimator. For all the variables we use internal instruments, except for remittances that are instrumented with the distance or migration instruments of Aggarwal, Demirgüç-Kunt, and Martínez Pería (2005).

* significant at 10%; ** significant at 5%; *** significant at 1%.

Figure 10.6 Growth and Institutions: Impact of a One Standard Deviation Increase in Remittances

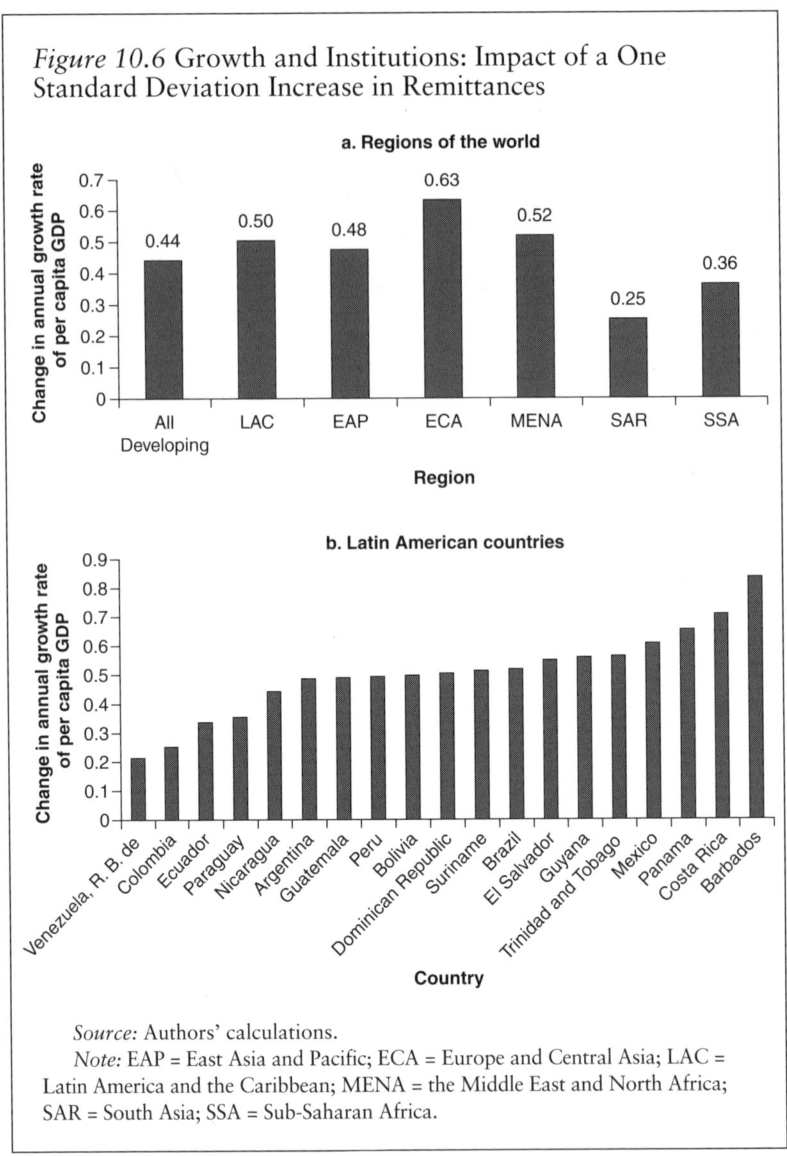

Source: Authors' calculations.

Note: EAP = East Asia and Pacific; ECA = Europe and Central Asia; LAC = Latin America and the Caribbean; MENA = the Middle East and North Africa; SAR = South Asia; SSA = Sub-Saharan Africa.

private credit. As in previous tables, each column corresponds to a different instrument set for our remittances variables. The results indicate that remittances promote growth, but that the effect declines as the financial system becomes deeper—that is $\beta_1 > 0$ and $\beta_2 < 0$. This finding is robust to the use of private credit or liquid liabilities as measures of financial development.

For instance, for Argentina the growth benefits of an increase in remittances[8] is 0.46 percentage points; for Peru it would be 0.39 percentage

Table 10.3 Remittances, the Financial Sector, and Economic Growth

Variable	Private credit			Liquid liabilities		
	[1] Exogenous remittances	[2] Distance instrument	[3] Migration instrument	[4] Exogenous remittances	[5] Distance instrument	[6] Migration instrument
Transitional convergence						
Initial GDP per capita	–0.453**	–0.420**	–0.301**	–0.497**	–0.401**	–0.296**
(in logs)	(0.13)	(0.12)	(0.11)	(0.16)	(0.14)	(0.12)
Macroeconomic policies and institutions						
Education	0.968**	1.025**	0.738**	1.026**	0.830**	0.651**
(in logs)	(0.25)	(0.24)	(0.20)	(0.26)	(0.21)	(0.21)
Financial depth	0.207	0.024	0.098	0.366**	0.275**	0.101
(private domestic credit to GDP, in logs)	(0.18)	(0.18)	(0.17)	(0.14)	(0.13)	(0.12)
Institutions	4.167**	4.368**	4.245**	3.552**	3.741**	3.997**
(ICRG political risk index, in logs)	(0.31)	(0.31)	(0.31)	(0.26)	(0.26)	(0.24)
Trade openness (TO)	0.304**	0.400**	0.379**	0.373**		
(real exports and imports to GDP, in logs)	(0.12)	(0.12)	(0.12)	(0.17)	0.472**	0.543**
Lack of price stability	–0.010**	–0.008**	–0.009**	–0.011**	–0.010**	–0.009**
(inflation rate, in log[100+inf.rate])	(0.00)	(0.00)	(0.00)	(0.00)	(0.00)	(0.00)
RER overvaluation	–0.011**	–0.011**	–0.012**	–0.011**	–0.012**	–0.013**
(proportional index in logs, overvaluation if >0)	(0.00)	(0.00)	(0.00)	(0.00)	(0.00)	(0.00)

(continued)

Table 10.3 Remittances, the Financial Sector, and Economic Growth *(continued)*

	Private credit			*Liquid liabilities*		
Variable	*[1] Exogenous remittances*	*[2] Distance instrument*	*[3] Migration instrument*	*[4] Exogenous remittances*	*[5] Distance instrument*	*[6] Migration instrument*
Government burden (general government consumption in logs)	–0.874** (0.16)	–0.857** (0.16)	–0.904** (0.16)	–0.964** (0.14)	–0.958** (0.15)	–0.893** (0.14)
Workers' remittances						
Remittances (workers remittances to GDP, in logs)	0.408** (0.14)	0.538** (0.15)	0.469** (0.15)	1.355** (0.16)	1.327** (0.16)	1.305** (0.15)
Remittances and financial development						
Remittances × Financial variable	–0.077* (0.04)	–0.100** (0.04)	–0.074* (0.04)	–0.351** (0.05)	–0.331** (0.04)	–0.314** (0.04)

Source: Author's calculations.

Note: The table reports the results of regressing per capita growth on the variables in the first column using the GMM system estimator. For all the variables we use internal instruments, except for remittances that are treated as exogenous, or instrumented with the distance or migration instrument of Aggarwal, Demirgüç-Kunt, and Martínez Pería (2005). Two financial variables are interacted with remittances in the regression: private credit, and liquid liabilities.

* significant at 10%; ** significant at 5%; *** significant at 1%.

points and for Brazil it would be 0.31 percentage points. These three countries roughly correspond to the 25th, 50th, and 75th percentiles of the distribution of our financial development proxy. It is worth noting, however, that our estimates in table 10.3 suggest that the impact of remittances on growth is always positive (the marginal impact of remittances on growth would turn negative for levels of financial development that are above the maximum value of that variable in our sample).

Which reasons can be behind these results? Although it is difficult to say from a single regression like this, one can hypothesize that the substitutability between remittances and financial depth is likely to reveal problems of access to credit by poorer households (especially those located in rural areas and devoted to agricultural activities), which may use remittances to finance high-return projects in their portfolio (for example, human capital accumulation). In other words, remittances would make the budget constraint faced by the poor less binding, and this would be more important in countries with less developed financial sectors where the poor will have even less access to credit. In fact, these results are in line with the findings of Giuliano and Ruiz-Arranz (2005), where remittances-driven growth is higher in countries with less developed financial systems.

Clearly, this should not be interpreted as an indication that countries should move toward shallower financial sectors. As is clear from table 10.3 (and more generally from the growth literature), a well-developed financial sector is a critical element in any growth strategy. If anything, this result would indicate that countries experiencing a decline in remittances can partially make up for it by further developing the financial sector.

Remittances, Macroeconomic Policy Environment, and Growth

We have already discussed above the arguments put forward by Burnside and Dollar (2000, 2004) that the effectiveness of international aid on raising the growth rate of the economy may depend on a sound economic policy environment that does not generate macroeconomic uncertainty. A similar argument is also made by Faini (2002a) for remittances.

To further explore this possibility, we follow Burnside and Dollar (2000) and use the coefficient estimates of the baseline growth regression reported in the first column of table 4.8 in chapter 4 of this book to construct a policy environment index that comprises trade openness, inflation, and government burden:

$$Pol = +0.329 * \textit{Trade Openness} - 0.0073 * \textit{Inflation} - 0.862 * \textit{Government Burden}.$$

In this setup higher (lower) values of *Pol* indicate a good (bad) policy environment, characterized by less (more) policy distortions, and to the extent that a good policy environment is a complement of remittances, we would expect a positive and significant coefficient for the parameter of the interaction term. Clearly in this index, trade openness is associated with a good policy environment, whereas inflation and government burden with a bad one.

Table 10.4 reports the results of the regression analysis where we replace the indicators of trade openness, inflation, and government burden with our policy environment index. The first three columns present the base results including the *Pol* indicator, whereas in the fourth to sixth columns we include its interaction with remittances as an additional explanatory variable. Inspection of this table indicates that the coefficient estimates for the growth determinants have the expected sign: (i) there is conditional convergence; (ii) growth is fostered by higher education, deeper financial markets, better institutions, and a sound economic policy environment; and (iii) growth is hindered by higher levels of real exchange rate overvaluation.

As seen in table 10.4, the parameter of remittances continues to be positive and significant with this specification. Our point estimates indicate that a 1 percent increase in remittances would lead to an increase in per-capita growth of about 0.2 percent. Moreover, when the interaction term is included in the regression, not only do we find that remittances still exert a positive impact on growth, but also that remittances are more effective in enhancing growth prospects in countries with better economic policies (as captured by our policy index). Our estimates suggest that a one standard deviation increase in workers' remittances will raise the rate of growth in the recipient country by 0.32 percentage points for countries in the 25th percentile of the distribution of policy environment. Growth benefits are only slightly larger for countries in the median and 75th percentile (0.35 percentage points and 0.38 percentage points per year, respectively).

Figure 10.7 reports the growth response to higher remittances conditional on the economic policy environment of the recipient country and region. We observe that, on average, the growth response in Latin America—an increase in the growth rate by 0.36 percent—is in line with the average response of the developing countries, as well as the Middle East and North Africa region. According to figure 10.7, the region that would benefit the most from a surge in remittances given its policy environment would be East Asia and Pacific, where an increase of one standard deviation in remittances would be associated with a growth acceleration of 0.42 percent. This finding conforms to the discussion in the second section, where we argued that the East Asia and Pacific region has the best policy indexes. Within the Latin American region, growth benefits would be higher for those countries with better economic policy environments—for example, Mexico or El Salvador (panel B of figure 10.7).

Table 10.4 Remittances, the Policy Environment, and Economic Growth

	Baseline regression			*Interacting remittances and policy environment*		
Variable	*[1] Exogenous remittances*	*[2] Distance instrument*	*[3] Migration instrument*	*[4] Exogenous remittances*	*[5] Distance instrument*	*[6] Migration instrument*
Transitional convergence						
Initial GDP per capita	–0.177*	–0.161*	–0.154*	–0.114*	–0.153**	–0.158*
(in logs)	(0.10)	(0.09)	(0.10)	(0.06)	(0.05)	(0.08)
Macroeconomic policies and institutions						
Education	0.349**	0.343**	0.341**	0.235**	0.277**	0.314**
(secondary enrollment, in logs)	(0.10)	(0.10)	(0.10)	(0.07)	(0.07)	(0.08)
Financial depth	0.364**	0.279*	0.287*	0.365**	0.278**	0.390**
(private domestic credit to GDP, in logs)	(0.16)	(0.17)	(0.17)	(0.13)	(0.09)	(0.11)
Institutions	4.057**	4.204**	4.094**	4.066**	4.279**	3.974**
(ICRG political risk index, in logs)	(0.35)	(0.36)	(0.36)	(0.46)	(0.20)	(0.29)
Policy index	0.998**	1.027**	1.008**	1.870**	1.646**	1.731**
(openness, inflation, government burden)	(0.16)	(0.18)	(0.18)	(0.19)	(0.16)	(0.24)
RER overvaluation	–0.019**	–0.019**	–0.019**	–0.015**	–0.018**	–0.018**
(proportional index in logs, overvaluation if >0)	(0.00)	(0.00)	(0.00)	(0.00)	(0.00)	(0.00)

(continued)

Table 10.4 Remittances, the Policy Environment, and Economic Growth *(continued)*

	Baseline regression			*Interacting remittances and policy environment*		
Variable	*[1] Exogenous remittances*	*[2] Distance instrument*	*[3] Migration instrument*	*[4] Exogenous remittances*	*[5] Distance instrument*	*[6] Migration instrument*
Workers' remittances						
Remittances (workers remittances to GDP, in logs)	0.213** (0.04)	0.245** (0.04)	0.243** (0.04)	0.460** (0.16)	0.339** (0.06)	0.388** (0.12)
Remittances and policy environment						
Remittances × Policy Index	...	...	...	0.144** (0.06)	0.058** (0.03)	0.092* (0.05)

Source: Author's calculations.

Note: The table reports the results of regressing per capita growth on the variables in the first column using the GMM system estimator. For all the variables we use internal instruments, except for remittances that are treated as exogenous, or instrumented with the distance or migration instrument of Aggarwal, Demirgüç-Kunt, and Martínez Pería (2005).

* significant at 10%; ** significant at 5%; *** significant at 1%.

Figure 10.7 Growth and the Policy Environment: Growth Impact of a One Standard Deviation Increase in Remittances

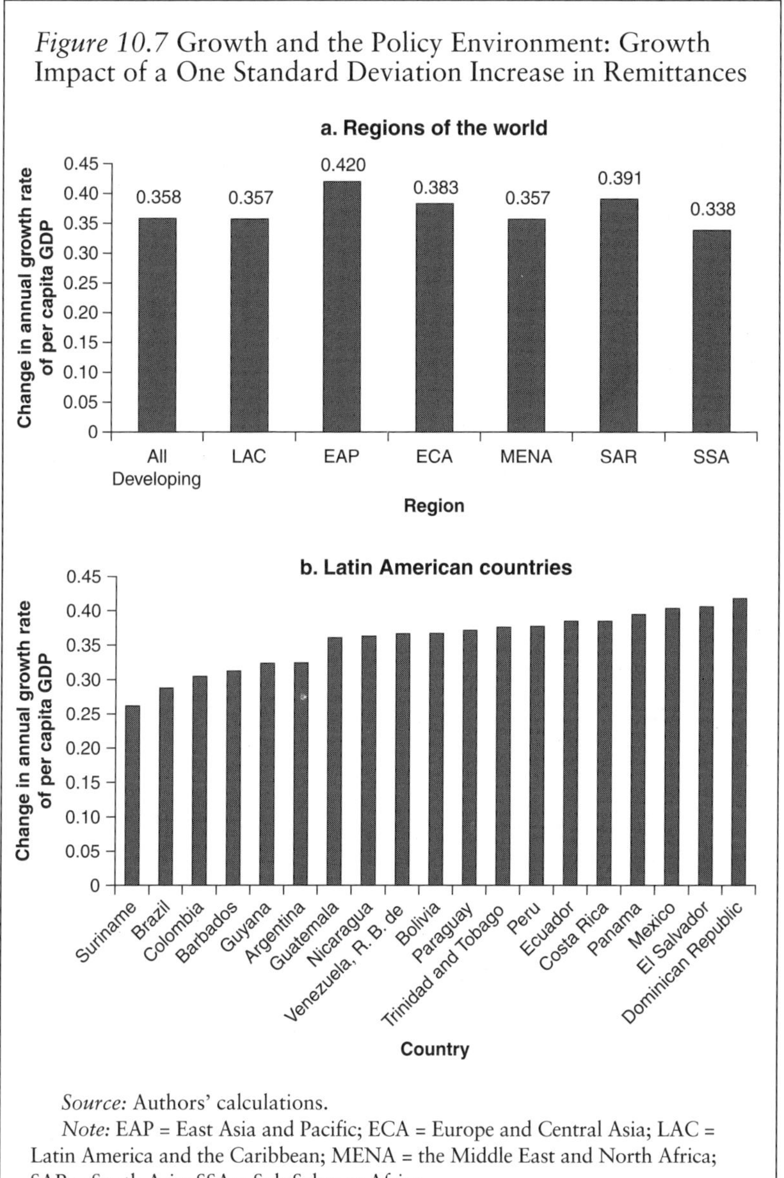

Source: Authors' calculations.

Note: EAP = East Asia and Pacific; ECA = Europe and Central Asia; LAC = Latin America and the Caribbean; MENA = the Middle East and North Africa; SAR = South Asia; SSA = Sub-Saharan Africa.

Remittances and Domestic Investment

The argument used in this chapter to justify the complementarity in the growth process between remittances and other policy interventions relies on the idea that when some conditions are present in home countries, those at the receiving end of remittances flows will have more incentives to invest the corresponding funds. It is thus natural to test whether the complementarities between remittances and other policies also extend to the determinants of domestic investment.[9] In order to investigate this possibility, we now proceed to estimate an empirical model that relates the investment rate to a set of controls, remittances, and an interaction between remittances and the variables used in the previous section to capture progress in the four different policy areas under analysis. That is, our model now is

$$\begin{aligned} \textit{Investment rate}_{i,t} = {} & \beta_0'Z_{i,t} + \beta_1 R_{i,t} + \beta_2 R_{i,t} \times \textit{Complement}_{i,t} \\ & + \mu_t + \eta_i + \varepsilon_{i,t} \end{aligned} \tag{2}$$

where Z is a set of control variables (see box 10.3), including the lagged investment rate, and the rest of the notation is as in equation (1).

Table 10.5 reports the results of this new exercise. Each column in the table corresponds to one of the areas identified above as a potential complement to

Box 10.3 Control Set in the Empirical Model for the Investment Rate

The empirical equation for the investment rate is based on the simple accelerator model relating the investment rate to per capita GDP growth and the cost of capital, which we proxy with the price of investment goods from the Penn World Table Version 6.1 (PWT6.1). This basic model is augmented with a number of variables aimed at capturing elements related to the investment climate. More specifically we also include among the explanatory variables, as a proxy for human capital, the ratio of total secondary enrollment (regardless of age) to the population of the age group corresponding to that level. Financial depth is measured by the stock of claims on the private sector by deposit money banks and other financial institutions, expressed as a ratio to GDP. The empirical model also includes the ICRG index of political risk to capture country institutional aspects, and the average annual CPI inflation rate as a proxy for the macroeconomic environment. Finally, the model also takes into account potential dynamics in the investment rate by including the lagged dependent variable in the control set.

Source: Authors.

Table 10.5 Remittances, Complementary Policies, and Investment

	Complement			
Variable	*Education*	*Institutions*	*Financial sector*	*Policy environment*
Persistence				
Lagged investment ratio	0.503**	0.648**	0.549**	0.589**
(in logs)	(0.02)	(0.03)	(0.02)	(0.02)
Growth				
Economic growth	0.041**	0.042**	0.033**	0.039**
(in percentages)	(0.00)	(0.00)	(0.00)	(0.00)
Macroeconomic policies and institutions				
Education	0.101**	0.056**	–0.005	0.027*
(secondary enrollment, in logs)	(0.03)	(0.02)	(0.01)	(0.02)
Financial depth	0.061**	–0.080**	0.062**	–0.031**
(in logs)	(0.02)	(0.02)	(0.01)	(0.01)
Institutions	–0.099	0.131**	0.260**	0.161**
(ICRG political risk index, in logs)	(0.07)	(0.06)	(0.08)	(0.05)
Price of investment	0.026	–0.041	–0.040*	–0.093**
(in logs)	(0.02)	(0.03)	(0.02)	(0.03)
Lack of price stability	–1.06E-03**	–1.23E-03**	–4.64E-04**	–1.37E-03**
(inflation rate, in log[100+inf.rate])	(0.00)	(0.00)	(0.00)	(0.00)

(continued)

Table 10.5 Remittances, Complementary Policies, and Investment *(continued)*

	Complement			
Variable	*Education*	*Institutions*	*Financial sector*	*Policy environment*
Workers' remittances				
Remittances (workers remittances to GDP, in logs)	–0.144** (0.07)	–0.491** (0.18)	0.076** (0.02)	0.067** (0.03)
Remittances and complementary policies				
Remittances × Complements	0.039** (0.02)	0.124** (0.04)	–0.023** (0.01)	0.030** (0.01)

Source: Author's calculations.

Note: The table reports the results of regressing the investment rate on the variables in the first column using the GMM system estimator. For all the variables we use internal instruments, except for remittances that are instrumented with the distance instrument of Aggarwal, Demirgüç-Kunt, and Martínez Pería (2005). The heading at the top of each column reports the variable used as complementary policy.

* significant at 10%; ** significant at 5%; *** significant at 1%.

remittances (education, institutions, financial sector development, and policy environment) and the reported results as based on the GMM-IV system estimator using the *Distance* instrument.[10] To a large extent, the results echo those found in the previous section for the determinants of growth.

First, remittances and human capital appear to be complementary factors in the process of physical capital accumulation. For instance, the investment effects of remittances are higher as the enrollment rate in schooling increases. Similarly, the marginal impact of remittances on investment is larger for countries with higher levels of institutional quality, and better policy environments as captured by our policy index.

On the contrary, and consistent with the findings in the third section, we also find that remittances and the development of the domestic financial market appear to be substitutes in the capital accumulation process. In fact, according to the estimates in table 10.5, the impact of remittances is positive and decreasing as domestic financial markets become deeper. The marginal impact of remittances on investment becomes negative and (in most cases) not statistically significant for higher levels of financial development (beyond the 85th and 90th percentiles). Thus, the largest increases in domestic investment driven by remittances take place in less financially developed countries. For instance, for countries with levels of private credit to the domestic sector (as a percentage of GDP) in the 25th percentile of the distribution (2.65 in logs), a one standard deviation increase in remittances would raise the investment coefficient by almost 1 percentage point of GDP—from an average of 20.3 percent to 21.3 percent of GDP. In turn, this higher investment would be transformed into an increase in the growth rate of the economy of 0.3 percentage points per year. On the other hand, for those countries with an average level of financial development, the marginal impact of remittances on investment is 0.015. In this case, an increase in the ratio of remittances to GDP would lead to higher investments of approximately 0.5 percentage points of GDP, and this would be transformed, in turn, to a growth increase of 0.17 percent per year.

Concluding Remarks

In chapter 4 of this book we argued that remittances are likely to have a positive effect on growth and poverty reduction. This chapter has extended the analysis and has explored the extent to which policy makers can enhance the development impact of remittances by implementing a number of policies that, in addition to being pro growth per se, can also result in an extra bonus in the presence of significant remittances flows.

The results discussed above suggest that the incentives to invest remittances in productive activities may be sensitive to some structural features and economic policies in the remittances-recipient country. More specifically, it has been found that remittances are more effective in raising investment and enhancing growth in countries with higher levels of human capital, strong institutions, and good policy environments.

It then follows that in order to maximize the development impact of remittances, countries need to (i) maintain sound macroeconomic policies, (ii) promote human capital development, and (iii) strengthen the institutional framework. The chapter has also explored whether a more developed financial sector may also complement remittances, but our results are more suggestive of substitution than of complementary effects.

Notes

1. Defenders of studies on remittances tend to argue that gaining knowledge about some related stylized facts can be extremely useful. For example, having a good idea of the impact of remittances on the real exchange rate can be of great value for those in charge of managing the exchange rate or the monetary policy of a country facing a surge in remittances inflows (chapter 7). Similarly, being able to understand the links between migration patterns and remittances flows (chapter 3) can also be useful in the preparation of medium-term macroeconomic frameworks.

2. We want to clarify that in principle it can be argued that for individuals with income or consumption levels below the poverty level, increasing consumption may be the optimal response to an increase in remittances flows.

3. All Mozambican mine workers to South Africa are forced to repatriate 60 percent of income for six months of the year, while Lesotho mine workers are forced to repatriate 30 percent for 10 months. Thereafter, they are assumed to only remit 15 percent of income per month.

4. Note that this does not imply that we treat remittances as an exogenous variable in our empirical models relating growth to remittances, but instead that policy makers treat them as given.

5. For example, *Economic Growth in the 1990s, Learning from a Decade of Reform* (World Bank 2005a), argues that the effectiveness of financial liberalization on growth depends to a large extent on the underlying institutions: intermediaries, markets, and the informational, regulatory, legal, and judicial frameworks. This same point is made by Calderón and Fuentes (2005), who explore whether the empirical evidence is supportive of this view, finding that in effect institutional quality seems to play a significant role in understanding the impact of both financial sector liberalization and openness to trade on growth.

6. To save space and lower the technicality of the discussion, we do not discuss the results of the specification tests (Sargan test of overidentification and test for second order serial correlation). Yet, it is worth noting that the tests do not reveal any particular problem with the specification of the model.

7. Although the results are not reported, we should note that when treating remittances as exogenous, the results were qualitatively similar.

8. As in previous exercises, we assume that remittances increase by one standard deviation.

9. Note in any case that failure to support this hypothesis would invalidate the results of the previous section.

10. A full set of results can be found in Calderón, Fajnzylber, and López (2006).

References

Aggarwal, R., A. Demirgüç-Kunt, and M.S. Martínez Pería. 2005. "Do Workers' Remittances Promote Financial Development?" Unpublished, World Bank, Washington, DC.

Banerjee, A.V., and A.F. Newman. 1993. "Occupational Choice and the Process of Development." *Journal of Political Economy* 101: 274–98.

Barro, R.J., and J.W. Lee. 2001. "International Data on Educational Attainment: Updates and Implications." *Oxford Economic Papers* 53 (3): 541–63.

Beck T., A. Demirgüç-Kunt, and R. Levine. 2000. "A New Database on Financial Development and Structure." *World Bank Economic Review* 14 (3): 597–605.

Bekaert, G., H. Campbell, and C. Lundblad. 2006. "Growth Volatility and Financial Liberalization." *Journal of International Money and Finance* 25 (3): 370–403.

Borensztein, E., J. De Gregorio, and J.-W. Lee. 1998. "How Does Foreign Direct Investment Affect Economic Growth?" *Journal of International Economics* 45 (1): 115–35.

Burnside, C.A., and D. Dollar. 2000. "Aid, Policies, and Growth." *American Economic Review* 90 (4): 847–68.

———. 2004. "Aid, Policies, and Growth: Revisiting the Evidence." Policy Research Working Paper No. 3251, World Bank, Washington, DC.

Calderón, C., and R. Fuentes. 2005. "¿Cuánto explican las reformas y la calidad de las instituciones el crecimiento chileno?" Central Bank of Chile Working Paper 314, Central Bank, Santiago, Chile.

Calderón C., P. Fajnzylber, and H. López. 2006. "Remittances, Growth, and Policy Complementarities." Unpublished, World Bank, Washington, DC.

De Ferranti, D., G. Perry, I. Gill, J.L. Guasch, N. Schady, W. Maloney, and C. Sánchez Páramo. 1992. *Closing the Gap in Education and Technology*. Washington, DC: World Bank.

Faini, R. 2002a. "Development, Trade, and Migration." *Revue d'Économie et du Développement*, Proceedings from the ABCDE Europe Conference, 1–2: 85–116.

———. 2002b. "Migration, Remittances and Growth." Manuscript, University of Brescia, Brescia, Italy.

Gallego, F., and N. Loayza. 2002. "The Golden Period for Growth in Chile: Explanations and Forecasts." In *Economic Growth: Sources, Trends, and Cycles*, ed. Norman Loayza and Raimundo Soto. Santiago, Chile: Central Bank of Chile.

Galor, O., and J. Zeira. 1993. "Income Distribution and Macroeconomics." *Review of Economic Studies* 60: 35–52.

Giuliano, P., and M. Ruiz-Arranz. 2005. "Remittances, Financial Development and Growth." Working Paper 05/234, International Monetary Fund, Washington, DC.

Kaufmann, D., A. Kraay, and M. Mastruzzi. 2005. "Governance Matters IV: Governance Indicators for 1996–2004." Policy Research Working Paper No. 3630, World Bank, Washington, DC.

Levin, A., and L.K. Raut. 1997. "Complementarities between Exports and Human Capital in Economic Growth: Evidence from the Semi-industrialised Countries." *Economic Development and Cultural Change* 46 (1): 155–74.

Loayza, N., P. Fajnzylber, and C. Calderón. 2005. *Economic Growth in Latin America and the Caribbean: Stylized Facts, Explanations and Forecasts*. Washington, DC: World Bank.

Maimbo, S., and D. Ratha. 2005. *Remittances: Development Impact and Future Prospects*. Washington, DC: World Bank.

North, D. 1990. *Institutions, Institutional Change, and Economic Performance*. Cambridge, UK: Cambridge University Press.

Perry, G., O. Arias, H. López, W. Maloney, and L. Servén. 2006. *Poverty Reduction and Growth: Virtuous and Vicious Circles*. Washington, DC: World Bank.

World Bank. 2005a. *Economic Growth in the 1990s, Learning From a Decade of Reform*. Washington, DC: World Bank.

———. 2005b. *World Development Indicators Database*. Washington, DC: World Bank.

Index

Boxes, figures, notes, and tables are indicated by b, f, n, and t, respectively.

I

J

K

L

N

R

ECO-AUDIT

Environmental Benefits Statement

The World Bank is committed to preserving endangered forests and natural resources. The Office of the Publisher has chosen to print ***Remittances and Development: Lessons from Latin America*** on recycled paper with 30 percent postconsumer fiber in accordance with the recommended standards for paper usage set by the Green Press Initiative, a nonprofit program supporting publishers in using fiber that is not sourced from endangered forests. For more information, visit www.greenpressinitiative.org.

Saved:

- 15 trees
- 11 million BTUs of total energy
- 1,328 pounds of net greenhouse gases
- 5,513 gallons of waste water
- 708 pounds of solid waste

2135 205